The Making of Israeli Militarism

THE
Making
OF
Israeli Militarism

Uri Ben-Eliezer

Indiana
University
Press

BLOOMINGTON AND INDIANAPOLIS

This work is a revised translation of *Derekh ha-kavenet:
hivatsruto shel ha-militarizm ha-Yisre'eli, 1936–1956*
(Tel Aviv: Devir, 1995)—LCCN 95-830759 /HE.

This book is a publication of

Indiana University Press
601 North Morton Street
Bloomington, IN 47404-3797   USA

http://www.indiana.edu/~iupress

Telephone orders   800-842-6796
Fax orders   812-855-7931
Orders by email   iuporder@indiana.edu

The paper used in this publication meets the minimum
requirements of American National Standard for Information
Sciences—Permanence of Paper for Printed Library
Materials, ANSI Z39.48-1984.

Manufactured in the United States of America

Library of Congress Cataloging-in-Publication Data

Ben-Eliezer, Uri.
  [Derekh ha-kavenet.   English]
  The making of Israeli militarism / Uri Ben-Eliezer.
    p.   cm.
  Includes bibliographical references and index.
  ISBN 0-253-33387-3 (cl : alk. paper)
    1. Militarism—Israel—History.   2. Israel—Armed Forces—
Political activity.   3. Arab-Israeli conflict.   4. Israel—Social
conditions.   I. Title.
  U21.5.B48   1998
  303.6'6'095694—dc21   97-46020

        1   2   3   4   5   03   02   01   00   99   98

As the book was going to press,
Professor Yonathan Shapiro passed away.
A friend and a mentor, he was the first to teach me
what political sociology is all about.
This book is dedicated to his memory.

CONTENTS

PART SIX
A Nation-in-Arms, 1949–1956

Preface

To write about Israeli militarism is to venture into an intellectual minefield. In Israel the term *militarism* evokes the idea of the special fate of the Jewish people—a defenseless nation—manifested in the recent past by suffering at the hands of the Nazis' fascist, militaristic system. Israel was widely perceived as a haven for the Jewish people, the only appropriate response to the horrors of the Holocaust. Such attitudes are hardly conducive to a discussion of the emergence of Israeli militarism in the crucial years of the state's gestation. These were years in which Israel portrayed itself as a nation engaged in a just struggle for national liberation, contending not only with a colonial power in the form of Britain but also with millions of Arabs who refused to recognize the new political entity in their midst and sought its eradication by any means.

Indeed, the protracted Arab-Israeli conflict, which has resulted in seven full-scale wars and innumerable lesser violent incidents, naturally has the effect of reinforcing the Israeli public's view that militarism is always the hallmark of the other side. I was aware of this problem when I chose the term *militarism* to encapsulate my thesis. The decision to take the plunge and use this particular word stemmed, finally, from my desire to explicate the rise and entrenchment in Israel of a phenomenon bearing social, political, and cultural meanings for which no other word is adequate.

Taking a broader perspective, the idea of militarism is readily usable. Specialists in the field have discarded the tendency to link the term to its archetypal examples, Japan and Germany; and, as the reader will discover, academic study of the phenomenon's manifestations, sources, and influences across a broad geopolitical and historical spectrum has produced a ramified professional literature. At the same time, this approach does not necessarily entail a correlation between the everyday meanings of militarism and the term's analytical use, the latter resting, of course, on a clear definition and solid theoretical foundations.

The term *militarism* was first used in France and Germany in the 1860s. From there it spread across Europe. Its appearance was connected with the fluid situation then prevailing on the Continent: the making of empires and the rise of new states, which were embroiled in conflicts generated by the demarcation of the globe into territorial divisions and struggles for territorial domination; the primacy of the national principle, initially perceived as a liberal, emancipator force but which, under the pressures of the global ethnic mosaic, also became the progenitor of violent conflicts; the growing strength of the bourgeoisie, or civil society, which, according to a certain point of view, does not accept states of emergency and wars with genuine enthusiasm; ethnic domination, frequently harsh and brutal; the rise of the masses as a sociological phenomenon; and the restructuring of armed forces into mass armies and of traditional warfare into total wars.

From the beginning, the ascriptive use of the term *militarism* implied an interest in two basic problems. One was the status possessed by the army in society, its political role, and above all its potential ability to intervene in government policy and in various arrangements of the civil realm. The second was the causes and possible prevention of war, in both the national and international arena. Gradually two distinct traditions emerged, the Liberal and the Marxist, each focusing on a different aspect of the phenomenon. In the Liberal tradition, *militarism* refers to a situation in which the army and its commanders accumulate sufficient political power to constitute a military regime. A system of interlocked arrangements—political, constitutional, and procedural—is supposed to prevent the army's intervention in civilian decision making and ensure its supervision by the civilian level. The Marxist tradition drew a connection between the means of production and the means of destruction in a society. Militarism from this viewpoint was a phenomenon that perpetuated society's inequalities and supplied the inexhaustible demands of the capitalist system, both locally and in the global market. Both traditions had their weak points: the Liberal tradition in its perception of militarism as a narrow political phenomenon tested by the single criterion of decision-making processes and the Marxist tradition in its deterministic outlook, which saw militarism exclusively through an objective economic lens.

The sociological approach to the study of militarism, which is expounded in the introduction to this book, avoids both pitfalls. To begin with, militarism is here placed in a broad political, social, and cultural context. Rather than treating reality as though it is driven by an ineluctable determinism, this perspective enables an understanding of the subjective interpretation offered by the participants themselves—an interpretation that is translated into the symbolic practices, organizations, and institutions that construct reality.

My principal thesis is that during the two decades beginning in 1936 the idea of a military solution to the Arab-Israeli conflict was gradually legitimized first within the Yishuv, the Jewish community in Palestine, then within the new state and crystallized into a value, a formula, and an ideology. More specifically, it was an outgrowth of the Yishuv's response to the Arab Revolt (1936-1939). But in time the idea of a military solution acquired a dynamic of its own that overrode its original, reactive character. In fact, in the decade that preceded statehood, the idea of a military solution to the national problem was carried by the young, "native-born generation." It was not yet shared by the entire Yishuv or espoused by the leadership. Only toward the end of the decade, particularly during the final months of the War of 1948, did the military solution acquire full legitimacy and become of decisive influence in setting policy. Thus one could talk not only about "cultural militarism" but also about "militaristic politics," the product of the cooperation that was achieved between the young generation, with its organized military frameworks, and the veteran political leadership, which generally advocated a moderate approach.

The relations between these two forces, representing the "military" and the "political," were gradually interwoven and characterized by a militaristic view of reality. In the years that followed, this way of looking at the world, which was embodied in methods and practices, was transformed into a substantive and comprehensive structure of society, more precisely into a mobilized society that I call a "nation-in-arms." From this point of view, the book will fulfill its purpose if it convinces the reader of the following thesis: in the course of Israeli history, military practices gradually became institutionalized and habitual, part of life's routine, until finally the idea of implementing a military solution to Israel's national problems was not only enshrined as a value in its own right but was also considered legitimate, desirable, and indeed, the best option.

The book's description and analysis are not limited solely to the social forces and practices that gave rise to Israeli militarism; an attempt is also made to explain how the interaction between the forces representing the "military" and the "political" turned militarism into a cardinal aspect of Israeli society. In this context a causal connection is found between two central trends that marked political life in the dozen years preceding the state's establishment. One was the attempt by military groups from the native-born generation to impose their militaristic viewpoint; the other was the untiring efforts by the political leadership of the state-in-the-making to impose its authority on a community which was ostensibly based on voluntary arrangements. The essence of the connection lay in the institutionalization of Israeli militarism and its enshrinement as a quintessential element of society—not least because the leadership was able to block the possibility that army officers would become the actual leaders of the country. Although this may seem an outrageous paradox, I ask the reader's indulgence: hear me out before rushing to judgment.

Recent years have seen the emergence of an academic debate in Israel between "New" and "Old" historians, between "post-Zionists" and "Zionists," and between radical and nonradical sociologists. As might be expected in a country which for years has been unable to resolve a deep internal dispute over how to settle the Arab-Israeli conflict, the academic debate has penetrated politics: the differences between the schools have become pegs on which to hang one's biases. As for myself, I share the alternative view of history, in particular because it supplants the *engagé* school of history, which was one of the foundations of Israel's nation-building process and, as such, vitiated scholarly research. I believe in critical writing which inherently reexamines accepted verities. However, my perspective is not political but academic. The book seeks to enhance our understanding of reality while allowing readers to draw their own conclusions.

The analytical use of the term *militarism* is by no means intended to determine who is the aggressor and which side is right in the Arab-Israeli conflict. This book is not a court of history. Nor should the fact that the study deals with one society, the Israeli, be construed to mean, or even suggest, that the author views the Israelis alone as being to blame for the Arab-Israeli conflict. Let me note, too, that the idea of militarism, although obviously related to military solutions and to war, cannot completely explain these phenomena. Still, it is undeniable that invoking the term *militarism* calls to mind a particular type of behavior, of organization, and of consciousness which arise under certain conditions and alter reality. Indeed, this book addresses a theme which is far more substantive than the immediate causes of a particular war or questions such as "who fired first" or "who gave the order." The real question is why human beings and human communities are willing to accept the destructive and deadly act of war not only complacently but often with astonishing relish.

Some will adduce a biological answer: humans are an innately aggressive species. But this book leads to a different conclusion; it insists on the importance of social organization, politics, and culture for an understanding of war. That same conclusion can also give rise to the hope—which this book will perhaps help bring to fruition—that militaristic blinkers will be shed in favor of an alternative view of reality, not to say a vision, which will hasten the day when "nation shall not lift up sword against nation, neither shall they learn war any more."

An earlier version of this book was published in Hebrew in 1995 as *Through the Gunsight: The Origins of Israeli Militarism 1936–1956* by Dvir Publication, Tel-Aviv. The English version of this book was prepared while I was a visiting scholar at the Jackson School of International Studies, University of Washington, Seattle. I would like to thank Resad Kasaba, Hillel Kieval, and Marty Jaffe from that institution, Ellis Goldberg from the Department of Political Science, and Paul Burnstein from the Department of Sociology for their support and help. Words are not enough to describe my deep gratitude to Joel Migdal from the Jackson School and to Baruch Kimmeling from the Hebrew University of Jerusalem, without whom this project could not have been realized. Special thanks as well to Linda Bevis, Charlotte *fon* Roberts, and Danny Bridge for being good friends to a visitor.

I would also like to thank my Israeli colleagues for their long friendship and support: Devora Bernstein, Sammy Smooha, Zvi Sobel, Ilan Talmud, and Yuval Yonai from the Department of Sociology, University of Haifa; Haim Hazan, Chana Herzog, Adriana Kemp, Avraham Kordova, Leon Shelef, Yehuda Shenhav, and Sasha Weitman from the Department of Sociology, and Eli Bar-Navi and Idit Zartal from the Department of History, Tel-Aviv University; Moti Regev from the Hebrew University; Nitza Berkowitz and Lev Greenberg from Beer-Sheva University; Charles Liebman and Shlomo Resnik from Bar-Ilan University; and Natan Sneider from the Academic College of Tel-Aviv Yaffo.

Welcome encouragement came also from Alan Silver of Columbia University, Roger Owen of Harvard, and Gershon Shafir from the University of California–San Diego. I take this opportunity to thank them. Joyce Robbins of Columbia University helped improve my English, while Ralph Mendel from Jerusalem did a superb job in turning a manuscript into readable English; their advice was useful and their patience never ran out. I'd like to thank, as well, the anonymous readers of the manuscript for their insightful remarks, and the staff of Indiana University Press for their impeccable editing work.

Finally, thanks to Inbar, to my children, Noa and Shir, and to Adri, for her true love.

The Making of Israeli Militarism

Introduction

The "Jewish Problem" and
the "Arab Problem"

Was organized violence always a feature of Jewish-Arab relations in Palestine/Israel? Was violence always considered a valid instrument with which to attain political goals? This book deals with a new perception of reality that emerged in the Jewish community in Palestine (known as the Yishuv) during the twelve years that preceded Israel's establishment and the first years of statehood. It held that the military way, meaning organized violence, was the desirable and preferable way to resolve the Jewish-Arab relations. I call this view of reality "cultural militarism," and "militaristic politics" is its concrete realization in decision-making processes. The subject of this book is the origin of Israeli militarism and the way it was institutionalized and became embedded within the whole nation.

In the wake of the Balfour Declaration (1917), in which Britain pledged to facilitate the establishment of a "national home for the Jewish people" in Palestine, the Zionist movement asserted its intention to operate through political negotiations. The Zionists sought Britain's assistance; they did not want a struggle against the Crown. This stand was articulated, for example, in a lecture delivered in 1939 by the chairman of the Jewish Agency Executive, David Ben-Gurion. Since Palestine's conquest by Britain in the First World War, Ben-Gurion said, Jewish settlement had rested on a political-juridical foundation, and the fulcrum of the Zionist lever was the right granted to the movement by Britain.[1] There was some truth in this, but it was not the whole truth.

Zionism's "founding fathers" did not rely entirely on diplomacy and legalism. In 1917 Jewish settlers constituted only 10 percent of the population in Palestine, and the Zionist leadership took this fact into account as it moved by degrees to cement the movement's standing in the new country.[2] The establishment of a Jewish state was at best a distant vision.[3] More concretely, the Jewish settlers adopted various strategies in the labor market which eventuated in a separate Jewish economy. They encouraged

the continued immigration of Jews to Palestine with the aim of altering
the demographic balance with the Arabs, and they transferred land away
from Arabs by purchasing property from *effendis* (landlords) and consoli-
dating their ownership by establishing small settlements. At the same
time, the national identity of the Jewish settlers was crystallized through
the concepts of "Jewish labor" and the "conquest of land."[4]

The Arab reaction was swift. As early as 1891, local Arabs expressed
their opposition to Jewish settlement in Palestine, which was then under
Ottoman rule. In a petition to the Sublime Porte, Arab notables in Jerusalem demanded a ban on Jewish immigration and land purchases. By
the end of the new century's first decade, Arab intellectuals and journalists in Palestine and throughout the Arab world had begun to speak of
the Jewish-Arab conflict in national rather than ethnic terms. The Balfour
Declaration only heightened the Arabs' fears and spurred them to take
political initiatives. Muslim-Christian associations sprang up, presenting a united Arab front against Zionism. Subsequently, political factions—the Husseinis and the Nashashibis, deriving from long-estab-
lished families—also came into being, reflecting the position that the
Jewish-Palestinian conflict was at bottom a national one. The masters of
the country and the architects of its destiny would be decided by the outcome of the conflict.[5]

In this period Ben-Gurion frequently invoked class slogans in his
analyses of the conflict. The socialist ideas he and his colleagues espoused served him in speaking about the liberation of the Arab *fellahin*
(peasants) from the effendis' yoke. When developments on the ground
undermined such class assumptions, particularly after the outbreak of
Jewish-Arab violence in 1929, Ben-Gurion interested himself in the Arab
national movement and met with its leaders, though he refused to recognize the Palestine Arabs as a separate people. Still, perhaps with an eye
on the demographic disparity between the two ethnic groups in Palestine, he declared that there was no conflict of interest between the Jewish
and Arab peoples; they could live together in peace and harmony in a
federated Land of Israel.[6]

Were such assertions only ploys? Should we take at face value the
comment of Berl Katznelson, one of the Yishuv's leaders at that time, that
Zionism had refrained from spelling out its aims vis-à-vis Palestine and
had deliberately voiced minimalistic goals?[7] Did Israel's founding fathers intend from the outset to realize their national goals by force?

Until the second half of the 1930s there is no clear evidence that the
Zionist movement considered force as such to be the means for implementing its national aspirations. Alternative possibilities were assayed.
In 1907, for example, the Poalei Zion ("Workers of Zion") party, one of
the two large workers' parties in the Yishuv, set up an organization called
Bar Giora, which had as its motto "In blood and fire Judah fell. In blood
and fire shall Judah arise." Two years later Hashomer (The Guard) was

established; it considered itself as much a political order as a professional military organization. In practice, however, the influence of these local, elitist groups was small. Hashomer never had more than a hundred members.[8]

During the First World War another attempt was made to achieve national goals by force of arms. Several Yishuv leaders conceived the idea of conquering Palestine with Jewish volunteers, who would enlist in the British Army. Wars are fertile breeding ground for ideas that advocate the use of brute force to solve political problems. It was in this spirit that the Zion Mule Corps was organized and fought alongside the British against the Turks. The volunteers, fired by a militaristic-nationalistic drive, declared themselves ready "to shed blood as an educational value for future generations." Their political leadership was no different. Rahel Yana'it, a leader of Poalei Zion, explained: "The primitive truth [is] that the right to a land is purchased above all with blood; that truth forces its dominion upon us at this historic juncture, and it marks . . . the road of the future."[9]

The Jewish battalions proved a disappointment. Failing to become the core of a military force to realize Zionism's goals with Britain's help, they eventually disbanded. But the militaristic symptom generated by the battalions produced a sharp counterreaction, primarily from Hapoel Hatza'ir (The Young Worker), the Yishuv's second-largest party. One of its leaders, Eliezer Yoffe, wondered: "We have as yet neither a nation nor a land, yet already we aspire to an army. Is this a primary need? Is it necessary to take people who are now in the Land out of it in order to guard it? It is like uprooting the trees from a garden to make a fence around the garden. But if the trees are uprooted—where is the garden and why a fence around it?"[10]

The failure of the battalions to become a decisive military factor led in 1920 to the creation of the Haganah (Defense), an illegal organization connected with the Histadrut federation of labor and Mapai (Land of Israel Workers Party), the ruling party of the Yishuv. However, the Yishuv leadership did not consider the military way to be a universal panacea for Zionism. It made no efforts to form an army or to purchase arms and ammunition. The Haganah guarded every settlement and protected the crops in the fields—but no more than that. All attempts to centralize its operations failed; influence lay with the district commanders, who tended to view events through a local rather than a national prism. Politicization was another impediment to the Haganah's military ability. Its leadership was keyed to parties and it was headed by functionaries rather than commanders with organizational ability and military know-how.[11]

The relatively moderate political approach of socialist Zionism soon spawned detractors. In 1923 Ze'ev Jabotinsky, a founder of the Zion Mule Corps and the Haganah, resigned from the Zionist Executive and set up the Revisionist movement. The Revisionists presented an alternative platform, explicitly demanding the Jewish conquest of Palestine by force of arms and the immediate establishment of a state. Jabotinsky emphasized the "cult of physical readiness" and the "psychology of shooting." Fulminating against his rivals in the Labor movement, he declared: "It is important to till the ground, it is important to manufacture, it is important to speak Hebrew, but unfortunately it is still more important to know how to shoot, otherwise we will have to forgo playing at settlement."[12]

Again, as in the episode of the battalions, a militaristic symptom worked its way into the life of the Jewish community in Palestine. The Revisionist movement was influenced by the atmosphere in nationalist Poland under the leadership of Marshal Jozef Pilsudski. In the early 1930s the movement also displayed sympathy for Mussolini's Italy. The members of its youth movement, Betar, which resembled the paramilitary organizations of the radical right in Central Europe, adopted outward symbols of an army: a uniform, parades, a cult of discipline, blind obedience to orders. In Palestine, the Revisionists established the Irgun (known also as the IZL, or National Military Organization), an underground movement whose members trained in the use of firearms. To the Irgun an army was not an unavoidable necessity but an attainable vision and an ideal. Gradually the Irgun—particularly after Menachem Begin became its leader—acquired autonomy and became more militant than the parent movement. It called for the immediate establishment of a Jewish state through the use of arms against both the British and the Arabs.[13]

In 1939–1940 Avraham Stern ("Ya'ir") led a group that broke with the Irgun and set up a military organization later known as Lehi (Israel Freedom Fighters), or the Stern Group (called by its detractors the Stern Gang). The interrelations of the two military organizations, Irgun and Lehi, and the Yishuv's political leadership proved to be a major contributing factor as the new military way evolved into an ideology from the mid-1940s on. Previously, the right-wing organizations had exerted only marginal influence in the Yishuv. The Labor movement—comprising the labor parties, the land-settlement movements, the socialist youth movements, the Histadrut federation, and the military defensive organizations—had the decisive voice in public life and politics, and it was far removed from the conceptual world of the Right.

Labor flinched at Jabotinsky's notion of the "Iron Wall"—that only by force would the nation realize its mission—and was appalled at his movement's "militaristic games." It looked with a mixture of incredulity and ridicule at Jabotinsky's idea of setting up Jewish battalions in Poland which would invade Palestine from the sea, march on Jerusalem, raise the national flag on its ramparts, and proclaim a Jewish state.[14] In the face of such ideas, Labor leaders espoused a pragmatic approach. They also thought that the Yishuv had to be strong, but power, they believed, did not necessarily spring from the barrel of a gun. They had good reason to spurn militarism. In the early 1930s the Zionist enterprise was flourishing. Jewish capital flowed into the country, Jewish urban centers developed rapidly, and Jews purchased land and built on it. With the approval of the British Mandate government, many autonomous Jewish institutions arose. The demographic gap narrowed, too: in the "quiet years" before the outbreak of the Arab Revolt in 1936, the Jewish population of Palestine climbed to 400,000, one-third of the country's total.[15]

Zionist leaders occasionally broached the idea of a "transfer" of the Arab population, but such notions had no impact on Yishuv politics.[16] Hard facts were what counted, especially in the realms of settlement, Jewish immigration, and economic consolidation. These facts in themselves were sufficient to rankle the Palestinians. True, land purchases by Jews did not solve the "Jewish problem": on the eve of the 1948 War less than 10 percent of the land in Palestine was in Jewish hands. But the Palestinians did not think in terms of percentages. In a predominantly agrarian society, loss of land has symbolic significance. Moreover, limited though it was, the transfer of land to Jewish ownership deprived fellahin of land which they had previously leased from effendis but which the latter now sold to Jews. It was inevitable that the Arab national movement should oppose Jewish settlement. The Arab Revolt of 1936–1939 was directed against the British overlords but also involved repeated attacks on Jewish life and property.[17]

The Yishuv leadership's response to these events was moderate and restrained. The Jewish community asked that the British recognize its right to self-defense, that the immigration quotas be increased, and that settlement activity be permitted. In November 1936 the Peel Commission arrived in Palestine. The local Arab community, at the behest of the Higher Arab Committee, boycotted the Royal Commission of Inquiry and subsequently rejected its recommendations, chiefly the idea that Palestine should be partitioned into two states. The Zionist leadership by and large accepted the commission's report. "The British proposal," explained Shmuel Dayan, a senior figure in Mapai (and the father of Moshe Dayan), "does much to destroy the 'illusions' regarding a large, expansive country." Another party member pointed out that despite twenty-five years of Jewish settlement and twenty years of British rule, the country was still heavily populated by Arabs. Both supported compromise, though many party stalwarts did not. But Ben-Gurion, Chaim Weizmann, and Moshe Shertok (Sharett) were relentless in their advocacy of the partition proposal and swung the Zionist movement behind them.[18]

Partition, though, was hardly the ideal of even the moderates among Mapai leaders. They seemed to grit their teeth when voicing support for the plan; they did not acknowledge the existence of a Palestinian entity deserving of a state. In his testimony before the Peel Commission, Ben-Gurion explained that the Jews were the only truly national group in Palestine. Besides the Jews, he said, "There is no other race or nation which—as a single unit—sees this land as its homeland."[19] Ben-Gurion's assertion may well suggest that even if the Jewish-Arab conflict had ethnic, economic, or religious roots or was the result of a mental divide, by the late 1930s it was beginning to become apparent that ultimately the conflict was between two national movements, neither of which saw room for the other in Palestine.[20] In any event, for reasons not related to the Jews, the Peel Commission's recommendations were never implemented.

In the meantime, the political crisis in Palestine worsened. In the face of the Arabs' guerrilla warfare against both the British and the Jews, British forces were sent into action and finally quelled the revolt. The Jewish leadership clung to a policy of "restraint" (*havlagah*), which ruled out the use of terror tactics or attacks on innocent civilians under any conditions.[21] This approach, however, did not have universal approbation, not even among the Zionist movement's traditional supporters. Beginning in 1936 a new dynamic, essentially force-oriented, emerged within the Yishuv. Initial unenthusiastic acceptance of the leadership's moderation metamorphosed into a full-fledged alternative policy which rejected *havlagah* and urged "reaction" (*tguva*).

The beginning of the period in question, which even the representative of the veteran leadership, Ben-Gurion, described as the time of "fighting Zionism,"[22] was marked by new military practices and methods. The period ended with the Sinai War of 1956, in which Israel, in collusion with the two great powers, invaded Egypt, captured the Sinai Peninsula, and reached the Suez Canal. In between, the two national movements fought the bitter, blood-drenched War of 1948. It developed into a war of conquest in which the majority of Palestine's Arab population was expelled and a Jewish state was born, though not within the boundaries designated by the United Nations. During these twenty years, a new perception of reality emerged within the Jewish community in Palestine, according to which the most appropriate, most efficient, and indeed, the only way to solve the "Arab problem" was deemed to be the military way. This new perspective, or ideology, can be defined as militarism. Its origins lie in the late 1930s and throughout the 1940s. With the establishment of the state, the leadership molded Israel as a "nation-in-arms," in which the whole Jewish population took part extensively in the project called army and war. Together, leaders and followers prepared for the "second round."

In recent years a number of historians have taken a new attitude toward the 1948 and 1956 wars, as well as toward the Jewish-Arab conflict in general. They are sometimes described collectively as "New Historians."[23] Challenging the basic premises of the established Israeli historiography, they have contributed to the creation of a new narrative. Their work is based to some degree on original findings, on the painstaking collection of details, and on a new interpretation of the facts. Overall, though, their work is confined to what can be called "narrative history" or "positive history," which excels in describing reality through accumulated facts rather than explaining it.[24] The present book, which is written from a sociological perspective, proposes to go beyond the limitations of narrative history in two ways: first, by analyzing events as they unfolded and took final shape, including the wars of 1948 and 1956, in the light of antecedent processes;[25] and second, by positing a theoretical and conceptual framework in an attempt to provide a comprehensive explanation for the abundance of historical facts and details.[26]

THE CONCEPT OF MILITARISM

Militarism is a multifaceted concept. The word lacks an unequivocal definition, and to complicate matters further, its day-to-day political usage suggests a value judgment. In fact, the term describes a relatively broad range of behaviorial patterns: an aggressive foreign policy based on the implicit threat of war; a propensity of the army to intervene in civilian life and politics, often by staging military coups and setting up a military regime; mobilization of society for military purposes involving extortion of human and material resources; an inordinate buildup of the army, usually spurred by a vigorous arms race; a dominant ideology that extols the armed forces and war; and a society that adopts military traits such as order, discipline, and hierarchy, or that reveres such values as the use of force, courage, and self-sacrifice.[27] The plethora of symptoms—some argue that true militarism entails their combined manifestation—does not necessarily indicate a conceptual lacuna. Rather, they reflect differences in the basic premises of students and scholars in the field. In any event, the multitude of expressions of militarism do not undermine the concept's importance for an understanding of the complex interaction among the army, politics, and society.[28]

As used in this book, *militarism* refers to a cultural phenomenon. It describes the viewpoint that organized violence, or war, is the optimal solution for political problems—a viewpoint that becomes habitual.[29] Militaristic politics ensues when this approach impacts directly on decision-making processes. The term's meaning can be illustrated with reference to Clausewitz's classic utterance on the relationship between war and policy. If war is, generally, the continuation of policy by other means, one option for action among many, as Clausewitz claimed, then the concept of militarism suggests a situation in which war, or the military solution, becomes the policy itself.[30] Of course, not every use of military force or resort to war attests to the existence of militarism. Militarism is not the opposite of pacifism, the total rejection of organized violence or war.[31] Militarism comes into being only when the use of military force acquires legitimation, is perceived as a positive value and a high principle that is right and desirable, and is routinized and institutionalized within society.[32]

Militarism should not be seen as a direct cause of war (which usually has many causes). It can, however, be seen as part of a mechanism that leads to a perception of war as a possible, available, and reasonable solution. In this sense, the concept of militarism contradicts the "neorealistic" explanation of wars, which for many years dominated the study of international relations. This explanation held that war is the outcome of a rational examination of the question: does the anticipated advantage of going to war exceed the anticipated disadvantage of refraining from war?[33] The idea of militarism hints at the possibility that an underlying conceptual foundation exists on the basis of which such decisions are made, that even a rational choice among operative alternatives actually rests on cultural assumptions and an interpretation of reality which legitimate and validate the use of organized violence or full-scale war. Militarism, in other words, is an ideology.

The study of ideology has made great strides in the past twenty years. Orthodox Marxism considered ideology to be a kind of justification of power relations and as existing in the superstructure, outside the material infrastructure. Contrary to past perceptions, ideology is itself conceived of today as a material substantiality that can constitute, reproduce, or transfigure reality. The interesting point, the linchpin in the work of scholars of ideology such as Antonio Gramsci, Louis Althusser, Raymond Williams, and Pierre Bourdieu, is that the image of reality which is created through symbolic practices, organizations, and apparatuses does not wield influence as a doctrine of supposed universal applicability or by virtue of its declarative force. Rather, ideology is effective precisely because it becomes embedded in everyday life, part of the "nature of things" as these are formed by habit and cemented by institutionalization.[34] Bourdieu, for example, objected to the term *ideology*, as he wished to demonstrate its manifestation in everyday life. He adduced the concept of habitus, expressed outwardly through speech patterns, body language, forms of thought, styles, customs, and habits, a generative mechanism that exists not as a result of study or of exposure to any sort of "logic" but is rather a product of everday experience.[35]

Israeli militarism, as will be seen, emerged neither from abstract systems and general ideas nor from doctrines or formal declarations. Its roots are traceable to concrete practices in the military realm which through the years became normative and habitual.[36] These symbolic practices, collectively to be called the "military way," were accompanied by the establishment of new military units. The new units signaled a shift from a static, defensive orientation to a mobile, offensive posture. The new military way was based on the assumption that it was possible and even desirable to resolve the Yishuv's national problems by means of organized violence. Its advocates were young persons from the native-born generation, the progeny of Israel's founding fathers, who came of age and crystallized as a sociological generation in the late 1930s and early 1940s.[37]

The new generation appeared on the historical stage in the context of the political crisis that afflicted the Yishuv from the late 1930s. The causes of this crisis were manifold: the Jewish community's impotence in the face of the Arab Revolt, the shift in British Middle East policy, the eruption of the Second World War and the German advance toward Palestine, and the cleavage within Mapai, the dominant party. A crisis is a conflict which does not find a solution, the conventional methods being perceived as ineffectual. From this point of view, every political crisis can be seen as a shaping and organizing event: it opens the way for new forces to enter the arena and realign the political process.[38] The young generation was engaged in this process. Its members belonged to generational units or to status groups, a mode of organizing that attested to the group's desire to acquire recognition, prestige, and influence.[39] Each of the various groups believed that it was best able to fulfill the national needs. Yet, out of their disputes, particularly the contest between those who volunteered for the British Army and those who joined the Palmach (Shock Squads)—the struggle between those "in uniform" and "without uniform," as it was known—the shared trait of the whole generation emerged: the idea that it was possible and desirable to solve the Yishuv's national problems by military means.

In the early 1940s the new perception of reality began to harden into an ideology, not least because of the support it received from political bodies, such as Mapai, the political party that fully supported the British Army recruits, and Hakibbutz Hameuchad, a kibbutz movement and a political organ, which backed the Palmach. The party and the kibbutz movement, rivals for domination of the Yishuv, believed that the new military way was a kind of resource which they could put to potent political use. They set up virtual private armies, of which they were the patrons. On the other hand, the massive support for the military way constituted a cornerstone in the process of the gradual emergence and consolidation of symbolic military practices, which were eventually transmuted into ideology.

Internal politics thus played a large role in determining the nature of the external, national conflict. During most of the 1940s, however, the new way of the young did not transcend the military framework and gained few supporters. Under what conditions does a new way of looking at reality become meaningful and dominant in the society? To students of ideology the answer is clear: symbolic forms become central or dominant to the degree that they are linked to the power structure within the society—constituting, preserving, perhaps even challenging power relations.[40] By the second half of the 1940s, the Yishuv's veteran leadership had recovered from its internal crisis and had begun to establish it-

self as the leadership of the "state-in-the-making"; as such, it launched
an intensive effort to impose its authority over the armed forces, which
were still reluctant to obey its orders.

MILITARISM AND PRAETORIANISM

Militarism, as the extensive literature on the subject demonstrates, involves two different phenomena, though there is often confusion about
the difference between them. One manifestation involves seizure of
power by the army and by supporting elements; the other, which is the
key to this study, entails the solution of political problems by military
means. The first phenomenon can be called "praetorianism," the second
"cultural militarism." Under certain circumstances, the latter enters into
the practical politics of decision making, thus producing a militaristic
politics.

Praetorians were the soldiers of the nine cohorts that were established
in Rome in 27 BCE by the Emperor Augustus. Initially they were the emperor's bodyguards, but gradually, beginning in the reign of Tiberius,
who became emperor in 14 CE, they became a powerful political force,
installing or deposing emperors virtually at will. Hence the term *praetorianism* denotes the army's possible intervention in politics under the
threat or actual use of arms.[41]

A key pioneer student of the process by which an army accumulates
immense political power and establishes a regime that uses military
means to solve political problems was the historian Alfred Vagts. Vagts
distinguished between the military way and militarism. The aim of the
former is to achieve a specific military goal as efficiently as possible
in terms of economic and human resources, whereas in the latter situation the military exceeds its narrow mission as an instrument to achieve
specific goals and intervenes in politics. Vagts posited militarism and
civilianism as the two poles of a continuum. His belief was that the two
poles were separated by the extent of the army's intervention in society.
In his view, then, the "problem of militarism" was bound up with the
nature of the regime and the degree of civilian supervision of the army.[42]

Many other scholars—notably Samuel Huntington, Morris Janowitz,
and S. E. Finer—took a similar approach, involving the so-called civil-
military relations paradigm. The spate of military coups in various parts
of the world, especially in the post–Second World War era, prompted
these scholars to address the question of how to keep the army from seizing power. For example, Huntington, in *The Soldier and the State*, posits a
low probability for military coups as long as the army officers are true
professionals, deeply committed to the military domain and indifferent
to politics.[43] Janowitz suggests that changes in the four branches of the
American armed forces—in their organization, their ideology, and their
tradition—endow them with a civilian-like character, reducing the like-

lihood of a military coup.[44] Finer, in *The Man on Horseback*, says that the maturity of the political culture and its ability to function democratically help a state avoid military coups.[45]

Although the three scholars disagree on many points, that should not obscure the common element which emerges in the civil-military relations paradigm. I refer to the basic liberal assumption that the two realms, the civil and the military, are analytically separate from each other, and to the well-known Clausewitzian assumption that the army is normally an apolitical instrument in the hands of statesmen.[46] Since then, the assumptions have been at the basis of numerous studies which posit a balanced system, with the army on one side and civil institutions on the other. Militarism and praetorianism are considered pathological phenomena, or aberrations, which disrupt the balance, usually when the civilian institutions are weak. Since both manifestations, militarism and praetorianism, belong to the same domain, the military, they are involved—so these studies maintain—in a symbiotic relationship: when one exists, so does the other; and similarly, if one is nonexistent, so is the other.[47]

Separation of the military and civil realms and of army and politics is characteristic of certain Western states. Probably no such distinction ever existed in the former Soviet Union or in Eastern and Central Europe and certainly not in the Third World or postcolonial states.[48] The distinction is not relevant for an understanding of historical cases such as Prussia-Germany, Japan, and France. Nor is it applicable to Israel, a democracy with no tradition of a viable civil society and liberalism.[49] This fact is not taken into account by most studies of army-society relations in Israel, which usually focus on the mechanisms that separate the civil and the military and on the forms of civilian control over the army. Thus if the Israeli army was used in various civil domains—absorbing new immigrants, teaching Hebrew, establishing agrarian settlements, disseminating the national culture—Israeli researchers consistently described this activity as nonmilitary use of the army and saw it as an example of how the army, being a civil institution, contributes to modernization, economic development, and nation-building.[50] Baruch Kimmerling argued that the divide was bridged by the ability of the political system to move efficiently from a "time of interference" to "routine time" and thereby to go on "living with the conflict" successfully.[51] Even Israeli scholars such as Dan Horowitz and Moshe Lissak who discerned a tendency toward the "society's (partial) militarization" invoked the opposite tendency, the "civilianization of the army," and concluded that the result was a kind of balance which supposedly precluded the emergence of militarism and praetorianism.[52] Or if the studies found cooperation between the political and military elites, it was pronounced "civilianism," the point being that this, too, worked against the rise of a military elite with vested interests, isolated and alienated from the society.[53]

All these studies, which have as their point of departure the civil-military relations paradigm, are vitiated by two major flaws: a view of the military as an organization which by definition is not involved in politics, and a lack of recognition that the military is an instrument of organized violence in society that is involved to some degree in violent actions and in war.[54]

An alternative to the civil-military relations paradigm views the army as an inherently political organ.[55] The army may display praetorian inclinations, expressed concretely as an attempt to seize power in the state, or a militaristic frame of mind by disseminating cultural militarism across the country (for example, through the socialization of new recruits in compulsory service) and by trying to induce decision makers to choose military solutions to political problems. Armies can operate in either way; they do not necessarily have to adopt both modes, as the civil-military relations proponents believe. After all, the classic militaristic armies—in Prussia-Germany, in Japan (until 1931), and in France (the latter known flatteringly for more than a hundred years, until the middle of the twentieth century, as *la Grande Muette*, the Great Mute)—displayed little inclination toward praetorianism.[56] Indeed, in all three cases the army was contemptuous of the politicians' officiousness and of the petty intrigues and compromises that characterize day-to-day politics. Yet, even though direct intervention in politics was at odds with the fundamental ethos of the army, in each case the generals had no qualms about disseminating a spirit of militarism in society or trying to influence politicians to adopt the army's perspective on reality. By this means the army cemented its status and ensured its influence in political life without having to resort to direct political intervention.[57]

Those and similar manifestations may be described as nonpraetorian militarism, a tendency to solve problems by the military way but without a military coup.[58] To this we should add that militarism does not begin and end with the army. Indeed, in the three cases just cited it was not the army alone that sought to idealize and glorify military solutions. Frequently it had the support of nonmilitary groups, such as youth movements, student societies, voluntary associations, religious groups, even women's organizations. Another possibility, as Alfred Vagts noted, is that political personalities without any military background pursue militaristic politics, a phenomenon he called "civilian militarism."[59]

Thus, if this book is to trace the emergence of militarism in Israel as an ideology in everyday life which came to exert a powerful impact on the country's destiny, it must also examine the social and political context in which connections exist between different groups and organizations, including the political leaders and the military chieftains. All are involved in politics in the broad sense of the term, not the politics of the allocation of resources and the competition to obtain them which exists within the framework of the agreed rules of the game but the struggle to determine those organizing rules or principles themselves.[60]

By examining the reciprocal relations and the struggles that took place between various actors, mainly the political and military leaders, the book identifies two sets of organizing principles which were integral to Yishuv and Israeli politics. One centers on the solution to the national conflict, in particular the attempt by the young generation to legitimate power-oriented, military solutions, in opposition to the more moderate veteran leadership. The second is related to the problem of authority. If the essence of politics is power, then the authority problem, in the tradition of Max Weber, concerns one of its crucial aspects: how rulers obtain consent to rule.[61] In the period under discussion, the right to command and the duty to obey were not clear and unequivocal, since the Yishuv had a fully formed political system but lacked sovereignty. Its leadership, which gradually became the leadership of "the-state-in-the-making," sought a modus vivendi with the military groups, which posted a potential and perhaps actual threat to its control. The possibility that such groups would try to seize power, as had occurred in other countries, where the army chiefs seized upon the situation of a national liberation struggle to depose the veteran political leadership, could not be entirely ruled out.[62]

That implicit threat brings us to the central thesis of this book: if militarism and praetorianism are not necessarily mutually conditional, there may be certain conditions in which a mutually beneficial realtionship can emerge between the military and political levels. The army's price for not intervening directly in politics and for not threatening military coups would be acceptance of its special status in society, its deep political influence, and its unintended dissemination of cultural militarism such that it becomes a cardinal principle in politics. In fact, the Israeli case raises the possibility that militarism and praetorianism may be diametrical opposites. Concretely, a kind of institutional trade-off was undertaken between central forces in society, by which the inculcation of the idea that it is possible and desirable to solve "the Arab problem" by military means was counterbalanced by the clarification and concomitant ordering of the relations of authority and by the diminished likelihood that the bearers of the sword would also hold the scepter.

Although the problem had been festering for some time, it was not until the 1948 War, following a series of internal struggles in which the basic assumptions of the political system were entrenched and with them the relations between the political level and the army, that cooperation between the two systems was cemented. The inverse relationship between militarism and praetorianism now emerged full-blown. The armed forces accepted absolutely the authority of the state's leadership, but at the same time they converted their tacit threat to seize political power into the exercise of concrete influence: their militaristic ideology became a central element of the leadership's politics. Thereafter, during the 1950s, with the special arrangements which exist in a nation-in-arms—which is characterized by a blurring of the distinction between army, politics, and society—the military solution was universally accepted as the legitimate and desirable way to end the Israeli-Arab conflict. It became part of the natural order and was preferred over possible political solutions involving diplomacy and compromise.

Thus the traditional theoretical approach, which juxtaposes militarism and civilianism, is challenged in this study by the hypothesis of an inverse relationship between militarism and praetorianism.[63] At the same time, I do not mean to suggest that the transformation of militarism into an organizing principle in Israel while the political leadership retained its place should be considered the exclusive explanation of the Israeli-Arab conflict in general or even of the wars that broke out in 1948 and 1956. It should be borne in mind that my analysis is limited to Jewish society. Moreover, the explanations adduced here are partial.[64] Nevertheless, the book takes issue with two approaches which for years were axioms of Israeli historiography and sociology on the Arab-Israeli conflict. Both have outlived their usefulness. The first thesis claimed that the events antedating Israel's establishment were in the main a reaction to a situation that was forced on the Yishuv by others, be they the British or the Arabs.[65] The second refused to acknowledge a connection between the Arab-Israeli conflict and internal Yishuv/Israeli politics, claiming that these were parallel lines that never met.[66]

The book's six parts correspond to the chronological sequence of events. Part 1 deals with the emergence of the military way, which was manifested in new military practices and methods, embodied in emerging military groups, and fraught with political significance. Part 2 deals with the reaction of the political parties to the new military phenomenon and with the changes undergone by the military way when it closed ranks with the Yishuv's central political forces. The major military groups, the Palmach and the British Army enlistees, were status groups which produced a particular culture and engaged in a struggle for recognition, prestige, and influence. Part 3 shows that these struggles transformed the new military way into a style and ideology. This development, in turn, was brought about by the interpretive reaction of the native-born generation to two major events that took place around this time: the Biltmore Declaration, which bore the promise of statehood, and the Holocaust, the Nazis' mass extermination of Jews in Europe.

About the mid 1940s the leadership of the dominant party, Mapai, recovered from its long crisis and began to constitute itself as the leadership of the "state-in-the-making." From that time, as part 4 shows, the leadership tried to resolve the problem of its authority over the military groups, which did not altogether accept its rule. It was not until 1948 that the relations between the native-born generation and its military units and the veteran leadership headed by Ben-Gurion were formalized. Part 5 discusses the institutionalization of the exchange that evolved during the 1948 War between the political and army leaderships, which created the foundation for an inverse relation between militarism and praetorianism. As the army acquired increasing influence during the war, the use of the military way as a solution to political problems became an accepted and desirable mode of action. As a quid pro quo, the army enshrined its obedience to the political leadership and its praetorian potential disappeared. As a consequence of this development, in the postwar nascent state the militaristic viewpoint was instilled in the whole nation. Part 6 shows that the state's Jewish population was constituted as a nation-in-arms. The social organization produced a situation in which differences between military and civilian were blurred, while the army and all things military became the linchpin of the national consciousness and the focal point of public life. For many years, Israelis were kept in a constant state of preparedness, mental and material, for war.

PART ONE

*The Emergence of a
Military Way,
1936–1942*

CHAPTER ONE

Quests

The origins of Israeli militarism lie in methods and practices which developed in the military realm during the decade leading up to independence in 1948. These methods and practices emerged in various places at the hands of various people, without planning or coordination. Primarily they constituted a reaction to the 1936 disturbances and the subsequent Arab Revolt. Moreover, they followed a serious crisis in the Haganah, the central military organization of the Yishuv, and a paralysis of the political leadership, whose moderate policies were broadly perceived as unsuited to the new circumstances.

The disturbances which broke out in Palestine in 1936 and evolved into the three-year Arab Revolt were a reaction to Jewish immigration and settlement and to the economic development of the Yishuv. The Haganah was unable to cope with the uprising. For the first time, the Palestine Arabs were seen to be capable of mobilizing manpower, resources, and military means in the pursuit of political objectives, to have overcome religious and tribal cleavages, and to have developed their own national identity.[1]

The debate in the Yishuv about how to respond was encapsulated in the catch-phrase "restraint or reaction." Domestic and external reasons alike had led the Haganah to pursue a policy of *havlagah* (self-restraint), which in practice meant defending Jewish settlements against incursions but not attacking the Arab civilian population. But the right-wing Irgun spurned Haganah's authority and advocated reaction, which took the form of attacks on innocent Arabs and raids on Arab population centers.[2] "Neither hollow phraseology, nor diplomatic talks and tea parties will win over world public opinion to the idea of a Jewish homeland," the Irgun declared, "rather the language of force and war, the language of bombs and dynamite."[3] An Irgun handbill termed Haganah's policy the tactics of ghetto dwellers. The Haganah, it said, had found a single cure-all: "Jews—give money. . . . Wear khaki, shoulder a rifle, but heaven forbid, don't fire it."[4]

A controversy arose between the Irgun, composed of native-born Israelis, and Ze'ev Jabotinsky, the Revisionist leader, who was cut off from the events in Palestine and still believed that the Jewish state would be established with the aid of Britain and not through a war against it. The controversy between the youths and their leader reached a peak at a conference of the Betar youth organization, which convened in September 1938 in Warsaw. There a coalition was formed between Betar members from Poland and the Irgun representative from Palestine on the basis of their common struggle against the British and the goal of conquering the Land. Menachem Begin, one of the prominent Betar activists in Poland, proposed the plan. In the spirit of the time, he expressed the view that the world's conscience should no longer be counted on and that a new version of Zionism should be adopted: military Zionism. Begin succeeded at the same conference in altering the oath of the Revisionist Party, "I will only raise my arm for defense," by adding: "and for conquering my homeland."

In the wake of the Betar conference the Irgun gradually became a military organization independent of any political party. Its texts made extensive symbolic use of the concepts of "rebellion," "sacrifice," and "conquering." These were placed in a poetic context, as an expression of the mood of the time, and were not considered part of a practical program. The Irgun nevertheless influenced the crystallization of the future Israeli militarism in two ways. First, it fought the British, showing that an armed struggle was possible, a phenomenon that was considered extraordinary in the Yishuv, which until then had aspired to realize its political goals with the British and not against them. Second, Irgun members did not accept the authority of the Jewish political leadership, showing that its approval was not necessary in order to put weapons to use. Indeed, toward the middle of the decade the Irgun would become a central military organization in the Yishuv, a partner in the Hebrew Resistance Movement, which would unite three distinct military organizations.[5]

The Yishuv's political leadership still maintained the policy of self-restraint. The British historian Christopher Sykes argues that the havlagah policy reflected a lack of confidence. In this view, the Jews did not believe they possessed the military prowess and courage to carry the war to the Arabs.[6] Sykes is right: the Jewish population was unprepared for the uprising and revolt of 1936, wrongly assessed its intensity and duration, and required British help to defend itself. These were the Yishuv's most turbulent years since the inception of the British Mandate. Normal life in both urban and rural sectors was badly disrupted, Jewish settlements were abandoned, and travel on the roads became virtually impossible. The flourishing economy, based on Arab labor, collapsed. Life and property were in constant peril, and fear became a way of life.[7]

The policy of havlagah did not derive from a lack of confidence alone. It was inspired by Chaim Weitzmann, who sought international approval, in particular from the League of Nations, then still a dignified and powerful organization. Among the Jewish settlers, though, it was not only the Irgun that felt frustrated by the official policy. Haganah activists also urged retaliation, and they gradually put their opposition to the official policy into practice. This practice had an air of professionalism. The Haganah's traditional military doctrine, based on passive defense, went hand in hand with self-restraint. Now new combat methods emerged. They were the first steps in the eventual emergence of the Israeli militarism.

OUTSIDE THE PERIMETER

In 1936, as the troubles intensified, Yitzhak Sadeh (Landoberg), then aged forty, arrived in the Jerusalem area. Sadeh had come to Palestine from the Soviet Union during the so-called Third Wave of Jewish immigration (1919–1923) and had joined the Labor and Defense Battalion set up in 1920 to promote communal agricultural settlement in the country.[8] Sadeh was not closely involved in public affairs and was never a political functionary, but in Jerusalem he volunteered for military duty and was sent to help defend an isolated settlement not far from the city. There he immediately gained prominence for his original military initiatives that included night patrols and ambushes.

Sadeh was equally successful in his next assignments, but the real turning point came in his mission at Kiryat Anavim, a kibbutz near the city, where a number of young Jerusalemites standing guard duty thirsted for reaction. Two of them, Zvi Spector and Israel Ben-Yehuda, had gunned down Arabs working in a field and thrown a bomb into a café in the nearby Arab village of Abu Ghosh to avenge the murder of three Jews outside a movie theater in Jerusalem.[9]

Sadeh's impact in Kiryat Anavim was tremendous. Meir Rabinovich, one of the young Jerusalemites, later recalled his first encounter with Sadeh. Sadeh woke him at 2 A.M., took him to a field, and ordered him to shoot out a light in the window of a house in the nearby Arab village. Rabinovich shouldered the rifle, aimed, and fired; the window went dark. "Brave lad," Sadeh told him. "From now on you will be a commander."[10] The young men were stunned by Sadeh's courage and his unconventional methods. Sadeh would choose the bravest and most devoted of them for his night patrols. One night Ben-Yehuda and Spector went with him on patrol. They shot at lights in the windows of Arab houses and laid an ambush for marauders. During an unexpected clash with an Arab squad, Ben-Yehuda was wounded and began to retreat, but Sadeh, hurling grenades at the Arabs until they fled, shouted, "No retreat, cowards!" The encounter in the hills made the three famous and admired, and the event became a myth of heroism. The idea that the Arabs could be dealt with by force began to materialize.[11]

Eliahu Ben-Hur (Cohen), Sadeh's partner in commanding Kiryat Anavim and in establishing the Nodedet (mobile patrol) that operated against Arab forces in the hills around Jerusalem, wrote in his autobiography that Sadeh was so overwrought following combat patrols that regular work became impossible.[12] But the young men were captivated by Sadeh and his methods. "To us he was an extraordinary man, even though he was older than us," one of them related. "He was one of ours, he had the same mentality as ours, the spirit of abandon. Like him, we did not want to remain in one place either, and we always said bitterly that we shouldn't wait for the Arabs to come to us, we should get to them first."[13]

Yigal Allon, the most famous general of the 1948 War, similarly recalled his first meeting with Sadeh, who had come to his village to propose that Allon organize a local unit: "I thought to myself: who is this bald, bespectacled, toothless man who has the effrontery to come and teach us combat doctrine—with the many impressive operations we already have to our credit?" But it was an offer that Allon couldn't resist. At night he and some friends set out with Sadeh for a nearby Arab village. They set an ambush and at dawn fired several volleys at houses in the village. Then, around a campfire, Sadeh explained the key tenet of his doctrine: do not allow the Arabs to be the masters of the night.[14]

The Nodedet's combat methods, which became known as "venturing outside the perimeter," were gradually adopted by the entire Yishuv, supplanting the traditional approach, which placed defenders behind a wooden guard tower and a searchlight.[15] In February 1939, for example, when the annual meeting of "security activists" convened in the Jordan Valley, little new was heard until Ben-Zion Yisraeli, a veteran settler, complained about the danger of relying on defense strategies and suggested offensive attacks outside the settlements. Thanks to his initiative, a military unit was formed in the region.[16] Yisraeli then tried to enlist the support of the Histadrut Labor Federation. "The Arabs control our land while we are enclosed within our fences," he complained.[17] The Histadrut met the challenge. A squad commander's course was organized, and Yisraeli himself took part, even though he was twice the age of his fellow cadets. The aim was to form a mobile force, unattached to any specific settlement. The initiative faced tremendous obstacles; the idea, however, was implemented.[18]

Sadeh and Yisraeli viewed reality differently from their chronological peers who had arrived in the century's first two decades. The two were more closely attuned to the outlook of the young generation, most of whom were born in the century's second decade and reached maturity in the late 1930s. The disturbances and the Arab Revolt affected each generation differently.[19] The formative years of the younger generation produced an ethos created by local experience: guarding fields and crops, fighting with Arab children, being given a weapon at the age of bar mitzvah. This was the childhood experience of prominent members of the young generation such as Moshe Dayan and Yigal Allon, as related in their autobiographies. Although they lived close to their Arab neighbors and partially emulated the Arab way of life, their outlook was tempered with suspicion, which frequently became hostility, and they reached maturity feeling that a confrontation between the two groups was inevitable.[20]

Yosef Tabenkin, the son of Hakibbutz Hameuhad's leader, noted that awareness of the hostile Arab surroundings had been an integral part of his childhood. During the 1929 disturbances, an Arab had threatened to murder him and his friends as they walked in the fields, and in 1936, when he was fifteen, he underwent arms training and did guard duty. As for venturing outside the perimeter, young Tabenkin said: "Our education and the situation in which we lived prepared us sufficiently to view the idea of venturing beyond the fence as something self-evident . . . innate in us because of our situation."[21] This example illustrates tendencies which the new generation acquired during childhood and adolescence. Now they served them as "provisions on their new journey" and would eventually influence the identity of the Israeli fighter, which evolved through everyday trials and experiences.

In 1937 the changes within the military became clear. Sadeh set up the Fosh (Hebrew acronym for "field companies"), which initiated violent clashes with Arabs. The Fosh expanded the strike-first approach, which its members hoped would constitute a middle course: neither Irgun terror, such as throwing bombs into Arab markets and killing dozens of men, women, and children, nor passive Haganah defense, which was confined to reacting to the other side's initiatives. In practice, an unanticipated dynamic took shape. The Fosh became a military unit whose members saw reality through the barrel of a gun and did not refrain from pulling the trigger.

Sadeh brought to the Fosh his cadets, known as Sadeh's Boys, who set the tone of the unit. Their distinctive esprit de corps and tendency to criticize the Haganah's traditional methods inevitably sparked disagreements and conflicts with veteran commanders.[22] Soon the Fosh signified a new military way that bore political meaning, as the military experiences crystallized into a coherent weltanschauung, a clear conclusion about how the Israeli-Arab conflict must be resolved.

A key development occurred in connection with the establishment in 1938 of Kibbutz Hanita high in the hills of Upper Galilee in the heart of an Arab-controlled region. The Hanita episode portended the shift that was about to occur in the Zionist conception: the ideal of the farmer on his land was overlaid with a politically based orientation entailing military strategy and conquest. That the "ascent to Hanita," as it became known, took place after the publication of the Peel Commission Report on July 7, 1937, is noteworthy. It constituted an attempt to expand the borders of the anticipated Jewish state beyond those recommended by the commission and agreed upon by the Jewish Agency Executive.

Hanita symbolized the way the settlement activity became part of a politics that sanctioned the use of force to achieve national goals.[23] There, Sadeh and the youngsters in the Fosh demonstrated their prowess. They decided not to defend the settlement—which more nearly resembled a military forward post than a kibbutz—from within the stockade but to meet the enemy on open land near Arab villages. A few days after the founding of the kibbutz, an Arab unit attacked the workers who were building the road to the new settlement. Two Fosh units headed by commanders, Yigal Allon and Moshe Dayan, took up positions on the attackers' flanks, held their fire until the right moment, then surprised the raiders from both sides.[24] The operation profoundly impressed Yishuv youth, who identified with the Fosh fighters' choice of force of arms to realize national aspirations. "They talk reverently about the heroes of Hanita," wrote the youth movement's journal, "and long to follow in their footsteps."[25]

Already discernible among Fosh activists and others who ventured outside the perimeter were the shadowy outlines of the fighter who arises from the society to solve national and territorial problems which are thought to be beyond the leadership's ability. Not for nothing did Nathan Alterman, a well-known Israeli poet, write his famous opus in honor of the Fosh on the theme of replacing plows with guns to conquer the land. This was the first idealization in the history of Jewish settlement of the fighter who aspires to solve problems his own way rather than leave the task to others.[26]

Idealization of the warrior had originated in Europe as nationalistic tendencies increased in the nineteenth century. No longer seen as a mercenary killer, the warrior was hailed as one who sacrifices himself on the altar of fatherland or national ideals, and the military was perceived to be fulfilling a national mission.[27] The Fosh too was viewed in this light: a national military body untainted by political party association and aiming at achieving national goals. As Eliahu Ben-Hur put it at the time, "An Arab's bullet bears no address. It hits and kills Jews from both right and left."[28]

Before formation of the Fosh, soldiering had been a part-time activity. Even the most distinguished military activists identified first and foremost with their political party. With the Fosh, military endeavor demanded complete devotion and the young men's conception of reality was entirely different, as reflected in a letter one of Sadeh's Boys wrote to his girlfriend around the end of 1938: "You know me well and you know that I am a 'sabra,' and that I am sometimes swept up by the current of a certain period, and then I forget the whole world."[29]

In the Fosh the new military way received organizational expression. The Fosh concentrated all the mobile patrols into one active corps of several hundred fighters. This corps transferred the fighting from the Jewish settlements to the fringes of Arab regions. Sadeh and Ben-Hur considered the establishment of a countrywide Fosh, which would be free from the authority of local commanders. This plan was not entirely realized. Nonetheless, the Fosh had its own headquarters, a cadre of skilled, professional commanders, and in 1938 a Fosh constitution was drafted, pointing to the formalization of the new national trend.[30] The Fosh also conducted various professional courses around the country. The official Haganah history stated that the courses differed from the Haganah's regular courses, not only in their content (many field and night drills, maneuvers, bayonet fighting) but also in their character. Indeed, a report drawn up by the commanders noted: "The maneuver [i.e., training] imbues the participants with a sense of the vast difference between passive defense—from within the position—and active defense in the field, with elements of assault."[31]

The report hinted at a possible blurring of the distinction between a political worldview and military plans. A more striking example of this possibility was the Avner Program, presented to Haganah headquarters in 1937. Drawn up by a prominent Haganah commander, the program was based on the prospect that Britain would depart the country in 1937, immediately allowing the Yishuv to struggle with the Arabs on its own through the establishment of an army and the introducing of Jewish sovereignty in Palestine. The program included detailed lists of the Arab population according to geographic location, as well as numerous maps with corresponding statistical tables. It described the phased takeover by Jewish forces of distinctly Arab areas, such as Galilee; the West Bank of the Jordan river, including Nablus, Jenin, Ramallah, and Jerusalem; and Jaffa, Lod, and Ramle. In these areas, the plan stipulated, the Arabs would be placed under a strict military government: night curfews, identification-card checks, and so forth.

Avner, which was an exclusively military program designed by a military personality, was not implemented. Nevertheless, it is indicative of a central conceptual change, being based on a new, power-oriented Zionist political conception. Many similar programs would follow, the best-known being Program D of 1948, which would give a formal, even practical, expression to the idea of conquering the Land by force. To a certain extent, Avner was ahead of its time. As its initiator himself stated, "Neither numbers nor equipment is the decisive factor, but the spirit, the correctness, the sacrifice, the patience, and the recalcitrance. . . . We must change our mentality. We must organize the militarization of the Yishuv in all domains of life: in settling the land, in education, in the press, and in public life. In the Yishuv, a regime of defense must reign."[32]

The Avner Program was the sign-post marking the possibility of a future Zionist cultural militarism. This possibility was discernible in the Fosh as well. The Fosh's organized violence was neither reactive, spontaneous, nor emotional and not necessarily revengeful, as in violence caused by uncontrolled passions. This is illustrated in an episode recounted by Ben-Yehuda. One night a squad of rookies led by him and Zvi Spector encountered an Arab force. "Fire!" the commanders roared, but no one obeyed. The Arab force fled and the unit went on its way. When they spotted Arabs harvesting the vineyards of a Jewish moshav, Ben-Yehuda and Spector inched their way forward and opened fire at close range, killing two of the Arabs. The recruits were then made to view the dead bodies close up.[33]

The desire to familiarize the soldier with killing and to turn this into an internalized disposition in such a graphic manner was new. In fact, this was the first time in the history of the Yishuv that a deliberate and willful murder of Arabs was carried out by non-Right young men; moreover, the murder was considered legitimate as long as it served the national purpose. Even the official *History of the Haganah*, which tends to understate the use of violence by Jewish military forces, notes that Fosh fighters were quite flexible in their interpretation of the "purity of arms" slogan and in their understanding of the havlagah policy. It mentions as well that there was a disparity between the views of kibbutz and moshav members, who understood military issues in terms of the relations they had formed over many years with their Arab neighbors, and the approach of the Fosh fighters, who pursued their own military methods.[34] This problem would reappear at the beginning of the 1948 War, when the military in many cases damaged the fabric of the neighborly relations reflected in agreements between Jewish and Arab villages and acted without taking the agreement into consideration. In 1937 the Fosh leaders claimed, in reaction to repeated accusations regarding the behavior of the military units, that their approach was unavoidable and that there was no other solution to the "Arab problem" than the one they had chosen. It was, then, in the Fosh that militaristic symptoms first appeared in the left-wing circles of the Yishuv, the beginnings of an "arms is the answer" approach. Not in vain did friends of Zvi Spector say that "he had a cruel streak, an un-Jewish streak, that was attracted to danger, and pulled the trigger without hesitation."[35]

Many Fosh youngsters were attached to the Special Night Squads (SNS), formed in 1938 under the command of the British officer Orde Wingate, which also exhibited a professional orientation and buds of cultural militarism. Wingate was the archetypal professional soldier who saw the world through the sight of a gun. Among the fighters he was rumored to have commented that the biblical Yehoshua's mistake had been that he had not mopped up the area sufficiently. Wingate's operations were renowned for their violence and brutality, for the routine use of killing as a method of collective punishment, for looting Arab villages, and for attacking innocent civilians. In one case he lined up all residents of a village, one of whom was suspected of a murder, and executed every tenth one. When Chaim Sturman, a well-known figure in Galilee and a personal friend of Wingate's, was killed, Wingate ordered the killing of

every Arab discovered in the vicinity of the raid.[36] These typical coloni-
alist deeds did not deter the Fosh commandos. On the contrary, it was
considered a great honor to participate in his raids, to learn and apply
his fighting methods.[37]

Anita Shapira, an Israeli historian, attempts to identify extenuating
circumstances for the development of the new conception of killing as
collective punishment. The Fosh fighters thought, she writes, that collective guilt should not be applied to the Arabs; however, if a village served
as a hiding place for an Arab force, it would be permissible to apply collective responsibility in the customary manner of the Arabs' blood revenge, whereby every tribe member was guilty if one tribe member committed murder. It is doubtful whether this forced revenge, which Shapira
attributes to the Fosh, ever guided the military unit. Shapira also claims
that the idea of collective guilt entailed a contradiction between the ideo-
political level, which made purity of arms the criterion for distinguish-
ing between Irgun and Haganah policy and which served as a central
value in the Yishuv's education, and the practical level, which did not
always honor the purity of arms principles. The two levels that Shapira
mentions were indeed present in the Fosh, but there was never a contradiction between them. On the contrary, it is in Fosh that we first find a
conceptual duality that held purity of arms to be a vital motif, but only
as long as it remained solely at the verbal level. A different, shadowy reality takes shape alongside, generated by concrete modes of military action divorced from moral considerations. In the 1948 War the disparity
between speech and the language of action would become a type of politics inherent in reality and not to be considered a flaw in its perception.
As early as Fosh, the will to operate efficiently and perfectly took precedence over any form of purity of arms. We see in Fosh the tendency to
gloss over military practices with verbiage expressing self-righteous
skepticism and anguished doubts, but never to let moralistic handwring-
ing interfere with the mode of action or compromise its effectiveness.[38]

The increased violence and attacks on innocent civilians led to a joint
meeting of the Fosh and a few members of the political leadership in
January 1939. At the gathering, Israel Galili, a senior Haganah activist,
spoke of the dangers latent in "excessive professionalism." Galili urged
his audience to beware of manifestations of a barracks approach and
to shun arrogance, haughtiness, and vulgarity. The notion of the professional soldier was alien to the veteran, socialist Haganah leaders; in the
same gathering, Yitzhak Sadeh warned against adopting the mannerisms
of English soldiers. The young commandos, however, did not share these
fears. One of them, referred to only as Zvi (perhaps Zvi Spector), fervently defended the pioneering character of the field companies, adding
that great things lay in store for them. Zvi rejected the diagnosis of the
Fosh's militaristic posture as "symptomatic of an illness." On the contrary, he argued, if anything it was symptomatic of a "counterillness," a

reaction to the "exilic ghetto mentality" of the heads of the Jewish Agency, reflected most acutely in havlagah.[39] Thus the young commandos unequivocally put forward their new professional military way as a political way able to solve the Yishuv's national problems.

BEWILDERMENT AND BITTERNESS

To understand how a new military way, fraught with political signficance, was created so quickly, it is necessary to recall that the Yishuv, its leadership, and its central military organization, the Haganah, were caught in a continuing political crisis, which encouraged new initiatives and solutions. At the London Conference of 1939, it became obvious that the British had, as the Yishuv feared, revised their regional policy and had decided to conciliate the Arabs after suppressing their three-year uprising. David Ben-Gurion's impression in the aftermath of the London Conference was that the revised British Middle East policy had placed the ball squarely in the Jewish court. "Here our work is finished. . . . We have to work to strengthen the Israeli front," he wrote in a letter. And again: "From this time the fate of Zionism depends solely on ourselves."[40] Such pronouncements were typical of the leader of the Yishuv. How did he intend to realize them?

Following the London Conference, the British published the White Paper (May 1939), which limited Jewish immigration to Palestine, thus delivering a blow to the heart of the Zionist ethos. A sense of solidarity swept the Jewish community in Palestine, a general strike was declared, and people took to the streets. The leadership proclaimed that the Jewish people would not tolerate the new policy; handbills were circulated calling on the public "not to submit, not to flinch."[41] Ben-Gurion, chairman of the Jewish Agency Executive and the ranking figure in the Yishuv, was a past master at producing effective slogans; he himself drew up the leaflet which declared, "We warn the government: when the scheme is revealed, the sword of Israel shall be unsheathed." At the end of April, Ben-Gurion convened the senior Haganah commanders to work out a plan of action. He had in mind organizing illegal landings of immigrants on the country's shores, and he spoke about an "aliya [immigration] revolt" that would use armed force.[42]

With emotions whipped up by the propaganda campaign, the Yishuv was ready to resist the White Paper by force. The public soon realized, however, that the leadership had no intention of going beyond a few demonstrative acts. Some ranking officials vehemently opposed a struggle against the British;[43] but others did not rush to translate the activist declarations into practice, and consequently the rage that had been directed against the British authorities was vented against them. "It was a week of delegations," Ben-Gurion wrote in his diary. "All of them with one

voice, expressing the same bewilderment and bitterness." The delegations, comprising different sectors in the Yishuv, heaped scorn on the policy of moderation; they demanded a civil revolt, dissolution of the political parties, and placing of power in the hands of an authoritative leader.[44]
Calls grew for Ben-Gurion's resignation in June 1939. The traditional
public institutions were unsuited to the new era and the old goals had
become irrelevant, the delegations complained. The last vote for the
Elected Assembly and the National Council had taken place in 1931; the
elections scheduled for 1935 had been repeatedly postponed, each time
with a new excuse.[45] Ben-Gurion and his supporters faced an unprecedented political crisis. To the demands for change—expressed in a new
term, *revisia* (revision), which was on everyone's lips[46]—Ben-Gurion retorted: "It is inconceivable that every person in the Yishuv should set up
his own committee. We have existing institutions, and they must not
be destroyed."[47] But the assault on the leadership continued. Ben-Gurion
charged that narrow political motives were behind the demands for the
leadership's replacement. In fact, the many public protest meetings bore
no clear sectarian character but rather a national, populist tone, not unlike events in Europe in the same period.[48]
Even Yitzhak Ben-Zvi, chairman of the National Council and a senior
figure in Mapai (later Israel's second president), who for years had accepted his exclusion from important decisions, suddenly took political
initiatives that infuriated Ben-Gurion, not least because they showed that
the ruling party did not speak with one voice.[49] The major rift, however, was within the dominant party, between the Mapai majority and
Faction B, which had been established in 1938 through an alliance between Hakibbutz Hameuhad activists and an urban opposition based in
Haifa and Jerusalem. A year later, the new faction was already disrupting
party activity and party institutions had become a mere formality. The
party rarely met and took no substantive decisions.[50]
The impact of the political crisis was felt in the military body of the
Yishuv, too. At the end of the 1930s attempts to reorganize the Haganah
were encountering numerous obstacles. Its members' calls to revise the
organization's structure and operating methods went unheeded, and the
breakthrough embodied by the Fosh was stymied. The Fosh was disbanded in early 1939 at the height of its strength in order to create the
Field Corps (Hish, in the Hebrew acronym). But operationally the new
unit was of no significance. The Haganah thus regressed, the attempt to
transform it into a centralized, national organization having failed.[51]
In July 1938 Yohanan Rattner, a nonsectarian figure, was appointed
chief of the Haganah National Command. His brief: to revitalize the Haganah and turn it into a professional organization. But he soon felt, as he
wrote in his memoirs, that he had fallen into an unfortunate situation.
The decision makers on matters of military were few: Ben-Gurion, Eliahu

Golomb, Shaul Avigur, and Israel Galili. Their personal influence and
power in the Histadrut enabled them to circumvent the Haganah National Command and those who stood at its head.[52]

A salient flaw in the Haganah was its lack of a professional military
staff. Mutual suspicion was rife: every military reform proposed by the
Left (the National Command was comprised of three representatives
from the right-wing middle-class sector and three from the left-wing Histadrut socialist sector) was construed by the Right as a plot to weaken its
hold on the organization. This was undoubtedly also how the nonsocialists viewed the endeavor to centralize the organization and make it a national body, thus weakening its affiliation with the cities and local councils, where the middle class exercised considerable influence.[53]

In March 1939 Eliahu Golomb, the Haganah's strongman, resigned
from the National Command. But to the nonsocialists' chagrin, his voice
remained decisive in military affairs, and the crisis deepened.[54] In his diary, Ben-Gurion used the word *disorganization* to describe the Haganah
Command, in which, as he saw it, there was no guiding hand and no
mutual trust and where crucial decisions went unmade and things were
in general neglected and opportunites missed.[55]

Agreement on reorganizing the Haganah was finally reached in
September 1939, but the crippling political and structural problems
remained until the National Command was disbanded in summer 1940
and the Yishuv-wide parity agreement, in effect since 1931, was an-
nulled.[56] More than a year would pass before the nonsocialists' return to
the Haganah. In the meantime, beginning in July 1940, many of the Haganah's rank-and-file and commanders enlisted in the British Army, and
the Haganah was further weakened for many years by the independent
character of the Palmach (set up in 1941 with its own headquarters).

The net result was that Britain's revised Palestine policy did not generate a commensurate change in the Yishuv leadership's policy. Indeed,
weakness paralyzed its military arm. In this crisis setting, a process
of de-authorization of the leadership began in the younger generation.[57]
Youth movement journals abounded with such statements as: "A new era
is needed, in which we will be the prime movers. . . . We will establish a
Jewish force of a kind that will demolish the White Paper and dictate
new papers."[58] Even Hashomer Hatza'ir, considered the most moderate
of the Zionist left-wing youth movements, vehemently demanded a campaign against the White Paper and a more militant national stance.[59] Arguments for the spontaneous organizing were expressed: "We shouldn't
wait for orders, we should act" and "There are times when influence . . .
is in the hands of those who act, not those who explain."[60]

Impassioned public demonstrations accompanied the slogans. On the
day the White Paper appeared, young people sabotaged the Mandate radio station, forcing a delay in the broadcast of the High Commissioner's
announcement. Several government offices were attacked, and in Jerusa-

lem a demonstration turned violent. When protestors left the prearranged route, dozens were wounded by police truncheons and, in the
first incident of its kind since the inception of the Mandate, a British
policeman was shot and killed by Jewish gunfire.[61] Some anti-British actions were carried out locally. In Haifa, student and youth movements led
by Meir Rabinovich (one of Sadeh's Boys) organized riots and demonstrations against the White Paper without official authorization. To the Haifa
Situation Committee, composed of elected officials and favoring a more
moderate struggle, they annouced that they had no intention of discussing the national campaign against the use of imported products, but
to prepare for throwing bombs. Among other activities, students staged
a sitdown strike at the Technion in Haifa, an act terminated by British
troops, who entered the university and arrested them.[62]

The anti-British frame of mind, heightened by criticism of the moderate line espoused by the official institutions, was further exemplified
in October 1939 when forty-three Haganah members were seized while
doing arms training and given lengthy prison terms. From their cells the
young prisoners let it be known that they were against any attempt to
resolve their case by diplomacy, terming it "acquiescence." They demanded the cancellation of a Yishuv-wide conciliation campaign aimed
at securing their release, urging instead that relentless public pressure
be exerted on the British and that the Yishuv "hold its head high."[63] The
"Haganah Forty-Three" perceived their imprisonment in nationalist
terms. As one of them wrote from prison, "I saw our incarceration as an
educational fact. . . . Our imprisonment reflected the liquidation of political Zionism [as opposed to practical Zionism]."[64] Upon their release,
many of the Forty-Three enlisted in military units, realizing in that way
their national aspirations.

The demonstrations of the young generation gained momentum at
the end of February 1940. Through a directive restricting land purchases
by Jews, the British made it clear that the White Paper policy would continue. This blow to another cardinal Zionist tenet triggered more than a
week of strikes and violent demonstrations. The youngsters did not shy
away from clashes with the police. Curfews were ignored and hundreds
were injured, some later dying of their wounds. For the youth this was
a formative period. The official journal of the youth movement Hano'ar
Ha'oved called on its members not to harbor illusions that lobbying and
diplomacy would get the land decree revoked. Such feelings were sec-
onded by Hashomer Hatza'ir: "Until now we received everything ready-
made, stamped with the [official] 'line.' Now a new way is needed."[65] The
daily *Ha'aretz* reported that in demonstrations against the White Paper,
high school students urged "permanent reaction and not a momentary
demonstration," and the slogan repeatedly chanted was "No speeches—
only deeds!"[66]

In time this rhythmic call would become the status symbol of the native-born generation and the most glaring feature of Israeli cultural militarism. In the meantime, the call for action was naturally directed to the political leadership. In late May 1939 it seemed that the young generation's expectations had been realized. Ben-Gurion began a meeting with representatives of right- and left-wing youth organizations (excluding the Revisionists), proposing a joint plan of action. His intention was to set up an all-inclusive, party-unaffiliated, quasi-military youth organization which would provide physical training and inculcate discipline.[67] The meetings prepared the ground for the central gathering on June 11, 1939, attended by thirty-seven representatives of youth groups. Ben-Gurion spoke about the weakness of the Yishuv, which was wracked by internal party conflicts. He expressed outrage at the demands to replace the leadership and called on his audience to act as the lever for realizing the leadership's main objectives. The young listeners were not easily convinced. "We followed the leadership almost blindly," one participant complained, "but they are not taking action." They questioned the authority of the leadership, which had been elected in an earlier period and for a different goal, and ridiculed Ben-Gurion's moderate ideas. Some were suspicious of the proposed youth movement and hinted that a narrow political consideration was behind the idea. A communiqué prepared after the meeting by the leadership said that the young generation must show confidence in the leadership and was obligated to display national responsibility and avoid violence. The announcement only reaffirmed the youngsters' fears: more than to activate them, the leadership aspired to control them.[68]

Ben-Gurion held additional meetings with youth representatives, trying to convince them to establish a single organizational framework. Repeatedly he implored them to accept the basic values of immigration, settlement, local manufacture, the Hebrew language, and Jewish labor.[69] But the young people had reservations. Ben-Gurion received a letter from the Union of Religious Students stating that talk about "unsheathing the sword of Israel," which then took the form of hikes in Jerusalem's neighborhood, undermined confidence in the leadership. There was no doubt, the students added, that "the forces latent in the youthful masses will find the way and the [proper] leadership, in spite of everything." Statements like these clearly demonstrate a process of de-authorization among the young generation toward the leadership.[70]

If Ben-Gurion actually intended to put the young people into action and not just keep them under his thumb, such plans remained unimplemented. That year Ben-Gurion suggested the "aliya revolt": to land immigrants on the country's shores, take over the city of Haifa using armed force, and declare the establishment of a Jewish state. One suspects that Ben-Gurion never seriously considered implementing such a fanciful plan.[71]

In Ben-Gurion's many meetings with youths during this period, a deep rift was revealed. One difference was the disparity between words and deeds. Whereas Ben-Gurion in those days, often engaged in "activist" speech but refrained from doing, the youths demanded less talk and more action. As a result of this gap, the Yishuv leader's contacts with the young generation were broken off for many years, almost until the 1948 War. He left for London, where he devoted himself for some years to diplomatic activity.

One condition for the emergence of a new sociological generation, according to Karl Mannheim, is the occurrence of unexpected events and rapid changes, causing traditional behavior patterns to be perceived as inappropriate.[72] This chapter has shown how the Yishuv's young generation interpreted the major historical events to which it was exposed, such as the Arab Revolt and the White Paper, differently from the adult generation. The difference between the veteran leadership and the young generation became more glaring. There were buds of a militaristic conception in the youths' new interpretation of reality, which hinted that it was possible and even desirable to solve political problems through organized violence. This undermined two basic Zionist assumptions, which had been sacrosanct until then: that a Jewish state would be established not only through Jewish action but with British help and that a peaceful agreement with the Palestinians would be possible. The next chapter will demonstrate the way the new military methods and practices were combined into a distinct organizational structure.

CHAPTER TWO

The Formation of
Military Structures

The new military practices wrought a transformation in the Yishuv's military structure. As we have seen, they also acquired great political significance by presenting a new Zionist way. This chapter deals with the continuation of the trend at the beginning of the 1940s. It discusses the establishment of new military groups, Special Operations, British Army recruits, and the Palmach, which thousands of youngsters joined within a short time. These groups saw the management of organized violence as a profession and a genuine vocation. Their perspective also had political significance, concerning both the best solution for the Yishuv's national problems and the question of who should rule in the Yishuv.

SPECIAL OPERATIONS

By June 5, 1939, when the Special Operations (S.O.) unit was established, the Arab rebellion had almost been quelled by the British; in other words, the S.O. was established not to defend against Arabs attacks but as a means of materializing a political assumption holding that the national problem should be dealt with by the military way. The S.O. consisted of Sadeh's Boys and other young persons who had excelled in the performance of independent military actions.

The decision to create S.O. came in the wake of acts of revenge against Arabs carried out individually by young Haganah members. One reason for its formation was to channel the thirst for revenge into a formal framework within which it would be controlled. In fact, S.O. also carried out unauthorized operations. On June 20, young activists under the command of Shlomo Shamir, a future battalion commander in 1948, and Yigal Allon, IDF's most famous commander in 1948, opened fire through the windows of a house in the Arab village of Libiya, killing and wounding men, women, and children. The Histadrut daily *Davar*, whose editors still hadn't come to terms with the new turn of the Labor Movement youth, wrote the next day: "A new crime was committed in the village of Libiya, a frightful crime which shows that its perpetrators have lost the last remnant of their capacity for sound judgment, and that the last spark of human feeling in them has been extinguished. . . . The memory of the Libiya action . . . will doom its destructive perpetrators to ignominy, whoever they may be."[1]

Revenge actions by S.O. personnel against Arabs became frequent. Following the murder of a Jewish locomotive engineer, S.O. activists set out for the village of Bild a-Sheikh to retaliate. They lost their way, but, not wanting to return without anything to show for their labors, they shot an Arab whom they happened to encounter. Subsequently another squad—including Haim Laskov, a future Israeli chief-of-staff—went to the village, dragged five Arabs from their homes, lined them up, and killed them all, firing-squad style.[2] The Revisionist leader Ze'ev Jabotinsky mentioned this incident later in a meeting with Eliahu Golomb to substantiate his contention that there was no great difference between the Haganah and the Irgun, whose members routinely attacked innocent Arabs.[3] Even if Jabotinsky overstated the similarity, S.O. did demonstrate the continuation of the new political tendency, first seen in the Nodedot and Fosh, according to which "the Arab problem" had to be solved by force. This approach was generally spurned, as one S.O. member noted: "We had to fight public opinion, the cowardice and timidity, the Yishuv mentality, our press, and the voice of morality and conscience."[4]

Following several similar incidents, along with complaints by Haganah National Command chief Yochanan Rattner, Ben-Gurion told the Haganah to draw up a "proposal for maintaining discipline in the security force, to prevent pointless killing." Shortly afterward, the National Command issued a directive prohibiting attacks on innocent Arabs.[5] But judgments handed down against S.O. men who were tried by the Haganah for killing Arabs were not implemented.[6] The following comment by Haim Laskov illustrates the youngsters' attitude toward the negative orders:

> Whoever gave us the orders for these operations was a great Zionist. We were instructed not to harm children, not to harm women, not, not, and not. It got to the point where if you managed to carry out the operation it was by some accident that enabled you to withstand all those nots. On the other hand, there was one action in which Yigal Paikovich [Allon] and David Shaltiel took part. They went up to a cabin, threw in their grenades and got out of there. Inside there were women and children. I wondered what would happen. Nothing happened. Someone said "pooh" and that was the end of it.[7]

The organized violence of S.O. was the continuation of a new collective-punishment approach. As in the Fosh, the political crisis situation made normal supervision of military activities difficult. The S.O. was unaffiliated with the Haganah National Command, in which moderate right-wing, middle-class commanders were also represented. When these commanders tried to have the unit disbanded, the young S.O. members were incensed.[8] The Secretariat of Mapai, the ruling party, was also divided politically on S.O. Some members objected to such a unit, and the Secretariat had to come up with several compromise formulations to forestall resignations and enable operations to proceed. Usually the objectors were apprised of S.O. actions only after the fact, to ensure that they did not torpedo them. Rattner later said that his resignation as chief of the National Command was prompted by the fact that S.O. actions were carried out without his knowledge and without the approval of the Haganah center.[9]

In fact, a new and not particularly democratic version of "civilian control" developed around S.O. operations. According to this formula, decisions on the use of organized violence for political aims were made in small informal forums without the consent or approval of any official institutions. S.O. members cooperated with the leaders of the informal forums rather than with the accepted institutions of the Yishuv or with the heads of the Haganah. At the same time, the young people enjoyed a considerable degree of freedom of action, and their independent initiatives received backing and protection from possible objectors by the leaders of the informal forums. In this way, S.O. sketched the outlines of a new pattern of cooperation with the decision makers of the political echelon and the executors of the military echelon on the basis of a shared militant view of reality.

The scuttling of the ship *Patria* demonstrates the emergence of this new tendency. The *Patria* affair signaled a shift in the S.O.'s focus from anti-Arab to anti-British targets, which included sabotaging the oil pipeline and sinking a British guardship. The operations were limited in number, particularly after the outbreak of the Second World War, when S.O. was formally disbanded. But November 25, 1940, marked a turning point. S.O. members scuttled the *Patria*, which was carrying illegal immigrants whom the British intended to expel to the island of Mauritius in the Indian Ocean. These were the last of the Palestine-bound Jews to leave Germany in ships organized by the Gestapo. The Yishuv saw the expulsion as part of the White Paper policy, which had to be opposed at all costs. The dynamiting of the ship caused it to list and sink, with the loss of more than 200 refugees.[10] The operation sparked a furor in the Yishuv. When *Hapoel Hatza'ir*, a Mapai journal, published an article condemning the "malicious hand" that had sunk the ship, Ben-Gurion's son, Amos, went to the journal's offices and slapped the editor, Yitzhak Lufben, in the face.

The *Patria* affair rekindled the debate between activists who wanted to continue the struggle against the White Paper despite the outbreak of the war and moderates who argued against anti-British actions for the duration of the war. Mapai and the Histadrut held protracted discussions on the operation's political and moral significance. Lufben said it was the blackest day of his thirty-two years in the country. The men, women, and children whose lives had been sacrificed had not been asked for their assent, he pointed out. But the Haganah's Eliahu Golomb spoke about purposeful sacrifices, and Eliezer Livenstein, a Mapai ultra-activist, called for the Yishuv and the diaspora to be educated in the light of this action.[11] Christopher Sykes, the British historian, later wrote about the myth of collective suicide that gained a foothold in the episode's aftermath.[12] Some members of the Mapai Center even spoke of "martyrdom."[13] And in the Mahanot Ha'olim Council, the young members said, "this is a great epic of Jewish destiny. Of immigration at any price. Of the recognition that the Land of Israel is the shore . . . although it was impossible to be sure of the effectiveness of the operation in advance, its accuracy was beyond compare . . . it's time we learn that in war nothing is obtained without martyrs."[14]

The debate in the leadership forums raised issues of principle: Should political problems be solved by force? Did anyone have the right to sacrifice others for a national cause? Was it legitimate to act against the British while the war continued? What were the decision-making procedures in the Yishuv? Speaking to the Mapai Secretariat, Yosef Sprinzak, a leading moderate, noted that no discussion by the official institutions had preceded the sabotage, which he labeled a "postfactum action": first comes the operation, he snapped, and only afterward is it deliberated by the official forums.[15] In fact, this was the first political argument in Yishuv history over the proper relationship between what may be called the "political" and the "military." The argument concerned matters of principle, and in the ruling party there was deep disagreement on the issue.[16] But with one slap, Amos Ben-Gurion showed how the younger generation felt about these fundamental questions. The young people despised vacillation and free political debate, stressing instead the value of action.[17]

Following the scuttling of *Patria* a wave of nationalistic political violence swept the Yishuv. Members of Hapoel squads beat a Jewish Agency official for not demonstrating what they regarded as patriotic sentiments. In September 1940 a bomb was thrown into the home of Professor Ernst Simon, and in January 1941 attempts were made to torch the houses of other famous professors—all former members of *Brit Shalom*, which espoused Jewish-Arab coexistence—who had denounced the scuttling of the *Patria*. The police investigation turned up Haganah involvement.[18] But more important than the question of responsibility is that the political violence hinted at the intolerance of public discussion on basic questions affecting the Zionist movement and the Yishuv.

BRITISH ARMY RECRUITS

Upon the outbreak of the Second World War, the Yishuv institutions organized a census of the younger generation and announced that "all assistance [to the British Army] is given most willingly."[19] The reality was different: objections to enlistment in the British Army were voiced immediately. Ben-Gurion told the Jewish Agency Executive that should there be a callup, the draftees would serve only in Palestine and the region, since it was beyond the Yishuv's powers to help the diaspora.[20] Ben-Gurion and his followers believed that serving in the British Army was tantamount to supporting the White Paper.[21] The left wing in the Histadrut labor federation went even further, saying that helping Britain conflicted with the Yishuv's needs.[22]

The Yishuv leadership faced a dilemma: was it best to aid the British in the war against the Germans or to fight the British because of their White Paper policy? Ben-Gurion's dictum is quoted in every history of the period: "We have to help the [British] Army as though there were no White Paper, and we must fight the White Paper as though there were no war." Yet at the time this dual imperative went unrealized; the Yishuv neither assisted nor fought the British.[23] At Ben-Gurion's behest, the Haganah barred its members from enlisting.[24] The Jewish Agency supported the mobilization of volunteers for specialized units, but the British wanted recruits for work details on the front, and here the Yishuv leadership put its foot down. Ben-Gurion sarcastically dubbed these tasks "wood-hewing and water-drawing."[25]

There was no rush by Jewish young people to enlist in the British Army, but as time passed a growing number of them wanted to take part in the war. By July, large numbers of volunteers flocked to enlist. Hakibbutz Hameuhad's young recruits declared that they would show the way. Israel Galili, from the Kibbutz Secretariat, tried to dampen their enthusiasm by reminding them that pioneering missions still awaited them at home, but the new recruits said that "the twenty years of liberal, labor-oriented, idyllic pacifism have ended."[26]

The motives of the recruits came as a surprise to the leadership. Yosef Sprinzak, who attended a party held in honor of new recruits, later recounted the experience with incredulity to his Mapai colleagues: the young people said that their recruitment would lay the foundations for Jewish military units, and they were enthusiastic about the prospect of going into battle.[27]

From mid-September 1940, volunteers were recruited also to the infantry units known as the Buffs (Royal Kentish Fusiliers), and three newly formed infantry companies were quickly manned. Around the same time, Haganah members had a change of heart about enlistment; hundreds joined up, some at their own initiative, without seeking the organization's approval.[28]

The kibbutz movement, however, was in no hurry to have its members join the British Army.[29] The kibbutzim feared that if volunteering were allowed on a personal basis, large numbers would enlist and their economic-farming interests would suffer. With characteristic ardor, the kibbutz movements reaffirmed their traditional stance that working the land was the mission of the self-fulfilling pioneer and that this mission could not be abandoned even in wartime.[30] But the younger generation found this outlook passé. At his farewell party, a new recruit and kibbutz member said: "During the long days of our life together, we got used to thinking about our work as being the front. In our eyes, work, guard duty, building our day-to-day lives, were the front. But now there is another front, in a different place."[31] To the young people this shift in perception was part of a rebellion against a whole way of life. Young kibbutz members, many of them graduates of youth movements, unable to accept the movement's refusal to let them enlist, left home and joined up.[32]

In July 1940, nearly a year after the outbreak of the war, the political leadership itself began organizing enlistment in the British Army. Nevertheless, the leadership did not fully support the move and organized the mobilization by the quota system. The leadership hoped that in this way it would be able to control mobilization. But soon it found itself confronting an unanticipated phenomenon.

By mid-1941 the war had reached the Mediterranean and the threat to Palestine was palpable. Around this time, Ben-Zion Yisraeli, a member of the Mapai Secretariat and one of the initiators of the concept of "venturing beyond the perimeter," reached the conclusion that enlistment should be based on volunteerism. He thought that some 20,000 people could be recruited by this means. Moreover, he himself set a personal example of his volunteer principles by enlisting at the age of fifty-four.[33] The impact this had on the younger generation was expressed by a member of the Socialist Youth: "To me, Ben-Zion Yisraeli's enlistment is a stirring phenomenon. . . . If this comrade enlists, then who of us cannot go, who of us is not duty-bound to go?"[34]

Yisraeli and some of his friends, the hard core of the volunteers, wanted to create a movement that would counteract all the forces trying to block enlistment: the kibbutzim, the youth movements, the Haganah, the cooperatives, and others, all of which were scrupulously adhering to the quota imposed by the Yishuv leadership.[35] The volunteers bypassed the organized bodies and appealed directly to graduates of the youth movements and young members of kibbutzim, urging them to enlist immediately. Their methods, which included posting notices on the bulletin boards of kibbutz dining halls, incensed many, but the nationalist message received publicity.[36]

The Jewish Agency's enlistment system was a bureaucratic maze, and Yisraeli and his group urged its elimination. "We have to distinguish between two concepts, mobilization and volunteering," Yisraeli explained. "Mobilization is carried out by the government. Volunteering is done by the people. We can carry out volunteering. . . . We must generate a movement. . . . I see the role of those in the offices as being to serve the movement and not to take it over."[37] Inevitably the volunteer movement spawned many enemies, owing to the style of its operations and its militant call to alter long-standing arrangements in the Yishuv.

Ben-Zion Yisraeli can be regarded as a "forerunner," in Karl Mannheim's terms: "It frequently happens that the totality of the perceptions that characterize a new generation first emerge and evolve in adults who are isolated from their own generation."[38] To the young people, Yisraeli was someone who refused to accept the existing order of things as self-evident and demanded their reform. The emotional aspect of the volunteering approach caught the youngsters' fancy: they were captivated by talk about a volunteering frame of mind, pioneering, free will, devotion and the importance of community. By emphasizing these values, the movement idealized the army and linked military service to the fulfillment of national aspirations, a connection which until then had not been obvious.[39]

The recruits' commitment to the army had a rational aspect as well. In the British Army they acquired the view that bearing arms is a true profession. Professional soldiers acquire their war expertise through education, preparation, and training. Their specialization imbues them with a sense of autonomy, which they seek to preserve by preventing ordinary citizens from interfering in professional military affairs.[40] Possessing this common demoninator, the professional military group strives to obtain an exclusive status in the right to bear arms and a myriad of other privileges. They flaunt their superiority through a variety of cultural means, such as, esprit de corps, which emphasize that they are a breed apart.[41]

As their military expertise grew, the British Army enlistees gradually became professional soldiers. At first they could join only sappers' units, part of the support system, and not combat units. Some joined noncombat technical units, or mixed (Arab-Jewish) units, whose level, military and social alike, was considered very low. The turning point came with their induction into the combat infantry, the Buffs, and later into Jewish battalions. The culmination of this process was the establishment of the Jewish Brigade, which saw action against retreating German forces in Italy. At the same time, a cadre of commanders emerged, some of whom won rapid promotion in the British Army and made careers out of the military.[42] In addition, professionals will protect their interests by presenting themselves as serving the needs of nation, state, or society rather than as seeking to acquire military expertise for its own sake.[43]

Indeed, the soldiers viewed these changes as part of an evolutionary process designed to fuse the ideas of a Jewish army and an independent Jewish state. In this sense we can regard their military organizing as a generational phenomenon, the embodiment of the worldview of the new generation, that the military way was best for solving the national problem. This perspective emerged as a reaction of the young to crucial historical events and as their criticism of the older, more moderate generation.[44]

With the perfection of their skills, their belief that political goals would be achieved by a military way took root. The process was encapsulated in the members of Socialist Youth who joined the army. At their first annual meeting, the main topic of discussion was the personal doubts and difficulties experienced by the enlistees. Those were the first days of the expanded enlistment, the days of the mixed units with their whole tangle of problems. A year later, in the second meeting, a new note was already being sounded, and the talk was about the problems of creating a Jewish army: how to get from the small units to the desired goal. "And we said . . . we have our own view about fighting for a Jewish army, not only from above—negotiations, political struggle—but also from below, from the rank-and-file soldiers." In the third meeting, they said: "Now we have arrived at a new phase: Jewish battalions."[45]

The real question is the political meaning of this new phenomenon. The idea that professionalism is a central factor in keeping soldiers out of politics has been strongly criticized as many professional armies have developed blatant praetorian tendencies.[46] In fact, armies are interest groups like any others, and their high-ranking officers are interested in guaranteeing the army's material and ideal interests. This, of course, points to their praetorian potential, which is likely to be realized if their demands are not met. In fact, it is precisely the professional traits which increase the chances of military intervention in politics. Professionalism turns the military group into a group with political and social advantages, one which sometimes finds it difficult to accept the notion that others, and not the military group, will decide what society's needs are.[47] Thus, on more than one occasion, although professional armies display a sense of duty to the national idea or to the nation, praetorianism has evolved when officers have perceived that the civilian leadership is in fact compromising, or even betraying, the national ethos.[48]

Armies and military groups thus bear a latent praetorianist potential. At the same time, they often contribute, along with other bodies and organizations, to the creation of cultural militarism and its dissemination in society, through conscription, for example, or through the development of a unique style. Armies and military groups can, as well, pressure the political leadership to subject its decisions to a militaristic orientation. By this means they can "make politics" and influence decision-making processes without any threat of praetorianism. Civil-military relations theorists do not entertain the possibility that a professional army could develop nonpraetorian militaristic tendencies. As mentioned in the introduction, they reduce the "problem of militarism" to types of governments and the absence of so-called civilian control over the military. But if militarism is a cultural phenomenon, then it is precisely a professional army which would have the means to disseminate it. In fact, it can exploit its singular traits—cohesion, autonomy, exclusivity, and naturally its presumption to represent all of society—to get across an unequivocal and, so to speak, professional message of the indispensability of the military solution for resolving political problems.[50]

The crux, of course, is the conditions under which the militaristic and praetorian potential can be realized. One possible avenue for praetorianism is related to the sense of alienation that an army may develop toward the public and the civilian leadership.[51] Such sentiments were not absent in the Israeli case. The soldiers' alienation was produced, to begin with, by the British command's deliberate disregard of the national identity of Yishuv enlistees, although in general the national identity of other recruits was played up in army journals, radio reports and movie newsreels.[52] The soldiers' frustration grew more acute because they were denied certain combat possibilities. In August 1940, when the Buffs was formed, the expectations of the Jewish soldiers soared, only to be dashed. The infantry companies were assigned guard duty, given meager training, and supplied with outmoded equipment. A few months later, hopes rose again, this time in connection with the formation of a Jewish division. But then the British government had a change of heart.[53] In August 1942 the British decided to form battalions by combining Buffs companies. Again anticipation ran high and there was talk of the Jewish army that would finally be established. But the British kept the new battalions away from the front, gave them poor equipment and sketchy training, and continued to assign the infantry to guard duty.[54]

As the Jewish soldiers' professionalism improved and their service was extended, the gap widened between their perception of their role and their lowly status in the Yishuv. The political leadership, the Histadrut, the kibbutz movements, the youth movements, and the other organized bodies that set the tone of the Yishuv were not unanimous in their support for mobilization. As one soldier wrote, "When I came to Tel Aviv on my weekly leave, I felt very uncomfortable walking along the street. I thought people were laughing at me. I had the feeling they considered me wretched for wearing a uniform, that they regarded me as insane and miserable. Why should this be? Because this is the Yishuv's attitude toward enlistment. Because it kept aloof, joked about it."[55]

In their many gatherings the volunteers were critical of the stand taken by the public and the official institutions toward enlistment. Recruitment activists tried to create an aura of prestige around army service, but with little success. Even Eliahu Golomb, the leading proponent of the Jewish military way, told the volunteers that he understood their desire to fight but that what was important was the overview, not one's personal perspective. Whoever thinks that only those in uniform are mobilized is thinking wrongly and is making things even more difficult, Golomb explained.[56]

Evidently the soldiers were disappointed. The Socialist Youth vented their feelings as follows: "We feel not like pioneers in the vanguard, but like the last of the forsaken, and some would add cheated.... Why do those who sent us not come? Tremendous bitterness is building up against them here, and the consequences could be appalling."[57]

The political leadership was aware of the frame of mind of the British Army recruits. Nevertheless, there was no immediate change in the leadership's attitude toward enlistment, which in its view served mainly British interests. Gradually, however, the leadership learned to recognize the political importance of the new military phenomenon that crystallized in the British Army framework and to understand the danger involved in disregarding messages that hinted at the soldiers' wish to influence the destiny of the Yishuv by military means.

THE PALMACH

Similar tendencies developed at that time in the Palmach, the military unit that was the quintessental embodiment of the native-born generation. This unit had its genesis in a quarrel. In December 1940, members of settlements in the Beit She'an region began working the contested Ashrafiya lands, which the British had refused to lease to the Jews. Hundreds of Arabs, armed with sticks and stones, tried to stop them. The ensuing fight saw many wounded on both sides, with one Arab killed. The British police broke up the melee and arrested twenty-five Jewish youths.

In jail the "Ashrafiya prisoners" met the "Haganah 43," members of the Haganah who had been caught by the British while doing arms training. Their conversations soon made it clear that the two groups tended to view reality in the same light. Following their release from prison, the young people discussed their reasons for taking part in the fight. One of them said: "We should see the affair as a link in the chain of warlike actions against the White Paper.... The public is not prepared for action. ... The steps taken by the official institutions do not conform with the will of our comrades as expressed here.... We have to find modes of action."[58]

The brawl over the Ashrafiya land and the ensuing protests against the Yishuv's political leadership formed the background to the emergence of the Palmach (Hebrew acronym for shock squads). Many of those who took part in the Ashrafiya fight later joined the Palmach and recalled the brawl as the primary mental impetus which had led them to volunteer for the new unit.[59] In the brawl, the first use was made of short-stick combat, a kind of fighting skill that the Palmach's members developed and turned into a status symbol. It symbolized the courage of the new Jew, ready to take on the Arabs face to face. Its political significance was made clear by Uri Brenner, the son of a noted Hebrew writer, who became a deputy chief of the Palmach: "An Arab who feels that there is an incommensurate reaction will be bolder.... We must strengthen the ability of each individual to stand fast in this kind of brawling. It is vital to train people well in the use of the stick. A different spirit has to be introduced."[60]

The Palmach was born out of the Haganah's weakness. By mid-1941, the Haganah's ranks were depleted. About 3,500 of its soldiers and commanders had joined the British Army, and the political infighting within its high command had vitiated its operational capability.[61] In fact, the Palmach was founded in the period when the right-wing, middle-class representatives had absented themselves from the Haganah National Command. They had left because of differences over control of the organization, and exponents of the activist view in the Haganah seized the moment.[62] But Levi Eshkol, a Mapai moderate leader, quipped: "The Palmach was born outside the National Command as far as I am concerned."[63] This statement points to the circumstances of the Palmach's creation: initiatives by military activists, above all by Yitzhak Sadeh, striving to realize a certain political line without first obtaining institutional approval for their initiative.

During 1941 Sadeh met frequently with security personnel and with young commanders to promote the idea of the Palmach. He even met with Avraham Stern, head of the tiny, persecuted rightist Lehi, which continued to fight the British despite the war. In a meeting with a leader of Hakibbutz Ha'artzi, Sadeh tried to convince him that the kibbutz movement should take part in the creation of a mobilized force. The decrepit state of the official institutions, he said, meant that in an emergency the Yishuv might be unable to act.[64]

Sadeh's success was bound up with the events of the period. The Yishuv lived in dread of a German invasion; Jews who had immigrated from Germany were especially fearful of reencountering the Nazis. The possibility of submission was voiced, but the young people felt that their hour had come. In a meeting of communes from the youth movement Hamahanot Ha'olim, the future writer Aharon Megged drew a distinction between healthy nations, willing to defend themselves, and degenerate nations without the will to fight back. Megged called for a brisk response against those who were readying the Yishuv for surrender and compromise. The Palmach, youngsters like Megged believed, represented the only logical solution to the situation.[65]

Sadeh brought many of his "boys" to the Palmach. The outlook of some of them had been shaped earlier, in the Young Turks circle formed by Galili in 1939 at the directive of Hakibbutz Hameuhad. The group, its members later said, sidestepped the official military framework and was meant to express the young members' criticism of the Haganah's methods and the leadership's moderation. When the Palmach was established, many of the Young Turks joined it.[66] Others came in through the Palmach's unique recruiting methods. Sadeh and a few of his "boys" went around to Galilee kibbutzim to recruit youngsters without any advance preparation, often in the face of opposition from the kibbutz or from Haganah district commanders, and frequently ignoring the quota regulations and other delaying factors.[67] Others got to the Palmach on their own. For example, when a young Haganah member urged the regional commander to organize units that would respond in the event of a German invasion of Palestine, he was told that such a unit already existed and was put in touch with Palmach commanders.[68]

Sadeh, the "old man," was in his fifties when he established the Palmach. He was, in the full sense of the word, a "forerunner" alienated from his own generation, who gave expression to the longings of the youthful generation.[69] The youngsters shared his interpretation of events and admired his originality and his flexible approach to Haganah procedures. For example, he decided on his own to liquidate the Arab who murdered the guard Alexander Zaid at Sheikh Abreiq.[70]

A romantic flavor permeated Sadeh's innovativeness. His relationship with his "boys," his followers, recalls Max Weber's descriptions of the charismatic community founded on the emotional element in social relations. Sadeh's "boys" were the core around which the Palmach evolved as a military unit.[71] Their initiative was undertaken without the involvement and backing of political party organs. Until that time, their participation had been a sine qua non for achieving anything substantial in the Yishuv.

The common social background shared by Palmach recruits helped bring about a uniform outlook. In the early period, many Palmach volunteers were from kibbutzim, and the kibbutz functioned as an exclusive social elite in the Yishuv.[72] Although the Palmach did not impose a rigorous selection process, natural selection was apparently at work. As one member wrote, "Was it essential to join the Palmach? On the kibbutz where I was born and raised it was a necessity. We were totally committed."[73] The archetypal Palmach member was a young, native-born kibbutz member. This exclusivity was one of the means by which the military way gradually became so esteemed.

The Palmach devoted its early years largely to improving its military professionalism. Anyone who peruses the organization's rules and training programs is immediately struck by the priority given this element.[74] The Palmach's founders regarded it as the highest stage in an evolutionary process of which the genesis was the military units of the late 1930s, the Nodedet and the Fosh. Despite disagreements regarding its character—a "fighting elite" to Sadeh, a cadre for the Haganah to Eliahu Golomb—professional prowess was the main emphasis.[75]

The British, too, played a role in the establishment of the Palmach as a professional military unit, alienated from party politics, with high professional standards. It was at their request that the Jewish Agency organized some forty young people to serve as scouts and interpreters for the Australian troops that invaded Syria. The youngsters' professional com-

bative approach and their familiarity with the geography of the region
enabled them to participate actively in the invasion, and there is no doubt
that their success played a part in the Palmach's creation. When cooperation with the British was institutionalized, the Palmach, numbering a
few hundred fighters, became a kind of trained, professional commando
unit. British instructors provided weapons, a budget, even food, and their
instructors were top-notch. April 1942 saw the opening of the "big
course" in which the entire Palmach received training in sabotage methods and reconnaissance tactics. Concurrently it was decided to double
the organization's size and increase its budget.

The second stage of training under British instructors was completed
in early June 1942. The Palmach's professional level continued to rise. In
August, with Palmach still under British auspices, the first central course
for squad commanders was held, and special units were formed: the German Section was readied to operate in enemy territory, the "Arabists" for
intelligence-gathering in Arab states. When the courses ended, the participants were not sent home: for the first time in the history of the
Yishuv, permanent bases were set up for the recruits.[76]

The Palmach thus generated a new role perception in the Yishuv: the
full-time fighter. Its organizational structure, with its own headquarters
and special budgets, open-ended enlistment, high level of training, and
innovative combat doctrine, was suited to the new professional conception. As among the British Army enlistees, military professionalism took
on a clear political meaning. The new perception was that Zionism's
goals could be realized in a military way.

The young people's self-image as professional warriors was flagrantly
at odds with the image of the pioneer as it was formed at the advent of
the century by the second and third "waves of immigration" to Palestine.
Nor did it correspond to the ideal of the "farmer-guard," the embodiment of the Yishuv tradition of static security. In the 1920s and 1930s, slogans referring to the "negation of the plow and the call to the sword" had
been confined exclusively to the political Right, which assailed the labor
movement's legitimacy. Now this same conception was adopted by the
younger generation, which was rooted in mainstream Labor Zionism.

We have already seen that the notion of "venturing beyond the
perimeter" conflicted with the concept of the farmer, rooted to the land
and guarding it zealously. The new idea was undoubtedly better suited
to members of the native-born generation than to their parents. In their
youth, the new generation crisscrossed the country on hikes, and their
attitude toward agricultural work and rootedness in the soil—concepts
that had signified the turning points in their parents' lives—was somewhat disparaging. The new ethos was found in a book that presented the
zeitgeist of the young generation: "Strange . . . you, the sabras, you do not
speak at all about the idea of holding the land . . . as though this notion
had never existed. And if someone does talk about it, you respond mock-

ingly: 'Zionism.' Jimmi, too, when he heard someone talking about it, would say with ridicule: 'Look, this guy has come to hammer Zionism into us.' "[77]

Sadeh vigorouly spread the Palmach idea. During 1942, he spoke at kibbutz movement conferences, demanding that recruitment to the Palmach continue. He did not always get a receptive response. "There is haggling everywhere," he remarked, "and this is amazing. . . . It makes the whole thing pointless." In the face of the interminable arguments about enlistment that broke out at kibbutz movement conferences, Sadeh presented a purposive approach: "I was not sent here and I was not invited. . . . You were undoubtedly discussing important matters. In Russia, can people meet together and discuss such issues? . . . Have we prepared ourselves [to fight] better than Chamberlain, of whom we were critical?" Sadeh thought that only one subject was worthy of discussion: combat. In contrast to the many garrulous speakers, he usually made do with a few sentences. His terseness made a tremendous impression, mirroring the new conception in which the emphasis was not on talking but on doing.[78]

But the direction that Sadeh had in mind was uncongenial to the leadership, a situation which in itself could generate a praetorian potential. An attack on a professional military organization by a political leadership seeking to undermine its autonomy and its exclusivity, and especially to negate its importance, may well bring about the military's tendency to intervene in politics.[79]

Indeed, the Yishuv institutions at first took a negative attitude toward the Palmach. This attitude was manifested in various spheres. For example, some new recruits were assigned to A Company, which was transferred from the north to the south of the country in view of the German invasion threat. Although they were pleased at being sent to the front, much to the inductees' surprise, they were sent south armed only with sticks. A Company was one of the Palmach's two veteran and respected units. Until the latest callup order, its personnel had come almost entirely from Hakibbutz Hameuhad; for them, the consciousness of the Palmach's necessity and importance was a "living need," in the words of their commander. The unit's expansion and its transfer to the Negev with sticks for weapons led soldiers and commanders alike to conclude that they were being deprived of the opportunity to shape the Palmach in a manner that would reflect their desire to fight. They aired their concerns at a meeting. The acting company commander tried to mute the protest but also said: "If they went to the front, to the 'first line of fire,' without the primary thing—weapons—that was a fatal mistake."[80]

The meeting helped bring into being a cohesive separate identity, of professional fighters espousing a clear political view who were being deprived of social esteem. Following the meeting, ten of the company's members, headed by a squad commander from a kibbutz and two platoon leaders, reached a practical conclusion and enlisted in the British Army in the hope of realizing their status image and seeing military action. There is evidence that an entire platoon was about to follow suit but was dissuaded from this course by Sadeh.[81] Of those who left and of the platoon leader who said that the Palmach's role had ended and that the time had come to fight, the editor of the Palmach bulletin wrote: "You did not go, but deep in your heart you half-shared his sentiments. You thought: in the Yishuv you are called a shirker, and when you come to town you 'swell up,' it's true, for all the world like a full-fledged army man in the underground, but you are deeply ashamed of your so-called uniform."[82]

"Sticks instead of guns" (in the words of a popular song of the time) remained embedded in the collective memory of every Palmach member, for this symbolic event bespoke a harsh reality larger than one isolated case. The reality for Palmach members in this period was incessant friction with the surrounding society. Palmach members had to carry with them at all times a certificate of release from the army. When fear of German invasion seized the Yishuv in 1942, the certificate did not prevent them from being branded shirkers.[83] Articles in the press denounced the Palmach. A well-known professor, Ben-Zion Dinur, later minister of education, wrote: "Whoever is of army age must go to the army and only to the army and nowhere else.... Anyone with eyes can certainly observe ... this type of the 'important' young man, with the release in his pocket and a look of secretive seriousness on his face and satisfaction in his heart and the hearts of his relatives."[84]

In 1942 most of the leadership was increasingly disposed to see enlistment in the British Army as the Yishuv's only hope in the event of an invasion. The Palmach, they felt, with its few hundred members, was irrelevant from this standpoint.[85] For this reason, Palmach members suffered from lack of esteem and low status. It seemed unlikely to see action, and its future prospects were questionable.[86]

This chapter has shown how the military way was carried forward with the establishment of new military structures and the creation of a new role of the full-time professional fighter. Certain attributes of the new path showed that it possessed a political thrust entailing a radical overhaul of the existing situation: ideas of lordship over the land and a craving for independence, including liberation from British rule, a solution of the "Arab problem" by using force, awareness of the young of their value as warriors, and criticism of the veteran Yishuv leaders, who refused to recognize the importance of the new military way. The military practices gradually took shape as a characteristic feature of a sociological generation. But they were still a long way from being institutionalized or becoming a central factor in the society at large.

PART TWO

The Military Way and Party Politics, 1940–1942

CHAPTER THREE

Hakibbutz Hameuhad
and the Palmach

Throughout 1942, clear affinities developed between the military units and the Yishuv's power structure, which was dominated by the veteran leadership. The two main political parties, the Mapai Majority and the Hakibbutz Hameuhad Secretariat, which formed the main leadership of Faction B, resorted to the military way in their competition for control of the Yishuv. The political use of the military was accompanied by a debate over mobilization priorities, the "in uniform" and "without uniform" controversy. The main question that the debate raised was whether to join the British Army and contribute to the main war effort of the period or to volunteer for the Palmach, the independent force of the Yishuv. The Mapai Majority inclined toward supporting enlistment in the British Army while not rejecting the Palmach, whereas Hakibbutz Hameuhad Secretariat opted for the Palmach although sharing in recruitment to the army. This and the following chapter deal with the background and causes of this sectarian linkage between political bodies and military units; they also consider the influence of this factionalism on the character of the new military way and its later transmutation into militarism.

The conflict between Mapai and Hakibbutz Hameuhad had its origins in the 1920s. Mapai won the support of the urban workers and at the same time completed the formation of its party apparatus, which gave total backing to Ben-Gurion as leader of the Yishuv. The main loser in these developments was Hakibbutz Hameuhad. In 1927 its leaders demanded that Mapai affirm that the kibbutz was the only socialist way, but Ben-Gurion and Berl Katznelson were unresponsive.[1] The controversy was exacerbated in the 1930s, particularly after another settlement movement, Hever Hakvutsot, joined Mapai, so that Hakibbutz Hameuhad was no longer the only kibbutz element in the party.[2] Toward the end of the decade, Hakibbutz Hameuhad's distinctive worldview led it to undertake separate political organizing within Mapai. Faction B was set up, composed of most of the rank-and-file and the secretariat of Hakibbutz Hameuhad. In July 1939, Yitzhak Tabenkin, the leader of Hakibbutz Hameuhad, resigned from the Mapai Center, followed by other committee members; he explained that his participation in the party institutions was fictitious and that the leadership did not involve him in decision making.[3] Speaking to the movement's secretariat, Ben-Gurion demanded that it cease acting like a political party.[4] But Hakibbutz Hameuhad continued to acquire extensive influence, not least in the military domain. Its aspirations to general Yishuv influence were blatant, as Israel Galili, the young Kibbutz leader, noted: "Our kibbutz [movement] harbors a great ambition to exert its authority and influence on the labor movement and it has the ability to shape the Yishuv."[5] In this way, two rival power structures were formed within Mapai, which struggled for domination in the Yishuv: the Mapai Majority, under the leadership of Ben-Gurion and Katznelson, and Faction B, under the leadership of Yitzhak Tabenkin.

As we have seen, owing to the political crisis in the Yishuv in the late 1930s, the military units evolved autonomously without substantive support from the institutionalized parties. Indeed, they were increasingly critical of the parties and their veteran leaderships. It was only a matter of time until both Hakibbutz Hameuhad and the Mapai Majority began to intervene in the internal working of the new military groups. Viewed as a resource that could be exploited for sectarian party politics, they did not refrain from taking various steps to link the military groups to them ideologically and organizationally. The crisis in the military groups—the fact that they did not receive moral and material support from the Yishuv—facilitated the connection formed between party politics and the military way.

HAKIBBUTZ HAMEUHAD AND MOBILIZATION

The orientation of Hakibbutz Hameuhad toward the military way was also economically motivated. In the early 1940s, the end of the major waves of immigration and increasing enlistment to the British Army produced a manpower shortage in all the land-settlement movements. Hakibbutz Hameuhad was worst affected. The structure of a large kibbutz was unsuited to temporary or seasonal manpower solutions. Italy's entry into the war had been an economic boon for the kibbutz movements: the absence of competition, the blocking of imports, the growing demand for agricultural produce, and above all the extensive needs of the Allied forces stationed in Palestine brought the kibbutzim unprecedented prosperity. They built factories, introduced new branches, and expanded their construction programs. Hakibbutz Hameuhad sought ways to cope with the manpower shortage. Some proposed mobilizing city youths to help the kibbutzim and raising the induction age to the British army to twenty-one. But these and other proposed solutions were found to be ineffective.[6]

Under the pressure of Hakibbutz Hameuhad, all the kibbutz movements began to send members to the British Army according to quotas set in conjunction with the Yishuv leadership. But the quota system kept mobilization at a low level while leaving the right to decide in the hands of the kibbutz movements. The Mapai Majority, together with its supporters in Hakibbutz Hameuhad, who resisted the policy of their secretariat, tried to have the system abolished. When the kibbutz movement balked, it was accused in summer 1941 of being hostile to recruitment. The Mapai activist Shmuel Dayan, for example, termed the kibbutz movement's call-up policy "shameful evasion" and urged that the draft be imposed without hair-splitting and without talk about the young generation, the foundation of the future.[7]

But the attacks on Hakibbutz Hameuhad were unavailing. Its leaders claimed that without the quotas the kibbutzim would fall apart, the Yishuv economy would collapse, and the country would be left without young people to defend it. Belonging to or joining a kibbutz, it was argued, was in itself a form of mobilization.[8] The quota system was not abolished, and when in 1941 a formal order introduced a general call-up, it took on a new significance: all young people, including moshav members, were made subject to the draft, but members of kibbutzim exempted. The kibbutzim themselves were appalled by this turn of events. As a member of one kibbutz explained, "It's understandable. . . . For us, the army has become the pressure point in a question of conscience. Every member who enlists and joins the army gives the others no peace."[9] The secretariat was aware of the problem. "If we pit the notion of going to a border settlement against mobilization," one member said, "they won't want to remain in the kibbutzim. They consider working there to be of declining importance."[10]

The newly formed Palmach was still not perceived as an answer to these problems. The young kibbutz members' insistence on enlisting further exacerbated the economic problem. Equally important, it threatened to undermine the authority of the kibbutz leadership. Some young women also wanted to join up, and the secretariat, trying to fight this trend, organized a meeting to propagandize in favor of women joining the Haganah.[11] There and in two subsequent sessions of the kibbutz movement's Council, the women were urged to show greater responsibility in work, not to view picking potatoes as something inferior, and to fight for their right—not to be inducted—but to drive a tractor.[12]

The young women did not relent, but neither did the secretariat. It claimed the women were enlisting because of a "psychosis" atmosphere which created the wrongheaded impression, shared also by the young men, that only the enlistees contributed to the war effort. Addressing a meeting of the kibbutz movement Council, Yitzhak Tabenkin said: "I know that there is a cult of the uniform, and there is something wrong with our people if they can't be inducted without a cult of the uniform. When I say to the fellow who wants to enlist in the army: serve as a commander in the northern Dead Sea area [i.e., the frontier], he shrugs off the proposal and doesn't go, but insists on his place in the army."[13]

The kibbutz movement, then, was in a qunadary. The younger generation believed that its aspirations would be realized through the military way; working the land and following the kibbutz life-style no longer seemed the only way to materialize national aspirations. The kibbutz movement's slogan of "who's for the farm and who's for arms" was seen as an evasive formula even by many of the kibbutz inductees.[14]

The Palmach was not presented as an alternative to enlistment in the British Army, even though its members came to kibbutz gathering to elicit support.[15] But in April 1942 Hakibbutz Hameuhad displayed a new attitude toward the Palmach. The danger posed by German field marshal Erwin Rommel's forces in North Africa was palpable, and the secretariat found in the Palmach a counterweight to the army, a solution to the young people's desire for military activism that did not conflict with the kibbutz movement's political or economic interests.

In early 1942 the Mapai Secretariat decided that half of those called up would go to the army and the rest to the Palmach and the Supernumerary Police. The objection to this arrangement voiced by Israel Galili was recorded in the minutes at his request.[16] Thus was launched the debate over "in uniform" or "without uniform"—the controversy over mobilization priorities. It was a debate more significant for its political ramifications than for its substance. In each of the kibbutz movement's four Council meetings that year the main subject was the general call-up, but in practice Hakibbutz Hameuhad lent its organizational, financial, and social weight to one cause: the Palmach.

In April the Council met at Kibbutz Givat Brenner and decided on the enlistment of 600 members, as follows: "At this stage, of every ten enlistees from Hakibbutz Hameuhad, three will volunteer for the army, three for the Supernumerary Police, and four to our units [the Palmach]."[17] This decision conflicted with a Mapai resolution, adopted two days earlier, which spoke of mobilization on a fifty-fifty basis. Mobilization priorities were also a bone of contention at the Histadrut Convention around this time. All the delegates had views on the subject, their opinions mirroring political affiliations. As one delegate noted, "The most shocking speech at the convention was Tabenkin's, and the most shocking act was that by Ben-Zion [Yisraeli], because it changed his life [i.e., his enlistment in the army]. . . . And the most tragic thing is that Tabenkin's formulation encounters Ben-Zion's self-fulfillment as an ideological opponent."[18]

Excitement and expectations in Hakibbutz Hameuhad ran high when young kibbutz members joined the Palmach. They were the first kibbutz generation, sons and daughters of the founders, who for their parents symbolized the new, liberated Jew not voluntarily transplanted to his homeland but rooted in it naturally. The journal of one kibbutz wrote:

"We know that the children of this soil will be among the finest defenders. This group proves that the blood bond with this land [is] an unbreakable one."[19]

In fact, these young people were not sent to the front but to other kibbutzim, in line with the new work-and-training program. Not everyone welcomed the arrangement. Eliahu Golomb, the Hagana leader, said that the transfer of people from Givat Brenner (one kibbutz) to a camp at Ein Harod (another kibbutz) and from Ein Harod to a camp at Givat Brenner would not have much impact on security.[20] Someone proposed that the Palmach members return to their kibbutzim after completion of the training program. However, Tabenkin, the kibbutz leader, was adamant: "If the Palmachniks go back to their kibbutzim, this framework will be meaningless and there will be no justification for preventing young people from enlisting in the army."[21]

The Palmach recruits were not impressed by Tabenkin's plans for their future. They suffered from a sense of social inferiority because they saw no action and were considered draft evaders. Their work in host kibbutzim further demonstrated their inability to actualize the military way they had chosen. In early July 1942, as Rommel's troops advanced toward Palestine, Palmach members stopped working and embarked on a full-time training program, but soon the majority resumed the work-and-training routine. A month later, in August 1942, the Yishuv was celebrating what was being touted as the greatest achievement of the British Army recruitment program: the formation of the Jewish infantry battalions. At the time the Palmach had fewer than a thousand members and its very existence was in jeopardy.

Nevertheless, Mapai was concerned about the strong affiliations that were created between the military unit and Hakibbutz Hameuhad. Some Mapai leaders had suggested that Palmach members be transferred to the army. The Hakibbutz Hameuhad Council, which met the same month in Kibbutz Na'an, came to the Palmach's aid. The intention was to turn the temporary arrangement of work and training into a permanent one and to present the Palmach as an alternative to the battalions. "Not a single Palmachnik will be inducted [into the army]," Israel Galili declared. "The Palmach's place in the scale of values is no less than the worth of our battalions."[22] The Na'an meeting dealt with the economic benefit the kibbutzim would derive from the Palmach members' work, though some had their doubts. As it turned out, the kibbutzim did quite well economically from this "human means of production."[23]

But not only economic concerns and the will to power guided Hakibbutz Hameuhad. In its view, supporting the Palmach was to support a Zionist line constituting a preparatory stage for a national-liberation war. In a lecture around the time of the Na'an meeting, Tabenkin presented his views on the relation between peace and war. He spoke of the unfulfilled pacifist dream that does not entertain the thought of using force and violence to attain goals. He heaped scorn on the League of Nations' "illusion" of solving international conflicts around a discussion table and rejected the reformist tendency in the Labor movement which aspired, in his opinion, to prove the justness of its cause in parliament rather than in war and struggle. "In every conflict," Tabenkin explained in his lecture, "no side ever gave up land, rights, possessions, or property out of goodwill, by way of logic and proof. No conflict . . . was ever solved without real struggle." Tabenkin appealed to educators to neither ignore nor disparage the war. He warned that following the war in Europe the Arabs would attempt to take over Palestine and the Yishuv and that relations with them could be resolved only through battle. Tabenkin's militaristic assumption that the solution by force of arms was the necessary, desirable, and ultimate solution in the national struggle was central to the link between Hakibbutz Hameuhad and the Palmach, which from this time espoused militant Zionism.[24]

The Mapai Majority could neither delay nor block the initiatives of Hakibbutz Hameuhad regarding the Palmach. The results of the Histadrut elections held in June 1941 meant that the Mapai Majority did not wield total influence in all Yishuv institutions and could not always ram its desires through in a vote.[25] In fact, cooperation between the two kibbutz movements, Hashomer Hatza'ir and Hakibbutz Hameuhad, gave them a majority in the Histadrut's Actions Committee. With it they had been able to block, for example, plans to transfer some Palmach personnel to the British Army's Jewish battalions. The situation in the Histadrut thus prevented the Mapai Majority from realizing its ideas concerning the army and the Palmach, and the political crisis was aggravated.[26]

"To wait for someone's approval—let us not wait, let us go ahead on our own," Tabenkin said.[27] In this spirit, Hakibbutz Hameuhad made loans and donated funds to the Palmach which were an important channel of influence for the kibbutz and a cause of discord with the Mapai Majority.[28] Hakibbutz Hameuhad also tried to co-opt high school graduates and youth movement groups training for kibbutz life to the Palmach. Benny Marshak, a secretariat member who had joined the Palmach, would turn up in military dress at meetings of the National Secretariat of Hamahanot Ha'olim. Assembling young people in schoolyards, places of work, and branches of youth movements, he would spark debates: Is this the time for work or studies? Has the time not come to undergo arms training?[29]

In October, Ben-Gurion returned from the United States to Palestine, bearing with him the Biltmore Program, which contained an open declaration for the establishment of a Jewish state. The program had been adopted in May at the Extraordinary Zionist Conference held at the Biltmore Hotel in New York. He moved immediately to deal with the situation in Mapai. Twice that month he met with the secretariat of Hakibbutz Hameuhad. Tabenkin recalled what went on at those meetings. Ben-Gurion claimed that Tabenkin had turned Hakibbutz Hameuhad into a political force, which was an aberration in terms of its original function. He told Tabenkin that he had returned to conduct a momentous Zionist war, having despaired of Chaim Weizmann and the World Zionist Organization, and that he considered Hakibbutz Hameuhad a partner in this endeavor. Tabenkin was unimpressed. He thought Ben-Gurion was driven by narrow political motivations and asked him sarcastically if, after despairing of Weizmann, he intended to go to war with Mapai moderates.[30] Ben-Gurion's remarks were unconscionable to Tabenkin, and his response was clear: "We have a war over the independence of the labor movement, in work, in the settlements, in the cooperatives, in educating children, pioneering youth, defense and security needs, mobilization and immigration."[31]

As Hakibbutz Hameuhad endeavored to influence the whole Yishuv, it found common conceptual ground with Hakibbutz Ha'artzi in the military domain. From the beginning of 1942, when Tabenkin first tried to win over Hakibbutz Ha'artzi to the Palmach idea, he resorted to class-based arguments. He labeled the actions of the middle-class sector in the Haganah "sabotage" and "subversion"; urged the dismissal of what he called the gaba'im (synagogue wardens), who had become power brokers in security matters; and told Hakibbutz Ha'artzi that in the military realm the two socialist movements could together bring to fruition the class war.[32]

Subsequently, this worldview would influence the character of the Palmach and its constitution as a "praetorian guard."[33] Meanwhile, the cooperation between the two kibbutz movements introduced party-movement politicization in the Palmach. It was rampant even in the organization's high command. In a joint meeting of the movements' leaders held in early 1943, Meir Ya'ari, the leader of Hakibbutz Ha'artzi, asked why his movement was not represented on the Palmach high command or among its senior commanders. His colleague, Ya'akov Hazan, demanded that a third of the places on the Palmach high command go to the movement and that Hashomer Hatza'ir representatives should take part in Palmach information activities.[34] These demands were partially met: a Hashomer Hatza'ir member was co-opted to Palmach headquarters, all of whose members, with the sole exception of the treasurer, were from Hakibbutz Hameuhad.[35]

Party-movement politicization also affected the appointment of Palmach commanders. In November 1941, only two Palmach company commanders were from Hakibbutz Hameuhad, but by the end of 1942 the number had risen to four out of six, and in 1945, when the Palmach battalions were formed, all their commanders were from Hakibbutz Hameuhad, not to mention the information officer and the editor of the organization's journal.[36]

WORKER-FIGHTER

Finding a formula to reduce the gap between the professional military framework and the socialist kibbutz movement was essential, since the high command of the Palmach's fully formed conception of the idealized character of their military organization did not meet the expectations of Hakibbutz Hameuhad. At the Council meeting in July 1942, Israel Idelson, from Hakibbutz Hameuhad Sectariat, had complained that the Palmach wanted a full-time soldier who could be easily transferred from place to place, and that this was to disregard the economic needs of the kibbutzim.[37] The Palmach high command also objected to expanding its ranks to bring about greater social diversification.[38] However, a large Palmach suited the old vision of a large kibbutz and also the political ambitions of Hakibbutz Hameuhad's leadership, which sought dominance in the Yishuv. Hence Tabenkin's assertion: "The Palmach is stringent in its conditions for selecting and accepting people, and this should be moderated. . . . It will be no answer if the Palmach comes in place of everything else, and we end up with only a select and superb handful [of people]."[39]

Hakibbutz Hameuhad Secretariat urged a restructuring of the Palmach so that it could accept young women who otherwise might join the British Army. Tabenkin complained that there were few women in the Palmach and that the training program was not geared to their needs.[40] The Palmach did not want to accept "individual" city dwellers who had a different background from the "veterans"; they had different reasons for enlisting and some of them reached Palmach via Yishuv mobilization orders. The Palmach journal gave expression to the doubts about the absorption of these "parachutists."[41] Palmach commander Sadeh agreed that such programs threatened the organization's military prowess, and Galili and Tabenkin were hard-pressed to convince him otherwise.[42] Tabenkin was actually concerned that the professional conception of the Palmach, wholly divorced from kibbutz socialist values, would foment what can be termed praetorian tendencies within the Palmach, that its members might use their weapons to impose their will in the Yishuv. By introducing a way of life combining work with training on kibbutzim, as well as through the idea of the "worker-fighter," Tabenkin and his colleages hoped to squelch such trends. But they encountered strong opposition from within the military unit.

Palmach members saw the work-and-training routine exactly for what it was—a program that was contrary to the conception of the full-time fighter, which had characterized the Palmach in its first year, and a return to the farming they had sought to escape. Even sick days, of which there were plenty owing to the unfit quarters in the harsh winter that year, were deducted from the month's fourteen training days, lest they prove detrimental to the agricultural work. Both kibbutz members and city folk refused to do agricultural work. The former asked why they should have to work in someone else's kibbutz in return for a few days of training and said that they saw the field of the military as being an equally original Jewish way; the latter could not get accustomed to farming and said they had joined the Palmach to fight, not to work.[43]

One center of agitation was B Company, which until mobilization order number 3 had drawn most of its members from Hakibbutz Ha'artzi. The company's objections to the work-and-training program prompted Palmach headquarters to convene meetings with representatives of the official institutions and the land-settlement movements. Later, Hakibbutz Ha'artzi Secretariat organized a meeting for its members in the Palmach, as did its counterpart Hakibbutz Hameuhad. All tried to dampen the raging spirit of the youth.[44]

One of the meetings is abundantly documented. Some young speakers accused the kibbutz movement of war profiteering by exploiting the idea of work and training to its economic advantage. All said they were disappointed by the new program's adverse effect on the Palmach's military professionalism. Instead of devoting itself to training, the Palmach was engaged in work, but nowadays work meant something very different than it had in the past, they explained. Shurika, who would become one of the most admired women fighters in the Palmach, said: "I came here to get an education in the life of partisans. . . . We did not enlist for a labor formation." The young Palmach members blamed the leadership for their situation. Their speeches revealed the existence of an elitist military group with a manifest-destiny orientation which they felt obliged to realize. Prevented from achieving its goals, the group had developed a sense of alienation from the general public and the Yishuv leadership. Some even drew conclusions: if the leadership lacks the funds to support the Palmach as a military unit which is not dependent on the work of its soldiers, they said, the money should be raised by coercion, through expropriations or organized fund-raising. A Palmach member gave voice to this frame of mind: "We are united in the view that the method of fund-raising practiced in the Yishuv is flawed and incorrect. . . . In the face of a public like this, sermonizing is not enough. . . . Obviously, as long as things continue to be arranged in the offices we will always be a minority, and that is exactly what riles us. We are not ready to accept things as they are. We are ready to do everything to change the facts."[45]

These statements suggest at least a readiness to threaten the use of arms to change the face of reality. Israel Galili's notebook contains a vivid account of the young people's praetorian spirit at the meeting. One member who condemned the petty bourgeois for refusing to help underwrite the Palmach said: "[We] are ready for arrests and battles. . . . There will be no peace in the Yishuv." Another noted: "There are differences here between the rank and file and the thinkers up above."[46] The atmosphere of recalcitrance and revolt produced a variety of demands; there was more than one call to fight the middle-class rightists, and the institutions were criticized for preferring a modus vivendi with them.[47]

These symptoms of praetorianism, resulting from the affront to Palmach professionalism, came as a surprise to the Yishuv's veteran leaders. They held talks with Palmach members to show them the light. In one of the meetings, Moshe Sneh, chief of the Haganah National Command, asserted that fund-raising of this kind meant breaking with the supervision and authority of the Yishuv institutions and the start of a degeneration like that of the Irgun.[48] Eliahu Golomb, the Haganah leader, told the young people in another meeting that, in effect, they were questioning the basic ground upon which the Yishuv was founded.[49]

Hakibbutz Hameuhad Secretariat convened all its members serving in the Palmach in order to persuade them that its approach was the right one. Tabenkin rejected the proposals to obtain money by force, stating that the needed funds would come from the working sector. Adducing the Soviet Union as a model, he said that there the army maintained itself by work and credit. He also called for an effort to induce Hashomer Hatza'ir to help make the Palmach a workers' army and provocatively asked his young listeners why they were contemptuous of this ideology.[50] The leader of the Israeli Left strove to link army and party-movement politics, even at the cost of weakening the Palmach's characteristic pure professional and national element.

The intervention of political bodies, parties, or movements in the affairs of the military is a common phenomenon, especially in struggles for national liberation. Attempts to block the intervention based on the argument that it will adversely affect professionalism and discipline are rarely successful.[51] The Palmach, too, inevitably succumbed to politicization. Palmach members and commanders protested and made threats but were not in a position to rebuff the initiatives of Hakibbutz Hameuhad, through which the Palmach was able to overcome its low social status, its material distress, and the political objections to its very existence.

Still, some were uneasy with the new situation, since the direct attachment between the Palmach and the kibbutz movement, with its particular values, would preclude the possibility of actualizing the professional military way. The dissenters "defected"—as those who remained termed it—to the British Army. In fact, the desertion rate was much higher than the 10 percent officially stated by the Palmach, and its impact was long felt. Two years later, a Hakibbutz Hameuhad security activist said that the Palmach had undergone a serious crisis in which it was idle, awaiting its eventual role, but at the time it was not clear that the role would be fulfilled, and many left.[52]

The idea that the Yishuv's political problems should be solved by force—not through the "kibbutz way" but through the "military way," as one of the "deserters" said[53]—prevailed not only among the deserters but equally among those who remained. The former, however, did not believe that the bond between the Palmach and Hakibbutz Hameuhad was productive and certainly not a suitable alternative to the advantages of serving in the British Army, which was a professional force isolated from society. In contrast, those who stayed thought that the military solution would come about through the unique path of the kibbutz movement and its cooperation with the Palmach. In this light, a Palmach journal depicted those who left as vacillators who sought only their own personal solution. Uri Brenner, who had received a kibbutz education, said later that those who stayed "viewed the issue from the perspective of the movement."[54]

Later chapters will consider the concrete effect of this movement perspective on the emerging cultural militarism. Certainly the party-movement politicization weakened the Palmach's professional foundation, its initial source of pride. Instead of fully realizing the idea of the nonsectarian, national professional soldier, the Palmach fighter gradually became a soldier of the faction, the party, the movement. Not completely, not declaratively, in some cases not even consciously, and not in a way that obligated everyone, since different political parties and settler movements were represented in the Palmach, but nevertheless the political affiliations were known and they were binding. The new identity of Palmach members also differed sharply from the image of absolute professionalism. Now they were worker-fighters, combining the plow and the rifle, emulating what was considered to be the Russian example. By 1942, this model was not extrinsic to the Palmach; it became more deeply embedded after the socialist youth movements joined the military unit two years later and the Soviet Union won the world war.

Tabenkin labeled the new military way "combatant antimilitarism."[55] But did the bond between the military unit and the political body, the penetration of party-movement criteria and the gradual consolidation of the trend to interweave the army and socialism, weaken the Palmach's militaristic and praetorian potential?

Through its massive support, Hakibbutz Hameuhad hoped to prevent the emergence of praetorianism based on a professional slant in the Palmach, to block the possible rise of a professional military elite alienated from the values and practices of the kibbutz movement. This motive for the military's intervention in politics may be called professional praetorianism. It occurs if the army is offended by decisions to scale it down, reduce its budget, or cut officers' salaries and deprive it of adequate armament or if its importance is not sufficiently recognized.[56] But military intervention in politics need not necessarily be triggered by the army's being a professional group isolated from society; it may derive from the army's very involvement in internal politics. Here the army is loyal to a party, class, movement, or ethnic group. To distinguish this case from the former, it may be called party praetorianism, a type of intervention that implies the possibility of cooperation between a political body and the military, leading sometimes to an attempt to take over the government through the potential or actual use of arms. The purpose in this case is to dictate a type of politics that serves the material or ideal interests of the party, political movement, class, or ethnic group. The involvement of soldiers in this case is usually the result of pervasive politicization in the army, inducing it to display loyalty to a certain conceptional cause and to the civilian group that represents it.[57]

The intervention of Hakibbutz Hameuhad reduced the Palmach's isolation and alienation and minimized the possible development of professional praetorianism. But it also paved the way for the possibility of party praetorianism. This was given expression in the Palmach's transfer to the kibbutzim, combining—with symbolic significance—work and training, and in the gradual blurring of roles between the kibbutz activist and the Palmach member, to the point where it was sometimes difficult to know whether certain individuals were acting as politicians or as soldiers. In any case, as long as the crisis in the leadership and the power struggles for control of the Yishuv continued, as long as Hakibbutz Hameuhad considered itself a political force with the self-styled role of leading the national struggle, the prospect existed that party praetorianism would arise in the Palmach.

Later chapters will show how the potential for party paretorianism affected the development and institutionalization of Israeli cultural militarism. It is important to note here that the worker-fighter arrangement did not signify an antimilitaristic approach. On the contrary, it helped blur the distinction between military and civil in a way that would bring about the militarization of society and spread the idea of the military solution to the national problem from the narrow confines of a military unit to the whole society. After 1942, Tabenkin, who claimed to draw inspiration from the Russian model, repeatedly came out with statements such as this: "In Russia, too, they do not distinguish between the war effort and the work effort."[58] But in fact, the worker-fighter concept more closely resembled the Prussian than the Soviet model. In eighteenth-century Prussia the soldier-worker resided in fortress towns and worked for his livelihood in order to conquer the frontier.[59] Moreover, when Tabenkin insisted on the Palmach-Russian analogy, he did not intend to send an antimilitaristic message, as when he spoke of the Palmach as "a camp of Jewish cossacks."[60] The Russian-born Tabenkin was well aware that in tsarist times the cossacks had been an elite unit that sought to expand the Russian empire's borders toward the northern Caucasus. The Palmach worker-fighter was thus the archetypal figure that would realize the vision of Greater Israel harbored by Hakibbutz Hameuhad. It was a model to conquer the land with a popular, militialike army which would complete the work of settlement.

Indeed, the socialist ideology which the Palmach inherited by way of the kibbutz was not presented and not perceived as an alternative to solving political problems militarily. In general, militarism and socialism are not mutually exclusive. Not by chance did Alfred Vagts, an eminent historian of militarism, coin the term *socialist militarism* to describe a philosophy that weds belief in a class society to use of armed struggle in order to realize the ideal.[61] Certainly militarism and socialism have not been at odds in twentieth-century attempts to turn socialism, or Marxism, into a type of regime which almost inevitably rested on centralistic, collectivist, coercive foundations.[62] In the Yishuv as well, militarism and socialism did not contradict each other.[63] Even the Russian example which Tabenkin so often cited was not presented as an antiwar socialist model. On the contrary, as Tabenkin himself said, "Russia did not err, but acted with reason in indoctrinating for the Red Army in every societal formation. Its mistake lies in the fact that the Red Army is not strong enough. . . . And here as well—our laws will be guided by the warrior . . . not by a farmer-and-worker type who only knows his work and neglects the gun."[64]

The following chapters will illuminate the militaristic content that marked the new image of the Palmach worker-fighter. At this stage, it should be noted that in those years Tabenkin, one of the Palmach's spiritual founding fathers, fervently preached militaristic solutions to the national problem of the Yishuv. He frequently resorted to circumlocutory and dialectic formulations such as this: "The meaning of education for war [is] to fight for the thing most diametrically opposed to war" and "Education for war versus pacifism is a war over a world without wars."[65] But what Tabenkin demanded concretely on behalf of Hakibbutz Hameuhad was not only the "militarization of our settlement enterprise," but the "militarization of the [entire] Yishuv—of every one of us." Thus a new conception, of a little Sparta, superseded the vision of the kibbutz as a humanist and socialist preserve. As Tabenkin explained to a gathering of teachers, "fighters' education must begin from kindergarten, not only from primary school, and even from the nursery." Moreover, "we should innoculate a child by taking him to spend nights in the mountains and valleys, to educate him to use the short stick and throw stones, to teach him to fight and to strengthen his body, and venture outside the perimeter."[66]

Those who deserted the Palmach in that period because of its affiliation with the kibbutz movement and joined the British Army could hardly be aware that the Palmach's party-movement politicization would not in the long run adversely affect its military way and its opportunities to fight. The historical irony is that it was precisely the Palmach, with its popular and militia elements and its "kibbutz way," that became the central carrier of the idea of military solutions for the Yishuv's political problems. Those who believed that the solution to the national problem should be realized in a completely professional way by a force like the British Army were able to wield less influence in the Yishuv.

The support of Hakibbutz Hameuhad for the Palmach was a major stage in the institutionalization and legitimation of the new military way. The Palmach was able to survive; not, it is true, along the narrow professional lines which had prompted its founding, but in a way that redressed its material problems and ended its alienation. The affiliation with Hakibbutz Hameuhad made the rise of professional praetorianism less probable. However, as long as the crisis within the political leadership persisted, the emergence of party-political praetorianism remained a distinct possibility. Nor should it be thought that only the Palmach gained from the support of Hakibbutz Hameuhad. The kibbutz movement was also a beneficiary. Its political power increased, and it became a key shaping force of the Yishuv. The link between the Palmach and Hakibbutz Hameuhad and the creation of a worker army was a fait accompli. The leadership of the Mapai Majority, still embroiled in the party crisis, was able to block some of the kibbutz movement's initiatives but not all of them. Instead, the Mapai Majority turned its efforts to the British Army enlistees in an attempt to influence the military way they represented.

CHAPTER FOUR

Mapai and Enlistment
in the British Army

Mapai, the dominant party in the Yishuv which controlled the Jewish Agency as well, was unable to articulate a consistent stand vis-à-vis the new military way which emerged in the late 1930s and early 1940s at the hands of the young generation. This situation was exacerbated by internal power struggles and lengthy absences of the party leader, Ben-Gurion. Not until the summer of 1940 did the leadership grasp its mistake. It then dropped its many demands to the British authorities about the character of enlistment, the new recruits' assignments, and the party's involvement in their affairs, and reached an agreement with them. Otherwise, Moshe Shertok said, thousands more would have enlisted without the aid of the Jewish Agency, "and we ourselves would have underscored our lack of authority . . . in Yishuv affairs."[1]

But the agreement still did not solve the leadership's authority problem, which was not only how to rule in the Yishuv but also how to achieve legitimacy for its positional primacy. In the meantime, the Revisionist movement urged its members to join the British Army, and most Irgun members enlisted. In exchange, the British granted the Revisionists parity in mobilization. Shertok explained to the British that this discredited the Jewish Agency in the public's eyes, but the British did not change their stance.[2] Opposition sprang up in the Yishuv to the leadership's dominant status in the call-up. Public figures such as Hebrew University president Yehuda Leib Magnes, Jewish Agency Executive members, and the mayor of Tel Aviv, all motivated by a liberal stance, denied its right to declare a national call-up or to take sanctions against evaders.[3] The mayor, for example, who belonged to the petit-bourgeois sector, followed the Revisionists and sent enlistees to a recruiting center unconnected with the Jewish Agency. This move incensed the leadership.[4] Its authority, however, was not measured at that time by groups which in any case did not support it. Far more problematic was the fact that Mapai was unable to impose its authority in military and mobilization matters even within the labor movement.

ATTEMPTS TO IMPOSE AUTHORITY

The quota system, as we have seen, benefited the kibbutz movements because it precluded individual volunteering, which went against their material and ideal interests. For a different reason, the quota system also served the interests of the Mapai leadership. It enabled the leadership to avoid having its authority tested by obligatory call-ups and allowed it to encourage mobilization through secondary associations which were loyal to the leadership, such as cooperatives, sporting organizations, and youth movements.[5] However, the split in the party soon led the leadership to realize that the quota system undermined its authority. As Shertok explained, "When one visits our settlements, one meets a good many lads who say, we are ready to go to the army. When you say to them, go, they say, it's impossible, we have to clear it with the kibbutz. When you come to the kibbutz, they tell you, it's out of the question, it has to be cleared with the kibbutz movement. At a higher stage they tell you to clear it with the Histadrut, and there they tell you that the kibbutzim have already fulfilled their quota." Excessive organization, Shertok maintained, had stifled the volunteering movement. In the midst of the Yishuv collectivism, he noted, there were manifestations of personal initiative, inner awakening, and an internal voice, and these must not be repressed.[6] Shertok spoke about the improbable constitutional problem which had arisen: who bore authority to decide on call-up in agricultural settlements, the Jewish Agency or the kibbutz?[7] But Shertok was not concerned about formalism, rather about Hakibbutz Hameuhad, whose actions threatened the authority of the Mapai Majority leadership.

In early 1941, when Ben-Gurion returned to Palestine following an absence of about ten months, he presented his program, "Guidelines for Zionist Policy," to the Jewish Agency Executive and declared his intention to further the idea of a Jewish state. Defining himself as a "Zionist preacher," Ben-Gurion spoke much about the tragic situation of Zionism. The movement had state roles to fulfill but did not command a state apparatus.[8] Ben-Gurion did not refrain from presenting the young generation as one factor that would bring about the desired change: "Zionist tension in the country," he said, "means first of all Zionist tension within the young people. The old generation is old. . . . Zionist policy is first and foremost a policy of power . . . and this is one of the things that was absent in Jewish theology. . . . Policy means power . . . accumulation of power, enlarging of power. . . . And the center of this power is the young generation. . . . If we demand all this, they will respond irrespective of all the frameworks, irrespective of all splits, parties, and class. Our appeal must be to Jewish youth!"[9]

Ben-Gurion uttered these clear statements during his five months of "preaching," when he sought to win over the Yishuv to his political programs. He hinted at forging a direct link with the young generation without organizational, movement, or party mediation, based on the military outlook shared by all the young people. His words, however, were not translated into concrete action. Ben-Gurion's biographer writes that when the leader of the Yishuv was asked by his colleagues in Mapai and the Jewish Agency Executive how he would implement his plan, he gave no clear answer.[10] Ben-Gurion indeed was content with slogans—"Zionist tension," "fierce war," "steadfastness," and others—which seemed to have a primarily political purpose: to reclaim authority for the majority leadership and amass all power in its hands. If not, why did the "Zionist preacher" devote most of his five months in Palestine to routine party activity and meeting with leaders of Hakibbutz Hameuhad?[11] The meetings led nowhere. Ben-Gurion asked the kibbutz movement's leaders, who were undermining his authority, to return to institutional activity, but they refused. The authority issue remained unresolved, and the Mapai Majority looked for a solution by forging a link with the British Army recruits.[12]

The mobilization order issued in May by the official institutions was the first universal call-up order in the history of the Zionist movement. Once the order was published, Ben-Gurion acted to enforce it. He publicized his positive attitude toward enlistment,[13] and in meetings with representatives of various organizations called on them to work for enlistment and to prefer the general authority over organizational loyalty. His listeners, though, remained skeptical. The policy espoused by the Mapai Majority encountered additional resistance because Hakibbutz Hameuhad activists held key positions in the Haganah. Put in charge of implementing a policy they opposed, they behaved like cats left to watch the cream.[14]

In the hope of altering the public's attitude toward enlistment and acquiring direct influence over the recruits, the leadership defined it as "the duty of volunteering." Shertok told a meeting of the Zionist Smaller Actions Committee: "We are not making do only with sanctions. We are spurring people to do their duty."[15] Lacking the means of coercion possessed by governments in sovereign states, the leadership attempted to obtain authority through this oxymoronic definition of the draft. It hoped in this way to overcome two possible problems concerning its authority: not to depict enlistment as an obligation only and thus risk a failure which would dramatize its limited authority without a state apparatus, but also not to make do with only the volunteering aspect, as this would grant absolute freedom to individuals and eliminate the possibility of using the draft to establish authority. Some social scientists and historians describe the Yishuv as an entity based on voluntary arrangements.[16] But the mechanism of "the duty of volunteering" suggests a more intricate picture. It was a political system that combined two opposing principles to control people and motivate them. If in those years the possibility existed of a clash between young fighters voluntarily enlisting in order to solve the national problem and the veteran leadership, which had its own view of reality, the formula of "the duty of volunteering" served as one of the political mechanisms that bridged this gap. The formula was not always effective, and intergenerational tensions did not disappear. Still, it frequently promoted cooperation between the young generation and the veteran leadership.[17]

The "duty of volunteering" formula seemed particularly well suited to the leadership's relations with the volunteer movements. The leadership could direct and oversee the movement's actions without corrupting characteristic principles of volunteering, spontaneity, emotionalism, and comradeship. Thus the volunteer movement spoke of "free volunteering" while the leadership talked about "discipline and obligation," but no friction developed between the two conceptions. As Berl Katznelson explained at a gathering of volunteers in September 1941: "How could we think it was enough if the institutions [merely] did their part? Enlistment requires a certain atmosphere, which does not exist, and which will be engendered in the first place by the volunteers themselves."[18] However, the rally that was supported to symbolize a turning point in the enlistment drive proved an abject failure in terms of its concrete results, and the leadership realized that it must place less emphasis on volunteering and more on obligation.

THE MAPAI SECRETARIAT AND THE PALMACH

On several occasions in 1942, the Mapai Majority complained that Hakibbutz Hameuhad had taken advantage of the party's paralysis to work independently in the military realm.[19] The Mapai Majority's support for enlistment in the British Army, which reached its peak with the formation of the Jewish battalions, was followed by the immediate countersupport of Hakibbutz Hameuhad for the Palmach. The crisis was further aggravated in September 1942, when Ya'akov Dori resigned as Haganah chief of staff. His letter of resignation denigrated the Palmach, emphasized the importance of enlistment in the British Army, and assailed the "peremptoriness with which civilians lay down rules and voice opinions" on military matters. By this he meant the involvement of Hakibbutz Hameuhad Secretariat in Palmach matters and the link that had developed between the army and party politics.[20]

On October 2, 1942, Ben-Gurion returned to Palestine after another lengthy absence, of some fifteen months. He referred to two major issues: the "Biltmore plan" and party organization.[21] He sought to create the impression that he wanted to realize this plan for an immediate revolutionary shift in Palestine policy. First, though, he met with several associates to discuss the situation in the party. A party meeting held that month at Kfar Vitkin decided to scrap the system of factions in the ruling party.

Ben-Gurion summed up this major political uproar in a single sentence in his diary: "In the afternoon [Sunday, October 25] I went to Kfar Vitkin; on Thursday, October 29, the conference concluded successfully."[22]

Ben-Gurion would now remain in the country, working with his colleagues to restore the leadership's authority. In a meeting at Eliyahu Golomb's house, Ben-Gurion asserted that only by retaining power could the party survive and that a watchful eye must be kept on Hakibbutz Hameuhad, which wanted control over the Yishuv.[23] The next day he told the Mapai Secretariat that henceforth "the party [must] be a genuine and substantive entity, with authority to act in matters it decides are within its authority; and no one and nothing must be allowed to curtail its authority or to assume that authority."[24] The word *authority* was repeated four times in that one sentence, and Ben-Gurion never missed an opportunity to hammer home the idea. In another meeting he said that the party should have unlimited authority over its members—greater than the state had over its citizens—over their body and their soul.[25]

Following the Kfar Vitkin conference, which put an end to the factions system in Mapai, the party majority tried to reinstate its authority in the military realm as well. First it tried to end the situation in which the Histadrut dealt with youth and military matters and to have decisions on these issues made instead by the Jewish Agency Executive and the National Council.[26] Second, the Mapai Majority prohibited loans to the Palmach; protest letters from Hakibbutz Hameuhad to the official institutions in the wake of the ban were ignored.[27] Yet another controversy involved the co-option of kibbutz training groups from youth movements to the Palmach. The Mapai Majority feared that this was another means by which Hakibbutz Hameuhad would extend its influence over the young. Speaking at a soldiers' meeting in Haifa, Katznelson said: "Some ask whether the party should prepare the young. We should prepare the young to fulfill Zionism in the next generation, which will follow us. . . . It is impossible for every bloc or faction to prepare its own youth for this task. Without the young nothing can be accomplished."[28]

Mapai's endeavors not to loosen the reins of power made a discussion of the Palmach's future inevitable. The Palmach, as an armed military organization, was perceived as an asset in which the party must increase its influence as part of its drive to acquire general authority and implement its declared goals. The Palmach-Hakibbutz Hameuhad link only made Mapai more determined to wrest control. Hence Ben-Gurion's assertion that he would certainly not turn over the affairs of the army, the Haganah, and the Palmach to Hakibbutz Hameuhad. Ben-Gurion's remark came in December 1942, the same month in which the Mapai Secretariat held its first discussion about the Palmach—a year and a half after the military organization's establishment. At the meeting, Katznelson emphasized that the Palmach should be considered very important if it fulfilled its own mission by remaining an instrument in the hands of Zionism and its authorized institutions and did not become an instrument to be used against those institutions.[29]

The Mapai Secretariat invited youth movement representatives to the December meeting to convince them not to join the Palmach. The status of the youth movements was on the decline because their members did not join any military unit, and many from the kibbutz training groups had left to enlist in the army.[30] Some of them wanted to join the Palmach, but the Mapai Secretariat warned that any change in the goal of the groups would harm the party. Following the meeting, the Mapai Secretariat published its conclusion: "The kibbutz training groups will remain within the existing framework." The youth movements that were subject to the influence of the Mapai Majority, Gordonia and the Scouts, accepted the decision, but in Hamahanot Ha'olim and Hano'ar Ha'oved, in which the influence of Hakibbutz Hameuhad was dominant, internal rifts grew and the situation reached a crisis point.[31]

At the time, about 150 participants in the kibbutz training groups wanted to join the army. Golomb, the senior figure in the Haganah, did not object and thus found himself at loggerheads with Israel Galili from Hakibbutz Hameuhad. Mapai leader Katznelson, for his part, expressed no particular sympathy for the Palmach. Calling for 200 Palmach personnel to be transferred to the British Army, he explained: "It is of the utmost importance . . . that the Palmach participate formally in the call-up. People should not flee the Palmach and become deserters, but take part in the call-up." The idea that the political leadership should control the Yishuv's military and have the decisive voice in its affairs was acceptable to Ben-Gurion and indeed to the entire Mapai Secretariat, which on December 9, 1942, had affirmed that it saw no objection to transferring part of the Palmach to the army.[32]

But Ben-Gurion, who was completely opposed to the Palmach phenomenon, wanted to go further. He decided to disband the Palmach, and a resolution to this effect was duly adopted by the party's Bureau, its highest institution, established after the Kfar Vitkin conference to enable decisions to be made without Faction B. Ben-Gurion told a Bureau meeting: "We propose the creation of a new framework, which will encompass all the youth organizations as well as nonparty youth. The budget exists. Affiliation and subordination will be on an individual basis. The goal will be a dual one: (a) Zionist education; (b) military training. The Palmach will also be part of this framework."[33]

Ben-Gurion, then, wanted to form an organization to replace the Palmach which would include the youth movements' kibbutz training groups. The new organization would engage in both settlement and military missions; it would not be party-affiliated, and membership would be on an individual basis, in order not to predetermine its character and its sectoral loyalties. Equally important, it would be completely under the control of the leadership.[34] The proposal, raised repeatedly in Mapai deliberations, was perceived as part of the organizational moves which would rehabilitate the party majority's standing and enable it to impose its authority on the young generation and the Palmach.[35] But the new organization was never created. The Mapai Majority lacked the power to implement its resolutions, and Hakibbutz Hameuhad set out to torpedo the idea.

The new prohibition on factions in Mapai left Hakibbutz Hameuhad Secretariat somewhat at a loss, but not for long. Following Mapai's decision to transfer part of the Palmach to the army and co-opt the rest to the mooted new organizations, Hakibbutz Hameuhad began considering how to prevent the Palmach's dissolution, even if this entailed taking far-reaching measures.[36] Next the movement convened another Council session, the fifth such gathering intended to promote the Palmach idea and curtail the increasing army enlistment by kibbutz members since the true scale of the Holocaust had become known.[37]

Two weeks later, Hakibbutz Hameuhad Secretariat organized a rally of hundreds of young people to express support for the Palmach and for the initiatives of the political body behind it. In terms of the period, this was a tremendous demonstration of strength, and the message was not lost on the Mapai Majority. The meeting's organizers gave it the bombastic title "Youth in the Face of the Diaspora Holocaust." Only one speaker, Haim Ben-Asher, a member of the Mapai Majority, called on the youngsters to shun insularity and join the fight against the Nazis. But his words made no impression. The youthful audience was more taken with the speeches of Hakibbutz Hameuhad leaders and of a few Palmach commanders and representatives of youth movements identified with Hakibbutz Hameuhad.[38]

A few days later, at the height of this charged atmosphere, kibbutz training groups from Hamahanot Ha'olim met to decide whether to join the Palmach. Idelson, from Hakibbutz Hameuhad, urged the young people to join only the Palmach, while Golomb, representing the Mapai Majority, argued that the Palmach was not everything. The vote on whether to join the Palmach was a tie, thus no decision was made.[39] In Hano'ar Ha'oved, too, supporters of the two major political forces were split on what the movement's graduates should do. The Mapai Majority had 2,000 of them enlist in the army.[40] But Hakibbutz Hameuhad also wielded some influence in the movement and was able to get four kibbutz training groups to join the Palmach.[41]

Hakibbutz Hameuhad did not succeed in its effort to channel the majority of youth movement graduates to the Palmach. Still, its counteroffensive led Mapai to abandon the idea of liquidating the Palmach. The party had to reconcile itself to the kibbutz movement's involvement in the Palmach. But to balance its inability to obtain monopoly on the organized means of violence in the society, Mapai devoted all its energy to increasing its influence over the British Army enlistees.

HAGANAH VS. THE VOLUNTEERING MOVEMENT

The decision to increase the dosage of "obligation" relative to "volunteering" in the "duty of volunteering" formula, following the failure of the October 1941 recruitment rally found expression in the leadership's increasing reliance on the Haganah. In view of the danger of a German invasion, Golomb drew up a plan "for imposing a regime of Yishuv-wide discipline." The plan was approved in April 1942 by the conventions of both Mapai and the Histadrut. A Center for the Mobilization of the Yishuv was set up, and a new Yishuv-wide call-up order was issued in June.[42]

The joint involvement of the volunteering movement, characterized by a communal, emotional, spontaneous approach, and the Haganah, with its formality, hierarchy, discipline, and obedience, produced friction in the mobilization drive. In March 1942 Shertok tried to resolve the problem. He brought the two sides together, trying to coordinate them and prevent dualities, but the tension persisted, each group trying to outdo the other. Volunteering activists, who by then had amassed considerable influence, sought to translate their military conception, formed during their years in the army, into a politically minded movement able to influence the public and the leadership. In 1942 they tried to form a federation of soldiers made up of democratically elected committees from army units. The elements of autonomous factionalism which were inherent in this process come through in a letter written by a recruit from one of the kibbutzim who objected to the phenomenon: "The soldiers have become accustomed to think of themselves as the nation's elect. The army must not be allowed to become the decisive factor in public life; the army has to be guided by the movement, the party, not vice versa. . . . I do not believe in the 'unique Hebrew' character of the Hebrew soldier. He is no nobler in character than any other soldier in the world. This is not an abstract question. Organizational frameworks are about to be set up which are supposed to give expression to this superior frame of mind, and I am not thrilled by the idea."[43]

Haganah activists regarded army enlistment as an arm of their organization; the volunteers, they said, should be subordinate to the Haganah and through it to the leadership. Galili, one of the Haganah leaders, explained that the volunteers' activity could be seen as positive and natural if they confined themselves to looking after the new recruits' cultural and economic needs and no more. This would make the recruits an operational arm for a policy for which they bore no responsibility and in the pursuit of which they must not intervene.[44] But the volunteers had no intention of giving in. They aspired to serve as a political force that would advance the idea of a military solution to the Yishuv's political problems. Ben-Zion Yisraeli said: "There are those who do not want ... company committees ... If the soldiers wish to organize, nothing can stop them. The movement continues to regard itself as the carrier of the idea of soldiers' activism and to encourage it in the units."[45]

Yisraeli hoped that he would succeed in curbing every scheme against his movement. This, however, was not to be, since Mapai leaders had changed their attitude toward mobilization and the recruits. In the Mapai Secretariat, Shertok briefed Ben-Gurion on developments during his stay abroad. Until now, he said, the enlistment drive had been accompanied by attempts to arouse the Yishuv through rallies, speeches, conventions, conferences, and much printed material. But none of it was effective without an orderly plan and clear arrangements.[46]

In the meantime, the leadership displayed its new approach by a greater use of punitive sanctions against those who refused to enlist. They could be fired from their jobs, their names and addresses could be made public, and they might be expelled from the Histadrut, political parties, and sports associations or even be subjected to physical violence. From the end of 1942 the sanctions were implemented with the help of the recruiters. Although lacking formal authority, the soldier-recruiters represented the "spirit of volunteering." They turned up at places of work, combed cafés and movie theaters, and visited and revisited the homes of potential enlistees. In some cases, threats to "shame the evader publicly and intimidate him" were carried out. People were beaten up in the streets or forced to drink cod liver oil; some had their faces smeared with excrement; a few were tarred and feathered. One person was forced to enter a closed box at high noon; another had a sign hung on him declaring his sins. Bombs were thrown into evaders' homes. In Jerusalem, there were five bombing incidents of this kind within two weeks.[47]

The atmosphere of the period is conveyed by Eliahu Lankin, an activist in the Revisionist movement: "I absolutely refused to enlist in the British Army, and I adamantly refused even when an atmosphere of moral and I would say physical pressure prevailed in the Yishuv, against youngsters of draft age. ... I remember that period as a nightmare, when young people would be removed from cinemas and cafés and set upon and subjected to all kinds of public outrages, and pressure would be exerted on them in all directions and all forms to make them enlist. ... And all this pressure came ... from Haganah circles, from what was called the Organized Yishuv."[48]

These were the first signs of a state-in-the-making, by definition characterized by the leadership's effort to impose its authority and acquire a monopoly on the means of violence in the society.[49] The British were the first to sense this development, speaking about "the saliently totalitarian, militaristic and national-socialist approach of the new Zionism."[50]

In fact, for various reasons the leadership was not yet able to wield authority fully. Not only did the right-wing military organizations refuse to accept its authority, but so too did Hakibbutz Hameuhad and of course the British, who at the begining of 1943 forbade the Jewish leadership to use violence against draftees.

The volunteering movement was in any case too independent and too political for the leadership's taste. Hence Ben-Gurion's remark about its organizer: "Ben-Zion [Yisraeli] now sees enlistment as the be-all and end-all. . . . Even if this were so, the Yishuv must not take this view of enlistment, because although it is an important detail, it remains only a detail. And if Ben-Zion pursues this course, he will fail."[51] In mid-January 1943 the Mapai Secretariat discussed the discord between the volunteering movement and the Haganah.[52] Three days later an internal Jewish Agency paper was drawn up summarizing the leadership's decision: "Subordination to Zionist authority. The soldiers' federation is subordinate to Zionist authority. [It] takes policy directives from the [Jewish Agency] Executive and orders from the [Haganah] Organization."[53]

The Haganah Archives contain the minutes of a stormy meeting which finally decided the fate of the volunteering movement. Ben-Gurion and the chief of the Haganah National Command, Moshe Sneh, would not countenance an organization which gave expression to soldiers' political opinions. On the question of authority, Ben-Gurion said: "It is not accomplished through ideology. It requires an apparatus and a structure. This is impossible within a democratic framework and it is out of the question to rely on soldiers' democracy. We have no other framework, and no other framework is needed, besides the Haganah."[54]

The volunteer soldiers were incensed at being barred from taking part in political activity and made subordinate to the weak but disciplined Haganah. At one of their protest meetings, to which Sneh was invited, a leading volunteer activist stated: "We have plenty to say to the Yishuv. We ought to have demands, and we do. The Jewish soldier needs a mouthpiece, the soldier's demands must be voiced, people must know that soldiers have their own views about Yishuv issues." The other speakers agreed that their organization still had political functions to fulfill in the Yishuv. "We are the carriers of the war for the Jewish people's struggle," one of them asserted. "We are an independent body, we demand that the Yishuv [fight] and we will force it to fight. . . . We should be the vehicles of the movement of the war for a Jewish state. . . . Today we are soldiers with true internal unity; we must transmit this soldierly outlook to the Yishuv."[55]

Frequently, writes Finer, soldiers clash with the civilian leadership, since they see themselves as more closely bound to the national idea and the nation than to the political leadership, which is elected in a temporary political arrangement. A constant concern of the army is that the leadership will compromise national principles or will try to realize them in a way different from that proposed by the military.[56] Indeed, the volunteers' protest only reinforced the leadership's impression that the young enlistees had a political agenda—a "soldierly outlook," as they called it—and that the military way had sown seeds of praetorianism. Sneh for one was stunned by the intensity of the political phenomenon when he met with the "volunteers," represented, for example, by one of the soldiers at the meeting he attended: "Here . . . an ideological unity is being formed among the soldiers. It seems to me that if the soldiers were allowed to impose a compulsory regimen in the Yishuv, such as placing it on a war footing . . . things would be different."

Sneh said he was appalled by the volunteers' insularity, and for a pioneering body insularity could prove ruinous. He was particularly struck by a statement uttered by one young activist: "We are not the army of the Jewish Agency but of the Hebrew nation." This undermined the leadership's authority, Sneh said, adding that he hoped the soldiers would leave two things to the official institutions: recruitment policy—there must be no discussion or decision on this by any soldiers' council—and political guidance. But the volunteers remained unconvinced. Why should 14,000 soldiers not be allowed to express opinions about recruitment? they demanded, rejecting Shertok's view that an army which is not a branch of the leadership constitutes a danger to the nation.[57]

The leadership's attempts to curb the potential praetorianism of the professional soldiers was no easy task, but they were finally successful. The volunteers' movement was not eliminated, but the leadership was able to channel the movement in the direction it chose. Ben-Gurion announced that he was giving the movement a new task: to educate the soldiers, organize life in the units, and tend to the soldiers' future.[58]

The Volunteers Committee, which had sprung up against the leadership's will, displayed political ambitions in its efforts to disseminate the "soldierly outlook" in the civilian society. It too had a praetorian potential, intensified by its aim of preserving political independence. But the political leadership's reaction to the challenge was swift. The protocols of the volunteering movement's meetings in the following years show that it directed its energies to establishing a library, putting out a newspaper, setting up a savings fund, organizing sports and cultural activities, and the like.[59] The movement's attractiveness seems to have waned after the political element underlying its military outlook was neutralized.

The Mapai leadership thus abandoned efforts to acquire influence in the Palmach but became an influential player in the arena of British Army recruits. In terms of a simple political calculation of profit and loss, Mapai's gamble paid off. In contrast to the handful of Palmach members—a few hundred at most—there were some 25,000 British Army recruits. In the face of the class-based workers' army of Hakkibutz Hameuhad, which tried during those years—without notable success—to shake off its sectorial label, Mapai's relationship with the recruits enabled it to present a conceptual alternative in the form of a national army, incorporating all strata of the society and standing for national, ostensibly supraparty, messages.

Some scholars attribute no factional political considerations to Mapai activists in this period. In the opinion of Yoav Gelber, the historian of Yishuv enlistment in the British Army, Ben-Gurion's actions against the volunteering movement were devoid of party interests. After all, Gelber maintains, the movement's founders were from Mapai, and by opposing them Ben-Gurion demonstrated that he preferred the principle of unity of command, via the Haganah, over the army's politicization by the Volunteers Committee.[60]

Gelber's analysis is problematic. He ignores the possibility that Mapai, as the largest party in the Yishuv, tried to consolidate its position precisely through a supraparty principle. In other words, it exploited the supraparty principle to achieve political control. Thus Uri Brenner, who became the historian of Hakibbutz Hameuhad, said that Mapai's claim that its activities among the soldiers were guided by principles of apolitical "statism" was rejected by Hakibbutz Hameuhad. Its argument was that no one could know the opinion of the entire body of soldiers and no one was entitled to maintain that the soldiers were not interested in politics or that they needed not political indoctrination but a revered national leader.[61]

Mapai was certainly politically active in the army and did not always bother to disguise this. Soldiers who in time became party functionaries in the army, along with activists who enlisted solely in order to further partisan political interests, distributed pamphlets and journals to the enlistees, organized meetings, and distributed thousands of leaflets. The soldiers were urged to heed the party and support a specific policy. This was a classic connection between army and internal politics, of which the recruit functionaries were the incarnation. The Yishuv often seemed to view enlistment in the British Army through the prism of sectarian party politics, with true military considerations in second place. Political intrigues, political organizing, and sheer agitprop became integral elements in the Yishuv recruits' army experience. It was all done to promote one party or movement or another, under socialist or nationalist ideological covers and with slogans extolling general unity and the national good. For those living in the Yishuv, this all seemed natural. Only the British, accustomed to the liberal ethos of separation between army and society, were astonished.

A letter from the British War Office to the Colonial Office noted two phenomena that had struck the censor in the correspondence of Palestine soldiers: the large quantity of material from political organizations that was being distributed in army units and the many letters sent by soldiers to political organizations in the Yishuv. The two phenomena, the War Office missive noted, attested to political intervention in military matters. The writer went on to explain that the individual army recruit was soon turned into the recruit of one or another political group. This group wanted to win over the recruits in order to gain power and rule over the Yishuv.[62] Overall, the army could not cope with the intensive politicization to which the Jewish soldiers were subjected. Not surprisingly the Palestine battalions were transferred abroad around this time and, as much as possible, distanced from Yishuv politics.

Nevertheless, Mapai's influence in the army grew in direct proportion to the resolution of its internal problems. Mordechai Hadash, a senior Mapai functionary in the army, could boast that "the mobilization in general, as well as the formation of the battalions, is basically a party enterprise. Party people implemented the enlistment, went themselves . . . [and] today constitute the bulk of the activists in the army and the battalions."[63] The greater Mapai's influence in the army, the greater its power in the Yishuv. When the Jewish Brigade was established around the end of 1944, Hadash could look back with satisfaction, knowing that he and other functionaries had contributed a great deal to their party's influence in the army.[64]

Thus, if a budding professional praetorianism was evident among the British Army recruits and in particular among those from the volunteering movement, Mapai succeeded in neutralizing the phenomenon. Just as the Palmach member was transformed from a full-time fighter into a worker-fighter under the aegis of Hakibbutz Hameuhad, enlisting in the British Army turned from personal voluntaristic enlistment to an organized call-up, under Mapai's control. The price of the institutionalization of the military way was the reduction of the danger, from the leadership's point of view, of professional praetorianism in the Yishuv; that is, the danger of an autonomous, separatist military way with its own corporatist military interests was reduced. But as long as the leadership remained split and two political bodies—the Mapai Majority and the faction led by Hakibbutz Hameuhad—struggled for control of the Yishuv, the possibility existed of party praetorianism. Such a development would involve, as we will see, the possibility that a military group, through party, movement, or sectarian loyalty, would volunteer "to help" realize a certain politics while suppressing another.

In this regard, Samuel Huntington is right that objective civilian control is a virtual impossibility. The great number of civilian groups, the different character of each, and their opposing interests practically rule out the possibility that they will all join forces as a unified bloc against the army. Thus civilian control is subjective, reflecting the balance of forces in the society and their underlying interests.[65] In pre-state Israel, the way in which the party/movement politicization of military organizations bonded army and politics reduced the chance of civilian control of the military, in the liberal sense.[66] Moreover, contrary to the claim of some Israeli political sociologists, who describe the army-politics connection in Israel as a functional link which serves certain clear and agreed upon "national security needs," the preceding chapters have pointed to the intrinsically political rather than functional character of a connection that was advocated by the political bodies which fought for control of the Yishuv and used the military way as a resource to augment their power.[67]

It is possible to discern the existence of a fusion or blurring in Israel between "army," "society," and "politics" after 1942. Practices indicating innovation and change are institutionalized through a process of objectification and legitimation.[68] It was party/movement politics of fusion that spurred the new military way, rescued it from its marginality, and gave it status and prestige.

PART THREE

*The Military Way as an
Ideology, 1942–1944*

CHAPTER FIVE

"In Uniform" and "Without Uniform"

Status Struggles

There is nothing romantic about soldiers, armies, or wars unless they are romanticized through social processes.[1] Such a process had been under way since the beginning of modern Jewish settlement in Palestine. But in 1942 it became a systematic, organized project. At that time several groups were active militarily. However, against the background of the Haganah's seemingly inveterate weakness and the inactivity among rightist organizations—Lehi had been liquidated by the British with the active help of the Haganah, and the Irgun was paralyzed, many of its members having joined the British Army—it was clear that either the Palmach or British Army enlistees would set the military tone in the Yishuv.

In earlier chapters we discussed the support of two political bodies for the new military way. Given the conditions that existed in the Yishuv, it was clear that the military way could not turn into an ideology without that support. However, this necessary condition in itself does not provide a sociological explanation for the transformation of the military way into an ideology, unless we also take into account the endeavors of the youngsters themselves, the members of the native-born generation, to enhance their status and disseminate their worldview.

Struggle for influence in the military arena commenced in a practical argument over priorities of mobilization. The question was whether Yishuv young people should enlist in the British Army or join the Palmach. But the argument rapidly developed into a symbolic struggle between those "in uniform" (the former) and those "without uniform" (the latter). In this way the military groups hoped to gain prestige, recognition, and control over the military sphere and thereby to influence the whole Yishuv. This chapter considers the symbolic struggle that occurred between the two military groups, how they were developed as status groups, and what support they received.

Status groups develop a distinctive style, through which they attempt to gain recognition, prestige, and influence.[2] The struggle between status groups is mainly a symbolic one. In the case under discussion, this style was based on acquired dispositions which the group idealized and publicized in order to prove that its military way was superior.[3] The first two sections of this chapter describe two distinct military styles and myths created by two status groups. The last section deals with the involvement of political bodies in this cultural production, which lent more validity and significance to the younger generation's messages and eventually turned the military way into an ideology.

PALMACH: STYLE OF A REVOLUTIONARY ARMY

Myths were created in the Palmach which glorified the military way of life. Two episodes were appropriated by the Palmach, although they weren't really carried out within its framework. One was the episode of the "Twenty-three Seamen," the group that was sent on a sabotage operation to Tripoli, Lebanon, and whose mysterious disappearance contributed to a heroic aura and creation of a myth around the mission. The other was the incursion into Syria, which the Palmach played up, even though militarily it was of marginal importance. Legends sprang up about the raiders, who numbered only thirty, and their deeds: "We will yet remember under a hail of lead, / How the Palmach marched in Syria."[4]

Like many military traditions, in which the exclusive right to bear a sword or a rifle becomes a status symbol, such as the sword-bearing of the Samurai caste, Palmach members tried to make a virtue of the fact that they could carry weapons at all times. When they were sent to the Negev in the tense period prior to the Battle of el-Alamein with sticks instead of rifles, their status image, as we saw, was severely impaired. It would remain so as long as they saw no military action. But the claim of exclusivity in bearing arms had a symbolic meaning: it helped underscore the Palmach's independence and power.[5] A symbolic use of weapons was made, for example, in review parades. When the British seized and imprisoned Palmach personnel who were transporting arms to such an occasion, Ya'akov Hazan, the leader of Hakibbutz Ha'artzi, was outraged at the high price paid for the symbolic use of weapons. But the parades did not cease.[6]

Palmach commanders seized every opportunity to demonstrate the organization's high military level, the proficiency of its troops, and its combat methods, including readiness for night fighting, mobility, reconnaissance tactics, and guerrilla training. Senior Palmach commanders trying to get young people to join played up the existence of special professional units, such as a naval unit, a German Section which trained its personnel to operate in enemy territory in the guise of German soldiers, and the Arabists, intelligence personnel who operated in Arab cities disguised as Arabs.[7] The professional courses in the Palmach enhanced its prestige, for cultural capital is acquired not only through internalized dispositions but also through objective and formal means, such as courses whose graduates receive attractive certificates out of which a military career can be made.[8]

Although the Palmach was portrayed as a professional army, after it became closely attached to Hakibbutz Hameuhad its professionalism was not practiced for its own sake. In addition to its self-styled combat image, the Palmach was also presented as a working army: a popular, egalitarian, revolutionary, socialist army. It is doubtful whether these descriptions were justified, but Palmach commanders even boasted that this pattern was unexampled in the world's armies.[9] Yigal Allon, the Palmach's commander, also evoked the motif of the unit's originality and independence when he described its combat doctrine: "It was not a doctrine which some expert or general brought with him from afar and instilled in the Palmach as a finished package. The combat doctrine was quarried out of the ground of our situation."[10] This was an attempt to create a tradition, as if the Palmach symbolized a kind of primacy or rebirth—and this, too, is characteristic of nationalist movements seeking to magnify their influence.[11]

As part of the ethos-making of a national, revolutionary army, the motif of equality was emphasized in the Palmach. A case in point is gender equality. Full equality certainly wasn't achieved, but many Palmach women were proud of their chance to participate in war preparations. Said one: "And what did we [the women] achieve? I will take the liberty of telling about myself. . . . I learned how to climb mountains, jump from rooftops, get past different obstacles. Some time ago I returned from Galilee. Each of us hauled nearly twenty kilos on our backs, and we went on foot." Another Palmach woman explained: "If necessary, I will sharpshoot, if necessary I will dress wounds. . . . I do not want to forgo this right to defend the land. I am like you, a daughter of the land."[12] As in many other armies, women's struggles for equality within the Palmach helped bring about the centrality, in the Yishuv's life, of the military way of which they demanded to be a part, and in which they believed they could function as well as men.[13]

The success of a status group in a certain field depends not only on the group's ability to acquire material and ideal resources. Such success is also closely linked with its ability to impose criteria for social evaluation and to serve as gatekeepers to determine the allocation of resources and rewards.[14] Against this background we can understand the Palmach's efforts not only to build up its own esteem but concomitantly to undermine the status of the British Army recruits. The Palmach's emphasis on professionalism became a true obsession in face of the lopsided competition on this subject between the Palmach and the members of the highly professional British Army. It was not by chance that Palmach commanders did everything they could to highlight the difference between their military prowess and that of the British Army recruits. They claimed that the British taught their troops to react automatically under fire but that in the Palmach, as one of its most famous members, Yitzhak Rabin, noted, the emphasis was not on a mechanical response but on the thinking fighter who was resourceful, could improvise, and was independent.[15]

Similarly, the emphasis on the Palmach's ostensible popular and revolutionary character derived in part from its desire to set itself apart from the ultra-professional British Army, with its formal hierarchy and its supposedly automaton-like soldiers. In the same vein, the Palmach made much of special relations which developed among the fighters. Publications of the Palmach's information department emphasized simplicity and camaraderie, cordial mutual relations between the commander and his subordinates, and pride but not haughtiness.[16] Of course, there was a good deal of pretentiousness in this demonstrative modesty. So much so that the Palmach commander himself felt constrained, during a speech in 1945, to apologize for the Palmach's haughtiness and uncontained pride.[17]

The communal relationships that evolved in the Palmach, based as they were on emotional bonds, contributed much to making it a closed, isolated status group. The character of the groupings comes through in this description by a female member of the Palmach: "The Palmachnik has no wife, no child, no kibbutz life. . . . You are enclosed within a defined framework. . . . The whole group sets the social tone. . . . No one made the Palmach, no one laid down rules, it's up to you as a Palmach member to make the rules."[18] The Palmach's communal character was interwoven with cultural production. Known as the "fellowship" (*hevruta*) and later as the "comradeship of fighters" and even the "circle culture," this communalism became one of the organization's cardinal status symbols. Through it the Palmach acquired much cultural capital, communalism being held up as the substitute for the formality and hierarchy of the British Army.

In a manner characteristic of status groups, Palmach members devoted much of their time to building up their ascription, mainly by depicting their innate traits as inherently valuable. An example is the pathos-laden attitude they took toward their young age or their place of birth: "Those born in Eretz-Israel [the land of Israel] are different . . . they have been fired with the freedom of the hills in the land and the heat of its sun. Here they stand, heads held high in pride and uplifted spirit, without fear of the foreign ruler. . . . With their feet planted firmly in this soil, they stand erect."[19] The fact that nearly all the Palmach veterans were from kibbutzim and as such were considered the Yishuv's social elite helped create the image of the Palmach's superiority. Even when city "individuals" began to join the rank and file (very few of them reached command level), kibbutz "lineage" was still regarded as a virtue.[20] A group's depiction of attributive status, such as age or place of birth, as a virtue suggests that it is attempting to accord itself prestige of ascription (not prestige of attainment) and, in this case, to lay down criteria that serve to determine hierarchy in the military realm.[21] The emphasis on the native status ascription was important, since pitted against the Palmach's "qualities" were several tens of thousands of British Army recruits, whose social background was quite heterogeneous.

The Palmach expressed its "qualities" in part through hiking, which demonstrated the difference between the younger and older generations. Members of the founding fathers generation, who had arrived in Palestine during the second and third waves of immigration, also hiked around the country. But for them the hikes did not possess a national meaning. Palmach members hiked not necessarily to behold the beauty of the landscape or to intoxicate the senses from nature. The Palmach hikes contained a symbolic element of mastery, of conquering, of ownership of all the land. As Benny Marshak, the Palmach's chief information officer (politruks), explained, its members had a tradition of not walking on paved roads or even on trails. Their goal was to conquer everything.[22]

In April 1942, seven young people were killed and fourteen injured in a hike organized by Hashomer Hatza'ir near Masada when a grenade exploded next to a bonfire. The disaster triggered a controversy: Were hikes necessary? Was this the time for such outings? These questions were posed by a Haganah commander in the organization's journal. The victims, he wrote, were not war casualties and their deaths were meaningless. The following number of the journal ran a critical reply to this broadside. Death on the way to Masada had meaning, this rebuttal argued. The finest of the nation's youths were drawn there by the force of memory, by the example of the heroes who preferred to die by their own hand rather than lose their liberty and dignity. The Masada episode thus added a "way of death" to the "way of life" of the native-born generation.[23]

In another case, following an attack by two Arabs on members of Gordonia who were on their way to Masada, the leadership banned trips to Masada, much to the dismay of the youth movements. "We should make Masada a memorial fortress to all who fought for the redemption of Israel and its resurrection in the homeland," the young people said, and the hikes continued.[24] Over time the hikes came to stand for the premise that no territory within the Land of Israel should be renounced. Articles in Palmach and youth-movement journals advocated conquering the land, extending the borders, expanding the frontier, demonstrating sheer presence, and reaching places where Jews did not usually set foot.[25]

As members of a status group seeking recognition and influence through uniqueness, Palmach members invested much time and energy in developing esprit de corps. Hence the tradition of the campfire, where customs evolved, songs were sung, and stories were told. Called *tshisba-tim*, these stories easily slid into the realm of the tall tale.[26] The Palmach member was also identifiable by his clothes. Previously, Palmach members had been branded shirkers because they had no uniform; but afterward this very lack became a valued resource, and the army "without uniform" became a status symbol, which clearly defined its parameters: "Our guys have no uniforms, but still, when one of the pack walks down the street, you suddenly sense: this is a brother. Khaki shorts, a shirt open to the belt, the sports badge, a tanned face. . . . Something in the total appearance [says]: one of ours."[27]

It was Yitzhak Sadeh who grasped the potency of the "Palmach spirit" and cultivated it systematically, under the rubric of "information and culture." In a course for information officers, Sadeh spoke about a "war by means of *kumsitzim*" (get-togethers around a campfire); culture must be "tendentious," he said, and it was essential to start conversations, to sing, and to hold social gatherings. In this way, the internalized dispositions of the native-born, which developed in the military arena and took on the form of a new Israeli style, not only were acquired through experiences but also were the result of learning and deliberate direction.[28] Gradually the Palmach started to "accumulate cultural dividends"—a sort of investment that later pays off in politics[29]—and to be regarded as the most authentic and important organization of the native-born generation. The Palmach, however, was not the only military group that accumulated cultural dividends at that time, and it was unable to achieve exclusivity in the military domain.

BRITISH ARMY RECRUITS:
PROFESSIONAL ARMY STYLE

The cultural production of the army recruits was based on their boasting about the professional training they received in the huge British Army with its great traditions. This training involved combat methods, order and discipline, social relations based on military hierarchy and "distance," and a perception of the army as a large, well-oiled, complex system. This character, the recruits claimed, was essential if a military force was to carry out its missions.[30]

Some soldiers proudly emphasized that they were cannoneers; others wrote home about wanting to be tank drivers.[31] No one doubted the professionalism of the British Army, but many were skeptical about the proficiency of the Yishuv inductees, whose professional progress in those years was indeed held back by the British themselves. As a result, they resorted to various status symbols to demonstrate their soldierly attributes. One such symbol was the uniform. So widespread was its use as a means to show off that one recruit felt the need to disparage songs glorifying the uniform, such as "How Fine You Look in That Uniform" and "Mother Is Sending You Ribbons." "One is dumbfounded," this soldier wrote. "Where does this spirit come from? Are we playing a game of uniforms? . . . The words [of the songs] are positively grating. Where is the [true] purpose for which we are here?"[32]

The army recruits were hard-pressed to cope with the Palmach's self-styled prestige. This, as we saw, was based on the Palmach's claim that its members' social background—native-born kibbutz members, youth movement graduates—transformed them into a quality group which could solve the problems of the Zionist movement. In contrast to the Palmach's relatively homogeneous makeup, the army enlistees included city dwellers, members of kibbutzim and moshavim, veterans and new immigrants, diverse age groups, multiplicity of ethnic communities, members of all sectors and political persuasions, educated and illiterate, rich and poor. The motif of unity is central to a status group seeking recognition and prestige; the British Army recruits accomplished this by invoking the "melting pot" metaphor. Their journals were full of articles that drew on this image and harped on the idea that at first the command wasn't Jewish, the commanders weren't Jewish, and the quartermasters weren't Jewish, but now, through direct contact and despite the many difficulties, the army units had become a "Jewish and Zionist melting pot for hundreds of lads from the Jewish people."[33] After the establishment of the State of Israel, this metaphor would become central in the new Israeli army, owing in part to the heterogeneous population, composed of many new immigrants who would arrive from all over the world.[34]

The soldiers relied on symbols to demonstrate what they defined as a "national mission." They added words before and after the word *Palestine* which appeared on their shoulder ribbon. They also insisted on speaking only Hebrew and chastised those who refused to comply as heretics and even traitors. They took pride in the establishment of a Jewish command[35] and fought for the right to fly the Hebrew flag. In this there was no difference between Laborites and Revisionists, between members of the Haganah and members of the Irgun, and if there were disagreements, the struggle with the British over the right to fly the flag became a unifying common denominator. In essence, the British Army served as a framework in which for the first time the national-Zionist ethos overcame the structural-class distinctions between Right and Left that marked politics and everyday life in the Yishuv at that time.

The "struggle over the flag" began in local incidents.[36] But it took on a different significance in the second part of 1943 when Jewish units sent to the Western Desert felt themselves to be inferior to others. These units were assigned noncombat roles, such as guarding unimportant positions and installations; they had been sent away from Palestine to prevent Yishuv parties from putting them to political use.[37] The British commanders objected vehemently to symbolic displays, in part because they considered them disparaging to soldiering for its own sake. But the demand to fly the national flag and its demonstrative raising by the soldiers in a continual struggle with the British focused attention on these units. Their national importance consequently increased, as one of their number explained: "The hoisting of the flag demonstrated that the Jews would not accept the trampling of their hallowed traditions."[38]

One episode produced a heroic description of flag waving, a militant response to the demand of a British officer—"the enemy"—to remove the flag, and the accusation: "He undermines our right to recognize that we are a nation and that this is our flag." It was recorded by soldier Haim Nadav in his diary. He added that "everyone is standing up for his honor and the honor of Israel." And in the end, "victory will be ours if we can prove that we have self-respect and know how to safeguard our flag, our people's honor."[39] Such pronouncements were meant to underline the enlistees' importance by fusing their way and the national goals at a time when the use-value of their mobilization was dubious, certainly in the eyes of the Palmach and its political patrons.[40]

From the Western Desert, news of the phenomenon spread rapidly and became a source of pride. The soldiers made sure that the ripples of their symbolic endeavor reached the Yishuv and its leadership. They put out pamphlets on the subject of the national flag, and their journals highlighted the "struggle." Their heroic deeds included secretly climbing up the flagpost to put up the flag, posting an all-night guard around the flag to prevent the British from lowering it, and standing for hours at inspection for refusing to turn in the "criminal" who hoisted the flag. These activities preoccupied them: unit committees held meetings about the flag issue, boycotts were imposed on Jewish officers who did not cooperate in the struggle, exhausting negotiations were held with the British on the subject, there were debates, stormy meetings, and sit-ins—all of it something of compensation for the fact that they saw no action.[41]

Thus in the years 1942–1943, whoever believed in a military way as a mode of action found himself engaged mainly in behavior meant to extol that way. What began as a military response to historical events evolved into a style of the new generation; it was cultivated by status groups, the Palmach, and the British Army recruits, endeavoring through their symbolic activity to achieve recognition and prestige.

This analysis conflicts with the nostalgic and idealistic descriptions of the emergence of Hebrew soldiery in the 1940s, as furnished, for example, in Amos Perlmutter's *Army and Politics in Modern Times*. Perlmutter, a classic representative of the civil-military relations school, depicts Israeli soldiering as revolutionary in character and different from other types of soldiering in that it lacks exclusivity, is not intended to protect narrow interests—of class or status—and is selflessly devoted to a general revolutionary movement.[42] My description, in contrast, is of two distinct exclusivist and corporatist military styles, one "professional-expert," the other "socialist-revolutionary," through which the two status groups sought a place under the Yishuv sun. For this, though, they also needed their political patrons.

STATUS POLITICS

A full understanding of the "in uniform" or "without uniform" struggle needs to consider the fact that the Mapai Majority on one hand and Hakibbutz Hameuhad and Faction B on the other aspired to enhance their power through their symbolic and practical support for the two military groups, and thus they were involved in the "status politics" which the military groups conducted.[43]

Hakibbutz Hameuhad helped the Palmach display its virtues and denigrated enlistment in the British Army. In early 1942, when the debate over mobilization priorities was still in the embryonic stage, Israel Galili told the Histadrut convention: "Great power is latent in a uniform. . . . But just as a uniform makes one stand out, it also conceals . . . the forces who for the time being are without a uniform. . . . We shall not forget the nights of the incursion into Syria, when our comrades assisted the invading Australian Army. . . . Are they worth less, are they to be deprecated in our eyes only because they do not wear a uniform? . . . I cannot fathom in what way . . . the combat value . . . is diminished [of] a comrade whose whereabouts are unknown after he went to sea. . . . Why should they walk about as inferiors? Superiority is not conferred by a uniform, even if it is the uniform of a great kingdom."[44]

Galili was trying to boost Palmach's image by evoking certain events which, as we have seen, had assumed mythical proportions. He further sought to enhance the unit's prestige by alluding to clandestine operations. Furthermore, Galili and his friends tended to present in a distinctive way the link between the Palmach and the kibbutzim. When young people of the kibbutz joined the Palmach, kibbutz members commented on the youths standing erect and proud, full of self-confidence, who knew how to take up arms when the need arose.[45] On top of the praises heaped on the Palmach and the virtues ascribed to its members as the first native-born generation was laid the ethos of the worker-fighter. As one kibbutz woman put it, "This is a kind of existence that still arouses me to great admiration. . . . The ideal and perfect fusion between the plow and the rifle. This is what we read about, talked about, and sang about for so many years."[46] As we have seen, through the idea of the worker-fighter, the kibbutz leadership tried to depict the Palmach as a working army, not alienated from societal needs, possessing socialist attributes—in contrast to a professional, militaristic army.

In essence, the two political bodies, Hakibbutz Hameuhad and Mapai, pitted the military bodies against each other, each praising the superior qualities of "its" force. Idelson, from the kibbutz leadership, said that a man volunteers only once for an army and having enlisted must fulfill all his obligations, whereas Palmach members in essence volunteered every day anew, since they might leave at any time. Idelson here evoked the volunteering ethos, central in the Yishuv, to increase the Palmach's importance.[47] Shertok, for his part, emphasized an organizational and professional foundation as the quintessential military experience: "When you are in the army, you are in the army all the time. It does not depend on whether the security committee does or does not have a budget for the Palmach. It does not depend on whether you have to work half a day and train half the time due to budgetary, kibbutz or other reasons. You are an army person at all times."[48]

In its cultural production, the Mapai Majority went so far as to publish a booklet naming all the enlistees. The point was to demonstrate the comprehensiveness of the phenomenon, which extended even to the Yishuv's social elite: members of the Mapai Center, lawyers, university lecturers, sons of Yishuv leaders, and graduates of the leading high schools.[49] Ben-Gurion, as well, who was at first not enthusiastic about the enlistment in the British Army, gave in to Shertok's entreaties and in late 1942 said in a meeting: "And I want to say to him [to Ben-Zion Yisraeli] ... that I am wholeheartedly, fervently [in favor] of volunteering for enlistment, for mobilization to the army, and I consider it a supreme precept."[50]

The endeavors of Hakibbutz Hameuhad and Faction B to enhance the Palmach's prestige infuriated the Mapai Majority. Katznelson offered a rationale of the opposition's status politics in explaining his support for the idea of transfering 200 Palmach members to the army. They created Palmach ideology as something lofty, unique, he explained, and therefore it was crucially important that it take part in the mobilization.[51] Golomb, until then considered a supporter of the Palmach, seemed to change his tune: "What is this boasting that we have created this mighty force? What is this pretentiousness that says, we are the Palmach pioneers? What does Faction B have to do with it?"[52] Around the same time Golomb appeared in a meeting of kibbutz training groups held in a kibbutz called Yagur. The young people's desire to join the Palmach drew an ironic response from Golomb, who said that perhaps Zionism should be renamed Palmach, and in fact everything should be called Palmach. He warned that the Palmach, too, must be at the disposal of the Zionist movement and not stand above everything.[53]

Mapai felt that the Palmach's status ambitions and its relentless campaign to gain recognition were turning it into an oppositional group, a situation liable to generate political unrest. Two years later, when Golomb was asked how he had felt about the Palmach at the time of the Yagur meeting, he replied: "Some among us think they are entitled to special privileges for doing their duty. I reject this. I also reject the idea that those who present themselves as the greatest patriots of the Palmach bring it any benefit. In my opinion, they do it harm. . . . They have got their terms confused. They thought that Palmach was the be-all and the end-all; Palmach is defense, Palmach is Zionism, Palmach is settlement, a world unto itself. I explained to these people that Palmach is not everything. . . . I found it necessary to clarify this at the time."[54]

Hakibbutz Hameuhad leaders hurled similar accusations at the army recruits. Probably no one did as much as Galili to boost the Palmach's prestige among the public. When the Jewish battalions were formed in the army, Galili complained that Mapai leaders praised the army recruits but had nothing good to say about the Palmach. Members of the latter, he said, had a gnawing feeling that they were undervalued as compared with their comrades who held equivalent positions in the army.[55] The mixture of haughtiness and whining often served the Palmach as a tactic of status politics.[56]

Cultural production and status politics were seen in various arenas: in kibbutz councils, in the press, in party discussions, and in the Histadrut. Members of the divided leadership disguised their political biases in professional terms to support "their" military groups. This was part of the politicization of the military groups that had already become habitual. Thus, speaking at a meeting of recruits from the Socialist Youth organization in April 1943, Ben-Gurion offered his opinion that there are means of force and means of training which are virtually inconceivable without a uniform, even if it is not a Jewish uniform and even if the highest authority is not Jewish. Only within an army framework can such training be given to 20,000 inductees or can an artillery company be formed. And to the "scoffers," as he called them, who retorted that the British Army units were not part of a Jewish force, Ben-Gurion replied with a parable: let us not be like the fox who cannot reach the grapes and therefore says that they are sour and inedible.[57] In later years Ben-Gurion would frequently intervene in military considerations; he refused to accept the idea that "civils," as he called them, did not have the right to intervene. This phenomenon, to which we have alluded, of the blurring of boundaries between the "civil" and the "military," had its beginnings in the party's political involvement in the military realm and in the "in uniform/without uniform" controversy which involved politicians, military personnel, and the heads of settlement movements.

The debate centered on the question of which of the two military groups represented the Hebrew army then taking shape.[58] The British Army recruits vehemently objected to any attempt to present only the Palmach as the national army. We can preserve our Hebrew character in the army, too, they said.[59] One of their political patrons, a member of the Mapai Majority, told the kibbutz movement's Council: "We have enlisted in a Hebrew army. Don't tell us we have joined the British Army. . . . Those who join up are part of a Zionist army."[60] Most of the army recruits believed that the Palmach did not meet the needs of the hour. For example, one of them explained that the Palmach numbered about 1,000, whereas the Buffs alone had 3,500 soldiers. Realistically speaking, what value did this number of Palmach members have when they were spread all over the country? What contribution could they make when the country was already defended by regular British Army forces?[61]

When the idea was being mooted of dispatching the Jewish battalions overseas and some soldiers expressed the hope that they would see action, spokesmen for Hakibbutz Hameuhad impugned their motives. At a meeting of Hakibbutz Hameuhad recruits, Galili said that he felt he was among friends and sensed their impatience—not only their eagerness to take part in the war but also their simple, human desire, out of boredom and dissatisfaction, to see new countries, to go abroad. This was a clear devaluation of British Army service; at the same meeting Benny Marshak shouted: "Let Jewish soldiers know, [it's] not the profession, not the salary, not even the romanticism, and not going to the front, because the front is here!"[62]

A striking expression of the status politics practiced by the young people and their political patrons involved their attitude toward the Holocaust. Reliable information on the systematic annihilation of Europe's Jews reached the Yishuv toward the end of 1942. Immediately the news was put to symbolic use by the military status groups. Hence the proposal to form an army unit called the "ghetto-destroyers' company."[63] The idea appealed to many recruits but was staunchly opposed by Hakibbutz Hameuhad Secretariat, which feared it would draw the youth away from the Palmach to the army. Speaking at a meeting of Hakibbutz Hameuhad Council, Idelson said that the only way he knew for destroying the ghetto was Zionism itself, along with the establishment of new settlements. Idelson added that there were some people who adopted an offensive tone in the "with uniform/without uniform" debate, maintaining that whoever did not enlist was a shirker. Others employed a more comradely tone, saying: "Let all of us go to destroy the ghettos, to actually encounter the enemy." But their intentions were similar.[64]

The Palmach and Hakibbutz Hameuhad opposed using the Holocaust to boost mobilization to the army while thwarting all other forms of recruitment. But their leaders did not refrain from invoking the Holocaust to promote their interests. Ostensibly, their conclusions were different. As one young activist wrote: "When the dreadful reports reached us . . . a powerful stirring seized us all. . . . Again every boy and girl is called on to forge a Hebrew force for work, for training, for camps [Palmach] where he will learn to love the land, withstand the enemy, expand settlement, [and] stand on guard for Zionism."[65]

To counter the ghetto-destroyer slogan, the kibbutz movements held information rallies for their young members. Addressing a Hashomer Hatza'ir gathering, a leading figure in Hakibbutz Ha'artzi said the slogan was deceiving and harmful; it alienated the soldiers from the Yishuv. Others branded it demagogical, a hysterical call to the front.[66]

Hakibbutz Hameuhad Secretariat confronted the ghetto-destroyer concept at a rally in mid-January 1943. The gathering was attended by a few hundred young people from Hakibbutz Hameuhad, the Palmach, and the youth movements. The purpose of the meeting was to increase the leverage of Hakibbutz Hameuhad in the struggle for control of the Yishuv and to strengthen the Palmach's position. As Moshe Tabenkin, the son of the leader of Hakibbutz Hameuhad, said: "There is little enlistment in the companies [Palmach]. What a frost around it! What an evil eye afflicts it on every side! . . . Therefore we have come out today in defense of the companies, and we intend to give their members a little of the encouragement that is given to their colleagues in the army from every public platform." Referring to the British Army enlistees, his brother Yosef left no doubt: "Uniforms, buttons, ribbons and stars are secondary hallmarks of power, and it is dangerous to admire them." The other speakers expressed similar sentiments. They assailed the disdainful attitude shown the Palmach by the official institutions and the dominant party, Mapai, particularly the fact that joining the Palmach was termed "organized evasion." In addition, lowering of the army draft age to nineteen, a decision made at that time by Mapai's leaders, was presented as "a knife in the back of the companies." No one protested the use of this metaphor, which was coined by General Ludendorff in the militaristic atmosphere of interwar Germany to rationalize the Wehrmacht's defeat in the First World War.[67]

Throughout 1943 the tragedy of the Holocaust was exploited for purposes of status politics. In a gathering of Hamahanot Ha'olim in February, Ben-Gurion asked what the Palmach was doing about rescuing Jews. Turning to Yitzhak Kafkafi, a key activist in the movement who toed the line of Hakibbutz Hameuhad, Ben-Gurion demanded that he stop mentioning the rescue of Jews as a pretext to get young people to join the Palmach and to be identified with Faction B.[68] Two months later, when Ben-Gurion tried to bring about the union of two youth movements as a means to amplify Mapai's power, he said that the overriding task was to save the remainder of the Jewish people from slaughter, adding that youths who did not live for this had nothing to live for. Ben-Gurion pushed to unite the youth movements, though it is hard to see how this was relevant to the rescue of European Jewry. But the Jews of Europe could not have been saved even by Palmach supporters. Asked about the appropriate response to the Holocaust, one of them said: "We achieved what we wanted . . . in the hike and the Masada assembly. For us this was a symbolic expression of our identification with the fate of the Jews . . . with those who refused to choose slavery."[69]

As time passed, the status struggles sharpened the differences between the two military groups and their conflicting military conceptions.

By 1948, as will be seen, the contradictory approaches had acquired the aura of full-fledged "schools." However, there should be no doubt about the significance of the disparities between the two groups and their messages. In fact, the paramount importance of the "with uniform/without uniform" controversy was that it placed the features common to the two groups at the forefront of people's consciousness, the shared perception that the Yishuv's national problems should be solved militarily. It is difficult to overestimate the impact which this view of reality exercised for a society lacking a military tradition, a history of battles, or memories of wars and national military heroes.

In this chapter we saw how bearers of arms attempted to obtain legitimacy for their activities and roles in the Yishuv. They did this through the development of a style and the use of stratification strategies designed to produce exclusivity and uniqueness, but mainly they were aided by the political bodies acting in the Yishuv. Preceding chapters showed how the welding of the "military" to the "political" served the political bodies as a resource in their struggle for control over the Yishuv. Now we have seen how the military groups themselves benefited from this connection. The military solution gradually became acceptable and legitimate, a sort of status convention that determined life chances and granted honor and prestige.[70] And when the cultural capital that the military groups had accumulated was invested in an attempt to influence politics and challenge power relations, the military way turned into an ideology.

CHAPTER SIX

The Holocaust and the
Biltmore Declaration

The Demand to Establish
a Jewish State by Force

Once the military way gained legitimacy and its importance was recognized, the young fighters started to demand that it be used to solve the
Yishuv's national problems. These demands were clear in their reaction
to two central events of the period: the Holocaust and the Biltmore Declaration. The reaction attested to the existence of military status groups,
in fact generational units, that sought to influence policy decisions. In
other words, these groups wanted to translate the capital culture they
had acquired into political influence.

The reaction to the Holocaust bore a spirit of revenge, which originated among British Army recruits. In their meetings and journals they
demanded the right to fight at the front and to exact revenge. As one soldier wrote, "Vengeance, this is the only word that rings in my ears, that
encourages me. . . . How I would like to carry it out!"[1] The desire to take
revenge exposed a conflict of interest between the young fighters and the
veteran political leadership. The latter procrastinated and deliberated in
reacting to the Holocaust; most of their activities took the form of solic-
iting funds for the European Jews and proposing the establishment of a
Jewish army abroad to fight the Nazis, without the participation of the
Yishuv.[2]

But the young people were of a different opinion. They suggested
establishing the ghetto-destroyers' companies.[3] The idea, first raised by
a Mapai member, Haim Shorer, had great appeal to many youngsters.
One wrote: "Companies of ghetto destroyers are to be formed in the land
of Israel. Will I be privileged to join them and redeem the blood of my
family?"[4] The veteran leadership balked, however, claiming that "ghetto-
destroyers' companies" was an empty and illusionary slogan. Some were
shocked by the exploitation of atrocities for propaganda purposes.

Yitzhak Gruenbaum, a former leader of Polish Jewry whose son was in a concentration camp, said that whoever wished to volunteer should go to Poland, not to destroy ghettos but to suffer along with his brethren and try to hearten them.[5] But there was more to the idea than the use of disasters as army recruiting propaganda. The proposal expressed a new worldview based on the peculiar attitude of the native-born generation toward the Diaspora Jews and the Holocaust.

THE SHAME OF WEAKNESS

In the leaflets disseminated to promote the idea of these companies, a new view of reality was revealed: "The Jews' response [to the Nazis] will be companies of Jewish soldiers . . . which will destroy the medieval walls built around the remnants of Jewish communities. Companies on whose flags will be inscribed: 'Revenge. . . . We won't cry, complain, or protest. . . . We will rise to revenge.' Dozens of companies of ghetto destroyers will embark on a war of attrition against the enemy."[6] Shorer's proposal and leaflets of this sort gave expression to the idea that the problems of the Yishuv and of world Jewry in general could be solved only by force. Shorer worked to actuate the slogan. He wrote to British officers and urged the Yishuv leadership to act in the spirit of his idea.[7] He even began signing up people for the ghetto-destroyers' company, and a few dozen young people registered.[8] The slogan's importance, however, lay not in its practical potential—Shorer was probably alone in believing that the idea was feasible—but in its symbolic significance: the proposal expressed an instinct of revenge mixed with a power-based military ethos completely detached from Jewish history. It also exposed the gap between the young fighters and the veteran leadership, a difference in mentality, in disposition, and in style. In part this was due to the negativity which the young people displayed toward the Diaspora from which the leadership had come. It is necessary to elaborate on this difference, because it contributed to the rise of militarism as the ideology of the emergent young generation.

The motif of "negation of the Diaspora" was part of the Zionist ethos of national rebirth, but after news of the Holocaust arrived, the new generation reconstructed the myth, recast it, and used it as a means to idealize the military way and to highlight its own importance as native-born warriors. The Yishuv leadership declared three days of mourning for the victims of the Holocaust, but this type of reaction enraged the younger generation. One woman soldier wrote: "We demand action but unfortunately at this time the dominant reaction espouses the ghetto approach, and its reaction consists of stopping work, prayer, closing places of entertainment, a fast day. The tried and tested panaceas, to pray, to fast, and no more. They will do that and then go home. Then they'll cry a little and be pleased: we did our part. God will do the rest and thus redemption will come. I sit and grit my teeth when I read these decisions. . . . I believe that there is one prayer, one help, one reaction: total activism, to forge a spirit of general mobilization."[9]

At that time, 1942–1943, "negation of the Diaspora" assumed a prominent place in their dispositions and attitude. They were the children of the land, young, strong, muscular, decisive, courageous, and proud—in stark contrast to the weak, pale, feeble, and obsequious Diaspora. This stereotypical contrast was constantly stressed in statements by members of the younger generation. They wanted to underscore their "qualities" and present their worldview as the logical and natural response to the poverty of the Diaspora life-style, to the behavior of the Jews facing annihilation. It was in 1942 that the expression "like sheep led to slaughter" came into widespread use. It represented the morality of the military groups justified negatively, through the emphasis on the us-and-them polarity, a common approach of status groups seeking recognition and influence.[10]

A conference entitled "Youth in the Face of the Diaspora Holocaust" gave the young people a platform to air their power-oriented beliefs. At the gathering, Moshe Tabenkin related that while passing a synagogue he had been appalled to hear the "weeping and wailing" (his actual words), since "it is not because we are in the right that we are being slaughtered. . . . The shame of our weakness is no less terrible. At this time 'negation of the Diaspora' has become for me hatred of the exile. Our weakness today is to blame. It is despicable. It is a crime!" The young Tabenkin had a well-defined response: "If we are not for ourselves, who will be for us? . . . Our healthy riposte is: a thirst for power, sensitivity for power, a 'craze' for power. True power. Ours. At our disposal." This statement was not exceptional; most young people used similar terminology.[11]

Through the Holocaust, then, the native-born generation disseminated the idea of military solutions to the Yishuv's political problems. The stereotypical portrayal of the Jews as weak and the way of power as normative was a recurrent counterreaction to the Holocaust on the part of the younger generation. In a seminar of Hamahanot Ha'olim, a young woman explained that in school they were taught about Jewish life which persisted in the Diaspora, and the emphasis was a positive one. We did not see, she said, the shabbiness of Jewish life, people who wanted to escape finding a solution, who were ready to let others do with them what they would, anything to end their suffering, to let others do to them while they did nothing. At the end of the discussion a conclusion was reached: "Spirit without action is inconceivable."[12]

On other occasions during that period, the young people explained that the only ones capable, in the face of the Holocaust, of offering a true message to Jewish youth in the Diaspora were those youngsters who remained whole in body and in spirit, who were raised on Hebrew soil and in a Hebrew culture—the youth who grew up in the Land of Israel.[13] The

Palmach journal would later write: "There was an inclination . . . to recoil
from everything that had a Jewish ring. Supposedly we held our heads
higher and therefore warranted a different definition. That is, by going
to the Palmach, we could feel that we were Hebrews."[14]

The motif of breaking with the past is shared by many national movements.[15] But in this case there was an extreme reaction to a devastating
event. In their response the young people demonstrated their importance
as people of action. They turned this disposition into an ethos, directed
not only against the Diaspora Jews but also, in essence, against their leadership and against the Yishuv's way of life. One person at the "Youth in
the Face of the Diaspora Holocaust" meeting warned against the prolix-
ity that was so common in the Yishuv and urged action. "We are a generation that demands deeds," another said, "and these should be made
manifest in the movement and the Yishuv."[16] Some years later the journal
Bama'avak (In the Struggle), which reflected the ethos of the native-born
generation, wrote that the new generation's "lack of spirituality" was
caused by a specific Yishuv condition. The spiritual life of the Yishuv was
exilic in nature, alien to the soul of the young people and unattractive to
them; hence their hostility to the life of the mind in general and their pull
to practical action.[17]

The British Army recruits, most of whom had not seen action, put a
high value on activism, and such formulations appeared in their journals: "Our soldier loves practical matters. Zionist propaganda directed
toward him, the prolonged speeches, the phraseology on the role of the
Jewish army . . . these things are not to his liking, he scorns them."[18] A
distinctive new idiom emerged in the Hebrew language, meant to demonstrate the characteristic activism of the new age. *Bama'avak* juxtaposed
the new Hebrew idiom and the conventional "Oxonian" Hebraicness
of the older generation, "that collection of mummified and florid clichés
which is so offputting to young people." In contrast, the "sabra" idiom
was said to be authentic, simple, and practical.[19]

This approach was perceived as the diametrical opposite to the moderation and forbearance displayed by the leadership in reacting to British
policy. For example, in a seminar organized by the communes of Hamahanot Ha'olim in late 1943, the youngsters claimed that an exilic approach was taking over the institutions, that they were reacting differently to events. The discussions revealed the existence of a broad gulf
between Berl Katznelson, the Mapai leader, who attended the seminar,
and the young people, who declared ardently that they had no wish to
continue the history of the Diaspora and to die a contemptible death.[20]

Half a year later, in another talk with teenagers, Katznelson spoke
of his grief at the young people's disdain for their heritage. "You have
become a Hebrew tribe totally detached from the Diaspora heritage," he
told them. "You are able to identify with Hashomer [the pre-Haganah
guards], with Wingate's units and with Sadeh's mobile patrol, but not

with Jewish issues. You do not find the shared destiny of the Jewish people to be relevant, and you claim that the experience of the previous generations has nothing to do with you."[21]

Katznelson, of course, was right. But the main point was that the young people took the old Zionist idea of negation of the Diaspora and used it to impose their military orientation and to influence society. This outlook held that utilization of force for its own sake attested to strength, hesitation in doing so to weakness. The Jews had been led like sheep to slaughter because they were weak. The Yishuv would suffer a similar fate unless the leadership adopted the practices of the young people or if the latter left the fate of the nation in the leadership's hands. The young people needed this sort of stereotypical, ultra-simplistic Zionist lesson of the Holocaust in order to promote their native worldview. In essence, exploitation of the Holocaust to construct a national and militaristic ideology began in 1942.

Anita Shapira, a historian of the Yishuv period, argues that the younger generation's tendency to accept simplistically the reality of its situation, with no moral soul-searching or questions, reflected an inability to cope with ideological questions and was proof of the diminished respect for political ideas among the young.[22] Shapira finds a gap between ideology and practices, but the analysis presented here suggests that this separation is problematic. The young people's production of culture narrowed and finally eliminated the gap between the level of the idea and the practical level by transforming the actions which were expressed through the military sphere into a symbolic action or an ideology. Indeed, the founding fathers generation, which established the Yishuv's political system, brought with it an idea-laden political culture and a clear and comprehensive doctrine. Yet the style of the young people was also the embodiment of an ideology, but in a different form. It was a simplistic and natural ideology, an ideology of practices, which seemed to derive from the constraints of the situation in which they found themselves.[23] As such, it was a direct reaction to events and could offer a clear and unambiguous a priori recipe for solving two critical problems of the Yishuv: its relations with the British and its conflict with the Arabs. This ideology of an absence of ideology would have considerable influence in the 1948 War, when Israeli militarism was finally expressed in deeds rather than in declarations. The point, though, is that this ideology of practices originated at the beginning of the decade, with the reaction of the native-born generation to the Holocaust and to the Biltmore Declaration.

A SENSE OF THE HEBREW HOMELAND

Since the Peel Commission, the idea of a Jewish state had gradually become part of the Zionist discourse. Ben-Gurion often spoke, especially in

1939, of the need for a state, and Berl Katznelson was also supportive of the idea.[24] Such declarations were not acccompanied by any attempt to flesh out the state idea with tangible content. Not until 1942 did the concept begin to become a reality: that October Ben-Gurion returned to the Yishuv with what became known as the Biltmore Declaration.

The Biltmore plan, which contained an explicit declaration of the Zionist aspiration for a Jewish state, had received recognition by the world Zionist movement several months earlier and was overwhelmingly adopted by the Zionist action committee in Palestine.[25] The general public was equally enthusiastic. Even the Irgun journal Herut found positive elements in the program.[26]

Still, it would be inaccurate to say that no one in the Yishuv objected to the Biltmore Declaration. Weizmann wrote to his assistant that the program contained all of Ben-Gurion's extreme ideas.[27] According to the historian Sykes, Ben-Gurion, unlike Weizmann, believed that it was necessary "to think big" and present programs that were both simple and stirring. Weizmann still believed that Zionism should proceed through peaceful evolutionary growth; Ben-Gurion thought differently.[28] The small but influential group called Ihud, whose members included Martin Buber, Ernest Simon, and other intellectuals, opposed the plan. Reservations were also expressed in the leftist Hashomer Hatza'ir, the youth movement of Hakibbutz Ha'artzi. In one of its assemblies, speakers maintained that the conception shared by the leadership and the British Army volunteers revealed a thrust toward a shortcut, force solution, as people had despaired of the idea of building the Yishuv gradually. One activist asserted: "Under our noses a comprehensive drive is under way to turn the Jewish fighting force into the instrument of a political goal which we oppose, an instrument for the establishment of a Jewish state. This is being done deliberately and in every sphere. There is a reflex of the Biltmore Declaration within the army."[29]

Such fears were in fact unfounded. The leadership was still a long way from accepting the idea that the state would come into being by force, through pressure exerted by the military and even with its own cooperation. Indeed, one reason for the tremendous support for the Biltmore Declaration was its utter impracticality. Thus Weizmann: "One might think that this was a well-considered decision reached after months of serious study. Permit me to tell you—this is far from the case. It is only a decision, like a hundred and one [other] decisions that are made."[30] It was neither its content nor its feasibility that turned the plan into the period's outstanding political symbol—it made no provision for political or military action—but its emotional freight and its apt timing. Attempts made to translate the Biltmore Declaration into more workable terms drew widespread objections. At the practical level, which hinted at the use of force to conquer the country, opposition came from those who still associated this idea with the Revisionists. And as for the possibility that the program would bring about the partition of Palestine between the two peoples who inhabited it and would stifle the Zionist enterprise in a dwarf state, this was anathema to many groups. Even Shertok, who viewed the program as a justifiable maximalist historical claim, was dubious about its feasibility.[31] The only ones who took the program seriously, though even they were not satisfied with its declarative and symbolic aspects, were the activists of the younger generation.

Cultural production began to influence events. If the Biltmore Declaration did not spell out the details of the independence it advocated, the young generation nevertheless perceived it as a concrete platform and depicted it as the means for resolving all the major issues of the Jewish people. As for themselves, the program held out the promise that with their military prowess, they could use force to establish a state immediately. Thus in late 1942 Nahum Sarig, a senior Palmach commander, addressing an assembly of Hamahanot Ha'olim atop Masada mountain, articulated the political conception of the young generation: "I do not believe in declarations. . . . Thus and only thus do I understand the concept of independence. It is not determined on paper. Even if our cause should gain massive support, we do not know how this will benefit us in practice. Let us not wait for the deliverance of an independence that is proclaimed on fading pages, for these are mere pieces of paper."[32]

Additional evidence of this desire to alter reality is found in the words of a Palmach member from 1943. Ben-Gurion, he wrote, has become the person everyone looks to, in whom everyone believes without limit. He satisfies the demand for an idol, yet precisely there the tragedy begins. Ben-Gurion's speeches say nothing about the actions that should be taken, and this lacuna turns the speech into a work of art lacking political substance. In the meantime, bitterness increases and there is insistent pressure from below for a new line, firm and uniform.[33] Another article criticized well-known Zionist leaders who were being careful not to read too much into Biltmore, their rationale being that "we waited two thousand years, we can wait a bit more." He then voiced the demand of his generation: "a Jewish state now!"[34]

By this time the demand to establish a state by military means was no longer confined to the Revisionists and the right-wing military organizations. A Palmach member who shared a prison cell with Irgun and Lehi activists wrote that the Palmach was receptive to some of the notions of these groups, particularly about the leadership's weakness, its moderate policies, and its efforts to neutralize and silence the younger generation.[35] He was referring to, among other events, the Struma affair. In early 1942 the ship, carrying illegal Jewish immigrants, was torpedoed near Turkey under mysterious circumstances; there was only one survivor. The young people were outraged when the leadership did not immediately blame the British for the disaster. Their representatives demanded that action be taken against the British and that Zionist policy be revised.[36]

Toward the end of 1942 and throughout 1943, British-Jewish relations in the Yishuv deteriorated rapidly. The British decided to put an end to what they considered a violence-ridden mobilization regime, and they shut down Jewish Agency recruitment centers. They moved to put an end to the illegal possession of weapons, such as the arms which had been in the Palmach's possession since the period of cooperation with the British. Two Haganah men were sentenced to lengthy prison terms for purchasing stolen British weapons. In early October 1943 British troops raided a kibbutz and found an arms cache. Tension ran high in the aftermath of an incident at Kibbutz Ramat Hakovesh toward the end of 1943. In the course of a weapons search, a fight broke out between members of the settlement and British soldiers. One kibbutz member was killed, others were wounded, and a large number were taken into custody.[37]

The young people demanded an alternative politics in meetings with the leadership. In an encounter of the youth movement Hamahanot Ha'olim with Ben-Gurion, there was grumbling about Mapai—that it was scornful of the Haganah and was groveling before the British.[38] The same complaints were sounded in the Socialist Youth organization. Until the 1940s, that movement had considered the conceptions of "nationalism" and "state" to be morally unsound. Now enlistees from Socialist Youth made the idea of establishing a state the movement's central motif. Complaints were voiced that the leadership was not reacting to the harsh British decrees and that Ben-Gurion's speeches, for all their activist rhetoric, were unaccompanied by action.[39]

In the conversation between Berl Katznelson and members of Hamahanot Ha'olim in 1943, the generation gap was obvious. No longer was the political leader and mentor able to persuade his audience. The youngsters railed at "weakness in the political institutions" and at a "leadership of betrayal" in viewing Biltmore as merely declaratory. The younger generation expects certain decisions, Berl was told, but its expectations were not being fulfilled. They added a warning that in most nations a spontaneous reaction begins from below. Berl was taken aback by the young people's mistrust and stinging criticism. What galled him most was their attitude toward the veteran leadership. Just a few years earlier Ben-Gurion's words had been sacred to them, whereas now he found alienation and suspicion. Berl all but accused the young people of incitement to revolt. He may have been carried away in his analysis, but the conversation pointed to the great political pressure that the young activists could exert on the leadership. Their aim was to ensure that the Biltmore Declaration would become practical policy based on their ideology, holding that the military way was the most efficient means to solve the Yishuv's national problem.[40]

Tempers were calmer and emotions in abeyance when members of Hamahanot Ha'olim confronted the famous philosopher Ernest Simon, perhaps because their polar attitudes raised few expectations to begin with. At the movement's invitation, Simon lectured on the ideas of his moderate political group, made up of German immigrants, which advocated a binational state in Palestine. In this dialogue between the moralist and the young people who would soon be on the battlefield, the young people's scraps of sayings, fragmented ideas, and internalized dispositions coalesced into a full-blown worldview: there is no guarantee that the postwar world will be a moral place; indeed, it should not be measured with a moral yardstick. The Jewish people have a high moral standard, and no one doubts that the current destruction unleashed in the world conflicts with that supreme morality. However, morality is not decisive. The primary question is whether the Jewish community in Palestine will become a power in the region.[41]

The young people thus proclaimed their refusal to imbue political decisions with moral considerations, yet in doing so they also expressed a particular moral code. Indeed, from that time no conflict was discernible between morals and deeds in their consciousness, nor, as time passed, in the practical policies that aimed at national liberation through a military solution. The "Arab problem" was not a question of substance demanding rational thought to find a solution; it was, rather, a technical matter, to be dealt with solely at the practical level, and to be resolved by means of the most effective technique. This perception of reality undoubtedly stemmed from the new circumstances in which the young people found themselves, not least the enhanced status their groups enjoyed as independent, highly prestigious military entities. They were not only ready in theory to use the weapons entrusted to them to realize national longings; they demanded the use of military force. It was only fitting, then, that one of the young people described their state of mind as a "sense of the Hebrew homeland" and another as a "sense of statehood."[42]

Driven by internalized dispositions and life conditions, the younger generation began to view the idea of a state as taken for granted. The journal of the Palmach's B Company wrote: "Our whole strength ... depends on the degree to which our generation will be able to relate to the imperatives of the state, as though the state were already in existence."[43]

Some cautioned against this drive for power. Ya'akov Hazan, the Hashomer Hatza'ir leader, claimed that the young people were behaving as though Palestine were already the Jewish state. The Palmach in particular, he said, had lost all sense of proportion.[44] Hazan noted that a change had occurred in the defensive approach which until then had characterized the Yishuv's security conception. Galili, too, warned that such feelings were deluding many youngsters and driving them to distraction. "Eretz-Israel," he asserted, "is the only place on earth where Jewish youth exists among its own people, but being among the people may breed an illusion. It may cause one to lose sight of the fact that we are still a minority in this country. ... The young people forget about the neighboring states and about the political forces operating in the region.

They live in the illusion of a functioning Jewish state, and from that illusion carve out their concepts of honor, national tactics, stratagems in the struggle, the power of coercion, and the strength of national obedience."[45]

Galili's apprehensions were well founded. The pressure to implement the Biltmore Declaration came from the young. Some time later, a young man (later known as Uri Avneri, a leading Israeli journalist) would articulate the significance of the Biltmore Declaration for his generation. The event that shaped the image of the Second Aliyah generation, he said, was the Balfour Declaration. All its thoughts for the future were based on belief in Anglo-Zionist cooperation. However, the generation that followed did not know the past. Its goal was to take control of the land and establish a state.[46] The official journal of the Right succinctly described the change that was taking place among youth affiliated with the labor movement: "Biltmore is part of the shift . . . that is drawing them closer to the phraseology of state-oriented Zionism. . . . We now hear frequently the words 'Jewish state,' 'Jewish army,' 'political Zionism' and so forth. We encounter broad circles of youth who are blindly loyal to the official leadership, [proclaiming] slogans such as 'military Zionism.' "[47]

But this was not blind loyalty. It was conditional on the leadership's abiding by the principle that the military way was the key to attaining a state. Youth movement and Palmach members held this opinion, as did the Jewish soldiers in the British Army. The Biltmore Declaration would continue to preoccupy the younger generation in the coming years. They would agree that Biltmore was a flexible formulation, amenable to every interpretation, and they would scoff at Zionist leaders such as Weizmann who were careful not to read too much into Biltmore and disseminated the spirit of "we've waited two thousand years—we can wait a bit more."[48] The young people were in a hurry. In face of the Holocaust and the Biltmore Declaration—more accurately, their singular interpretation of these events—they demanded that the leadership adopt their way. Even if these demands were not always clearly formulated and not always presented as ultimatums, they compelled the leadership to respond. Politics is more than decision making; inherent in power is the ability to disseminate symbols and invest them with legitimacy.[49] From this point of view, the young warriors became a political force not to be underestimated. Galili understood this when he noted: "I know them from the Palmach. . . . I know them from the army, [I know] they feel suffocated, that they want to burst out. But can this be a basis for political judgment? This alone? . . . Can this be the basis for our political decisions?"[50]

In many nationalist movements that was indeed the basis for political decisions. Not only Galili, but the whole leadership understood this and were disturbed by its implications. The young people's demand for military solutions to political problems constituted a criticism of the leadership's traditional moderate policies, its tendency to act by means of negotiation and diplomacy. Nor did the youngsters believe that the leadership embodied the nation. On the contrary, through their interpretation of the Holocaust and the Biltmore Declaration, they themselves claimed to represent the nation and to be its savior. This sense of "manifest destiny" is found in state armies, underground movements, and national liberation forces. It tends to arise if a moderate leadership is perceived as being incapable of solving major political problems.[51]

"CANAANITES" AND "FIGHTING NATION"

Among those present at a meeting of the right-wing Betar movement held in Warsaw in September 1938 was a young man from Palestine named Uriel Halperin, later a major Israeli poet under the pen name Yonatan Ratosh.[52] Halperin and some other young Revisionists had urged an armed struggle against the British in the 1920s. In the latter part of that decade, they had formulated an integralist nationalist outlook and had fiercely attacked the labor movement's pioneer-socialist approach. Indeed, the group expressly advocated fascist stands and declared its sympathy for Nazism, which it saw as successfully countering communism. Halperin's articles in those days preached violent, brutal conquest, and his poetry evoked "blood" and "fire" and "a conquerable land." Compromise with the Palestinian Arabs was ruled out. Following the publication of the Peel Commission report of July 1937, which recommended partition, Halperin published a series of articles in the journal *Hayarden* under the general title "Looking toward Government." Zionist diplomacy, he claimed, had run its course and the way to fight Britain was by force of arms. His articles had an enormous impact on young members of the Irgun and Betar.[53]

Returning to Palestine from Paris after the outbreak of the Second World War, Halperin founded a movement called the Committee for the Consolidation of Hebrew Youth. In its first publication, "Letter to the Hebrew Youth," Halperin urged Yishuv youngsters to set aside their organizational differences, seize on what they had in common, and be aware of the abyss dividing them from Diaspora Jewry.[54] The Committee for the Consolidation of Hebrew Youth first expressed the native-born young people's wish to overcome the structural split in the Yishuv along party lines of Left and Right. According to Halperin/Ratosh's brother, he and some of his friends who had been born or raised in Palestine considered themselves Hebrews rather than Jews. They began holding meetings to spread this idea in the early 1940s. Palmach members who attended were as enthralled by the idea that the Land of Israel might be liberated by force by its native sons as they were outraged at the leadership's policy of compromise. In 1942 the Committee for the Consolidation of Hebrew Youth decided to expand the framework. A few of their number joined the Palmach and Lehi to preach the Hebrew national concept to receptive young people in those organizations.[55]

Eliahu Beit-Tzuri, one of the two Lehi agents who were involved in the 1944 assassination in Cairo of Lord Moyne, the resident British minister of state in the Middle East, belonged to the new movement. At his trial he explained to the British judges that the Hebrews were the real owners of the Land of Israel, that their aspiration for independence antedated the British occupation, and that the Hebrew's presence in Palestine was not dependent on the mercy of foreigners. The young Eretz-Israelis were striving to win indepedence by expelling the foreign power, Beit-Tzuri said. He added that they were not fighting to uphold the Balfour Declaration or for the sake of a national home but for the most important concept of all: a free and independent Land of Israel.[56]

The movement's members would be called "Canaanites," meant as a pejorative name. But the name stuck and was accepted even by them. They emphasized their complete break with the Diaspora and denounced Yishuv authors who were using modern Hebrew to write on traditional Jewish topics and thus implanting the Diaspora values in the Land of Israel. In particular they decried the Yishuv's sectoral division into Right and Left, instead declaring their desire to foment a Hebrew revolution based on a common national identity.[57]

Halperin and his movement were in harmony with the frame of mind of the younger generation, which perceived itself as a social category in its own right, and with the distinction between "Hebrew" (*ivri*) and "Jewish" (*yehudi*). Similarly, the Canaanites were at one with many other young people in considering the national rather than class question to be the central problem of the Yishuv and in believing that only by force could the land be wrenched from the British and the Arabs.[58] It was also around this time that the first works began to appear by young people who would later be known as the writers of the "1948 generation" or the "Palmach Generation." They first gained recognition in 1943-1944, often with contributions to the daily press. Their works, which stirred up considerable controversy, dealt with the collective experience: the life of the second kibbutz generation, enlistment in the army or the Palmach, youth movement experiences, resistance to the British. But their writing was also suffused with Canaanism, reflecting the outlook of those born in the Land of Israel, contrasted with their parents who had been immigrants, and the attitude toward the Holocaust: the unavoidable comparison between the free, proud, and healthy young Israeli and the Diaspora Jew, bent and sickly, a victim of the Nazis.[59]

True, the Canaanite movement was small; it did not establish a strong political organization, and its activity was largely confined to café discussions and fringe publications. But its impact cannot be gauged by these criteria alone. Culturally, the Canaanites influenced the whole generation. Halperin himself tried to win over the poet Haim Guri, a renowned young writer of the Palmach Generation. Guri notes that he was constantly torn between a Jewish emotional identity and the feeling that something new, of a "Hebrew" character, was taking shape in the country.[60] Yet the Canaanites' Hebrew nationalism turned out to be absolutely divorced not only from Judaism but from the Zionist movement as well; few of Halperin's contemporaries were willing to go that far. They shared some key elements of Canaanite thinking but stopped short of revolt against the official leadership. Some, though, went a long way toward translating the Hebrew experience of the young generation into concrete military action.

In January 1943 an underground radio station announced the establishment of a new movement consisting of a core-group of activist Hebrew youth from Right and Left. "We have extended a hand to one another, young people from all camps," the announcer stated, and went on to pledge that the organization would coordinate all activist circles and serve as a meeting place for all Hebrew youth who strived for the establishment of a state. He asserted that youth had no faith in the leadership which was conducting secret talks with the British and demanding that the young people sit idly by: "We can wait no longer! We demand action from the leaders of the Yishuv."[61] This was the first radio broadcast of Am Lohem (Fighting Nation). Although small in numbers and short-lived, Am Lohem played a significant role in legitimating the idea of the use of force to resolve Yishuv problems. This was one of the origins of an Israeli cultural militarism that would ignore the division between Right and Left, as the editors of a pamphlet emphasized.[62]

The Am Lohem movement sprang up in several places separately, one of which was the Palmach, in particular its Jerusalem-based F Company. This company had a reputation for carrying out independent operations. On one occasion it sabotaged vehicles of the British transport company Steele Brothers. In another incident, the company threw a bomb into a printing house, where the *Orient,* a journal published by several German immigrant associations, was printed. This journal was critical of the nationalistic and militaristic spirit which its sponsors believed had seized the Yishuv leadership and the Haganah.[63]

In 1943 several members of F company joined Am Lohem. Their recruiter, a Haganah officer, explained the background: "During conversations we said that some sort of jolt was essential in order to lead the Yishuv to unity of thought and action. To us it was clear and obvious beyond any doubt that the leaders in the Yishuv could not, under any circumstances, carry this out."[64] Not many Palmach members joined Am Lohem. But the organization's spirit was shared by many young people. In a course for Haganah and Palmach information officers in July 1943, as one of the lecturers recounted, almost all Palmach members asked him why the Jewish Agency had not used force against the British and had demanded that the Haganah launch an armed struggle.[65]

Another core of Am Lohem formed at Moshav Nahalal, the first and most prestigious moshav in the Yishuv. Again it was Am Lohem's national and militant outlook that appealed to the moshav members.[66] At the same time, some Mapai members who served in the British Army joined Am Lohem as well. They formed a group which espoused a "soldierly outlook," according to its members, to realize the national goals for which young people had joined the army. The group wanted to fight against the wave of sympathy for the Soviet Union displayed by Faction B, and the antiactivist spirit which they claimed Hashomer Hatza'ir recruits had brought to the army. They set out to show the Yishuv that the military struggle for a Jewish state was not the sole preserve of the Revisionists.[67]

The majority of Am Lohem members were from the Irgun. As already mentioned, throughout the war years the Revisionist movement urged its members in the Irgun to join the British Army. The Revisionist soldiers viewed enlistment as part of the struggle for independence. At the end of the war they promised, "We will be the first in the game, like the legions of Pilsudsky."[68] The views of Marshal Pilsudsky—a Polish national hero in the interwar years who commanded legions in a regular army, traded socialist revolutionism for integral nationalism, and believed that only military force could establish a strong and independent state—were tremendously influential in the Revisionist movement.[69] Such rhetoric was alien to the soldiers who came from the Labor movement, but their extended stay together in the army brought some of them to the understanding that the national-military element was shared by all and that independence would eventually be won by force. In those years the Irgun was in the midst of a prolonged crisis. Some of its members left and founded Lehi; most of the others joined the British Army. Following the death of Irgun leader David Raziel, in May 1941, while on a mission in Iraq for British intelligence, the organization virtually disintegrated. Raziel's successor, Yaacob Viniarski (Meridor), had authority on paper only. Under his leadership the Irgun's main business was collecting members' dues, using terror methods, and carrying out "zealous operations," such as attacking clubs of the Palestine Communist Party, torching stores that sold foreign-language newspapers, and threatening Jewish owners of grocery stores who put up signs in Arabic as well as Hebrew.[70] The crisis was aggravated when the Irgun leader was forced to relinquish his position as the organization's military commander.[71] Given this background, it is clear that Am Lohem was not founded by the Irgun, as was claimed by Haganah headquarters, but as a consequence of the crisis in the Irgun and to take action against the British, which the Irgun failed to do during the war years.

The connection between the Irgun and the Palmach was forged by dropouts of the former who decided to hold a dialogue with members of rival military organzations. In these meetings, as one participant said, everyone spoke a single language: same feelings, same thoughts, same plans.[72] Another rightist who came to Am Lohem was Binyamin Luvotzky (Eliav). A leading figure in the Revisionist movement who had been Jabotinsky's secretary, Luvotzky immigrated to Palestine in 1940 and noted similar outlooks of the activist wings on the Right and the Left.[73] In an article Luvotzky published in June 1943, he set forth his credo: the differences between the Yishuv camps, Right and Left, have already been blurred, and the old accounts should be closed and forgotten. A single dividing line passes within every party—between the "small-minded leaders" and "young people thirsting for action."[74] Luvotzky would later say that he was influenced by the activist stream in Mapai. Palmach journals also had a powerful impact. Reading them, he asserted: "Here is our partner on the other side."[75]

Indeed, Am Lohem was intersectorial in its recruiting efforts and took care not to be branded with a narrow party label. As one of the founding fathers of the organization noted: "Our approach was not party-political but activist. We were soldiers of the Hebrew nation; that was the basis."[76] A leaflet circulated by Am Lohem stated that youth no longer believed in negotiations, no longer accepted Weizmann's leadership of the World Zionist Organization, and that "if the order is not given by the [official] institutions, the young people will know how to carve out their own path."[77] In other words, the threat existed that the younger generation, with its armed organizations, would attempt to shape policy according to its lights. In one pamphlet, Am Lohem even stated that its members were determined to put a stop to the leadership's inaction and to perform "revolutionary deeds."[78] It sounded promising; the expectations, however, were not fulfilled.

Am Lohem carried out sporadic operations, but these had little impact. The group got publicity from radio broadcasts and pamphlets. Their broadcasts called the Biltmore Declaration the "necessary minimum" and urged Ben-Gurion to dissociate himself from Weizmann's mistakes and move away from the middle of the road.[79] Over time, particularly in the final months of 1943, Irgun involvement in Am Lohem grew. Irgun leaders wanted to use Am Lohem as a stepping stone to reorganize their own movement and resolve its crisis. They also publicized their involvement. On November the Irgun journal printed extracts from Am Lohem radio broadcasts and put out a leaflet. "The incarnation of the fighting nation had appeared," the leaflet stated, "and the Irgun would no longer be alone in its fateful war, its ideas have been accepted by allies from other camps in the nation."[80]

The Irgun's involvement in Am Lohem was bound up with a plan to kidnap the high commissioner. With its help, Am Lohem prepared a bunker in which to hold him. They monitored his movements and set a date for the kidnapping. The plan was postponed several times and eventually canceled,[81] in part because Palmach members in Am Lohem decided not to take part in the operation. They met to discuss the matter, argued it out, and finally sent one of their number to inform their company commander about the plan.[82] The Palmach leadership took the matter seriously. Moshe Sneh, chief of the National Command, put out a circular describing the Am Lohem movement as a clandestine group with political-military goals which made it a branch of the Irgun. It was deceiving young people with false slogans about a united youth and terror against the authorities. Sneh ordered everyone in the Haganah who had been in contact with Am Lohem to break all ties with the group within seventy-two hours or face severe punishment.[83]

Palmach members who had joined Am Lohem were put on trial. All received light punishments. The leadership apparently grasped that this was the most effective way to deal with the phenomenon. After all, the youngsters had displayed national feelings, and heavy punishments might have triggered widespread sympathy for them and a generational protest against the veteran leadership. For the same reason, other Palmach members who had been involved in Am Lohem were not tried. Yitzhak Sadeh, the Palmach commander, was afraid that if they were placed on trial they would leave the Palmach and join the Irgun, and some of them later confirmed that this fear was not unfounded. The military way had become the common demoninator of all the organizations, and any attempt by the leadership to restrain them severely could prompt a massive rush to the rightist organizations.[84]

Some thought the Haganah could benefit from the existence of Am Lohem. One Haganah officer who belonged to Am Lohem was able to convince the Haganah's chief of staff, Ya'akov Dori, that Am Lohem could induce the Irgun to accept the authority of the official institutions. The two went to Sneh, but he vetoed futher cooperation.[85] Sneh understood that Am Lohem, even if largely inactive, was the embodiment of a mood that many young people found alluring; its ambition to achieve political goals through military means not only reflected a cultural militaristic orientation but also created a praetorian potential which constituted a threat to the Yishuv leadership. Another leader who grasped this was Natan Peled, of Hashomer Hatza'ir. In his view, the Am Lohem affair proved that if the Palmach were to lose its socialist-class foundation, it might slide into separatist antinationalist activity, either "deliberately or inadvertently."[86]

Earlier chapters showed how the native-born generation, in its various military groupings, developed meaningful methods and practices that can be termed the military way. These practices acquired legitimacy with the help of major party-political organs. When the young generation tried to apply its conception to practical politics—after the fact of the Holocaust had become known and the Biltmore plan had been presented to the Yishuv—the military way metamorphosed into cultural militarism. The Canaanites and Am Lohem were a product of this change. The new ideology was still confined to the younger generation; it was not yet shared by the general public or the leadership. But it was nonetheless meaningful, since it was translated into concrete demands, was put forward by young people from rival political camps, and constituted an assault on the leadership's authority.

...

PART FOUR

*The Military Way and
the State-in-the-Making,
1944–1947*

CHAPTER SEVEN

Saison

The Imposition of
Authority as a Principle

A political elite, in particular one based on social homogeneity, a high
level of organization, and one clear ideology, usually plays a central role
in the process of state making.[1] Toward the end of the 1930s and the beginning of the 1940s, the division of the political elite between the Mapai
Majority and Hakibbutz Hameuhad and Faction B inhibited the elite's
ability to act and brought about the weakening of its authority. One problem common to any political leadership is that of authority. How can the
elite gain legitimacy and convince others that its rule is desirable? Why
should others accept it? Toward the middle of the decade, as the Second
World War was nearing its end and it was obvious that the Palestine question would become central in international politics, the Yishuv leadership tried to solve its authority problem. This chapter deals with its attempts to impose its authority on the armed forces and the effect this had
on the place of the military way within the community and on the militaristic ideology which emerged at that time among the native-born generation.

After the Mapai convention at Kfar Vitkin in late 1942 decided to
eliminate the party's faction system, Hakibbutz Hameuhad boycotted
party institutions. Ben-Gurion warned them: "The strike cannot last
long. Life goes on; things will be done without you."[2] And indeed, until
the final split in 1944, the majority group continued to gather strength.
It gradually gained power in the party, in the Histadrut, and in the
Yishuv's formal institutions, while edging out Hakibbutz Hameuhad. So
low was the status of Hakibbutz Hameuhad that even its initiatives toward the Palmach and the younger generation tapered off. Gone were the
stormy days of 1942 when the kibbutz leadership had equal footing with
Mapai on matters of security.[3]

With the end of the internal conflict in the dominant party and the
decline of Hakibbutz Hameuhad, Mapai set about establishing itself as

the leadership of the state-in-the-making. In practice, it attempted to impose on the Yishuv a new principle of rule, more sweeping than in the past. First, Ben-Gurion and his colleagues decided to bring the military bodies under their control and prevent them from possibly imposing their will by force. The state, by definition, monopolizes the means of violence in society; a state-in-the-making strives to achieve this monopoly.[4]

This principle guided the leadership as it gradually changed its attitude toward the Palmach. In a meeting of the Socialist Youth organization at this time, Ben-Gurion described the "in uniform"/"without uniform" debate as reprehensible. There was no fundamental difference between the two groups, he asserted; the Yishuv needed both, and most important, both groups had to derive their strength from a single political source.[5] Ben-Gurion repeatedly emphasized how crucial it was to separate "deciding power" from "executive power." He had emphasized this in the past, but as long as the leadership was divided and absorbed in power struggles, this kind of separation was only a slogan. Now he hoped it could be realized.

Another reason for Mapai's more tolerant approach toward the Palmach was probably the growing tension between the Yishuv and the British authorities in 1943. When the British closed the Jewish Agency's recruitment centers, Ben-Gurion wrote in his diary, "Let them not go to the army, in the meantime," and he told the Mapai Secretariat that a war against the White Paper in Palestine was even more important than the issue of mobilization to the British Army.[6] And when Ya'akov Uri, from the Mapai Secretariat, stated that enlistment should be solely in the British Army and that the Palmach was not an adequate substitute, Ben-Gurion had reservations. He put forward as an alternative a more comprehensive conception, in which the Palmach was expected to integrate itself firmly: "It will not be good if to all the existing parties another party is added, a 'Palmach party' and an 'army party.' It would be better if there were one party, for both the Palmach and the army. . . . We needn't consider the Palmach as something that contradicts the army or the army as something that contradicts the Palmach. No one will benefit from this. Uri should not get used to appearing as anti-Palmach; it's bad enough that we have people who appear as anti-army."[7]

When the leadership alluded to the importance of a single overall authority which would control the military way and all the armed forces, it was not only the Palmach that was meant. In February 1944 the Irgun circulated a leaflet including the following statement: "The time has come to take the Land of Israel for ourselves as a state."[8] Not long before, Menachem Begin, the new Irgun commander, had declared that although the world war hadn't ended, a truce no longer existed between the Hebrew nation and the British administration in the Land of Israel.[9] Meanwhile, the Irgun began to recover from its prolonged crisis. Its initial actions were relatively moderate, but within a few months it carried out more aggressive, frequently violent actions. It planted bombs in offices of the British Criminal Investigation Department (CID), raided the British broadcasting station, attacked police stations, and staged daring robberies, demonstrating know-how and resourcefulness.[10]

Lehi ("Stern Group") also began to act. Since February 1942, when the British caught and killed its leader, Avraham Stern, Lehi had been paralyzed. A series of escapes from British prisons by Lehi activists gradually brought about its rehabilitation. Lehi became more able militarily. Its members began to carry guns and for a time developed a custom of shooting British policemen and officials as part of what they called "the little war," as opposed to the world war.[11]

THE STIGMATIZATION OF RIGHTIST ORGANIZATIONS

The Irgun's "revolt" and Lehi's raids, while aimed at the British, also defied the authority of the Jewish leadership, which aspired to concentrate power in its hands and to monopolize the means of violence in the society. Of the two groups, the praetorian threat of the Irgun was far greater than that of Lehi. The Irgun was the military arm of an organization which also operated a political party, a youth movement, even a workers' union. The Yishuv leadership grasped the difference, explaining that the fight against the Irgun had to differ from the fight against Lehi, since the latter was very small, had no party behind it, and was out to fight Britain, whereas the Irgun's goal was not only to expel the British but also to seize control of the Yishuv and depose the leadership.[12]

Stopping the Irgun's military activity was more easily said than done. The Irgun entrenched itself and became stronger, winning support from different sectors of the Yishuv. Leadership members talked of applying sanctions against the Irgun and ceasing all cooperation with the Revisionist movement, which gave the military organization political backing. It was clear, however, that this wouldn't solve the problem of authority.[13]

It was Golomb, the leader of the Haganah, who urged the use of violence against the Irgun. The first law of a separatist phenomenon, he told the Mapai Council, was that at some stage the breakaway organization sets its sights on the government and fights with all means at its disposal for its overthrow. An organization like this, he said, could become an example for others and spark internecine political struggles among armed groups.[14]

Throughout the year, members of the leadership met with Irgun representatives. However, Menachem Begin, the organization's leader, refused to abandon the anti-British struggle. He also denied that the Irgun had ruling ambitions but admitted that his movement objected to Mapai's "monopolization of the Yishuv."[15] Around the same time a serious incident occurred that demonstrated to the leadership the danger latent in military organizations that would not accept its authority. A few Lehi people entered a branch of Hashomer Hatza'ir in Tel Aviv to propagandize for their movement; when the youth leaders tried to evict them, the intruders opened fire with pistols, seriously wounding one Hashomer youngster. It was difficult for Haganah members to remain silent about this event. Golomb met with a leading Lehi figure, Natan Yellin-Mor, and threatened a sharp reprisal if such incidents should recur.[16]

Following the collapse of the dialogue between the Yishuv leadership and the Irgun, with the latter refusing to accept the leadership's authority, the Jewish Agency Executive finalized its policy against the Irgun and Lehi in April 1944: isolation, preemption, and seeking public assistance in capturing those who were armed. These resolutions marked the peak of the first stage of the campaign against the two organizations.[17]

This stage was accompanied by a propaganda attack. The Yishuv's political leadership undermined the image of the Irgun and the Lehi as freedom fighters acting in the national interest. Instead they were presented as criminals and "breakaways" who chose to exclude themselves from the "Organized Yishuv," "a gang of madmen," "cast-offs and decadents who are stabbing the Yishuv in the back."[18]

Stereotyping and exaggerating the potential danger of some political groups, defining their deeds as crimes and deviance, are well-known methods used by leaderships and political institutions.[19] The campaign against the breakaways was intended primarily to affirm the principle of authority. It was directed not only against the "deviants" themselves but was also meant to deter others whose views were close to theirs but who had not yet joined them.[20] The Irgun hoped that its violent operations would appeal to Yishuv youth loyal to the leadership and thus undermine its rule.[21] Yishuv leaders were aware of the danger, as Golda Meyerson (Meir) said: "I don't know what they [we] will explain to our youth, to the Palmach . . . kids who read Sternist literature. They [Palmach youngsters] said they have to be opposed, but they are bowled over by their literature." At this meeting several Mapai speakers, including Meyerson, suggested that Lehi activists be physically liquidated. Such ideas agitated their Mapai colleagues, but all agreed that force was needed. The reasoning was that young people saw the acts of terrorism as heroic deeds.[22] A report by British intelligence on the violent actions of the breakaways in this period also noted that the Jewish community derived increasing satisfaction from these operations and that their success would induce young people to flock to the Irgun and the Sternists.[23]

In those same months, Lehi's appeal increased greatly. Its members surprised the public with their determination to sacrifice their lives for the national cause. Their trials in British courts served as a stage for them to publicize their message and gain sympathy. Their sparring with the judges kindled the enthusiasm of many young people.[24] This fact worried Hakibbutz Hameuhad leaders. Speaking at a meeting of the Ahdut

Ha'avodah Council—in essence Faction B reorganized at the initiative of Hakibbutz Hameuhad—speakers such as Idelson and Galili stated that Jewish fascism was gaining many adherents among the "organized youth" and the Palmach.[25]

This general anti-British mood worked in favor of the rightist military organizations. They were also aided by the fact that the Palmach did not lift a finger against the British; in fact, at that time it had never once seen military action, and its members were eager to fight. The breakaways exploited the situation. They presented themselves as people of action who offered a military answer to the political problems of the Yishuv. They addressed the Palmach directly with the slogan "We are doing what you wish you were doing."[26] In this spirit, an Irgun commander explained to members of the leadership that Hebrew youths detested servility in the face of the foreign ruler and that the Irgun was the mouthpiece for the frustration of these young people. "We know," he added, "that your youths also understand this and in their hearts sympathize with our fight. The day will come when your youths will erupt too."[27]

The leadership knew that there was an element of truth in this. At meetings of Palmach members who had taken part in actions against the breakaways, it became clear that Palmach members needed ideological fortitude to battle against anti-colonialist fighters.[28] The same was true of the youth movements. On November 14, 1944, the leadership organized a convention of 150 representatives of the movements, at which Ben-Gurion called on them to cooperate with the British and to join the hunt for the breakaways. To imbue the campaign with the most inclusive national-military character, Ben-Gurion recruited all youth movements (with the exception of the right-wing Betar) and not only the socialist groups.[29] Initially some of the youth-movement representatives said they could not accept all of Ben-Gurion's ideas regarding the campaign against the breakaways, and some refused to sign a statement urging cooperation with the British in eliminating terrorism. But Ben-Gurion, now the acknowledged senior representative of the state-in-the-making, was able to overcome resistance to his proposal. The statement, entitled "War of Jewish Youth against Terror and Its Perpetrators," took the line that the breakaway groups were violating national discipline and subverting the general authority and therefore they had to be stopped.[30]

Obtaining the endorsement of all the youth movements for the statement was clearly a victory for Ben-Gurion, but he knew that expressions such as "national discipline" and "the rule of all" were too abstract. Not all the youth movements would follow the leadership for the sake of these principles, in particular with regard to the campaign against the breakaways, who according to the leadership exploited the young people's veneration of force and worship of arms in order to attract them.[31] As for the Palmach members, they lacked not ideological fortitude but military action. As early as May 1944, in the first countrywide meeting of the Palmach, its commander, Yitzhak Sadeh, delivered a strongly anti-British speech, implicitly criticizing the moderate Jewish leadership. Turning to the Haganah's chief of national command, Moshe Sneh, who attended the convention, Sadeh declared to thunderous applause: "We are ready for action; we ask to be sent into action!"[32] The enthusiastic audience had no way of knowing that they would soon be called on to act nor of imagining that their quarry would be very different from their expectations. It would be the first time in Yishuv history that a connection between the use of organized violence and obedience to the leadership was forged.

THE *SAISON* AFFAIR

The use of a military unit, stated to be expert in the use of violence, against political rivals marked a turning point for the leadership which gradually came to represent the state-in-the-making. There would be no more compromise and concession, no more turning a blind eye to the political dangers represented by the breakaways and their military actions. The basic problem was noted in a letter from Golomb to the Lehi commander, Yellin-Mor: "We are in a quandary [about] . . . what is more dangerous, [taking] vigorous action against Lehi . . . or refraining from action."[33]

In the fall of 1944 young men wearing khaki and high boots began appearing in the cities. This marked the beginning of the "hunting season," the *saison*. They trailed Irgun people, removed Irgun wall posters, protected people who had been threatened by the Irgun, and beat, kidnapped, and arrested Irgun personnel, hiding them in prearranged sites, including kibbutzim. These operations were conducted by the Palmach and the Haganah's security service. More than 200, perhaps 300, Palmach members were recruited for the operation. All the commanders were from the Palmach.[34] In short order the Irgun's archives and arms caches were uncovered. Its apparatus was broken and its ability to raise money dried up.[35]

Palmach members who were involved took pride in their operational ability and military prowess. Allon, the Palmach comander, said that in all the reports from the field there was not a single case in which an operation against the Irgun ended in failure.[36] The Palmach seemed intent on taking the opportunity to demonstrate at long last its military skills. For a status group which was fighting for recognition of its ability and achieved it, among other ways, by developing an innovative military style and which had encountered much opposition to its independent existence, the saison was a turning point. It was a first chance to obtain recognition and support from the Yishuv leadership.

Perhaps for this reason the Palmach acted against the breakaways not only efficiently but also brutally. Brutality exercised by a group serves as a means for the group to demarcate its difference from the objects of the brutality and to flaunt its superiority over them.[37] In fact, one way in which groups whose status is undermined try to preserve their position is by attacking and persecuting those perceived to be the source of the threat. Status struggles are generally much fiercer than other conflicts, since it involves struggles over abstract principles and morals which acquire supreme and decisive value.[38] Thus Palmach journals were engaged in underscoring the difference between "us" and "them": "They [the breakaways] have commanders, they have pistols, bombs too, and they are 'doing things.' ... The public which is eagerly awaiting a war by Jews for the realization of Zionism is drinking thirstily from their turgid and ugly waters. ... And here, secretly and relentlessly, people sense the sacred work and are honing their weapons for the great test. They possess vision, political logic, national responsibility, and moral purity."[39]

For some time Yishuv leaders had deliberated whether to cooperate with the British against the Irgun.[40] A series of meetings with Irgun leaders removed all doubts. "They want to impose their way on everything," Sneh said after one such meeting.[41] By November, Irgun members had already been handed over to the British. On November 6, Lehi agents in Cairo assassinated Lord Moyne, the senior British representative in the Middle East. The murder caused a storm in Palestine and abroad. It also played into the hands of the Yishuv leadership, which could now more easily call on the public to help the British in the war against the breakaways.[42] Since Lehi had agreed in the meetings between Yellin-Mor and Golomb to lay down its arms and since in any case it held no political aspirations, only Irgun members were arrested and turned over to the British.

The most resolute utterance against the breakaways came at the Sixth Histadrut Convention in November 1944. Ben-Gurion explained his program against them, which contained four clauses: (1) removal of breakaways from jobs and schools, (2) denying them shelter and haven, (3) forcible resistance to threats and blackmail attempts, and (4) cooperation with the British police against them. Until then the Yishuv's political leadership had been incapable of organizing a boycott as sweeping as this; now, as the recognized leadership of the state-in-the-making, it had gained more confidence. Every one of Ben-Gurion's measures was carried out.[43] However, there was also another military organization whose loyalty the leadership wanted to examine.

The Palmach at first objected to the idea of turning over Irgun members to the British. Allon, the Palmach commander, proposed a one-time operation to arrest 300 Irgun activists.[44] He dubbed the raid "Operation [St.] Batholomew's Night." Did this allude to a plan to perpetrate a massacre, like the murder of French Huguenots by Roman Catholics in 1572, the event from which Allon took the code name? In fact, no physical liquidation was carried out.[45]

Allon's plan was based on his belief in the Palmach's skill and operational capability. Haganah's chief of staff, Yaacob Dori, who was not one of the Palmach's proponents, rejected the plan;[46] so did the political leadership. Not even Galili, a fervent Palmach supporter, accepted Allon's idea, explaining: "Young people have a penchant for clear solutions, clear policy. They see every issue as a decisive battle, be it against the government, against the breakaways or against the Arabs. In the matter of the breakaways, for example, they would like [to see] a decisive battle, for the entire strength of the Yishuv to be mobilized and the entire problem eliminated. . . . Do you think the problem can be eliminated simply by declaring the breakaways to be . . . the enemy and [therefore] subject to eradication and annihilation?"[47]

Not even Galili, then, was inclined to adopt a simplistic formulation holding that force alone was the deciding factor and shaper of reality. The Palmach, however, viewed the opposition to Allon's plan as a vote of no confidence in its military ability and as additional evidence of the disparity between those who espoused military solutions to political problems and the moderate leadership, which preferred to cooperate with the occupiers. Palmach activists derided the political leadership for being "thwarters of direct action," and Sadeh wrote: "A war to the end, but . . . by us, with our strength."[48]

The Palmach's opposition to handing over Irgun people put to the test the leadership's power and authority. At the heart of the conflict between the Palmach and the leadership were two conflicting principles. On the one hand, the Palmach followed the principle of volunteering, which had guided the military groups since their establishment and according to which those within a military framework follow their own will and outlook and use available means to realize national aspirations. On the other hand, there was the principle of obligation, which the leadership attempted to enforce and according to which the military is required to obey the orders of the leadership of the state-in-the-making with no questions asked. The conflict reached a peak when Allon, whose program was not accepted, resigned as commander of the saison. His resignation attested to both the modicum of power which the military had accumulated in the Yishuv and the gravity of the crisis.[49]

But the crisis did not bring about a decisive rift: eventually an agreement was reached between the representatives of the military and the political leadership by combining the two seemingly contradictory principles. The compromise formula, the "obligation of volunteering," satisfied both sides. The Palmach maintained its definition of volunteering, the cornerstone of its military operations, and thereby preserved a certain degree of military autonomy and a certain freedom of action for military activities, while the principle of authority and obedience to the leadership was brought to the fore. Despite their objections, Palmach members accepted the verdict and obeyed the leadership's instructions.

In the saison the combined definition was successfully imposed. A statement of the General Staff said: "The operation shall not be assigned to the organization [the Haganah] but to volunteers, and not by order of the organization's command."[50] The operations carried out by the volunteers were well organized by the Haganah under the leadership's supervision. But the volunteering principle was preserved. To the obligation of volunteering was added the "organization of volunteering." Palmach companies were assigned quotas, their commanders even receiving lists of the names of those recruited for the saison. Only after these people had been taken to the cities were they permitted to opt out of the operation.[51]

With the mechanisms of the obligation of volunteering and the organization of volunteering, Palmach members were obliged to cooperate with the British and turn over the Irgun members to them. Even Allon justified the operation with these words: "In the conditions of those days the [choice] was simple and cruel: [to be] with the whole Yishuv, despite its mistakes, or against it. With a bitter heart, but with a sense of responsibility, all the comrades heeded the discipline [inherent in] Yishuv authority."[52]

In January and February 1945, more than 100 Irgun personnel, including most of the top command, were kidnapped and handed over to the British. Jewish Agency liaison officers supplied the British police with the names and addresses of another 500 or so. Among those abducted and turned in were Irgun staff officers who had been active in the Am Lohem organization and had advocated closer Irgun-Haganah relations.[53]

The saison afforded the Palmach an opportunity to show its stuff. Some Palmach personnel were cited for their fine work, and a report of the Haganah's intelligence service enumerated the Palmach's achievements: most Irgun branches were eliminated, its arms caches were depleted, its operational ability was paralyzed, its influence on the young generation declined, its members' arrogance was tempered, and many were turned over to the British police.[54] The effective blow to the breakaways gave the Palmach a stamp of approval for its military way. So when the order came from above to end the saison, bitter complaints were voiced in the organization: Why? After all, the Irgun has not been totally liquidated. The frustration was palpable in a song aimed at the leadership: "Listen, liquidation is a pipe dream, / Don't believe what you might hear. / This is it, the end of the *saison*, / You know you have a grand illusion."[55] A controversy developed, pointing to the fact that the right to command and the duty to obey did not yet fully characterize the relations between the young fighters and the political leadership.

To clarify the controversy and to put an end to the saison, representatives from the national institutions and the Haganah attended a meeting of saison activists called by its commander, Shimon Avidan. Palmach members objected to the termination of the saison. The Irgun is not totally liquidated, they claimed, and we should not stop the job before it is completely done. The leaderhip's answer was surprising. It hinted at the need to stop the operations in order to unify all forces against the British. The activists were not convinced. One of those present later recalled that thirty of them spoke and not one favored calling off the operation. Finally, Sneh's patience ran out. "I have spoken!" he exclaimed, repeating the words four times. This event was supposed to show the young people who really had the power to decide in the Yishuv, but Sneh's pathetic repetition later became a means of derision, part of Palmach folklore that symbolized the problems that accompanied the leadership's attempts to constitute its authority over the armed forces.[56] In the *Palmach Book* Allon wrote that the saison did not refer to a "hunting season." The true interpretation, he claimed, was this: "Once more the leadership needed the Palmach, and once more it has gained seasonal attention." This gloss demonstrates that Palmach members were embittered over not being included in the political decisions.[57]

A few years later, when Israel's defense minister, Ben-Gurion, tried to disband the Palmach, the unit's leaders reminded him of the saison events as evidence of their loyalty and obedience to the Yishuv leadership. But even then their words displayed the dilemma that accompanied their behavior during the saison: "What actually happened in the saison? In the matter of the breakaways, we accepted authority. There was a debate, a clarification; not a polemic, we didn't vote, we never decided anything by vote, we were either persuaded or not, but we accepted authority."[58] In practice the Palmach discontinued the saison operation. But it couldn't accept its position as no more than an operational instrument being used temporarily and conditionally according to the leadership's will. If the leadership hadn't promised the Palmach members at the meeting that they would soon act against the British, it is probable that the Palmach would not have accepted the order to terminate the operation. The leadership, aware of this possibility, turned to a different angle to examine the question of to what extent the military organization was willing to accept its authority.

THE PALMACH'S TRANSFER TO THE JEWISH BRIGADE

The creation of the Jewish Brigade in September 1944 as part of the British Army, along with the increased possibility of face-to-face contact with the enemy, gave the Jewish soldiers what they wanted and fulfilled their status aspirations.[59] The establishment of the brigade thrilled the political leaders, who perceived it as a major stage on the way to the state. Ben-Gurion, taking his leave of soldiers who had enlisted in the unit, said: "This is not the end; it is not a brigade that we need but a Jewish army, and I believe this will come to pass, and not only a Jewish army but a Jewish state, and I believe it too will arise."[60] Shertok's address at a Mapai meeting in Haifa indicated clearly the change that had occurred in the leadership's policy. For years, he said, there was a debate in the Zionist movement about the final goal. The leaders had deferred every decision as long as a Mandate regime existed which allowed them to move toward their final objective, but the world in the aftermath of the victory would be different. The leaders could not be content with bringing about the annulment of the White Paper. "Our demand is a Jewish state throughout the Land of Israel," he said. "The decision—in the very near future; implementation—as soon as possible."[61] The tone clearly indicates that by 1944 the leadership had changed, become more decisive, more confident of its power, and aware of the importance of the armed forces at its command and the goal to which they would be activated.

In September 1945 Ben-Gurion, hinting at the possibility that a Palmach group would join the Jewish Brigade, said: "It is essential that the recruits from this country should include our finest pioneer group.... I am not mentioning numbers, whether they are 50 or 100 of our elite people . . . and the best of the young people we can recruit." Thus was rekindled the "in uniform/without uniform" debate over which mobilization was preferable: to the Palmach or to the British Army.[62] A month later Shertok tried to persuade the secretariat of the Histadrut's Actions Committee to consent to the recruitment of some Palmach members to the Jewish Brigade. It would be a valuable symbolic act, he explained. But this was precisely why Hakibbutz Hameuhad objected. Asked how many Palmach members he thought should join the British Army, Shertok refused to give a figure saying: "The Palmach [is] our own independent creation. We are placing an alien stone in a foreign setting. It should be in our interest that the Palmach feels it is lending a hand to establish the brigade, that it has a part in this."[63] Hakibbutz Hameuhad leaders rejected the plan completely. At a meeting of the Ahdut Ha'avodah at that time, some claimed that the plan contained a hidden scheme to disband the Palmach, despite Shertok's insistence that the idea involved a symbolic transfer only.[64]

Clearly the supporters of the Palmach's transfer to the brigade were not seeking to strengthen the latter, just as the opponents of the symbolic move were not concerned about the Palmach's military level. The debate was part of the political struggle for control in the Yishuv. But the internal political reality had changed since the "in uniform/without uniform" debate first surfaced in 1942. Ahdut Ha'avodah indeed resolved "not to give even anything symbolic," but the movement was not strong enough to prevent the transfer. Ultimately the Palmach's German platoon was transferred to the brigade.[65] Although militarily the transfer was insignificant, the leadership saw the episode as a test of the principle of authority. Indeed, from 1944 on, it began to fight against the involvement of party and movement political bodies in the army and in security affairs in general. Accordingly, the leadership also downplayed its involvement in these spheres and presented itself as operating according to general, national, supraparty rules.[66]

Later chapters will clarify how the leadership's problem of authority helped institutionalize cultural militarism as an important element in the Yishuv's politics. The Jewish Brigade, in any case, managed to see action in the war. Sent to northern Italy, it was integrated into Allied combat units and during two months on the front fought the retreating Germans. Subsequently, with the war's end, the brigade became part of the Allied occupation forces in Europe. Many of its members served a number of years in the British Army, acquiring rich military experience and hoping that they would become a central force in the process of establishing a state. When the soldiers returned home, however, they discovered that not the Jewish Brigade but the Palmach was the object of esteem and prestige.

Although the cooperation between the Palmach and the leadership of the state-in-the-making was still characterized by arguments and controversies, the saison signified the begining of a tacit understanding that obedience was conditioned on the leadership's acceptance of the the military way as the legitimate means for solving the national problem. This understanding evidently strengthened the tendency, carried on by the native-born generation, to turn the military way into an ideology in which the practical foundation was considered superior to theoretical knowledge. As the journal that expressed the mood of the young generation stated, "The most dangerous enemy for our generation is ideology. It destroys all purposeful thinking. . . . The young people in the Land of Israel do not get excited by ideologies—for them the word has become pejorative. . . . [Our] ideology will be an ideology of deeds."[67]

So powerful was the emphasis placed on the practical element in the worldview of the new generation that Galili complained to the Ahdut Ha'avodah Council that this posture was making Palmach members absolutely, almost blindly, obedient to the political leadership. Palmach members who were asked why the breakaways had to be quelled had replied: "We are a state-in-the-making, our political representation is a government-in-the-making, whoever rebels against it is rebelling against the kingdom and must be liquidated." On the same occasion, one young person present raised a question of conscience: "If we are supposed to fight these groups because they object to the existing political line, there are others who oppose the Biltmore-Jerusalem program, so why shouldn't we fight them?" The "others" were Ahdut Ha'avodah, the new socialist party that opposed Mapai, the dominant party. The implementers of the saison, Galili maintained, would carry out any other order as well, whether or not they agreed with it, only because it was based on a power-oriented and military solution to political problems. Galili continued to explain that there were young people who thought the Arab problem would be solved by liquidating them, and that they had the strength to do it.[68]

On another occasion, Galili spoke his mind about the new mood among the younger generation: "I think this kind of thinking derives from the simplistic view that has its source in the illusion that . . . we have sufficient strength to take our problems in our hands and resolve them by liquidating them. An end to the breakaways, an end to the Arabs." With his acute instincts Galili grasped the nature of the phenomenon: it was a militaristic ideology that praised the use of force as an effective and appropriate solution for every problem. The British, breakaways, Arabs, even left-wing opponents could become victims of its sanctification.[69]

Weizmann, president of the World Zionist Organization, on a visit to Palestine for the first time since 1939, took note of the changed atmosphere in the Yishuv. Shocked by the assassination of Lord Moyne, he told the Jewish Agency Executive at a meeting in Jerusalem that the Yishuv's political climate had changed for the worse. He was especially upset by the younger generation's anti-British sentiments. "Forgive me, but you don't know the Yishuv," Ben-Gurion retorted. "The young people who have grown up here are as proud of themselves as American youth. . . . They do not see themselves as part of a small and wretched nation, they do not regard themselves as lepers, yet they are rejected." The young people who had been raised in the Land of Israel, Ben-Gurion continued, loved the country and liked to wander about in it, and they found it hard to accept when the British restricted their movements or placed political difficulties in their way. If you knew the Israeli youth, he told Weizmann, you would certainly admire their potential.[70]

These exchanges, which clearly served Ben-Gurion in his prolonged dispute with Weizmann, also showed that the diametric opposition in outlook that had vitiated relations between the younger generation and the veteran leadership was reduced. They confirmed Weizmann's observation that a change of mood had indeed occurred, not only among the youngsters but also among the leadership. In his autobiography, Weizmann wrote about "the negative features I have referred to: here and there a relaxation of the old, traditional Zionist purity of ethics, a touch of militarization, and a weakness for its trappings; here and there, something worse—the tragic, futile, un-Jewish resort to terrorism, a perversion of the purely defensive function of Haganah; and worst of all, in certain circles, a readiness to compound with the evil, to play politics with it, to condemn and not to condemn it, to treat it not as the thing it was, namely, an unmitigated curse to the National Home, but as a phenomenon which might have its advantages."[71] Weizmann, the advocate of diplomatic compromise and the political approach, belonged to the old order. He believed that the realization of the dream of a state could be different from what he saw with his own eyes. Upon his return to England in March

1945, his assistant, Doris May, noted that Weizmann was painting a dark picture of the psychology of the younger generation in the Yishuv and was fearful of the demons which he had not been able to contain.[72]

The Yishuv was in the midst of a powerful metamorphosis. It could be discerned in the endeavor of Ben-Gurion and his colleagues to achieve sweeping control. At the same time, in a manner not divorced from this, the use of mililtary action for political purposes was given legitimation. Weizmann, in a sense, showed prescience when he claimed that the new phenomenon attested to an understanding that had been reached between the armed forces and the leadership based on a common ground of activism. But at the time he spoke, this understanding, or formula, involving conditionality between military execution and obedience to the leadership, was not fully consolidated, and its implementation—as the saison affair showed—encountered great difficulties.

CHAPTER EIGHT

Unification of Forces

The Hebrew Resistance Movement

The joint struggle of all the Yishuv's military groups against the British was a clear sign of the existence of a state-in-the-making. The Hebrew Resistance Movement demonstrated the leadership's ability to unify all the military groups under a single command. It also marked the first use of organized violence by the leadership against the British. This chapter shows how the Resistance movement reinforced the reciprocal and conditional relation, first seen during the saison, between obedience to the leadership and the adoption of the military way as an efficient means to solve the national political problem.

The change of government in Britain following the world war gave hope in the Yishuv for a different British policy toward Palestine. The newly elected Labor Party, after all, had always been pro-Zionist during its years in opposition. The expectation was that Labor would now revoke the White Paper and implement the Balfour Declaration.[1] But these hopes were quickly shattered. By late 1945 the political leadership under Ben-Gurion realized that the Labor Party would no longer act as it had while in opposition and that in any event the civil service bureaucracy would continue to dictate policy. The new foreign secretary, Ernest Bevin, declared in Parliament that the opposition between Jews and Arabs could not be resolved by a compromise and therefore it was necessary for Palestine to be placed under international guardianship. The result was mounting sentiment in favor of using military means to put pressure on the British.

David Horowitz, a leading Zionist official, would later write: "Belief in legal, constitutional methods of political action was shaken. . . . There was a tidal wave of bitterness. . . . A sense of helplessness, despair, and revolt began to take hold among youth."[2] The younger generation believed it was called upon to change the situation. Every period has its mission, Yitzhak Sadeh wrote in an article that urged direct action against the British. Sadeh, who consistently expressed the mood of the younger generation, called for military action wherever possible.[3] The youth movement journals made similar demands.⁴ This time the young people who demanded an armed struggle got what they wanted.

The Mapai leadership had emerged greatly strengthened from the split in the party, making significant gains in the voting for the Elected Assembly and in the Histadrut Convention in 1944. The contest for the leadership of the state-in-the-making, waged by the two large labor parties, seemed to have been decided. The leadership still did not enjoy full control of all the military groups but hoped that the violent struggle against the British, a turning point in Zionist policy, would bring about such a unification. As always when he intended to be the sole decision maker on issues over which the leadership was divided, Ben-Gurion intimated that he was thinking of resigning. Once again his colleagues hastened to express their support for him. "The Yishuv and all its operative agencies are behind you," they said, "and without you the battle is inconceivable."⁵ Ben-Gurion and Sneh, chief of the Haganah National Command, could count on the support of the Palmach and Haganah, but now they sought a broad front which would also include right-wing military organizations.

NATIONALIST ORIENTATION
OVER CLASS ORIENTATION

The possibility of cooperation between the rival camps first arose, as we saw, in the Am Lohem organization in 1943. This was not an isolated case. In December 1944, Ya'akov (Yasha) Eliav, a senior Lehi commander, escaped from a Jerusalem jail. He had thought for some time that the Yishuv needed a new organizational framework comprising the Palmach, the Irgun, and Lehi. The Lehi Central Committee, gradually recovering from the death of its founder and leader, Avraham (Yair) Stern, and the arrest of many of its activists, gave Eliav the go-ahead for his plans. After his escape, Eliav met with Palmach commanders. The encounters only confirmed him in his belief that the young people in all camps favored a military solution to the Yishuv's political problems.⁶

From January to May 1945, Eliav was involved in Haganah-Lehi contacts. Eliahu Golomb proposed a complete Haganah-Lehi merger, and the latter's Central Committee discussed the idea.⁷ Eliav's letters shed light on the new conception, which in his view was shared by the entire young generation. In a letter to Moshe Dayan, who also took part in the talks, Eliav pledged that "the new [Lehi] boys will bring fervent faith and unbounded self-sacrifice. . . . Cooperation can be effected along the lines of Zionist activism."⁸ He also assured Golomb: "And to those striving for progress and liberation from subjugation . . . I shall offer my strength . . . it will not be long before the false barriers fall."⁹

Golomb, the principal decision maker in the Haganah, developed close ties with Lehi's Natan Yellin-Mor, and this facilitated the talks between the two sides.[10] After years of persecution and ostracism, Lehi had concluded that without the Haganah and the Organized Yishuv, the independence they coveted would not be attained.[11] However, Lehi still deliberated the question of who wielded authority. As for the Irgun, it had recovered from the saison and resumed its activity. It attacked police stations and other British targets. The Irgun kept stepping up the violence, and in May 1945 the Irgun and Lehi decided to coordinate their operations. They set up a kind of special headquarters, worked out operational guidelines, and began carrying out joint actions against the British. The Haganah felt threatened by the Irgun-Lehi ties, which undermined its authority.[12] In the series of meetings which followed, the Haganah's Galili and Sneh tried to find a formula for cooperation with the two organizations. Finally, Lehi and the Irgun announced jointly that they insisted on retaining their independent status, in return for which they would pledge not to carry out uncoordinated operations.[13]

This was evidently satisfactory to Sneh. In September he cabled Ben-Gurion, who was then in London, about the latest developments. Informally, Sneh let Ben-Gurion know that he had been successful in bringing the breakaways under Yishuv authority and that they had undertaken to obey his orders.[14] Ben-Gurion replied that he would enter into an agreement with them on one condition: "One authority and total discipline . . . in the first place, among the soldiers."[15] The agreement establishing the united Hebrew Resistance Movement was signed on October 23 and was based on two central elements: obedience and action.[16] The military organizations agreed to submit to the authority of a joint command, which was formally answerable to the political level. The essence of their subordination was based not on prohibitions but on what must be done, and otherwise had little potency. Ben-Gurion wrote in his diary: "It was agreed to establish a resistance movement headed by Sneh. . . . [The breakaways] will do nothing on their own. If the operation ends, they are free to do as they wish."[17] For the first time, the reciprocal relation between military action and obedience to the leadership, between the materialization of the young generation's wishes and the fulfillment of the leadership's will, was formulated officially and explicitly. The armed forces would obey the leadership on condition that it would make the military solution the centerpiece of its political action.

The Yishuv seemed to be embarking on a new path. It was the first time in Yishuv history that the rightists and the leftists had cooperated and national interest was given preference over class interests. According to an article in the Haganah journal, "The differences over the means and methods of the struggle are obsolete. Now there is a united, fighting Yishuv whose sons are acting with a deep sense of a shared destiny."[18]

The major effect of the creation of the Hebrew Resistance Movement was that the military groups discovered the existence of a common ground among them: the indispensability and centrality of the military way as a means of realizing national goals. Galili deluded himself in thinking that the Resistance movement would only oversee the breakaways without also legitimating their militaristic worldview. More perceptive was Mapai official Abba Hushi, who warned that the Revisionist line could become dominant in the Yishuv. "Whoever advocates a certain way of action," the future mayor of Haifa said, "is also bound to advocate partnership with those who have long held the copyright over that way of action. Whoever proposed coordination with the breakaways was, in effect, affirming their way."[19]

The Palmach, too, demanded action against the British. In the aftermath of the saison, its prestige had grown, and kibbutz training further enhanced its status. In the military sphere the Palmach established formal battalions, signifying growth and greater efficiency.[20] In the summer of 1945 a fierce quarrel in the Haganah over the Palmach's superior standing helped further entrench the latter's position. The chief of staff, Ya'akov Dori, an inveterate opponent of the Palmach, was forced to resign; he was succeeded by Yitzhak Sadeh, the Palmach commander.[21] Through Sadeh's initiative and with the support of Sneh, the Palmach had a tremendous impact on the Haganah. The Palmach held the key positions, its instructors ran professional and command courses, and its members comprised the bulk of the cadets in those courses.[22] The distinctive Palmach military spirit, at the time called "activism," spread through the entire organization.

The Palmach treasurer, the only Mapai member on the organization's general staff, noted that Palmach members, although they were from different political backgrounds or politically unaffiliated, all adopted the same political outlook once in the unit. This is part of the burgeoning of ideology in everyday life. It does not occur through a conscious altering of political views but through shared lives and experiences among people who have spent many years together. Even those from Hakibbutz Ha'artzi, known for its relatively moderate views on Jewish-Arab relations, became as activist as the others according to their own assessment.[23]

Fear of this militaristic perspective led the leaders of the state-in-the-making to prohibit a Palmach assembly which had been called for July 1945. They were apprehensive about demands for military action, which were certain to be made at the gathering, and about the criticism they would have to bear for not making use of the military force at their disposal.[24] Intergenerational tensions indeed intensified; they subsided only when the Palmach was finally activated. Then, as one Palmach poet put it, the floor was given "to comrade revolver . . . to comrade submachine gun."

The start was relatively mild: a clash between armed escorts of illegal immigrants and British troops in the north of the country. On October 9, the Palmach freed immigrants interned at the British Atlit camp.[25] Atlit was hardly a classic military operation, but it allowed the Palmach to vent long-standing frustration. As Yigal Allon wrote, "This was what we had been looking forward to and had insistently demanded of the official institutions."[26]

The opening of violent action against Britain had another interesting aspect. When Sneh cabled Ben-Gurion requesting authorization, the latter chose to respond not in the usual code but in his own terminology. In this way, operations were executed without formal authorization or approval from the leadership of the national movement. (As will be seen, a similar situation arose during the 1948 War. Ben-Gurion gave no official sanction for the expulsion of the Palestinians. Still, he did all he could to encourage this process. In both instances, it was the lack of formal consent that facilitated the operations. It allowed the doers considerable latitude and reduced the possibility of international pressure on the political leadership.[27])

In any event, the raids against the British fired up the Yishuv, and the Palmach urged more actions.[28] In the next operation of the Resistance movement, the "Night of the Trains" (November 1, 1945), the railway line in Palestine was sabotaged at 153 places. This complex and sweeping attack was the first combined operation of all three military organizations. Yitzhak Sadeh wrote that the time had come "to cross the Rubicon" and the railway action indeed represented that crossing.[29]

Ben-Gurion, back in Palestine after an absence of eight months and after years during which the majority of his time was spent abroad, encountered head on the new approach of the younger generation.[30] The idea that it was necessary to establish a Jewish state without Britain's approval and indeed through the expulsion of its forces was not acceptable to all in the leadership. But the new dynamic was not easily contained. The idea of a forcible solution gained more adherents with each military operation; the voices of moderation grew fainter.[31]

The spearhead of the activist spirit in the Haganah was Sneh, the head of the Resistance movement, who persistently demanded more authority from Ben-Gurion. Members of the Jewish Agency Executive were increasingly apprehensive about Sneh's activist approach and regularly warned against the large powers he was amassing.[32] To curb his growing influence, they decided at the beginning of 1946 to establish a committee (later called the X Committee) to deal with security issues and thus limit individual powers. Sneh, though, was not seriously constrained by the committee, having the support of the Haganah and the Palmach.

On December 11, 1945, it was decided to escalate the struggle. Implementation was placed in the hands of the Palmach, which already had some impressive military operations to its credit. These included raids on British police and radar stations; attacks on bases of the Palestine Mobile Force (PMF), in which four Jewish fighters were killed; "Wingate Night," in which the Palmach tried to seize control of Tel Aviv and show that it was possible to bring in illegal immigrants openly; and the most complex and bombastic Palmach operation of that period, the "Night of the Bridges," on June 17, 1946, when eleven strategic bridges in various parts of Palestine were blown up.[33]

With each new military operation, Palmach influence increased. Its high command repulsed attempts by the Haganah to have a say in the planning and execution of the Resistance movement's actions. Gradually, Palmach headquarters became the operations staff of the Haganah organization. Allon, the Palmach commander, became a permanent fixture in consultations held by the inner circle of the Haganah National Command, and it was the Palmach that executed most of the operations of the Resistance movement. Not surprisingly, senior Haganah personnel, such as Yohanan Rattner and Yigael Yadin, resisted the Palmach's encroachment and even resigned.[34]

Operational decisions during this period show where influence lay in the Yishuv. Sadeh and the Palmach high command planned the operations, and Galili and Sneh presented them to the X Committee for approval. Unrepresented on the committee were the right-wing, middle-class sector, the Revisionist movement, and both the Irgun and Lehi. After authorization, often following pressure by the doers, the plans' operations were returned to the Palmach for execution. The Palmach thus served as the body in which the plans originated and to which they were sent back. Allon wrote: "We are already used to the idea that many actions in the Yishuv's war originated in an initiative from below, which obtained its authorization in the supreme institutions following intricate moves to secure their approval."[35] After years of crises and forced inaction, the Palmach had become an influential political body. Was there a chance that its prestigious commanders, with arms at their disposal, might seek concrete and formal political power? Could they make the attempt with the backing of their political patrons? From a sociological point of view, these questions are essential: possession of arms confers power and creates the temptation to use that power politically.

CONTRADICTORY CONSCIOUSNESS

The military operations carried out by the Resistance movement brought about a change of attitude in the Yishuv toward the Irgun and Lehi. For example, following the "Night of the Airplanes"—the most successful Irgun-Lehi raid within the Resistance movement framework, in which British aircraft were destroyed at several airfields—kibbutz members helped the perpetrators escape.[36] Another example: on April 25, Lehi operatives blew up a bridge near Acre and withdrew to a kibbutz, where they were greeted warmly and invited to spend the night.[37]

Such responses would have been unthinkable only a short time earlier. The Irgun journal celebrated the birth of a new era: "Something has happened. All the Yishuv forces that constitute the nation's armed branch have gone on the offensive. . . . Do you remember the summer months? . . . Even in those mad days we did not lose faith that one day we would fight shoulder to shoulder with our wayward brothers. That day has arrived."[38] The Irgun, of course, utilized the Hebrew Resistance Movement to gain legitimacy, as expressed, for example, in a song composed after the airfields operation: "Without a road the unit marches / Out of the battle they proudly step / Only thus is the state conquered / With vision, machine gun, and grenade."[39]

Right-wing propagandists couldn't resist the temptation to claim over and over that the Palmach had adopted their approach.[40] In fact, the Palmach had difficulty keeping up with Irgun actions, a situation it found humiliating. The Irgun and Lehi were not constrained by the same limitations as the Palmach; they took full advantage of a loophole in the Resistance movement agreement and independently procured arms and solicited funds. The ever-bolder Irgun and Lehi operations deeply impressed the public. The Resistance movement's operations officer, who belonged to the Palmach, remarked: "Our main preoccupation was to go mad with envy all the time because the Irgun and Lehi were doing something. Our feeling was that the struggle should have been more aggressive, more intense, less hesitant. We always felt somewhat inferior. We were consumed by envy."[41]

Palmach young people found themselves in a state of what might be called "contradictory consciousness."[42] On the one hand, they sensed the considerable similarity between them and their peers in the right-wing military organizations: all favored a military solution to the national problems. On the other hand, they had the tendency to obey the leadership and were ready to confront anyone who challenged its authority. Gradually a syndrome of "verbal criticism and concrete obedience" developed among Palmach members. It received institutional expression in a multitude of meetings and conversations held by the Palmach. Palmach members felt that it was their right, even their duty, to criticize the moderate approach of the leadership, for example, the long intervals between military operations. At the same time, they chose to separate criticism from obedience. This pattern was seen by the leadership as a kind of safety valve which reduced the possibility that the young fighters would translate their outlook into a concrete politics of opposition. Legitimation of the duality of criticism-cum-obedience, however, should not be considered as only the result of manipulation by a leadership which aspired to keep the positions of power for itself. It was an institutional trade-off: at the price of forgoing decision making, the young people secured influence, the right not to respond blindly to orders, and the ability to voice their opinions emphatically. The criticism-obedience syndrome joined other patterns (such as the obligation to volunteer), which characterized the relations between the young fighters and the leadership and made cooperation between them possible despite their conflicting points of view.

The more frequent and complex the operations of the Resistance movement, the more the young people's militaristic worldview seemed to combine with obedience to the leadership. This created a foundation for mutual understanding between the generations. In this spirit, after the Night of the Trains Ben-Gurion commented in a phone conversation on the talent, ability, and perceptiveness of those who carried out the operation.[43] Golda Meir spoke admiringly of the Jewish community's youths, who were ready to sacrifice their lives.[44] But just when it seemed that the gulf between the fighting young people and the leadership was narrowing, one of the sabra's sources of satisfaction came to an abrupt end: the leadership decided to halt the military operations.

DISCIPLINE FOR INACTION?

On the day after raid on the bridges, the Irgun abducted six British officers as hostages for the life of an Irgun man whom the British had condemned to death. The same day eleven Lehi operatives were killed while attacking the Haifa train station. The British reacted harshly. In Operation Broadside ("Black Sabbath") on June 29, 1946, thousands of Yishuv officials and activists were arrested, including members of the Jewish Agency Executive. Appalled by the escalation in violence, Weizmann announced that he would resign as head of the World Zionist Organization if the resistance operations were not halted immediately. The political committee that ran the movement acceded to his ultimatum. One who objected strenuously to the halt in operations was Sneh. Those in control of the Zionist Executive, he scoffed, could not rid themselves of a sense of mental and ideological inferiority vis-à-vis the British. He resigned as chief of the Haganah National Command and went secretly to Paris, hoping to persuade Ben-Gurion to resume the military action.[45]

Sneh said that he knew the youths and the fighting organizations supported his stand. He was right. "The move by the chief of the National Command reflects the feelings of [this] organization," the Haganah journal wrote, adding that the resignation of Sneh was pressure toward returning to the line of action.[46] The anger of the young people and of those who claimed to speak for them was directed mainly at Weizmann, the embodiment of moderation. Sadeh wrote: "We are proud of our president. He belongs to the great liberal presidents of the last century.... He is a charming personality.... He is one of the great scientists.... Our president is learned, a diplomat, a tribune, but he is no commander-in-chief. And life nowadays requires that the leader of the campaign be more than a statesman and a scientist."[47]

There was nothing vague about what Sneh wanted. His wish reflected

the worldview to which Weizmann's moderate policies were the antithe-
sis. The interruption in operations and the breach of the implicit bargain
by the leadership juxtaposed two political orientations: the militaristic
approach, holding that violence is an acceptable and efficient instrument
to solve the national problem, and the diplomatic approach, based on
a belief in negotiations and compromise, which Weizmann embraced.
Weizmann explained the significance of his ultimatum in a letter to Shertok: "It is not a secret that I am an ardent opponent of political violence.
... Our only strength is moral fortitude. ... It is the duty of our leaders
to explain to the young generation that they must concentrate on building the land."[48] But the young generation heaped scorn on the attitude of
the elderly leader. In a tone harsher than that of Sadeh, the Irgun journal
wrote: "To all those with trembling hands, enough! Go, for heaven's sake,
go, and turn the leadership over to young hands."[49]

Golda Meir, who was not among those arrested, related that after
Black Sabbath she was troubled by the fear that unless the leadership took
the initiative, the breakaways were liable "to take matters into their own
hands."[50] With the collapse of cooperation between the Palmach and the
leadership and concomitantly of their agreement on military operations
and obedience, some in the leadership began to actively distrust the Palmach. Allon's later writing on that period confirms that their suspicions
were well founded: "In the Palmach there were good and true people who
reached a point where they denied the moral right of the Zionist leadership to continue heading the struggle. They proposed that the Palmach
should carry out actions on its own."[51] A Palmach song, "The Brigade is
Waiting," written around this time, was a variation on this theme: "The
brigade is poised again and waits here / What is it waiting for? Why,
why here? / It's waiting perhaps in case they should by chance deign / To
summon it even for some two-bit job again / Because, friends, after all we
used to be the spearhead / . . . But suddenly a rotten state of affairs— /
The spearhead is standing a bit off to the side . . . / Since the night of Atlit
it's looking! / Since PMF! Since Vitkin! Since railways and bridge! Since
the destruction of the radar . . . / The brigade is poised / In anger and
gloominess / Hurt by its silence— / Shall its way yet be illuminated?"[52]

The Palmach's reaction of anger and gloominess to the termination of
the revolt left no room for doubt: the carriers of the Israeli military approach acted as political agents and pressured the leadership into acting according to their lights. It was at this time that the first issue of
Bama'avak appeared, reflecting the spirit of the native-born generation, already phrased in slogans such as "We are tomorrow's forces!" "The Haganah first!" "Give the floor to the Land of Israel generation!" and "All
powers to the defenders of the Yishuv!" The journal demanded that responsibility be placed in the hands of the military leaders, since the political leadership had demonstrated that it was incapable of waging a true
struggle.[53]

In a poem Sadeh wrote for the journal of Ahdut Ha'avodah, he took
the split further, expressing the young generation's claim that there was
a rift between youth and the leadership: "The country of Israel is a fact /
Its youth, too, are a fact / And if our youth had a straight and erect back
/ Our life would be filled with content. Our life here is not gracious / And
that decides the content of our war and its style! / Neither leadership
nor even congresses set the content / The leadership has a choice: to walk
ahead or be dragged at the end / To climb to the peaks or to slide down
the slopes / And our youth will ascend and reach the top."[54]

The crisis in relations between the fighting youngsters was exacerbated on October 8 when the same journal published Sadeh's article "Discipline for Inaction," the article Ben-Gurion would cite after the outbreak
of the 1948 War as his reason for blocking Sadeh's military promotion.
"The leadership, too, has obligations," wrote Sadeh. "It is up to the leadership to decide. . . . But our leadership does not decide. . . . Without [mili-
tary] action, there will be no discipline. . . . Discipline is important for
marching in a procession, but discipline for inaction?"[55]

Sadeh's article showed in no uncertain terms that the young people
and those who sided with them posed a potential threat to the leadership which had called off the revolt and had thus violated the understanding between them. It was the most cogent expression to date of the
sentiment, which was gaining even more public suppoort, that military
actions were needed. As a member of Hakibbutz Hameuhad explained,
despite its weakness and fear the Jewish Agency would again have to declare a revolt against Britain, because a new reality has emerged in the
Yishuv, based on a tradition of war and a fact of war.[56]

This statement was not without foundation. Not only had there been
active military organizations in the Yishuv for more than ten years, but
with each act of violence the Resistance movement had expanded its ring
of participants and thereby broadened its public support. When the British searched for arms in Sharon region settlements, Haganah members from the whole area were alerted and rushed to the scene. Nine Jews
were killed and more than sixty wounded in the ensuing clash. This became the pattern. Whenever the authorities carried out arms searches,
large numbers of unarmed Jews tried to block them, in some cases paying
with their lives.[57]

The funerals of Palmach and Haganah members killed in resistance
operations turned into large national demonstrations. They were attended by the leaders of the Yishuv, senior rabbis said the memorial
prayers, Jewish soldiers and policemen bore the coffins, and crowds of up
to 50,000 followed. Jewish officials sanctioned the new approach and hon-
ored those who were willing to die for the cause. The British saw things
differently. Nicholas Bethell said that from Britain's viewpoint the Palmach warriors killed while attacking a police station were simply Jewish
terrorists.[58]

But the Jewish public was no longer interested in what the British thought. Now, at the end of 1946, a new round of mass demonstrations took place, marked by clashes with the army and police. A number of Jews were killed in the confrontations and hundreds were injured. The phraseology of the time sheds light on the new public mood. The Voice of Israel called the British "oppressive rulers" and likened their actions to "pogroms." Even phrases such as "Hitlerism has seized the rulers" were voiced.[59]

Not surprisingly, the decision to end the revolt incensed the public as well as the fighters. It hinted at the possibility that the leadership would choose an alternative, moderate approach. Certainly the British hoped so. At first they had reason to be pleased: Sneh resigned and the Resistance movement was disbanded. But it soon became clear that the Jewish Agency Executive was not leaning toward moderation. The main subject on the agenda of the Twenty-Second World Zionist Congress, held in Basle in December 1946, was whether to attend the London Conference called by the British in an attempt to resolve the Palestine crisis. Weizmann, who was in favor but found himself in the minority, made an impassioned plea. "This is not the way," he said, responding to an earlier speech by Sneh. "This is not the way in which Zionism was born." He appealed to the youngsters not to try to hasten the redemption by un-Jewish methods. The military struggle, he said, was a form of idolatry which endangered all the achievements of the Yishuv. "Zion," he declared, "shall be redeemed in Judgment—and not by any other means."[60] It was a lost cause. Weizmann was voted out as president of the World Zionist Organization and his bitter rival, Ben-Gurion, assumed the security portfolio of the Jewish Agency Executive. The fact that this post, which had not existed in the Zionist Executive (except for a brief period in 1939), was given to a leader as central as Ben-Gurion showed that the Zionist movement and the Yishuv were embarking on a new path. Direct attacks on British targets had been terminated, but the struggle was channeled into other realms: immigration and settlement.

THE NEW ZIONIST APPROACH

Ben-Gurion was in Paris on Black Sabbath. After hearing the details, he went to the local office of Hamosad Le'aliyah Bet, the organization in charge of Jewish immigration to Palestine, and declared: "We will hold a council of war here." He began by calling for more and bigger ships for sending immigrants to Palestine. Until then most of the "illegals" had been transported in small vessels and had usually arrived safely. Ben-Gurion now decided to turn the campaign to political use.[61]

Illegal immigration operations were organized by the Mosad with the active help of the Palmach. The Mosad purchased the ships, brought them to the port of departure, and loaded them with refugees. The Palmach provided most of the commanders and crews. The Palmach organized resistance when ships were intercepted on the high seas, and it was responsible for receiving the ships that broke through the blockade and for sabotaging British naval facilities that were scattered along the coast. Thus the political leadership under Ben-Gurion decided policy, the Mosad, a secret organization of the Haganah operated in Europe, organized the operations, and the Palmach carried them out. The relations that developed among these bodies intensified the part that the military way had fulfilled for some time in Yishuv politics.

The campaign of active resistance to the British during the period of illegal immigration was organized mainly by David Nemeri and Palmach commander Yigal Allon. Both were known in the Haganah for their militancy. They dictated an aggressive line against the British and demanded military retaliation for their interception of illegal immigrants. They ordered the ships' captains to resist every boarding attempt by the British. The orders were "Don't stop, don't answer British orders, proceed to shore."[62]

But the rickety vessels could not compete with the British Navy, which considered itself the ruler of the high seas and had the warships to prove it. Only a few immigrant ships got through. But this did not deter Allon and Nemeri.[63] Their insistence on continuing the operations and the violent resistance even though it was clear that very few immigrants would reach shore reflected the influence of the militaristic spirit on the Yishuv's doers. To display military prowess seemed more important than achieving the goal.[64]

The Palmach was worried about possible political opposition to its tactics and politics. Its concern turned out to be justified. Not long afterward, the heads of the Political Department of the Jewish Agency, Golda Meyerson and Moshe Shertok, tried to order an immigrant ship, which was approaching Palestine, to avoid any fight with the British.[65]

To prevent such interventions by the official political leadership, Allon issued standing orders to the military escorts on board the ship. They were to act without asking for permission.[66] To ensure that his policies would succeed, Allon visited Europe at the beginning of 1947 for firsthand briefing of Palmach members at immigration bases in France and Italy. Some of Allon's interlocutors raised the humanitarian issue of whether refugees should be exploited to make political and military gains. Even Palmach emissaries, who had firsthand exposure to the problems of the would-be immigrants, told Allon that orders which might endanger them after they had already endured so many hardships should come from the political leadership and not from the military.[67]

Mosad members, it turned out, were more moderate and cautious than the native-born Palmach commanders and took greater care to prevent loss of life among the refugees. The Mosad personnel did not agree with the policy of automatic resistance without prior consideration for the consequences. But Allon and his colleagues had a different outlook. The desire to prove that they could break through the blockade using military skill became an obsession.[68]

Nor did Allon and the Palmach command want to miss the opportunity to mold Yishuv politics in their image. Whenever a ship showed signs of hesitation owing to the difficult conditions of the men, women, and children on board or because of British obstinacy, Allon ordered the resistance to proceed despite everything. One historical account offers a somewhat understated description: "The Palmach had the feeling that the political leadership of the Yishuv and the Zionist movement was a bit hesitant and needed prodding from below. Indeed, it was the Palmach that pushed for bold action and for decisions."[69]

To realize his aims fully, Allon supported the illegal immigration struggle with military operations in Palestine. For example, following the capture of the *Exodus* and the expulsion of the refugees from Palestine, Palmach units raided two British Army installations on Mount Carmel and sabotaged British ships used to deport refugees to Cyprus. Palmach circulars sent to the ships noted the possibility that the refugees would come under British fire. "I am convinced from the bottom of my heart," wrote Allon, "that these victims will not die in vain. The blood that is shed belongs to fighters sacrificing their lives in a war for the liberation of their people." Allon was intoxicated with the path of force and its political potential, regardless of the price. No one asked the refugees if they agreed to be made use of to realize political goals, to the point of placing their lives at risk.[70]

Yet despite the Palmach's independent politics, no rift developed with the leadership. Allon's policies were aided by the leadership's ambivalence about how to deal with the illegal immigration issue. However, this ambivalence should not be construed as a sign of weakness or impotence; rather, it was a tactic employed by the leadership. At the beginning of the chapter we noted the significance of the leadership's decision not to decide on resistance operations. Later chapters will show this politics of smoke screens repeating itself with regard to the fate of the Palestinians in the 1948 War. The leadership left their fate unresolved, as it were, and so made it possible for organized violence, perpetrated by the young fighters, to determine events without explicit orders. A similar pattern is seen in the period of illegal immigration: to win the Palmach's obedience, the leadership was deliberately silent, permitting the military wide latitude through which it exercised a powerful influence on Yishuv politics. Cultural militarism, as defined earlier in this book, involves turning the use of force into a preferred political instrument. The illegal immigration operations, as they were executed and managed by the Palmach, advanced the militaristic conception in the Yishuv, if not by declarations then by symbolic practices which became habitual and gained legitimacy in terms of "this is the way, and there is no other way."

The same phenomenon was manifested in the sphere of land settlement. The focus on land settlement in the mid-1940s hinted at a switch from a struggle against the British to another target, the Palestinians. It signaled a return to the idea of conquering the land by force. When a small right-wing organization sought, after Black Sabbath, a way to approach the young people in the Palmach and in the youth movements, it found it more pertinent to speak about "waves of defeatism prevailing in various sectors of the Yishuv, mainly in the old generation, who display a willingness to discuss partition proposals." There was also a concrete plan: "We hereby turn to all the youth movements that support the idea of a Hebrew state in its historic borders, regardless of their political or social-ethnic affinities, with a proposal for real cooperation . . . against every partition plan or concession of any part of the homeland."[71]

The idea of conquering the land by force and so blocking the possibility of political compromise leading to partition was not foreign to the Palmach. The youth movements also joined the Palmach because they shared the idea that the "land cannot be divided." As the journal of Hamahanot Ha'olim explained, "Our existence in this country—as a minority in numbers and in land—imposes on us a war different from that of every other nation. A war of conquest, settling, breaching borders, the settlement of every bit of land that belongs or could belong to us. . . . We shall defend the right of that creation with arms, too. The right of immigration and settlement throughout the land. . . . One does not divide one's homeland."[72]

The "settlement way," as the youngsters called their plan, was regarded as an antidote to the idea that the land could be conquered and independence obtained by the state and not through settlement. The "state way," the youngsters claimed, would bring about partition, since it was based on trust in the power of the state and the support of foreign powers and depended on negotiations and diplomacy. The settlement way revived the old idea that conquering the land was a prerequisite for sovereignty. It was a conquest to be carried out not by a regular, professional state army but by popular, socialist forces, albeit armed, but acting consciously and voluntarily.[73]

The aspiration to control the land found expression in settlement. This was a politics that held that borders are not determined in conference rooms, that states are not achieved by politicians but by fighters and settlers who seize the frontier.[74] In this spirit, the Secretariat of Hamahanot Ha'olim declared: "We are not a political party, but still we cannot be silent about partition. For us, [this] is not a political question. It is something instinctual, which sprouted and took root in the movement, an agreement forged between the movement and the land . . . this is our mission."[75]

The idea of conquering the land by force in order to prevent partition was also evident in strategic planning. As early as 1943 the Haganah had submitted to the Zionist Executive a program which did not consider settlement as an end itself but as a key means to effect "the process of the Zionist conquest of the country." The document called for coordination between settlement operations and military actions by the Haganah, suggesting that the British restrictions on land acquisition by Jews and the fact that the majority of the land was owned by Arabs should be ignored.[76] Such ideas were a few years ahead of their time. In 1943 the Yishuv was not strong enough—not least because of the leadership's internal problems—to implement this program.

From 1945 on, the picture changed. Following a lengthy period of near dormancy, forty-nine settlements were established within two years. The agricultural-economic aspects of settlement had become secondary to strategic-military-national considerations, as settlement activities were backed by the Haganah's Plan B, which was directed against the Arabs and was formulated in September 1945. In this plan, as in the plan of May 1946, the Palmach was assigned mainly attack missions and had approval to operate anywhere in Palestine.[77]

The two military plans hinted at a phenomenon that was fully revealed in the 1948 War, as the Palmach's strategic approach and its political views fed each other and in effect became one. The young people would then take up arms to prevent the partition of Palestine into two states. But in 1945–1947, the militarization of settlement was perceived as an instrument within which to secure that political goal.

In July 1946, the British government tried to work out a joint plan with the Americans to solve the Palestine problem. A committee of experts was formed, headed by the British minister Herbert Morrison and the American ambassador Henry Grady. Its deliberations produced a proposal for a federated Palestine—in essence a partition plan—with Jerusalem and the Negev to remain under British administration. Arabs and Jews would reside in quasi-cantons, with 40 percent of the land allotted to the Arabs and 17 percent to the Jews. This was a revised version of the Peel Commission proposal of a decade earlier.[78] Neither the young fighters nor the leadership could accept the plan. As for the leadership of the state-in-the-making, it was under attack by the young activists and by Ahdut Ha'avodah, the party identified with Hakibbutz Hameuhad, for its political moderation. The criticism was intensified because of the leadership's agreement to attend the London Conference on Palestine in September 1946. To Ahdut Ha'avodah this was servility, groveling, and self-abasement. Its leaders thundered at Mapai that they could not achieve a Jewish state in London.[79] The leadership hoped that the new settlement activism would serve to offset such charges and demonstrate that the leadership was committed to the new way.

In a cable to Palestine dated September 14, 1946, Ben-Gurion ordered the establishment of twenty-four new settlements, of which at least twelve were to go up immediately in the Negev.[80] In a lightning operation, eleven such "points" were founded in the Negev in one night. Considerable resources were involved in the military-style operation. The organizer was the Haganah high command; Palmach units acted as escorts, and several of the sites were inhabited by Palmach settlement groups. The settlers were ready to defend the sites with arms, if necessary, but the British, faced with faits accomplis, did nothing.[81] This was an instance of the beginning of cooperation between the young fighters and the leadership, and Levi Shkolnik (as Levi Eshkol, a future prime minister) proudly told a Mapai Council meeting: "We have grown, we have matured, we have emerged from the infancy of a nascent project, we have made important achievements, we have attained a strong core of Jewish independence."[82]

Following this operation, it was decided to establish settlements in areas that would be outside the Jewish zone in the event of partition. On September 1, 1947, when the United Nations Special Committee on Palestine (UNSCOP) issued its report recommending a two-state solution, Jewish and Arab, the Palmach immediately reacted with a military operation in which new settlement points were established in the Negev. As a sure sign of the new conception, the traditional settlements were replaced with unique paramilitary settlements (*heahzuyot*), not meant to be permanent but to serve as "wedges": they enabled military control to be maintained over an extensive area and facilitated conquest of the frontier.[83] In this way, both the young fighters and the political leadership hinted that reality would not be determined by means of political committees, diplomacy, or compromises entailing a partition of the land between the two nations living on it. The determining factor would be force and facts on the ground, utilizing first military settlement and ultimately war.

What came to be viewed as reality, a product of practices to which everyone was accustomed, did not always receive verbal approval. Many in the older generation of the labor movement were loath to admit that the character of settlement—and indeed of the Zionist enterprise itself—had changed. In one of his talks, Galili grumbled about the traditional conception. Zionist activity, he said, consisted of many links: settlement, immigration, building, political action, and negotiation, and in this chain there was also a link called struggle. If the need arose, force was used; force was not unacceptable, but it was not always used.[84] By presenting such an ideological outlook—Clausewitz in Zionist dress, as it were—holding that organized violence was only the continuation of politics but by no means a substitute for it, Galili ignored the fact that the military solution had taken root in the Yishuv and that the traditional distinction between the labor movement's "act of building" and the "way of force" of the breakaways was disappearing.

The struggle against the British by all the military groups of the Yishuv through cooperation with the leadership constituted a new stage in the transformation of the military way into a militaristic way. For the first time the Yishuv deliberately chose the way of force to achieve political goals; for the first time cooperation took place between political rivals, united by the national-military cause into one movement. Even so, cooperation was far from smooth and the question of the leadership's authority was not entirely resolved. The breakaways had no use for national authority, refusing to halt their military operations as ordered by the leadership. Difficulties remained with the Palmach as well, and the question of authority would remain an open wound as long as the leadership was not fully willing to adopt the military way.

In the meantime, reeling under the onslaught, the British realized that they would have to relinquish control of Palestine. After UNSCOP recommended the establishment of two states, Britain announced that it would cease to exercise the Palestine Mandate and would withdraw. It was in the crucible of war that the problem of militarism and the question of authority within the Jewish community were finally resolved.

PART FIVE

Militarism and Praetorianism, 1947–1949

CHAPTER NINE

Political Praetorianism
in Wartime

During the 1948 War the political leadership, in conjunction with the armed forces, implemented a new type of politics. Previous chapters dealt mainly with the conditions and the circumstances that created cultural militarism. This chapter and the next, on the 1948 War, show how cultural militarism was implemented as militaristic politics.

Preparations for the anticipated war were mental as well as material. Ben-Gurion played a central role. In 1946, speaking to the Political Committee of the Twenty-Second Zionist Congress, Ben-Gurion had urged a new approach, involving more materiel and "preparedness of a completely new kind."[1] On this and many subsequent occasions Ben-Gurion was resorting to hyperbole when he said that the Yishuv was threatened with annihilation. Not that Palestine was a placid oasis where there was no danger at all, but the exaggeration served Ben-Gurion's purposes. For the same reason he thought it expedient not to mention that the Palestinians were displaying little inclination to fight for their cause. Their unity was a fiction, and their combat potential in terms of manpower, resources, and weapons was limited.[2]

The better to execute his plans, Ben-Gurion assumed the Jewish Agency's security portfolio, which had been unfilled for many years. He changed the word used to describe the post from *haganah*, meaning "defense," to *bitahon*, meaning "security." This switch was important. The old term signified a defensive orientation based on maintaining the status quo; this approach had characterized the Haganah organization in the past. Now the strong man of the Zionist movement and the Yishuv wanted to express the change and to give his full support to the stand which called for a decisive solution: "A decision based on force, a Jewish military decision."[3]

Putting words into action, upon his return to Palestine Ben-Gurion embarked on what he called a seminar, teaching himself everything he could about the military. To make it clear that the Yishuv's primary mission was to establish a Jewish state and to prevent, by force of arms, the creation of a Palestinian state, he reiterated on several occasions during this period that there was a substantive difference between the politics of the two struggles—against the British and against the Arabs. The former, although it included military operations, was basically political, whereas the latter was fundamentally military.[4] Ben-Gurion thus stated overtly that there was only one way to solve the Jewish-Arab conflict. His comments revealed for the first time a militaristic perception of reality on the part of the veteran political leadership.

To make his point, Ben-Gurion did not hesitate to criticize the Haganah for not being prepared for events to come and for not understanding "the mission."[5] Whether Ben-Gurion's criticism was justified is a moot point. His aim was didactic. He wanted to focus public thinking on the new path upon which the political leadership and the military generals, with himself at its head, were embarking.

In essence, Ben-Gurion's perspective presented a sharp departure from the two-states solution. In the months that followed, Ben-Gurion made numerous declarations about the new path. The following are a few examples. On May 13, 1947, Ben-Gurion told a meeting of the Jewish Agency Executive which was held in the United States: "We want the Land of Israel in its entirety. That was the original intention."[6] A week later, speaking to the Elected Assembly in Jerusalem, the leader of the Yishuv wondered: "Does anyone among us disagree that the original intention of the Balfour Declaration and the Mandate, and the original intention of the hopes harbored by generations of the Jewish people, was finally to establish a Jewish state in the whole Land of Israel?"[7] Speaking to the Mapai Secretariat in June, Ben-Gurion stated that it would be a mistake to forgo any part of the land. We have no right to do that, he said, and there is no need for it. As for those who say that there should be a compromise with the Arabs—such a compromise had already been achieved. The Jews say they have the right to Trans-Jordan, but that territory has already been declared an Arab state. Therefore "we have the right to the whole of western Palestine."[8]

In his speeches during this period Ben-Gurion explained that he had supported the idea of partition for so many years because it held out the promise of a Jewish state—and because agreement to partition did not necessarily entail support for the creation of an Arab state alongside the Jewish one. The intention, he said, was to establish a state in part of Palestine and then to build up the country until it became possible to confront the Arab majority. Now, in 1947, even before a genuine Arab threat had emerged and before the United Nations' adoption of the partition resolution that November, Ben-Gurion had reached the conclusion that it was time to actualize the original intention.

Even if the Jewish leadership accepted ostensibly the partition resolution, in truth it did not think for a minute of leaving the establishment of the state and the demarcation of its borders in the hands of the United

Nations and the Great Powers. The leadership would take advantage of
their help but placed no faith in their diplomacy. The true intention was
disclosed in various forums. Thus Ben-Gurion promised the Histadrut
Actions Committee in early December 1947: "There are no final arrangements in history, there are no eternal borders, and there are no ultimate political claims. Changes and transformations will still occur in the
world."[9] A week later, at a meeting of the Mapai Secretariat, Ben-Gurion
said he agreed with the complaints being voiced in his party that the
partition plan was a setback to the aspirations of the Zionist movement
and that the proposed borders were unsound politically and militarily.
He also assured his listeners that the boundaries of Jewish independence
were not final.[10] The importance of these statements is that they anticipated any substantial confrontation with the Palestinians. They were intended to prepare the ground for the possible use of military force as a
means to obtain control over the entire Land of Israel and to prevent the
establishment of a Palestinian state in any part of that territory.

Perhaps the major characteristic of the period is that its reality was
determined by the military modes of operation which had been forged
through the decade. It was not policy that determined the military operations but the opposite: those modes gradually became the policy. A first
hint of this was apparent at the beginning of the war. The Arabs objected
vociferously to the partition plan and threatened to take military action to block its implementation. In practice, however, they made hardly
any preparations and certainly took no action to realize their threat.[11]
The Jews, in contrast, made no declarations about war and even said that
they were willing to accept partition, but in practice they began to prepare, energetically and comprehensively, to prevent the resolution's ap-
plication.

Beyond torpedoing the resolution, the plan was to appropriate the
whole of western Palestine. Ben-Gurion explained this to a meeting of
the Mapai Council in February 1948 which discussed the Jewish presence
in the so-called Jerusalem Corridor. When someone interjected that "we
have no land there," Ben-Gurion replied: "The war will give us land. The
terms 'ours' and 'not ours' are only concepts of peace, and in war they
lose all meaning."[12] On another occasion Ben-Gurion described to the
head of the Jewish National Fund a plan which called for the Haganah
to conquer the Negev (the southern desert) and expropriate the land there
for settlement purposes. The official laughed and replied that the Middle
Ages were over and armies no longer stole land. But Ben-Gurion advised
him "to disabuse [himself] of conventional thinking." To Yosef Weitz, director of the JNF's lands department, who was also present, he said: "We
will not buy land in the Negev. We will conquer it. You forget that we are
in a war." Ben-Gurion also ridiculed the JNF officials "who are still accustomed to land registry and do not believe in the new ways of acqui-

sition." These statements are important because they were made at the very beginning of the war, reflecting a frame of mind and pointing to intentions.[13]

Some were alarmed at the leadership's militaristic tendency. In early October Mapam leader Ya'akov Riftin criticized Ben-Gurion and Golda Meir for making aggressive statements toward the Arabs and hinting at the possible use of the Haganah to achieve political decisions on territory and borders. At a meeting of the Mapai Secretariat, Ben-Gurion tried to allay such fears, but at the same time he and his followers began to implement the very politics which Riftin had warned against.[14] To begin with, they enlarged the Haganah. It soon became an army of fourteen battalions, organized in four brigades. There was also the Palmach, which had its own headquarters, and auxiliary forces such as the naval battalion and the intelligence unit. It wasn't only size that counted but also motivation and political outlook. The Palmach, the British Army veterans, and certainly the Irgun and Lehi had basically the same political approach: that it was right and proper to resort to military force to solve the national problem. All these groups were also ready to realize their worldview.

The first concrete expression of the military solution was seen in reprisal operations. Though neither side alone can be held responsible for the terrible violence, once unleashed it followed a foreseeable pattern of conflict involving ethno-national groups inhabiting the same territory, and it was nearly impossible to stop. The reprisal raids executed by the Jewish armed forces were fraught with implications. They banalized the conflict, made it part of everyday life, and contributed to the emergence of the "no-choice" syndrome. The reprisals also helped stereotype the Arab as the enemy who had to be taught a lesson no matter what the cost. As the Haganah's information bureau put it, "There is no thought of returning to the approach of restraint which supposedly existed during the Arab Revolt of 1936–1939. . . . We reiterate . . . that the aggressors will pay a heavy price for their attacks everywhere."[15]

Indeed they paid; in fact, both sides did, and heavily. In December 1947 Haganah and Palmach units began raiding Arab villages and blowing up houses. At the end of that month, in retaliation for the massacre of Jews perpetrated at the Haifa oil refineries—a massacre which was itself the Arabs' reaction to the Irgun's killing of six of their number at the site—Haganah forces attacked the village of Balad ash-Sheikh near Haifa and killed more than sixty Arabs, including women and children.[16] In January 1948, to take another instance, units of Givati Brigade operated against the village of Arab-Sukrir in revenge for the killing of eleven of their members. The soldiers were ordered to annihilate the village and to kill all the men.[17] The Irgun and Lehi also executed many revenge operations. During December they planted barrel mines around the gates of the Old City of Jerusalem and in Arab cafés in Jaffa, killing dozens or perhaps hundreds of Arabs.[18]

The reprisal escalated the conflict. Each side tried to outdo the other in violence, in killing, in satisfying the lust for revenge. A cycle of violence was born. Even if the two leaderships, the Jewish and the Arab, were not always in control of events, they certainly encouraged the revenge operations and in most cases organized them. Thus, on December 19, Ben-Gurion instructed two senior Haganah commanders not to be satisfied with a military reaction to Arab operations but to adopt the method of "aggressive defense": to deal a crushing blow, destroy the village, expel the inhabitants, and usurp them.[19]

One should not be misled by the term *aggressive defense*. Such expressions were mere semantics whose meaning—and irrelevance—were well understood by the armed forces when they began to translate words into deeds. In any event, if Ben-Gurion had given this type of order in April or June 1949, when the conquest of Palestine and the expulsion of its Arab residents was well under way, it would not have made much difference. But coming at the very outset of the war, it shows more than anything else that the later problem of the Palestinian refugees was caused not only by the war but was also, at least in part, the product of deliberate intentions, the product of the cultural militarism that already existed in pre-state Israel.[20]

This cultural militarism was articulated at a meeting held on January 1, 1948, between Ben-Gurion and his aides. Fundamental differences emerged between the Arab affairs experts, the so-called Arabists, and the military. The former tended to belittle the danger posed by the Arabs and to warn against excessive use of force. "We must not rely on force alone," one of them said. "We must find a way to reach understanding with the Arabs." The Arabists' perception of reality had been formed in the course of their extensive contacts with the Palestine Arabs, familiarity with their way of life, and concern to maintain the good relations which had been cultivated for many years. The army commanders, however, were eager to retaliate against Arab attacks without giving peaceful solutions a chance. In the meeting, Haganah officers, among them Yigael Yadin and Yitzhak Sadeh, complained that they were not being permitted to take offensive initiatives. It was not enough to react, they said; counteroffensives were essential. In the initial stages of the war these and other commanders often brought about the expansion of hostilities into tranquil areas and into Palestinian villages which had not contemplated fighting the Jews.

The differences which emerged at that meeting were the result of a reprisal operation executed by the Palmach on December 18, 1947, in the village of Khisas, in the north, a village that had not been involved in attacks against Jews. Twelve villagers, including women and children, were killed when their homes were dynamited while they were still inside. The operation outraged Nahum Horovitz, an Arabist from Kibbutz Kfar Giladi, who was known for his close ties with the local Arabs. Fearing that years of promoting good relations would be wiped out, Horovitz went to Tel Aviv and met with Ben-Gurion and others. He demanded that the commander of the Palmach's Third Battalion be punished for his part in the murder of the women and children.

The Khisas raid sparked fighting throughout Upper Galilee, just as similar operations triggered hostilities elsewhere. This episode illustrates the point of view of the Haganah high command, which would become politically influential as the war progressed. In the meeting with Ben-Gurion and his aides the majority of the Arabists were of one mind regarding Khisas. One of them argued that the operation had been a serious mistake and that many villages, for example in the south, would have remained quiet if not provoked by Jewish attacks. But the young commanders backed the action. Allon explained: "It is impossible to avoid injuring children—because it is impossible to separate [them] and to enter the house for that reason. Now only collective punishment is possible; a call for peace will be interpreted as weakness." Moshe Dayan agreed, adding that economic warfare against the Arabs should also be used in the struggle.[21]

The Arabists continued to insist on their distinctive interpretation of the events and remained at odds with the military. On February 19, for example, they reported that in many locales the Arabs had no desire for war and that there were enormous differences between villages which supported the Arab forces and those which sought only peace.[22] About a month later the Jewish Agency's Arabists submitted a proposal to Ben-Gurion calling for the establishment of an Arab state alongside the Jewish state. The Yishuv, they said, should act so that "the Arabs will remain with a way out and we will be able to look for points of contact."[23] In a sense, the Arabists presented an alternative to the new militaristic way, which saw reality through the barrel of a gun. Gradually, however, their voices faded and they were swept up in the prevailing current.[24]

The revenge operation at Khisas, in any event, showed the possibility of a meeting of minds between Ben-Gurion and the army based on agreement on how to solve the "Arab problem." Indeed, the approach taken by the Haganah officers in the meeting with Ben-Gurion revealed the existence of a conceptual foundation on which the politics of the leadership could build. But the Palmach's action at Khisas raised another quandary: the question of the discipline owed to the leadership. In a cable to Shertok, Ben-Gurion made it clear that the Palmach commander had acted contrary to an explicit order. Ben-Gurion believed that this was symptomatic of a wider problem, which the operation had brought into the open.[25]

"REVOLT" OF THE GENERALS

Besides learning about the Haganah's military ability at the seminar he organized, Ben-Gurion also saw firsthand the politicization which was rife in both the Haganah and the Palmach. As he put it, "They have turned the [Haganah] organization into a party and not into an army which serves the nation."[26] Since the mid-1940s, after the effects of the conflict within Mapai had become muted and the party had split, the leadership under Ben-Gurion had been endeavoring to bend the armed forces to its authority. That was the background to the saison and to the subsequent creation of the Hebrew Resistance Movement. But these efforts were not always successful. Cooperation between the civilian leadership and the military high command, as we have seen, was conditional on various formulations, such as the "duty to volunteer," "verbal criticism vs. concrete obedience," "discipline for doing and not for nondoing," and so forth. In practice, the armed forces relentlessly pressured the leadership to adopt their outlook and their way of doing things. However, the political level did not yield, as seen, for example, in the decisions to end the saison, suspend operations against the British, and disband the Resistance movement. That the Palmach laid down conditions in the saison and the breakaway groups did the same in connection with the Resistance movement only confirmed to the leadership the existence of a praetorian potential in the armed forces.

After assuming the security portfolio and concluding the seminar, Ben-Gurion was determined to place not only security but also discipline and the subordination of the armed forces above all else. His first problem was with the Haganah. In a meeting of the Yishuv's Security Committee about a month before the outbreak of hostilities, Ben-Gurion said: "The question of authority. That is a serious question. . . . If someone looks for the source of a mistake, it was the absence of civilian rule over the [Haganah] organization. . . . The organization ruled itself."[27]

The authority problem became meaningful when, for the third time in the decade, another "in uniform"/"without uniform" debate arose. When the British Army veterans returned home, they found that they were unable to obtain senior positions in the Haganah, while the Palmach was closed to them completely. Closure is a typical measure taken by a status group which seeks to preserve its preferential position.[28] The veterans tried to change this situation and obtain recognition and prestige. They invoked their combat experience and the high level of training in a large, professional regular army which operated in accordance with formal rules and procedures. Their spokesmen liked to explain the differences between them and the Palmach in terms of two schools: underground and regular.[29]

The Palmach would have rejected this description, but its activists also drew a sharp distinction between them and the British Army veterans. In their portrayal, the true military ideal rested on partisan, militia, and egalitarian foundations.[30] The "in uniform"/"without uniform" row in its third version erupted in the first joint Haganah-Palmach officers' course, which opened in February 1948. Most of the instructors were British Army veterans, and they tried to inculcate British training methods. There was, for example, the "battle drill," which was meant to accustom the soldier to act automatically in battle. Such methods were foreign to the Palmach; the course participants were outraged. Serious friction ensued, and the course commander wrote that the Palmach's objections to the training methods were tantamount to the "creation of a state within a state."[31] Later, when Yadin, the acting chief of staff, testified before the Committee of Five, he spoke of a clash between the "Haganah and Palmach party" and the "army party."[32]

As in the earlier status struggles, which began in 1942 in conjunction with the perceived threat of an invasion of Palestine by Rommel and resumed in 1944 with the formation of the Jewish Brigade, in the 1948 version the political parties intervened in the status struggles and in the production of culture. Mapam, which had been established in 1948 by the union of two kibbutz movements, Hameuhad and Ha'artzi, claimed that Ben-Gurion wanted a professional-career army in which the distinctive Palmach shirt would be replaced by a uniform, Haganah commanders by professionals, and pioneering voluntarism by complacency and career.[33] The new army, Mapam suggested, would be cut off from the society and its needs, its internal structure suited not to battlefield requirements but to internal ruling purposes. Mapam cautioned against the danger of professional praetorianism, but the leadership ignored the warning.[34]

In contrast to the previous crises, Ben-Gurion and his colleagues now represented the embryonic state and considered themselves entitled to recognize the military hierarchy and reformulate the army's guiding principles. To Mapam's chagrin, Ben-Gurion drew on the British Army veterans as the foundation for the regular state army—large, professional, and complex. His statist conception also sat well with some of the principles which the British Army veterans espoused: formalism, bureaucratization, hierarchy. It was precisely the ideas entertained by the Mapam-Palmach, in favor of a militia- and class-based political army, that Ben-Gurion thought dangerous and liable to bring about a praetorian force. The Palmach fighter possessed high self-esteem, regarded himself as a thinking soldier, demanded to be convinced that the order he was given was justified, often questioned it, and lent an ear to his political patrons. In contrast, the British-style "professional soldier" sanctified the idea that the will of the political leader was equivalent to an order: "Your wish is my command."[35] The British style facilitated Ben-Gurion's efforts to create substantial relations with the army and to obtain legitimacy for its rule.

Immediately after the "seminar" period, Ben-Gurion began to suspect the Palmach of showing indiscipline and anarchism. In a diary entry from late January 1948 he described behavior of this kind which had been reported to him by the head of the Intelligence Service. Members of the Palmach's Fourth Battalion had appropriated an Arab taxi and ordered the driver to take them somewhere. When he refused they killed him and threw his body into a river. The Palmach men said the driver had belonged to the Arab gangs, but it turned out that he had collaborated with Haganah intelligence in Galilee.[36] A week later Ben-Gurion referred to this incident at a meeting of the Mapai Council: "Never have I hated war and militarism more than I do now. . . . Whoever abuses a non-Jew will also abuse a Jew." The solution, as he saw it, was to place the Palmach within a framework of iron discipline.[37]

Ben-Gurion associated militarism with indiscipline. In our terms, an army could be disciplined but militaristic, in the sense of helping to obtain legitimacy for the frequent use of violence as a political tool. Ben-Gurion was actually referring to the possibility of praetorianism. He took a similar approach in remarks he made in February to the Mapai Council about the Haganah and Palmach: "There is always a danger with people who have arms and constitute a force . . . and [if] that force is not subordinate to a supreme authority, they constitute a great danger to the public and to themselves. . . . Never have I been more against militarism . . . than in this year. . . . The new force . . . must be established on a foundation of iron discipline, as in any well-run army, in which an order is an order, and which asks no questions but does exactly what it is commanded."[38]

Ben-Gurion diligently collected "facts" and testimonies about the Palmach's lack of discipline.[39] Most of his barbs were directed at Palmach Headquarters, an organized body which in effect had acted autonomously since May 1941. Its members were a united, cohesive group. They had been friends from an early age, native-born Israelis who had spent much time together in soldiering and shared the same political views, which were not necessarily compatible with the leadership's policies. Ben-Gurion may have known how the Prussian General Staff became a powerful political force in the nineteenth century. Created as a centralistic tool to prepare the army for war, it soon accumulated vast political power and displayed flagrant praetorian and militaristic characteristics.[40] Perhaps he also knew about the immense political power wielded by the French General Staff on the eve of the First World War. That body had not only great prestige but sweeping political influence and great autonomy.[41]

In any event, even during the "seminar" period, on April 10, Ben-Gurion had written in his diary: "They [Palmach HQ] have a separate budget. Once their budget is approved no one can intervene in [its] economics. They alone set the courses, they delegate emissaries, information officers."[42] More than a year later, when, as minister of defense, he was disbanding the Palmach, he would write to the army chief of staff that the arrangements which had ensured the separate organization of the Palmach and the independence of its command, including special means of recruitment, ties with youth groups, and independent appointment of commanders, had never been approved by the government or by the Haganah's National Command. Moreover, he added, all attempts to adapt the arrangements within the Palmach to the general procedures of the army encountered overt and covert resistance—overt by the Palmach and covert by Mapam, which considered itself the Palmach's patron.[43]

After the eruption of the war Ben-Gurion tried to intervene actively in the composition of the Palmach Headquarters. In February he ordered Ya'akov Dori, the Haganah chief of staff, not to approve any appointments to the Palmach Headquarters without his prior confirmation.[44] Another strident dispute arose over control of the Negev. The Palmach considered the Negev's expanses to be virtually its own extraterritorial domain. Ben-Gurion, however, sought to reduce the Palmach's influence there by appointing his people to key positions.[45] The Palmach's Negev Brigade objected strenuously to these moves and was able to thwart most of them. On March 5 Allon met with Ben-Gurion to discuss the subject. In reply to the latter's question as to why a different regime existed in the Negev from the rest of the country, Allon replied decisively: "There is brigade pride. The brigade has accomplished much until now; it will continue to do so."[46] Ben-Gurion's reaction is found in his diary: "I expressed astonishment at those who do not distinguish between the past . . . and the needs of the war now. They mixed mysticism with mystification. The Negev does not exist for Palmach HQ, but the opposite."[47]

It is interesting to consider the use Ben-Gurion made of the term *needs of the war* as an argument with which to reduce the Palmach's potential praetorianism. The method by which Ben-Gurion eventually tried to resolve the conflict was to insist that all shared a common element—the "needs of the war"—which they must sanctify as supreme. Gradually the idea of the "needs of the war" would become a verbal cover for a self-initiated war of conquest carried out in cooperation between Ben-Gurion and the army, a development that would narrow their differences.

In the meantime, one apogee of the struggle that Ben-Gurion waged against the Palmach was triggered by a circular distributed in May by an officer named Havlin, the organization's acting commander. The document ordered Palmach brigades to take orders only from the Palmach Headquarters. Ben-Gurion was outraged. He summoned Havlin and ordered him to retract his order, which was tantamount to mutiny against the legally constituted authority of the army. Ben-Gurion himself directed all Palmach brigades to accept any authorized order issued by the supreme command or by the provisional government and its authorized representatives. Ben-Gurion liked to mention this episode on every pos-

sible occasion, as it served his purpose of asserting the principle of obedience.[48]

Palmach disciplinary infractions contributed to the incessant friction
that existed between the Palmach's Harel Brigade and Etzioni Brigade,
both of which operated around Jerusalem. The bad feeling reached a new
peak on June 6 when members of Harel Brigade removed the staff officer
of Etzioni and his driver from their jeep at gunpoint, beat them vigorously, searched their belongings, and confiscated their vehicle and sixty-
seven rifles. Ben-Gurion said that the Palmach's isolationism was the
cause of such incidents; he demanded the removal of the person responsible, though adding that the real blame lay in the background circumstances.[49] Ben-Gurion continued to fill his diary with entries about Palmach indiscipline. Leaving aside the question of how serious these events
were, Ben-Gurion used them to drive home the importance of discipline
and authority in the army of the new state and to hint at the potential
praetorian danger latent in the Palmach.[50]

A major source of friction between Ben-Gurion and the Palmach and
its political patrons was the question of army appointments. When the
Committee of Five was set up to investigate this issue, under what some
called the relations between the "military" level and the "civilian" level,
even Yadin, whom Ben-Gurion regarded as a nonpartisan soldier,
claimed that the defense minister was not appointing officers to senior
positions on professional merit.[51] Ben-Gurion made the question of obedience paramount in appointments. When he objected to Sadeh's appointment as a brigade commander, he cited Sadeh's criticism of the leadership in the article he had written to protest the decision to suspend the
struggle against the British. Sadeh's opinions there, Ben-Gurion argued,
disqualified him for service as a commander, as they suggested possible
disobedience to the leadership.[52]

By now Ben-Gurion was referring to the Palmach as a private, factional army. He also warned about a conspiracy between a military unit
and a political party, stressing that all military forces must be under
the control of the state and not that of political parties.[53] Such apprehensions were not unfounded. As we saw, from 1942 Hakibbutz Hameuhad
viewed the Palmach as a class-workers army. This approach continued to
be voiced, particularly by Yitzhak Ben-Aharon, from Hakibbutz Hameuhad Secretariat, who put forward an alternative ideology to Ben-Gurion's
statist army. "There is a class and worker element in the Haganah," Ben-
Aharon told a joint meeting of the Mapai and Mapam leaderships. "Pioneering has made the whole corps. We shall not establish an army on the
British model. Palmach is an instrument for the pioneering spirit."[54]

The major step Ben-Gurion took during the first months of the war
to reduce the power of Mapam-Palmach was his decision at the end of
March to disband the Haganah's National Command and remove its
head, Israel Galili. The National Command included equal party repre-

sentation. It was the formal channel through which the political parties penetrated the Haganah and acquired influence in the organization. Galili was suspected by Ben-Gurion of owing his major loyalty to his party, Mapam, and of serving as a go-between for the party and its high-ranking army officers. Ben-Gurion explained that he had decided to dissolve the National Command within the framework of restructuring the security apparatus. His real intention, though, was to minimize Mapam's influence within the army, to establish a direct link between himself and the army and to neutralize the elements liable to interfere with his direct control.[55]

Mapam warned about the implications, especially among the soldiers, of Galili's dismissal and the disbanding of the National Command.[56] Speaking to Mapam's Political Committee, Ben-Aharon sounded an encouraging note: "True, Ben-Gurion is dismissing [Galili], but as long as we have friends in the supreme command we have to instruct them how to behave."[57] How serious Mapam was about realizing this threat is another matter. But to Ben-Gurion the threat itself was sufficient to justify the feeling he afterward described: "Then for the first time I had the shadow of a suspicion that there was some sort of factional party politics in the army."[58]

In fact, Ben-Gurion and Mapam entertained identical suspicions: each believed the other was trying to politicize the army. But Ben-Gurion claimed to be promoting suprapolitical statism. "I do not want to set up a party-based army," he said. "I want to deal with security."[59] Like the term needs of the war, the abstract notion of security also served Ben-Gurion to demand total discipline and complete obedience. The army accepted the linkage between the "needs of war" and obedience to the political leadership because it was given, in return, the right to largely define "security needs."[60]

Some historians, assiduously building an idealistic image of Israel's first prime minister, would afterward claim that he took on the military groups in order to create an apolitical, uniform, state army. Ben-Gurion was said to have been farsighted in standing above party intrigues, even coming out against his own party, and taking a comprehensive and disinterested view of events.[61] But the reality was different. Ben-Gurion did not seek the depoliticization of the army (as those historians claimed) but its de-partying. The reason for that was twofold: to create a strong ethnic army ready to fight the national war and to sustain the leadership's position within the new state.

Statism was not some idea that floated about randomly. It was a means of domination that Ben-Gurion wanted to impose in order to realize his will to rule over the whole society, directly and all-inclusively. It was not by chance that the order establishing the Israel Defense Forces (IDF), promulgated on May 26, 1948, was enacted hastily and asserted no principles to define and consolidate government-army relations.[62] Nor was it an oversight on Ben-Gurion's part that he did not appoint a replacement for Dori, the IDF's first chief of staff, who for most of the war lay ill in bed. Ben-Gurion's rivals branded his behavior during the war as "dictatorship."[63] This overstated the case, but it is certain that the supraparty statism which Ben-Gurion wanted to impose in the army, centering on the principle of disciplined obedience, was intended to grant him broad powers in military matters and beyond. To that end he was ready to revise the "security regime," to reestablish its source of authority, and to reformulate its structure.

Ben-Gurion's plans were not so quickly realized, however, for the army torpedoed them. On May 3 a delegation of chiefs of branches in the General Staff met with Ben-Gurion to explain the difficulties his plans would entail. It may be inferred that they saw as a threat the extra powers Ben-Gurion had assumed, his intervention in professional army matters, and the way he had clipped the wings of the General Staff. A second meeting followed, and the officers submitted a letter to Ben-Gurion threatening to resign within twelve hours and disclaiming responsibility for the consequences if Ben-Gurion persisted in his demand to dismiss Galili.[64] Ben-Gurion called the letter "irresponsible" and the resignation threat a "political mutiny." The letter confirmed his view that the veteran Haganah officers and Palmach commanders intended to intervene in political decisions.[65]

It was not the first time in the decade of the 1940s that officers had tried to influence policy. But now the commanders of the army had issued a distinctly political ultimatum, and during a war to boot. The commanders' potential praetorianism was related to a professional problem: army officers do not like it when civilians intervene in professional matters. But the potential praetorianism also had a political slant. Most of the officers were connected with an opposition political party which exercised considerable influence on developments within the army. Ideological differences also played a part. The representatives of the native-born generation, cetainly in the Palmach and the "Haganah party," sought to conquer the land by force. That ambition had been translated throughout the decade into military initiatives which were intended to influence the political leadership to adopt the army's view.

The officers had long been apprehensive that the political leadership would not be able to resist the temptation to establish a state in only part of Palestine and would concede the rest under pressure of the United Nations and the Great Powers, or because of difficulties in the war and high casualties. Although Ben-Gurion did not stint on militant declarations at the begining of the war, the senior officers were suspicious, as they had been throughout the decade, knowing that the leadership did not usually implement its tough declarations. The dialogue that took place before and during the war between Ben-Gurion and Jordan's King Abdullah gave rise to fears within the military that the West Bank would become part of Jordan and that the Negev, the apple of the Palmach's eye, would also be given to the Jordanians as part of a deal. Similarly, the younger generation was perturbed at the government's failure to formally annex Jerusalem or indeed any of the territories that were captured in the fighting. In fact, this reflected a cautious policy which held that no purpose would be served by becoming embroiled with the United Nations. Although the apprehensions of the young fighters gradually proved to be unfounded, in May, on the eve of the declaration of the state, they were the underlying cause for the "mutiny" by the senior army commanders.[66]

In an attempt to end the political crisis, which had blown up toward the end of a truce in the war, Ben-Gurion agreed to reinstate Galili. The praetorian threat, then, had done its work. Ben-Gurion also assured the Mapam leadership in a meeting held on May 24 that he and Galili would work as a team.[67] Ben-Gurion, it turned out, needed the support of the officers and could not have succeeded otherwise. This was an interesting revelation to both sides, and it guided their relationship.

THE *ALTALENA* AFFAIR

Another episode occurred which showed that even though Ben-Gurion was defense minister and head of the elected government of a new state, he did not yet enjoy the confidence of all the armed forces. There were other military groups which, like Mapam-Palmach, thought they could promote their political agendas by military means.

Since the dissolution of the Hebrew Resistance Movement and the Irgun's bombing of the King David Hotel, relations between the leadership of the state-in-the-making and the breakaways had deteriorated. They had been further aggravated in 1947 when the Irgun and Lehi persisted in the struggle against the British and the leadership reacted by taking measures against them that were known as the "little saison."[68] Even after hostilities began, the breakaways refused to accept the state's authority. Ben-Gurion, with his all-inclusive statist approach, wanted to integrate them into the nascent IDF, citing two reasons. First, they had military prowess, deriving in large measure from the Revisionists who had been in the Jewish Brigade, soldiers with broad military experience who should be mobilized.[69] Second, their induction into the army would neutralize their praetorian potential. As Ben-Gurion had explained in early November 1947, the breakaways displayed a new element not previously seen among the Revisionists or other right-wing groups: not only did they refuse to accept public responsibility but they also used guns to impose their will on the people.[70]

As with the Palmach, Ben-Gurion realized that the nature of the relationship with the breakaways would be determined by the interplay between the two circles of the conflict. There was the "internal" conflict, in which struggles for control of the Jewish community were waged across

the decade, and the "external" conflict at the national level. In the contacts which the sides held during this period, Ben-Gurion and his emissaries made it clear that military cooperation between them was conditional on their acceptance of authority. In Ben-Gurion's words: "A front
is authority. One front—one authority."[71] Ben-Gurion demanded the full
integration of their forces and their pledge not to take separate actions or
steps involving, as he put it, "the use of force or the threat to use force,
whether directly or indirectly."[72] But the Irgun, too, and far less subtly
than the Palmah, believed that its continued existence would prevent the
leadership from acting with moderation and particularly from implementing partition. Menachem Begin, commander of the Irgun, was under
pressure from his followers to relinquish the organization's independence only if the state would wage a total war of conquest. If not, he
must preserve the Irgun's independence at any price.[73]

The differences between the sides did not prevent them from trying
to find a compromise based on the common denominator whose existence was asserted by Begin himself: "We accepted, for the sake of fighting unity, the principle of the Resistance movement, according to which
we would propose war plans and implement them with the approval of
the Haganah command."[74] Begin was right. It had been the formula of
the Resistance movement, which had entailed the conditionality of two
principles: discipline owed to the leadership and military action. Article
7 of the agreement, which was signed between the political leadership
and the Irgun at the beginning of March, demonstrates the new conditionality. It asserted the necessity of cooperation for carrying out military
operations, not for preventing them, and stipulated that if the political
situation were to change, each side would be entitled to consider changing or canceling the agreement.[75] The Irgun, then, like the other military
groups, pursued its traditional line of making obedience to the leadership contingent on the use of military force as an instrument of policy.
The political leadership in effect accepted that principle.

On March 28, 1948, the chief of the National Command informed
army commanders that the agreement with the Irgun had gone into effect. On April 9 the Irgun perpetrated the massacre at the village of Deir
Yassin, just outside Jerusalem. The operation was condemned by the leadership but did not constitute a reason to annul the agreement—perhaps
because the operation, excepting the element of massacre, did not deviate
from the general line which the leadership drew up that month of conquering Arab villages and evacuating their inhabitants. Another possible
reason was that the operation had been approved by the Haganah, which
also provided support during the capture of the village.[76] At all events,
the agreement had its ups and downs and was accompanied by mutual
suspicions, recriminations, and tensions. Nevertheless, agreement made
it possible for the members of the breakaway organizations to enter the
IDF at the beginning of June.[77]

But this did not put an end to the authority problem. The Irgun announced that it would accept the government's authority within the borders of the State of Israel but would seek the conquest of the whole Land of Israel.[78] Again obedience was made conditional on military operations. Both the Irgun and Lehi took advantage of the fact that the leadership did not formally reject the United Nations' idea to internationalize Jerusalem, claiming that their agreement with the leadership did not apply to Jerusalem, which was, in their view, not inside the State of Israel.[79] The two organizations thus tried to pressure the leadership to annex Jerusalem. The result was a sharp rise in tension between them and the leadership and between them and the IDF and the Palmach, certainly after the U.N. mediator, Count Bernadotte, decided at the end of June to include Jerusalem within the Arab area.[80]

The frictions arising from the conditionality between accepting authority and using the military way to achieve political goals reached their peak in the affair of the *Altalena,* an Irgun ship, which reached Israel on June 19, 1948, during the truce. Besides new immigrants it carried a large supply of arms and ammunition. The leadership claimed, and the Irgun denied, that the ship's arrival was a breach of their agreement, and debate later developed over the question of who was at fault.[81] It is known that the Irgun had informed the government of the ship's arrival a month before it appeared off the Israeli coast.[82] Begin then conducted protracted negotiations with representatives of the leadership over its fate. One of his requests was for the IDF to help unload the cargo. The Irgun wanted to divert the arms shipment to Jerusalem. Galili, who led the talks on behalf of the leadership, stated that the arms must first be handed over to the IDF, which would ensure that some of them reached Jerusalem. Always an opponent of the political Right, Galili saw an opportunity to do it damage. He told Ben-Gurion that in his view the Irgun was unwilling to turn over the arms unconditionally, adding his interpretation that "the Irgun command continues to operate and exist inside the state and is striving to bring about relations of 'parity' and 'agreement' with the state."[83]

This time Galili and Ben-Gurion saw eye to eye. Ben-Gurion decided that the time had come for the new state to flex its muscles to demonstrate, even if symbolically, the principle that obedience was owed to the leadership. The government therefore sent an ultimatum to the Irgun to hand over the arms to the IDF unconditionally. When the Irgun balked, Ben-Gurion declared the organization to be in mutiny and ordered a military operation. Dan Even, commander of Alexandroni Brigade, was ordered to block the Irgun's attempt to unload the ship's cargo near Netanya, north of Tel Aviv. Even's units sealed off the area. In these conditions violence seemed inevitable. The ship slipped out to sea and set its course southward toward Tel Aviv.

Ben-Gurion summoned a cabinet meeting in which he spoke of an insurrection which was endangering the state and the army. "The moment the army and the state submit to a different armed force," the prime minister explained, "it will all be over."[84] Speaking to the Provisional State Council, Ben-Gurion reiterated the same statist principle according to which no state could tolerate the existence of weapons which were not under its control. The Irgun, he said, wanted to use the arms aboard the *Altalena* to realize its political ambitions. In other words, Ben-Gurion suspected the Irgun of displaying praetorianist tendencies.[85] In the meantime the ship, now off the coast of Tel Aviv, was shelled by an IDF cannon; IDF units, including male and female clerks from the nearby Palmach HQ, fired at it with rifles. Twenty-eight people were killed and dozens wounded. The *Altalena* sank and the explosions of the ammunition it was carrying could be heard for days afterward.

Did the Irgun intend to foment a rebellion and topple the fledgling government by force of arms? Was this a saliently praetorian manifestation, as Ben-Gurion claimed? Was it an attempt to exploit a sensitive political, military, and social situation to execute a putsch, as Galili said?[86] Intentions aside, the important point is that Ben-Gurion and his government turned the episode into a symbol which was meant to teach, by example, the importance of the authority principle. As for the Irgun, the question that should be asked is not whether it rebelled but why did it not rebel after the *Altalena* affair. As in the saison, some of its activists urged the organization to fight back. But the Irgun's commander was against this. What were his reasons?[87] This question hints at the possibility that the leadership found a way to resolve the problem of the armed forces which did not completely accept its authority. A similar problem existed with the Palmach.

PALMACH AS PRAETORIAN GUARD

By June 1948 Ben-Gurion was vigorously demanding that the Palmach be disbanded. He also wanted to integrate the Palmach into the new IDF structure, dispersing its members on the various fronts in a manner which would bring about its dissolution. As Ben-Gurion put it, all were soldiers of the Israel Defense Forces and a single law applied to all battalions and units.[88] Twice, on June 16 and 19, Ben-Gurion called in Allon to broach the idea of disbanding the Palmach.[89] Allon would have no part of it. A few days later Allon stated: "That brigade was not established by some offhand remark and it must not be disbanded by some offhand order. That brigade will have its say."[90]

In this power struggle Ben-Gurion was not about to throw up his hands without a fight. He decided to go public. Speaking to the Mapai Council on June 19, he stated that an attempt was being made to give one party a monopoly over the Palmach, to turn it into a kind of military brigade owing allegiance to a party. It was untenable, he explained, that most of an army should be subordinate to the general control of the people but that part of it should be answerable to some other authority, overt or covert.[91]

In the meantime the *Altalena* affair occurred and the Palmach's issue was left in abeyance. However, for the Palmach's commanders the affair served as an opportunity to illustrate their role as a praetorian guard. Allon gave a colorful account of this at a meeting of commanders held in late June. "A miracle has occurred," he said, "and the Irgun has had a disaster in which one of their ships ran aground opposite the headquarters of the Palmach. . . . The program of the breakaways today is no less and no more than to establish the Kingdom of Judah as against the Kingdom of Israel, to breach the outposts and get there in full force, and to set up the Kingdom of Judah in Jerusalem. And the successor to King David arose, Menachem [Begin], and he did make war against David Ben-Gurion the King of Israel. . . . Something very great happened here, when a few staff officers and a few girls working there in the offices and guarding the gate . . . succeeded . . . in smiting Jewish fascism at the fifth rib, or as we say today, beating it to a pulp."[92]

In a meeting with Ben-Gurion at Kibbutz Na'an on September 14, Palmach commanders expressed clearly, even proudly, their praetorian outlook. The same Shalom Havlin whom Ben-Gurion had earlier suspected of breaching authority said: "We must also remember that Jewish fascism exists. There is Jewish reactionism. It is there. . . . We saw its tip in the *Altalena* episode. Would the *Altalena* operation have been possible without the Palmach?" To which Allon added: "If Begin becomes prime minister, I will not submit to him as long as I live. . . . It was enough for me to hear Meridor's [an Irgun leader] slip of the tongue at a meeting with journalists, when he said that with a hundred men he could have taken the government."[93]

The idea of the Palmach as a praetorian guard was categorically supported by Mapam. In May the party had called for the creation of an armed Histadrut force, an army that would demonstrate class loyalty and could prosecute a war against the political Right. Mapam leaflets distributed in Tel Aviv called for an armed force to be forged which would be attached to the working class and defend it.[94] The party's leaders explained that there was a class and working-class problem in the country, that the Irgun wanted to seize control, and that only an army based on the Haganah and the Palmach could save the day.[95] At a meeting of the Histadrut's Actions Committee, Mapam leader Hazan said that the Palmach Headquarters had repulsed the danger of an Irgun takeover in Tel Aviv. The right wing, Hazan said, had no restraints and no need for complex Zionist calculations: the moment it could seize power in Israel, it would do so.[96]

Ben-Gurion recoiled from the reasons by which the Palmach and its political patrons justified its continued existence. "I am told," he said to Palmach commanders, "that there should be loyal brigades. But I must first of all ask: loyal to whom? Is the Palmach's distinctiveness based on a separate affiliation, in contrast to all [other] army units?" He added: "Can you imagine a State of Israel which has an army of the whole state, but in the army one part is subordinate to another authority, not that of the state"?[97]

Ben-Gurion seemed to be looking for any reason to attack the Palmach. At the end of June he announced a round of new appointments of officers, all of them British Army veterans, to key positions in the General Staff and combat units. When the appointments were made public, the heads of the General Staff branches again threatened to resign. The members of "the faction," as Ben-Gurion called them, told the prime minister and defense minister that he faced "shock and ruin in the old way" and demanded that the cabinet be informed of their resignation.[98] Ben-Gurion claimed that they were not acting in good faith. He suspected them of something very like political praetorianism—of presenting a clear challenge to the state leadership, undertaken with Mapam's backing. "A kind of political mutiny in the army and a matter of unparalleled seriousness," he said.[99]

Was there any basis to the claims of Ben-Gurion and his colleagues about Palmach praetorianism? This question is no more sociologically significant than that of the Irgun's supposed rebellion in the *Altalena* affair. The point is that Ben-Gurion's accusations and suspicions were part of the reality that guided the behavior of those involved; they also brought about the reduction of the constant friction among them. In any event, one of the ways in which the second "revolt of the generals" was more serious than its predecessor was that it transcended the narrow confines of the senior IDF level and was referred to the cabinet. The latter was asked to decide the affair, and to that end it established the Committee of Five to investigate Ben-Gurion's accusations of a political mutiny in the army. Here was the moment of truth for civil-military relations in the new state. Testimonies were heard over four consecutive days. They reinforced Ben-Gurion's view—he was present throughout—that political-party motivations underlay the revolt of the generals, an intrigue by Mapam, as he called it, aimed at seizing control of the army and ousting him.[100]

But the committee reached different conclusions. Its findings were a stunning surprise to Ben-Gurion. One of the subjects examined by the committee was whether the minister of defense was entitled to wage war and appoint commanders at his exclusive discretion. The committee concluded that Ben-Gurion's excessive powers in these matters should be curtailed—in effect, that the political and military levels should be separated. As Moshe Shapira, a committee member, explained: "I accept the view that Ben-Gurion should be the guider but not the implementer."[101] The committee also recommended that a small war cabinet should be created to mediate between Ben-Gurion and the high command. In addition, it proposed the appointment of two directors-general, or deputy ministers for defense, to operate in conjunction with the minister of defense.[102]

Ben-Gurion's reaction was characteristic of his behavior in such crises. He resigned, not only as defense minister but also as prime minister. Nor did he retract his resignation until his associates in the leadership implored him to return and pledged their unwavering support. The committee's recommendations were not implemented. Galili was forced to pay the price and left the high command altogether. But of far greater importance is that a singular situation was created, which was succinctly summed up by Itzhak Gruenbaum, interior minister and chairman of the committee: "This means that [there is no] dividing line between Ben-Gurion and the army."[103]

One can understand why Ben-Gurion's political colleagues surrendered to his ultimatum. But why did the army, which had the weapons, follow suit? Why did the General Staff assent to Ben-Gurion's refusal to accept the conclusions of his associates in the leadership, even of a cabinet-level state committee? Why did they, too, not demand the separation of the political and the military, as the committee recommended? Why did the Palmach, whose leaders were in constant consultation with Mapam, reconcile themselves to Galili's forced resignation and to the probability that the Palmach would be disbanded? The breakaways, too, had not rebelled following *Altalena*. True, Ben-Gurion had his own methods for getting his way; still, it is difficult to accept that reality is determined solely by the manipulations of a single individual.

There was another reason why the army did not revolt and why praetorian tendencies, on both the Right and the Left, did not materialize. That reason was the war, or, more precisely, its management. It is more than interesting that the sharp conflict between Ben-Gurion and the native-born generation, in its different generational units, was blunted and indeed effectively disappeared in July, when hostilities resumed at the end of the truce. This fact should be considered in conjunction with another: now that the internal conflicts had been largely resolved, the Israeli combat posture was no longer defensive. It was evidence of a new political line which would determine the character of the entire war. Israel was now implementing a militaristic politics. This form of politics also provided the solution for the authority problem which had long plagued the leadership. In short, the militaristic politics adopted by the leadership neutralized the army's praetorian potential. The external conflict replaced the internal one.

CHAPTER TEN

Militaristic Politics
in Wartime

Until the end of March 1948 the Yishuv, which was still arming and organizing and wanted to gain time, engaged in bloody clashes with Palestinian irregulars who were reinforced by a few hundred volunteers from the neighboring countries. The Arab force was unorganized, was poorly trained and equipped, and lacked even the advantage of numbers. The Arabs controlled the roads, however, and their presence enabled them to cut off many Jewish settlements. They also recorded some significant achievements in battle. The war's outcome was hardly a foregone conclusion at this stage.[1]

The Haganah had begun to revise its strategy in February. Haganah units, which were organized at brigade-planning level with tactical execution by companies, carried out hit-and-run raids on villages deep inside Arab territory. These self-initiated operations were another stage in the transformation of the military way into a central instrument of policy.[2] But the crucial milestone in the use of the military for political purposes was Operation Nahshon, which began on April 6, 1948. Its declared goal was to open the road to Jerusalem. In fact, however, it was a first effort by regular military forces to capture territory, "cleanse" it of Arabs, and prevent them from returning.[3] Operation Nahshon marks the incipient realization of a type of politics I call militaristic. Not because it aimed to establish a state by force of arms but because it was founded on the premise that the only way to establish the state was by the use of arms and the capture of territory beyond the boundaries designated for the Jewish state, despite the political leadership's solemn assent, to the U.N. partition resolution.

Galili, chief of the Haganah's National Command, explained the concept to graduates of an officers' course on April 8. Asked whether the Jewish forces would fight only in the areas allocated to the Jewish state by the United Nations and what the fate would be of the dozens of settlements that lay outside those boundaries, Galili replied: "We are fighting and we shall fight for all the territories that have been conquered by Hebrew settlement to this day. . . . The boundaries of our state will be deter-

mined by the boundaries of our strength. . . . The political borders will
match the borders of the areas that we shall liberate from the enemy, the
fruits of our conquests."[4] That same month, after the two main Arab
forces were beaten—at the approaches to Jerusalem and in the Haifa
area—a mass exodus of Palestinians was under way from towns and villages. Some fled out of fear; others were expelled by the Haganah, which
was executing a military operation code-named Plan D.[5]

CONQUEST AND EXPULSION

Plan D is part of the evidence that the Jewish forces did not only react
to Arab violence. The plan called for seizing territory on a countrywide
scale, "cleansing" villages, capturing Arab towns, expelling Arabs from
cities of mixed Jewish-Arab populations, and forging territorial continuity between the various Jewish enclaves.[6] As earlier chapters showed,
Plan D was preceded by offensively oriented military operations which
held that the fate of the region would be decided by force of arms: the
Avner Program in 1941, Plan B in September 1945, and Plan May in 1946.
By late 1947 two staff papers had been formulated which spoke of
"cleansing" Arab areas, "active defense" along the borders, and imposing
a political solution by military means.[7] Plan Joshua, which preceded Plan
D, was also based on the implicit assumption that the whole country was
a single territorial unit which must be captured. The multiplicity of plans
turned offensive military strategy into a value and contributed to the entrenchment of the political conception according to which a state would
be established by force and not by diplomacy, as the only solution to the
"Arab problem" was the military one. Plan D may have been couched in
language which was vague and generalizing, but the attendant operative
orders which went out to the brigades show that the General Staff had a
political goal: to expand the state's territory beyond the boundaries of the
partition plan.[8]

   In this they were of one mind with the political leadership. Its view
that the state's borders would be determined not by diplomacy but by the
strength of the army was voiced in a meeting of the National Administration (Minhelet Ha'am) held on May 21, 1948. To Pinhas Rosenblitt's
remark that it was impossible to avoid the question of demarcating the
state's borders, Ben-Gurion replied: "Everything is possible. If we decide
here to say nothing about borders, then we will say nothing. Nothing is
a priori." Not conceding the point, Rosenblitt said that a legal question
was involved. Ben-Gurion retorted that people create legal systems. The
possibility thus emerged that the military way would determine reality.
Ben-Gurion went on to offer an example: if the army were to capture
Western Galilee or both sides of the road to Jerusalem and those territories were to become part of the state as a result of their conquest, why
should an undertaking about borders be given now? After this, the Na-

tional Administration voted not to introduce the question of borders into the proclamation of the state.[9]

The decision not to decide was consciously superseded by politics that relied on the army's modes of operation. In the meantime, Operation Nahshon was followed by a series of offensive thrusts. In all of them, territory was captured, villages were destroyed, and the inhabitants fled or were expelled. Major operations were undertaken by Harel to consolidate control in Jerusalem, Hametz to capture Jaffa, Yevussi around Jerusalem, and Yiftah in Upper Galilee. In these and other offensives, dozens of villages and some towns fell to the Jewish forces. Plan D only hinted at the mass expulsion of Arabs. Still, directives to the effect that if a village resisted the local armed force should be destroyed and the population expelled across the borders were sufficient to actualize assumptions which the young fighters had internalized through the decade of the 1940s.[10]

In some cases the expulsions were accompanied by absolute silence on the part of the leadership or even expressions of amazement.[11] One of those who was most amazed during this period was Ben-Gurion: "How did tens of thousands of people leave in such panic, and without sufficient reason, from their town, their houses and their property? What brought on this flight? Was it only an order from above? . . . Was it really fear?" Ben-Gurion's amazement was short-lived. That same day, in a meeting of the Arab Affairs Committee, he laid down a rule: "It is not up to us to be concerned about the return of the Arabs."[12] A few weeks later Ben-Gurion again confided his astonishment to his diary, wondering how it had come about that the inhabitants of Jaffa had left the city. The next day the defense minister moved new immigrants into the houses of those who had departed.[13]

The flight of the Arabs began at the end of 1947. The Jewish leadership understood immediately that the opportunity which had arisen must be fully exploited. The leadership used diverse means to encourage and intensify the Arabs' flight: leaflets, radio broadcasts, harassment by loudspeakers, and whispering campaigns to generate an atmosphere of fear and panic.[14] Arab hysteria had its own reasons; one of them surely stemmed from incidents of soldiers' brutality toward civilians, most notoriously at Deir Yassin. With the approval of the local Haganah commander David Shaltiel, Irgun and Lehi forces raided the village on April 9, ignoring the nonaggression agreement which was in effect between the village and the adjacent Jewish neighborhoods in western Jerusalem. The massacre that ensued, in which about 250 men, women, and children perished—an altogether extraordinary outcome, even in terms of ethnic conflicts, which can be blood-drenched affairs and produce civilian casualties—spurred the exodus of Arabs throughout the country.[15]

So, while the political leadership was amazed, the ethno-national army went about its work. At the end of April the second wave of the Arabs' mass exodus began.[16] Allon, commander of the Palmach, appraising the military situation in eastern Galilee, recommended a series of measures designed to bring about the area's conquest and the expulsion of the local Arabs. In operation Yiftah, led by Allon, dozens of Arab villages were captured and razed to the ground. The large towns of Safed and Beit She'an were also taken, and Arabs who did not flee were expelled.[17] Afterward Allon would command other operations in which large numbers of Arabs were expelled. Following Operation Dani, for example, in which some 60,000 Arabs were expelled from Lydda and Ramleh, Allon noted in his report that one of the benefits of the "departure" (Allon's chosen term) was that long lines of refugees clogged the roads and blocked the advance of the Arab Legion.[18] The human tragedy made no impression on Allon, although he belonged to Mapam, a socialist party, and was a kibbutz member, two institutions that were usually linked with a moral approach. Certainly it paled in comparison with the strategic advantages that accrued from the refugees' flight or with the vision of the conquest of the whole land, a goal to which Allon and his colleagues had aspired for years. Benny Morris notes that Allon, in all his operations, made a point of not leaving an Arab population in the areas he captured; he had the reputation of wanting to ensure that the rear areas behind his forces' forward lines would be "Arab-clean."[19]

Other senior army commanders were also eager to capture territory, level villages, and expel the inhabitants. Operation Ben-Ami, the Haganah's last large-scale operation before the establishment of the State of Israel, brought about the conquest of areas in western Galilee which were not earmarked for the Jewish state in the U.N. partition plan. As far as we know, the Carmeli Brigade, which carried out the operation, was not explicitly ordered by either the Haganah or the political level to expel the Arab population. Nevertheless, the brigade's commander, Moshe Carmel, did just that. Readers of the book Carmel published in 1949 about the operation in Galilee will find no boasting about conquests and expulsions. On the contrary, Carmel offers a depressing account of the Arabs heading north: long lines of refugees, horrific scenes of dying infants, lost women, exhausted old people. Unlike Allon, Carmel saw the human tragedy, but he too did nothing to stem the tide of fleeing refugees, a tide which he himself had generated.[20]

The disparity between Carmel's deeds and words was typical. His account suggests no moral dilemma, no soul-searching, no battle ethics. The ability to identify with the refugees' fate was not translated into actions which might have prevented or relieved their plight. Carmel and other commanders were guided by an ideology of military doing that was unaffected by words. The origins of this duality lay, as we saw, in the Fosh and later in the Palmach. It was given stark expression in 1948 and would become known in later Israeli culture as the "shooting and crying" syndrome.

In the south the Palmach's Givati Brigade carried out the conquests and expulsions. Its commander, Shimon Avidan, like Allon a member of Mapam and a kibbutz member, also did his best to empty Arab villages of their inhabitants. For example, it did not stand the residents of the village of Zarnuqa in good stead that they maintained friendly relations with their Jewish neighbors and were therefore considered traitors by other Palestinians. They were expelled, their village was pillaged, and their land was parceled out among the local kibbutzim.[21] Such operations by the brigade commanders were highly effective. By mid-May, when the Jewish state was formally proclaimed, it was in fact already in existence owing to the military gains which had created territorial continuity. Four of the five mixed cities had been voided of Arabs: Tiberias, Haifa, Safed, and Jaffa. Key neighborhoods had been captured in Jerusalem, the fall of Acre was imminent, and about 100 Arab villages had been vacated in various parts of the country. By contrast, the Palestinians had not captured even one Jewish settlement.[22] It was not that the Palestinians were more moral than the Jews or that they were less aggressive; they were simply weaker militarily.

WHO GAVE THE ORDER?

The efficient ethno-national army had an enormous impact in constituting the new reality. Did the army also determine that reality, to the chagrin of the leadership? The brigades were largely autonomous in planning and executing operational actions. Their commanders were even authorized to decide which villages to capture and destroy.[23] This involved a division of control and the use of forces at the microlevel, in a manner that did much to determine reality.[24] In fact, this was a salient expression of politics that relied on the army's strength and its officers' readiness to "determine facts on the ground"—as indeed was the case in cities like Haifa, Tiberias, and Acre and in dozens of villages which were captured on local initiatives by commanders who took advantage of the Israeli forces' numerical superiority.[25]

Books published after the war under the auspices of the brigades are revealing about how, through scores of actions at the local level, an irreversible totalistic reality was created. The village of Zarin, for example, was captured by Golani Brigade. Following the breakthrough into the village came vehicles carrying explosives and combat engineers. At first light the houses in the village were blown sky-high, as the brigade's book relates. Elsewhere villages were "softened up" with mortar or even artillery fire before the ground forces entered. Anyone who was not killed or wounded fled. Often those fleeing were cut down by machine-gun fire.[26]

In the north, after the details of the ambush and massacre of the Yehiam convoy became known, units of Carmeli Brigade's Twenty-first Battalion attacked the Arab villages that formed a wedge between Kibbutz Yehiam and the town of Nahariya. The brigade's commemorative

book states that the operation was a punitive action, with the enemy fleeing and leaving behind houses and other property. All the Arab villages
in the area were captured and destroyed in the revenge mission. Large
amounts of explosives were used, and house after house was blown to
bits.[27] Long afterward a resident of one of the villages described the
events. On the day the village was captured, the resident said, the Jewish
forces ordered all those who remained in the village to assemble by the
church. They took a few youngsters away from the church and killed
them. Then they ordered others to bury them. The next day all the residents were evacuated to another village, where many evacuees from the
surrounding villages had gathered. Those who tried to return to the captured villages risked death.[28]

Atrocities were perpetrated by both sides. It is, however, the Israeli operations which were applied at the local level which concern us here. The
"specialists" in razing Arab villages that got in the way of Jewish territorial continuity were the Palmach units. For the Palmach, engaged also
in status struggles with other corps, this was a chance to demonstrate its
military prowess and its commitment to an unpartitioned Land of Israel.
Probably it was Ben-Gurion's incessant suspicions about the Palmach's
lack of discipline and his questions about its combat ability that made its
commanders determined to prove themselves. In the final reckoning, the
combined operations of the army and the Palmach, which were supposedly purely military in character, acquired great political significance by
altering the political, geographic, and demographic reality in every part
of Palestine.[29]

Sociologically, one of the most interesting aspects of the conquests
and expulsions was that even though the policy was not explicitly articulated, either orally or in writing, everyone knew about it. In most cases,
whether before or during an operation, neither the political leadership
nor the General Staff issued guidelines regarding the fate of the Arab residents, but the expulsions took place. The young commanders in the IDF
and the Palmach had no need for concrete orders; they were motivated
by an ideology which had coalesced during the decade of the 1940s.
Overruning villages and killing or expelling the inhabitants seemed to
them a logical or necessary "military action" which overrode all moral
inhibitions. A case in point is the behavior of Amos Mokadi, commander
of Golani Brigade's Twelfth Battalion. During the capture of the Galilee
village of Nasr a-Din, the Arab fighters emerged from their positions surrounded by their children and wives. Although no order was given, the
Israelis held their fire. Long afterward, Mokadi recalled that he had been
fearful and hesitant: if he let the village men go, the order to destroy the
enemy would not be fulfilled, but on the other hand women and children
were in the way. "And then I gave an order, and it was quite difficult, that
everyone who comes out of the position is a fighter, and therefore—fire!"
For an instant, Mokadi was confronted with a moral dilemma, but he did

not let morality get in his way. And he concluded: "We burned the houses in the village. That lowered the morale of the Arab fighters in Tiberias and raised our morale."[30]

There was more to it, though, than the fact that policy was not explicitly enunciated. Throughout the war, Ben-Gurion and his colleagues employed moderate rhetoric, presenting Israel as a nation seeking not only peace but an alliance with the Arabs.[31] An Israeli historian claimed that the gap between declarations and deeds stemmed from a kind of cognitive dissonance in security affairs within the leadership.[32] The truth is that the gap was integral to the politics practiced by the leadership at the time. The Israeli leaders walked softly and concealed a big stick.

The politics of the time was not based on a political decision or an operational order. Hence it is undocumented. It was the product of informal cooperation between the political leadership, principally Ben-Gurion, and the army. The ideology of the young fighters, which had often been expressed through criticism and protest directed at the moderate leadership, was now supported by it. Still, not everyone in the leadership was privy to the secret. Some were deceived, while for others silence was the sign of consent. Weitz, director of the JNF's lands department, wrote in his diary: "Spoke with Shkolnik [Eshkol] on the question of evacuating the Arabs from various blocs of ours. He knows nothing about it. Who then is the directing hand?"[33] At a meeting of the Histadrut's Actions Committee on June 16, the chairman, Yosef Sprinzak, referred to a phenomenon which he found unacceptable. He had heard certain things, he said, but was unable to clarify who had decided them. Taking the destruction of the town Beit She'an as an example, Sprinzak said he knew that the decision had not been made by the Actions Committee, the Jewish Agency, the National Council, or the members of the cabinet. Who, then, did decide? Sprinzak admitted that in recent weeks he had been one of those in the dark. Meir Ya'ari, a senior figure in Mapam, echoed Sprinzak's remarks, though he also spoke about "decision-making processes" according to which the army created facts on the ground with the government's tacit consent. Ya'ari said that in Beit She'an he had met a commander and asked him some questions. The latter replied that after all the inhabitants had been evicted, the order had been given to destroy the town. Ya'ari then tried to discover the source of the order. The battalion commander, it turned out, had received an order from the level above him. So had the brigade commander. Ya'ari was not sure, at that meeting, whether to call it an "order from above" or "shutting-up from above." Everyone swore that no transfer was intended, he stressed, but everyone was also well aware of the consequences of their deeds.[34]

Cabinet ministers also asked tough questions. In early July, for example, Bechor Shetrit asked whether a policy existed regarding the mass arrests in Arab villages, the working of their lands by Jews, and the isolation of the urban Arabs in special neighborhoods. Shetrit in fact exposed the policy of an "absence of policy." The prime minister, in reply to Shetrit's question, continued to insist that he had heard nothing, seen nothing, and knew nothing. The same Ben-Gurion who since the days of the "seminar" had made a point of acquainting himself with the minutest details relating to the military, who knew about the appointment of junior officers or the number of mortars in a particular settlement, suddenly pleaded ignorance. In any event, the prime minister said, with feigned innocence, that the army had not been ordered to destroy Arab villages or to burn houses.[35] Three days later, when the governor of Safed asked Ben-Gurion for a large quantity of explosives with which to destroy the town's houses, Ben-Gurion's diary entry gives no hint that he was surprised by the request.[36]

Not even the most thorough investigation would have disclosed the source of the orders for the conquests and expulsions. The simple fact is that no such orders existed. It was the ethnic and militaristic frame of mind and mode of operation that actualized it. However, some members of the leadership could not countenance this. In another meeting of the Histadrut's Actions Committee, held on July 14, more questions were asked about the decision-making processes in the new state. "I suddenly hear," Sprinzak said, "that even before the surrender process is complete, there is already a civilian evacuation, but here nothing is known of this. This is an impossible situation." Moshe Aram, another representative, explained: "Everything stems from the same [policy] line which we know nothing about." Aram related that even before the capture of Lydda and Ramleh, he and his comrades had tried to prevent the expulsion of the inhabitants, at least the women and children. They thought they had succeeded, but the reality was different; the "political line" had been decisive. Some of the participants in the meeting tried to get to the bottom of the political line. Hazan explained that the acts of theft and looting were an inexorable instrument which was meant to bring about the expulsion of all the Arabs and the realization of the political line without documents (meaning without written orders). Another member claimed that there was an undeclared but very effective intention that no Arabs should remain in the State of Israel. Israel was destroying their economic base, he explained, and even if it declared that they could return, and even if they wanted to return, they would have nowhere to return to or would be unable to make a living.[37]

The political line which the Actions Committee discussed at length was a manifestation of the young fighters' cultural militarism, which finally became a central element in the politics of the leadership. This transformation, however, did not occur because of the army's seizure power in a society characterized by inept and weak civilian oversight mechanisms, as Vagts and the civil-military relations school might say. What became dominant, rather, was the common view that the "Arab problem" should be resolved through the military way and its actualization.

Ben-Gurion continued to declare, from every possible platform, that no one had authorized the destruction of Arab houses and the expulsion of their occupants. Sometimes, though, the exception proves the rule. When Ben-Gurion wanted to prevent an expulsion, he did so easily. Take the events of July 18, 1948, when Carmel ordered the evacuation of the entire population of Nazareth. Learning of the imminent expulsion, Ben-Gurion immediately sent a countermanding cable, presumably because of his concern about the Christian world's possible reaction.[38] In other cases, Ben-Gurion brought his full influence to bear to expedite expulsions. Ezra Danin, the Arab affairs expert in the service of the Jewish Agency, described the exodus of Haifa's Arabs. Ben-Gurion, standing with a group on the balcony of a hotel in the city to watch the departing convoys of Arabs, said: "How many are left? If they want to go, why are you delaying them? Let them go."[39] In his diary, Yosef Weitz, who was deeply involved in the tranfer politics, noted that he warned Ben-Gurion about concentrations of Arabs in various parts of the country: "What is the remedy [Ben-Gurion asked]—Harassment—I replied—Harassment using every means and preventing their return across the border.— How?—he asked. I explained to him part of my plan.—Who?—he asked—I told him. . . . He made a note of it and promised to act in accordance with my proposal."[40]

Ben-Gurion's silence on the expulsions was of course particularly thunderous during the conquest of Lydda and Ramleh. After the towns were captured, the senior commanders met with Ben-Gurion at operational headquarters. According to Yitzhak Rabin, who was operations officer at the time, Allon asked Ben-Gurion, in the presence of many witnesses, whether he should expel the inhabitants of the two towns, but Ben-Gurion did not respond. Later, Ben-Gurion, Allon, and Rabin left the room. Allon repeated his question. With a vigorous wave of his hand toward the east, Ben-Gurion seemed to approve of the expulsion of 60,000 people. Ben-Gurion, then, kept mum. Allon and his staff, which was in effect the Palmach high command, acted.[41]

One of the controversies in Israeli historiography revolves around the connection between the idea to transfer the Palestine Arabs, which was broached in the Zionist movement long before the 1948 war, and Plan D and the mass expulsions during the war.[42] Those who claim that the transfer notions never gelled into a Zionist master plan of organized, planned expulsion until the war may be right.[43] Still, it is difficult to accept that the expulsion of the Palestine Arabs was a product of the war and its e ents, as Morris, for example, argues in his important book about the mass exodus of the Palestine Arabs. Whether or not there was an explicit decision of expulsion—in the manner of the behavioralist perspective which demands "smoking-gun" proofs—is not crucial for the understanding of the events of 1948. The explanation for the transfer lies not in any particular decision or its implementation but in the consciousness that led to it. For the army commanders the expulsion of the Arabs was a "natural" and "necessary" outgrowth of the idea of conquering the land by force which had evolved over the decade. It was something self-evident for which no clear orders were required, since it had come into being gradually and was reproduced constantly through modes of operation. The reprisal raids against villages, their conquest and destruction, and the expulsion of most of their inhabitants—it was all due to the entrenchment of the militaristic ideology. How else explain the fact that within such a brief period, no more than a few months, and without the existence of clear orders and guidelines, between 600,000 and 750,000 Palestinians departed the country and some 200 villages were laid waste? Indeed, there was no Zionist master plan to evict the Palestinians. However, the decade that preceded the establishment of the state saw the rise of a cultural militarism which paved the way for the advent of militaristic politics in 1948, applied by the army and the leadership.

Responsibility for the implementation of the political line, the militaristic politics, was borne also by the major political parties. The expulsions made little impression in Mapai; its institutions hardly discussed the subject. If there were calls for a discussion, the leadership found ways to block it. It was only after the expulsions in Lydda and Ramleh that Sprinzak said: "We are getting all worked up after the event." He was right. Discussions took place after the facts had been determined by the army. However, Sprinzak's being "worked up" never led him to make any concrete effort to reduce the scale of the expulsions or stop them.[44]

Mapam, by contrast, did hold discussions about the events. Its members even voiced criticism of the army and the leadership. Some regretted the prominence of senior commanders of the party in the expulsions, the pillage and the general brutality of the war. "As far as combat goes," said Mapam leader Meir Ya'ari, "the system created a wonderful generation . . . courageous and heroic. . . . But at the civilian-moral level, the generation did not pass the test of war: the youth we cultivated in the Palmach, even kibbutz members, sometimes make the Arabs their slaves; they shoot Arabs, defenseless Arab women, and not in battle. Is it permitted to kill prisoners who surrender?"[45]

Mapam, though, was two-faced. Together with criticism of the soldiers' behavior and of the expulsions went a vigorous effort to prevent the refugees' return. If they let the Arabs back into the villages they had captured, Mapam leaders told the Histadrut's Actions Committee, the Arabs will become enemies, a fifth column.[46] Indeed, Mapam did not decry the new line publicly because the party was implicated in it and reaped its fruits. Mapam kibbutzim took over Arab land, crops, and abandoned property. To obscure the political ramifications entailed in the destruction of the villages and the confiscation of the Arabs' property, Mapam preferred to speak about "looting."[47] Weitz recorded in his diary his reaction to statements made by figures in Mapam: "Meir Ya'ari was furious about the evacuation of the Arab villages, as though he doesn't know that all his comrades in the kibbutzim are involved in this with genuine devotion."[48]

By their ambivalence, both Mapai and Mapam effectively gave legitimation to the conquests and expulsions; their spokesmen implied that the military way and a forceful solution were a necessity which had been imposed on the Yishuv. It was not that one could choose a certain mode of action from several possibilities; it was, rather, a kind of ineluctable dictate of fate, for which the other side was responsible, for if the Arabs had not behaved as they had, it might have been possible to achieve co-existence and reconciliation.[49]

NO REFUGEES WANTED

As though to test that thesis, the question of the refugees' return had begun to be raised about the middle of 1948. Thus a new aspect was added to the militaristic politics of conquest and expulsion.

The first initiatives to prevent the refugees from returning were taken by the army. IDF units were ordered to prevent attempts by refugees and their families to sneak back across the lines to their homes, "even by fire."[50] The heads of the army formed a kind of lobby, trying to adduce persuasive reasons to keep the refugees out. By this approach, they not only influenced the politics of the time; they determined policy. On June 13 Yigael Yadin, the acting chief of staff, ordered the IDF's brigades "to prevent absolutely" attempts by Arabs to reap their crops. A few days later he ordered the fields to be harvested, and if that were impossible, to destroy the crops.[51] On August 14 Yadin wrote to Shertok: "In view of the spread of diseases among the Arab refugees, I propose that a total quarantine be declared in all our areas of conquest. By this means we shall be able to stand more vigorously against the demand for the return of the Arab refugees and against the infiltration of Arabs into abandoned villages."[52]

The political leadership also helped determine facts on the ground, usually without a declared policy. Immediately after the truce came into effect, Ben-Gurion and his colleagues discussed the problem whether to "erase" the Arab neighborhood of Abu Kabir, adjacent to Tel Aviv. Two days later, on June 5, Weitz submitted to Ben-Gurion a plan for a "retroactive transfer" which included practical steps to prevent the refugees' return.[53] Typically, Ben-Gurion did not adopt the plan, but neither did he reject it. At a cabinet meeting a few days later, Ben-Gurion spoke of the urgent need to populate Jaffa. Jaffa will be a Jewish city, he said; war is war, and the return of the Arabs to Jaffa is not justice but foolishness.[54]

Gradually, a consensus of rationalizations emerged for blocking the return of the refugees. The leadership argued that it was not to blame for their departure and therefore would not take responsibility for their return.[55]

The politics that prevented the return was also manifested in the power exercised by the state through its bureaucratic apparatus and its orders. On August 8, a military government was established in the occupied areas. An Arab Affairs Committee was set up to introduce order and organization into the hasty army expulsions and prevent the return of refugees.[56] A new reality was thus forged, undoubtedly an aberration in Jewish history, involving an occupation army, orders and commands, prisons and exile, rational methods of coercion, all underpinned with legal foundation, but there is no more striking proof of the institutionalization of the cultural militarism in the new state than the formal decision not to allow the refugees back. Even if the refugee problem was engendered in the storm of war, the decision to block its resolution was calculated and tendentious. As early as July 21, the cabinet decided that no Arabs were to be allowed back for the time being.[57] On August 18 the policy was articulated even more clearly and comprehensively: the return of the refugees must be prevented by all means, villages still standing should be destroyed, Jews should be settled in abandoned villages, the Arabs' fields should be cultivated and their lands confiscated for the benefit of the state.[58]

Hence arose the policy to settle new-immigrant Jews in abandoned villages. Jewish settlement already was perceived by the native-born generation as an instrument for conquering the country. Now the state had become involved. The state encouraged the kibbutz training groups and the newly arrived immigrants to settle in the "abandoned" areas.[59] Various bodies were active in this regard, including Weitz's Transfer Committee;[60] the lobby of the land-settlement movements;[61] the Histadrut Labor Federation, whose officials worked hard to prepare accommodations for new immigrants in places that "had become vacant" of Arabs, as they put it;[62] Ben-Gurion himself, who worked energetically to get the villages settled;[63] and the army, which at the end of the year was already engaged in "curbing infiltrations" into the new Jewish settlements.[64] The overall goal was presented in a meeting of the Mapai Central Committee: "The war and the [newly established] state have opened new possibilities for us in the area of settlement and immigration . . . which previously had not existed. We could not even dream of them. . . . In order to fill the land, which is now empty, with settlements, we must achieve 400 [settlement] points. Naturally we are speaking mainly of Arab land. . . . We want to enter an existing [site] or to completely eliminate the existing Arab village. . . . We want to make use of the opportunities which have presented themselves and of the validity given the state."[65]

Settlement was a way to legitimate the army's creation of the new political facts. As one of the commanders of the Negev Brigade put it, "True, we have conquered the Negev militarily. But the real truth is that we have not yet conquered the Negev, not until the soldiers are replaced by settlers and Beersheba is Jewish, not until . . . fighting settlements are scattered there."[66] This form of settlement attested to an incipient civilian militarism, or "combative settlement," as Weitz called it in a meeting of the Histadrut Actions Committee.[67]

MILITARISM AND THE ABSENCE OF PRAETORIANISM

The conflict described in earlier chapters between the "way of settlement" represented by the young generation and the "way of the state" represented by Mapai and the leadership now vanished. Indeed, the longer the war lasted, the tighter the cooperation became between the political leadership, headed by Ben-Gurion, and the army. Trade-off took place, which was the linchpin of their relationship. In return for the leadership's practice of militaristic politics, which revolved around the army's operations, the army neutralized and discarded its potential praetorianism.

Until May the outcome of the war was in doubt. The Jews had many military successes, but the invasion of the Arab armies, the fighting at Kibbutz Ramat Rahel in Jerusalem, the fall of the Old City of Jerusalem, the failed attempts to capture Latrun, and the high price in killed and wounded hindered the leadership's efforts to put its intentions into practice. However, by the time of the June truce, the situation had altered radically. In mid-June, Ben-Gurion told a cabinet meeting that the November 29 resolution was dead. In the same meeting Foreign Minister Shertok took the floor to present the guidelines of Israeli policy. They turned out to be maximalist: not to concede one inch of ground from the November 29 borders and to add to that territory the areas which had been conquered under the pressure of bitter necessity. By bitter necessity, Shertok explained, he meant nonconcession of those areas which bitter experience had taught must be under the state's control to enable a proper defense. This legitimated every conquest and expulsion. Ben-Gurion then added two firm points. The first, as mentioned, was that the November 29 resolution was dead; the second, which hinted at the emerging new politics, was phrased in the following words: "The matter will be decided by force. The political question is now a military question."[68] But these were not merely declarations. Beginning in June, the military way became the central political way of the leadership.

As part of Ben-Gurion's incessant attempts to impose his authority on the army, he monitored the military closely. This is another example of civilian militarism, the political leadership's adoption of the military worldview, including military symbols, as the foundation for its operations.[69] Ben-Gurion, the "politician in khaki," frequently visited the theaters of combat and was in direct touch with the heads of the General Staff

branches, the commanders of the fronts, and even the brigade commanders. He often decided on Israeli-initiated operations and urged the army
to execute them. He was involved in strategic planning, which bore a
heavily political character, including expansion beyond the partition
boundaries to the north, east, and south.[70]

The army, though, needed no outside prompting. To meet the Arab
invasion, the Haganah formed twelve brigades, as well as artillery, engi-
neering, signals, and air branches. The Palmach was turned into three
full brigades and a number of auxiliary forces. This power did not come
into being overnight; it was the fruit of years of planning. The invading
Arab armies had no organized brigades at the time. Combined, they had
perhaps nine or ten brigades, but they were not as strong as the one Israeli
army.[71] The latter kept pushing for more offense, more conquests, for operations that would disable the implementation of the partition plan. On
these questions there was a meeting of minds between the army chiefs
and Ben-Gurion, as could be seen, for example, in their joint meeting
on June 18. Despite the high tension that prevailed between the sides because of Ben-Gurion's intervention in professional military matters, all
those present agreed that Israel must take the offensive.[72]

The operation they agreed on, to begin as soon as the truce ended,
was aimed at the conquest of Lydda, Ramleh, Latrun, and Ramallah—
hence its original name, Operation LRLR. Operation Dani, as it was otherwise known, was assigned, and not by chance, to the Palmach brigades
commanded by Allon and his staff, whom Ben-Gurion strongly suspected of harboring praetorian tendencies. The warning order for the operation was issued on June 20. However, a few days before the attack was
to begin, Ben-Gurion decided on new and puzzling appointments that
outraged the General Staff. Its officers were on the horns of a dilemma,
according to Zvi Ayalon, one of the heads of branches who resigned. By
the end of the first truce, he recalled, Israel had already passed the difficult stage of the war. The army was ready to take the initiative, but Ben-
Gurion's wrongheaded decision, in Ayalon's view, could prove ruinous.[73]

But Ben-Gurion's timing was deliberate. He wanted to demonstrate
that a connection existed between the politics of conquering new territories and disciplined obedience to the political leadership and its head.
The army commanders, including the "rebels," knew this. And if they
did not grasp it immediately, it certainly became clear when they discovered that the conclusions of the Committee of Five had not been implemented. However, the essential role of the army high command now also
became clear. At the height of the crisis, on June 29, the U.N. mediator
Bernadotte submitted his proposals for resolving the Palestine conflict.
The nine-point plan (and an appendix on the borders) implied that Israel
would have to give up its military conquests. Ben-Gurion was furious. He
had no intention of accepting either that proposal or another, submitted
by Bernadotte a few days later, to demilitarize Jerusalem. His indirect re-

ply to both plans was given in collaboration with the army: the IDF took full advantage of the four-week truce to recruit manpower, integrate materiel from abroad, and conduct intensive training.

This was the background to the implicit bargain between Ben-Gurion and the high command, which became more deeply rooted following the end of the "generals' revolt" in early July. It should be emphasized that Ben-Gurion's "understanding" with the military took shape not because of the Committee of Five, not because of the enactment of "basic laws" in place of a constitution, and not because of legislation to regularize relations between the army and the political level. The understanding was made possible by the intention to launch extensive military offensives in order to prevent the establishment of a "partition state." Thus a clear connection was forged, in the security discourse, between two elements: the leadership's adoption of militaristic politics, based on its cooperation with the high command, and, as the quid pro quo, the armed forces' relinquishment of the underlying praetorian threat which had characterized the armed forces throughout the decade of the 1940s.

The course of events beginning in July shows that this interrelationship had become solidly entrenched. On July 9 the IDF launched its offensive. Concurrently, Ben-Gurion recovered from his "illness," which had been brought on by the conclusions of the Committee of Five, and returned to lead the state and the army. The most significant result of the Israeli post-truce blitzkrieg, undertaken with a professional army some 80,000 strong, was the ground gains. By the time of the second truce, which came into effect on July 20, approximately 1,000 square kilometers of land had passed into Jewish hands. Addressing the State Council on this subject, Ben-Gurion exuded self-confidence: "After the further manifestation of our military ability and our new territorial gains ... who shall determine how far we will go and the conquests of which we are still capable?"[74]

The military groups shared with the political leadership the wish to create political facts through the army and nullify Bernadotte's plans. This was perfectly clear in Ben-Gurion's statements. He did not hesitate to lash out at the Palmach for its ties with Mapam, yet at the same time he praised its military prowess and the courage and tenacity of its fighters.[75]

It was in fact the conclusions of the Committee of Five, which were not applied, that enabled the trade-off between the defense minister and the army. The committee's recommendations brought home to both sides that despite everything they must work together because there was no substitute for cooperation between them. The heads of the army and of the Palmach continued to complain that Ben-Gurion had assumed excessive powers in military affairs, even after the second "revolt of the generals." However, they could not really object to a politics that exalted them and let them make use of their skills and actualize their deep-rooted ideology. Moreover, the defense minister himself drew certain lessons from the committee's conclusions. He intervened less in developments within the army. And following Galili's forced resignation he saw to it that no Mapam officers were dismissed while the war continued. The result was that Mapam leader Ben-Aharon, the great proponent of the idea of an antistatist socialist army, noted with "great satisfaction" that the commanders on all three fronts—Carmel, Allon and Avidan—were members of Mapam.[76]

The breakaway groups were also partners to the leadership's militaristic politics. On June 1 an agreement was signed for the Irgun's countrywide integration into the IDF in special companies. After this the organization took part in the conquest-and-expulsion operations, and in exchange—certainly after the *Altalena* affair—its members obeyed the leadership. Ben-Gurion, for his part, treated the Irgun as he did the Palmach. It was divested of its praetorian tendencies cautiously and by stages. Still, in the battles of the "Ten Days" in June, both the Irgun and Lehi fought like all other soldiers. They added more than a brigade to the IDF, a significant upgrading for an army which was based on twelve formations.[77] Neither the "holy cannon" that hit the *Altalena* nor the women at Palmach headquarters who fired at the ship eliminated the praetorian threat of the right. That was accomplished by the leadership's militaristic politics.

Contrary to the opinions of some scholars, the relationship, particularly at the informal level, between Ben-Gurion and the various military organizations which emerges here does not attest to an attempt by the prime minister and defense minister to bring about a liberal-style division of powers between the military and civilian levels. Certainly no process occurred that led to "civilianism" over "militarism."[78] Ben-Gurion himself made this clear. When Yadin, the "nonpolitical" soldier, demanded the separation of army and politics in the name of pure military professionalism, Ben-Gurion replied: "You, Yigael, are always generalizing. You divide the world into two: you are political figures, we are soldiers. I do not accept that. I consider myself to be with the army. . . . Like each of you, I am part of the army. . . . I do not agree to be left out, I do not accept that these are soldiers and those, politicians."[79] Indeed, the cooperation between the political leadership and the army took shape on the basis of the linkup between the "military" and the "political," which in its special form drew a distinction between praetorianism and militarism, the institutionalization of the latter coming at the expense of the former. The weakness of the praetorian element augmented the power of the political leadership and its head, but the institutionalization of the militaristic principle accorded the army prestige, autonomy, and influence. As for a "civilian" component, or a "civil society"—one that is separated from state and army under conditions of ethnic conflict and cleavage, which are in turn translated into militaristic politics—it was simply nonexistent.[80]

The militaristic politics which was pursued by the defense minister and senior IDF officers occasionally generated friction between Ben-Gurion and the cabinet. Following the second truce, ministers asked for information on military developments and for a discussion of the war's management. The result was the formation in July of a consultative ministerial committee on prosecuting the war, but in practice the committee was neutralized by Ben-Gurion.[81] An event that sheds light on the entrenchment of militaristic politics in Israel occurred in a cabinet meeting held on September 26. Ben-Gurion described to the ministers his plan to conquer the entire West Bank, involving warfare against Jordan's Arab Legion, but to his surprise the ministers rejected his proposal. They were fearful of a campaign which would violate the truce and would represent a clear attempt to frustrate "Bernadotte's testament." Ben-Gurion, who was forced to give in, said the decision was an "everlasting mistake." In his diary, though, another aspect of the episode emerges. "Fortunately," he wrote, "they [i.e., the ministers] did not have to vote for us to execute the majority of the operations that were carried out during the year." Ben-Gurion, then, did not usually submit the plans of conquest that he conceived with the army for cabinet approval, and on this occasion he was quick to recognize his mistake.[82]

Following this incident, Ben-Gurion was far more cautious in his dealings with the cabinet. Usually he would formulate plans with the General Staff, then ensure the support of his party's ministers, and only afterward seek the cabinet's approval.[83] On more than one occasion Ben-Gurion completely disregarded cabinet resolutions. For example, after the U.N. Security Council had resolved that a ceasefire should take effect, Ben-Gurion ignored the cabinet's same view and ordered the IDF to keep fighting.[84] The picture that emerged was of an army creating facts on the ground with the prime minister's approval, while the cabinet often rubber-stamped decisions it had not made. This confirmed a tendency which had existed through the decade, its origins lying, as we saw, in the S.O. operations and in the sinking of the *Patria*. Informal cooperation between the political leader and security activists sidestepped possible checks by the government or other elected bodies.

The cat-and-mouse games between Ben-Gurion and the cabinet went on for months. On November 7, for example, Minister Shapira asked about the army's actions in conquered villages in the north and the south. The prime minister evaded the question.[85] Three days later, to ensure that there would be no further interference from the cabinet, Ben-Gurion brought about the passage of a resolution barring ministers from voting against government resolutions in the Provisional State Council.[86] The ministers, though, were not cowed and decided to set up a committee

of three of their number to investigate the army's actions in the conquered areas.[87] When the cabinet discussed the powers of the inquiry
committee, Ben-Gurion succeeded in getting a resolution passed stating
that he was charged with the task of investigating allegations about
the army's misconduct against Arabs in Galilee and the south.[88] Still the
ministers did not give up. On November 25 Bechor Shetrit, who held the
minorities portfolio, asked why the army was uprooting Bedouin villages
in the south without prior coordination with his office.[89] On December 5
the ministers chose an additional committee of five ministers to examine
policy.[90] However, it was also finally neutralized and dealt instead with
settling new Jewish immigrants in abandoned Galilee Arab villages. Instead of probing policy, the committee became an instrument to abet the
official ethno-national line.[91]

While the government was not in control of events, the high command continued to press unremittingly for the continuation of the war
and the conquests. Carmel urged more operations in Galilee,[92] while in
the south Allon employed a quasi-lobby for the same purpose and even
tried to get Weitz's intercession.[93] Army commanders also continued to
exert pressure in meetings with Ben-Gurion. On October 6, for example,
Ben-Gurion met with a delegation of senior officers, who supported his
plans for an offensive in the Negev. That same evening the government
approved the decision "to break through with force to the Negev"—a
clear act of defiance against "Bernadotte's testament." Ben-Gurion himself said it was "the gravest decision since we decided to proclaim the
establishment of the state."[94]

The decision to conquer the Negev delighted the Palmach. As has
already been mentioned, the Palmach's great fear was that the political
leadership would hand over the Negev to Abdallah as part of a compromise settlement. When the country was divided into military fronts,
Allon wanted the Palmach command to be given responsibility for the
Egyptian front in order, as he put it, to prevent the "selling of the Negev
cheaply." Now Allon, in close consultation with Ben-Gurion, led his staff
and brigades in a sweep to conquer the Negev. The shared premise of all
those involved was that the best, indeed the only, way to deal with the
Arabs was by warfare. Ben-Gurion reflected this line of thought when he
wrote in his diary: "Even if we conquer the whole land as far as the Jordan [River], the Arabs will not accept it because their fear will grow. The
war will continue." And, about a month later: "The end of the war. Will
there be an end? . . . And if peace is established, was there ever a war
which was not preceded by peace?"[95] Integral to the militaristic viewpoint was a deterministic and fatalistic perception of the Arab-Israeli
conflict by the defense minister and the army. It was a point of view
which would prevail for many years.[96]

When the order was given to disband the Palmach on October 7, Allon
and his staff were busy preparing to conquer the Negev in Operation

Yoav. Allon did not even take the time to try to get the order rescinded or deferred. Uri Brener, a rear-echelon Palmach officer, wrote to Chief of Staff Dori in the name of the organization's commanders on the 10th that the order was a painful blow. It was not difficult, he added, to imagine the effect it would have on the Palmach's units or the bitterness it would arouse. Dori replied on the following day that some of the formulations in the letter were unbecoming to the military, but it was clear that these were the final notes of a requiem. The Palmach was disbanded without undue turmoil, quickly and efficiently.[97]

Mapam generated a minor furor when the Histadrut, meeting on October 15, discussed the fate of the Palmach. Yet even its activists did not unleash their full fury against the decision. There was no hiding the fact that the members of Mapam's Political Committee were frightened of being condemned and stigmatized for not belonging and not being partners in the effort. "Things will be done to uproot us and depict us here as a 'leftist *Altalena* party,' " warned one of Mapam's leaders. Mapam, he said, should not leave the government at this time, "because that is just what they are waiting for."[98]

Operation Yoav, the IDF's most extensive operation, began on the day after the Histadrut discussed the disbanding of the Palmach. "Yigal [Allon] is liberating the way to the Negev," Ben-Gurion said proudly. On the same day he issued his "Letter to a Palmach Comrade" in which he responded to the controversy in the Histadrut and reiterated his firm opposition to the Palmach's continued existence.[99] Operation Yoav was executed by an army that by now numbered some 90,000 troops. Its commanders, Allon and his staff, who were the informal Palmach high command, won honor and glory. Allon was lauded as the war's most distinguished commanding officer.[100] The conquests, though, did not end with Operation Yoav, as Ben-Gurion wrote in his diary: "We must ready ourselves to eliminate Gaza." On the same day the army launched Operation to the Hill (El Hahar) to expand the Jerusalem Corridor southward.

The big operation in the Negev whetted the appetites of other officers. Carmel kept pressing in the north[101] and Moshe Dayan urged an attack on Jerusalem.[102] The pressures in Galilee led to Operation Hiram, which began on October 28 and was also designed to create borders going beyond the partition lines. On the same day Ben-Gurion instructed chief of staff Dori to implement the order to disband the Palmach.[103] The two aims thus converged: complete authority was obtained over the army, as reflected in the dissolution of the Palmach Headquarters, and in return a war of conquest was launched in which the Palmach played the leading role. Nor was this the end. Even as Operation Hiram proceeded, Ben-Gurion and Allon began to plan the conquest of the entire West Bank.[104]

The politics of forceful conquest and violent military actions is defined as militaristic if it is perceived by those who apply the policy as desirable and legitimate. In the period under discussion, the IDF's journal *Bamahane* offered justifications for the campaign of conquests: "The pursuit of the enemy, which will bring us as far as Sinai, the Litani [River in Lebanon], the Jordan . . . represents the crushing of an invader who has no connection with this land. Our right, our duty, and our destiny send us on his trail as far and as deep as possible. . . . We have never given up, nor shall we ever give up the vision of Greater Israel. The partition always seemed to us a severe concession. . . . We shall not fear nor recoil from territorial advances by our forces. . . . We shall not allow the partition boundaries to serve as a line of defense or as a kind of sacred magic circle in which every vermin will hide after taking our blows. The duty to strike at invading armies is more important than any theoretical lines that were ever set."[105]

Ben-Gurion, too, gave verbal expression to the militaristic politics which had been introduced at his inspiration and which more usually took the form of action rather than words. Speaking to army commanders, he explained clearly: "It has been said that war is the continuation of policy by other means. That is not always correct. . . . Beginning from the first truce, our military activity constitutes a kind of political act."[106]

Foreign Ministry officials occasionally complained about this perception of reality which had imposed itself on policy, overriding their political plans. As one senior ministry official put it, "After all, B. G. [Ben-Gurion] takes a severely skeptical attitude, almost of dismissal, toward such political programs. The impression is that he wants to resolve most of the problems by military means so that no political negotiations or political activity will be worth anything."[107] In his consultations with the Foreign Ministry, Ben-Gurion was generally accompanied by army officers, particularly if the subject was the future of the conquered territories. Predictably, the officers took militaristic stands, along the lines expressed by the chief of operations Yadin: "If we are talking about borders, there is in my view only one factor—the military one—and all other factors are secondary."[108]

In the meantime the armistice talks had begun at Rhodes. The commanders' disappointment at the suspension of the offensive was mitigated by their active participation in the talks. Here was the start of "military diplomacy"—that is, diplomacy conducted by representatives of the army, in which military considerations were given the highest priority. Very quickly, differences emerged between the officers involved—Yadin, Dayan, Makleff, and others—and the Foreign Ministry's representatives to the talks. According to the army, the officials did not grasp the fact that the military viewpoint took precedence over the political viewpoint.[109] In his memoirs, Yitzhak Rabin explained that he had not been very impressed at the time by the charms of diplomacy, by the "give-and-take," the bargaining. Like all the IDF's commanders, he wrote, he too was imbued with a sense of the young army's might and prowess.[110]

In short, the armistice talks did not prevent the army from continuing to pressure Ben-Gurion to resume the offensive. Ben-Gurion ordered Allon to send forces to the south and create facts by force in order to rebuff U.N. plans for Beersheba and the Negev. Again the pressure succeeded, bringing about Operation Lot and later Operation Horev.[111] These operations, involving the largest concentration of forces in the IDF's history, were marked by the political initiative displayed by the commanding officers.

This, however, was not all. On December 27, without orders from the General Staff and without a decision by the political level, Allon and Rabin advanced into Egypt. In his biography, Rabin describes the thrill experienced by the troops at the decision to take the war into the territory of an Arab state for the first time in modern Israeli history. The forces advanced, in the absence of coordination with the General Staff, to El Arish. The failure to coordinate led to attacks on the advancing forces by Israeli aircraft, in which some IDF soldiers were killed. As a result, the position of the forces became known and the General Staff ordered them to withdraw. Allon did not give up so easily. On the 31st he flew to Tel Aviv and protested to Ben-Gurion against the order, but to no avail. The disappointment of the commanders—the "clan," as Yadin called them—was intense. The soldiers were equally upset, and according to Rabin they shouted: "El Arish is within our grasp. We can capture most of Sinai, the Egyptian army is cut off and surrounded." However, Ben-Gurion, facing heavy pressure from Britain and the United States, did not yield and his view prevailed.[112]

The creation of facts by the army continued into March 1949 in Operation Uvda. Rabin asked for and received permission to leave the "diplomatic game" at Rhodes so that he could help plan the operation. Operation Uvda again displayed the army's tendency to act politically. The brigades were ordered to advance toward Eilat but to halt if they encountered enemy forces. The army, however, got around the order by bypassing Jordanian troops or, if they did meet up with them, by firing from a distance, ostensibly for self-defense, and then pressing on.[113]

In his diary, Ben-Gurion wrote that he admitted to the army that until the second truce the war had been of a purely defensive character—albeit, using offensive methods—but that since then the campaign had been a political operation undertaken by other means.[114] He also wrote that peace was essential—but not at any price. It was an opinion shared by many of Israel's future leaders. At all events, the fighting tapered off, and Ben-Gurion could write with pride: "In a short time the Israel Defense Forces redeemed ten times and more the area which had been redeemed beforehand during three generations." Indeed, the labor movement's myth of "another dunam and another goat"—referring to the gradual and moderate acquisition of the land—was shattered by the military conquests. In his diary Ben-Gurion looked back with satisfaction. Only a year had gone by since Operation Nahshon, the war's turning point, and a completely new reality had emerged.[115] The army's commanders also had every reason to be pleased. True, the war was over, but the importance of their military way for politics had been demonstrated absolutely, they believed.[116] Ben-Gurion and Allon, the statesman and the soldier, the key figures of the war, found time to visit together the Arava, which is in the southern desert. On the way, Ben-Gurion asked Allon how the hills of Edom, in Trans-Jordan, could be conquered. When Allon, nonplussed, asked the prime minister whether he was interested in taking the hills, the latter replied: "Me—no. But you will one day conquer them."[117]

PART SIX

A Nation-in-Arms, 1949–1956

CHAPTER ELEVEN

A State Army
Constructs a Nation

In the 1948 War, particularly after the end of the first truce, reality was determined in accordance with the assumption that Israel's national problems, in its relations with the Arabs, should be resolved by the military way. The large army, product of the union of all the pre-state military organizations, did its utmost to block the restoration of the status quo ante. The campaigns of conquest, the expulsion of the Palestinians, and the prevention of the refugees' return ruled out the possibility that two states would come into being west of the Jordan, as the United Nations had resolved. Policy at that time reflected the alliance which had been forged between the young army officers and the veteran political leadership. Concurrently, a new factor made its presence felt. It was the state, which constituted the Israeli Jewish population as a nation-in-arms in the postwar years. This chapter shows how militarism, whose origins and institutionalization were discussed earlier, was transformed from an ideology espoused by elite groups into a project of the entire Jewish community living in the State of Israel.

Statism (*mamlakhtiut*) was the action principle invoked by the state's leaders in order to transfer most functions—which in the pre-state era were carried out by voluntary bodies, usually attached to political parties—to state responsibility and control. The state would thereby concentrate the bulk of power in its hands, and become a "strong state."[1] The process included, for example, the attempt to eliminate the different educational tracks, the formation of an independent state bureaucracy, and, most crucially, a monopoly on the means of violence, so cardinal to every state.

Practically, it did not rely solely on saliently statist instruments. It also sought to blur the distinction between state and society and to reduce possible differences between them. Ben-Gurion called this process "statist pioneering." The success of statism, he and his colleagues believed, depended on the partnership of the Jewish population and its identification with and mobilization for the goals set by the state. This was pioneering of a new kind; no longer perceived as the prerogative of the chosen few, it was an element which should be foisted on the the whole nation.[2]

The army was seen as the embodiment of the new statism, the main instrument of the principle that sought to fuse the society's pioneering values with the *raison d'etat*. As early as August 1949, when Ben-Gurion met with Yadin to formulate the basic principles which should form the foundation of the new army, the prime minister spoke of professional and organizational efficiency and a spirit of pioneering.[3] Ben-Gurion envisioned the new army as combining the values of the Palmach, based on volunteering, community, and the youth movement spirit—in short, an army that was not divorced from the society—with the values which had been imbibed by the British Army veterans: discipline, order, obedience, hierarchy, and formalization. The result would be an army that was both militialike and statist.[4]

Even the army's personal makeup reflected the new conception. At the end of the war the General Staff consisted primarily of officers from the "British school." At the same time, representatives of the rival "school" still held many senior command posts.[5] It was Haim Laskov, head of the army's Training Branch and the very embodiment of the British school, who was not afraid to cultivate instructors and officers from the Palmach. Yitzhak Rabin recalls in his memoirs: "I reached the front feeling lonely, and skeptical about my future. Until Haim Laskov . . . solved the problem. Previously Laskov had been the spearhead in the great debate against the Palmach . . . and insisted on the advantages of the British methods. Now he asked me . . . to take command of the battalion commanders' course. . . . I couldn't believe my ears when I met with Laskov to discuss the matter and he told me: 'Collect all the Palmach commanders. Whoever is ready to stay in the army—I will see to it that he will be posted as an instructor or a trainee in the battalion commanders' course. . . . I will see to it that they do not lose rank or status. Together we will formulate the IDF's new combat doctrine.' "[6]

As a system of domination, statism represented a collectivist, nonliberal, guided democracy.[7] The new pioneering was pioneering of everyone, but was organized from above, by the state. It was a useful concept to keep the population in a constant state of mobilization. Not surprisingly, a popular phrase of the period was "pioneering tension."[8] That tension was considered essential, a means for turning a population, mostly of newcomers, into a nation.

Like many other states, Israel was forged through the struggle of a national liberation movement which likely drew inspiration from an ethnic past and which certainly strove to establish a political framework—a state. Once the state existed, however, its leaders did not regard the *ethnie* as an objective category which would in large measure determine whether it would crystallize into a nation. Instead, they viewed the *ethnie* as being susceptible, in varying degrees, to manipulation, invention, domination, and mobilization.[9] As the prime minister of Piedmont once said, "We have made Italy, now we have to make Italians." Or as Ben-Gurion put it in April 1951 during the election campaign: "I see in these elections the shaping of a nation for the state; because there is a state but not a nation."[10]

Usually, states construct nations through various means, including the school system, youth organizations, the media, and the army.[11] As for why, among all the possibilities, the Israeli nation was constructed (or reconstructed) primarily by the army, the answer was supplied by Ben-Gurion. It was because of efficiency, he told the Knesset, the Israeli parliament: "I have been a Zionist all my life and I do not deny the existence of Israel, heaven forbid . . . but . . . even the English nation was not always that nation . . . but was composed of different tribes . . . fighting one another. And only after a development of hundreds of years did they become one nation. . . . We do not have hundreds of years, and without the instrument of the army . . . we will not soon be a nation. . . . We must guide the progress of history, accelerate it, direct it. . . . This requires a framework of duty . . . a framework of national discipline."[12]

Israeli military sociologists have accepted that rationalization. Relying on nation-building and modernization theories in which the army was perceived as an agent of development and integration, they have written about "the many and varied functions of the Israeli army" and its "role expansion" in the civil sphere. The army was said to assist with immigrant absorption, act as a melting pot for Jewish ethnic groups, help conquer the wilderness, further settlement, educate for good citizenship and love of country, and foster culture.[13] The Israeli military sociologists did not accept the possibility that the army's involvement in these spheres and the blurring of the boundaries between army and society attest to the society's militarization rather than to the army's civilianization. They preferred to deal with the army's integrative role and to ignore its instrumental role as a means of organized violence.[14]

Ben-Gurion presented the army as an efficient instrument to forge a nation. However, he was speaking not of something technical but of something substantive. Turning a population into a nation through the army was intended to bring into being a nation of a particular kind. In fact, Ben-Gurion did not just complain about "the problem [being] that we are not a nation," he also liked to explain why this was a problem: "[There should be] a desire to fight, and an ability to fight. In order to want to fight, there must be a nation, and we are not a nation."[15]

Such notions were not without historical precedent. Post-revolutionary France, Prussia following its defeat by Napoleon, and Japan in the early years of the Meiji Era (1868–1912) are examples of states which constructed a nation for the purpose of war. The distinctive feature of the wars which France waged for more than twenty years was that the French possessed national passions which their adversaries lacked. It was the war of a nation, a fact given legal affirmation by the 1792 *levée en masse*, the conscription of the entire male population which later led to Napoleon's "Grande Armée." The nation-in-arms would later extend this idea to include the moral and material contribution of the home front to the war effort, and the resultant blurring of differences between soldiers and citizens.[16]

Prussia, even more than France, is a historical example of the calculated manufacture of national feeling which might help win wars. Most striking in this regard were the reforms carried out within the Prussian Army following its defeat by Napoleon in 1807. The new army included both regulars and reserve forces, units that observed strict discipline and a supplementary popular militia, less hierarchical and less rigid, of which the reserves were a part. Alfred Vagts aptly called the fomentors of the changes in the army (among whom was von Clausewitz) "Prussia's military Jacobins." Comprehensive mobilization enabled the state to give the conscripts, who came from every part of the country and were suspected of religious, ethnic, regional, and certainly class pluralism, a nationalist-militarist indoctrination. After their discharge, the soldiers transmitted the values they had absorbed to the general society.[17]

In time, the demand that the population identify with the idea of war was not made by the army alone. A whole array of civilian organizations operated energetically in Prussia-Germany to further the militaristic orientation: youth groups, student associations, societies for the navy (*Flottenverein*), the Church, associations of discharged officers, and others. Some of the German professoriat were called upon to guide the "mobilization of the minds." Much of their effort tended toward injecting meanings into the war; they revived Hegel's idea that war had a cleansing effect on society, and they contributed to the German obsession with *Einkreisung*, the fear of a two-front war.[18] Nor did the army sit idly by. Generals, von Clausewitz's faithful disciples, transformed their mentor's doctrine from a means to a principle, from a military strategy to a goal in its own right. General Ludendorff, for example, claimed that politics was the continuation of war, a kind of topsy-turvy version of the original. Van Der-Goltz, early in the century, wrote a book called *The Nation in Arms* (*Das Volk in Waffen*), since he considered the population's mobilization and total organization the key to success in war.[19]

In Japan, the imperialist thrust for territorial aggrandizement generated a new orientation. As a Japanese military academy report explained, "A characteristic of modern war is fighting with the total strength of nations. War in earlier times was decided by the side with the strongest military power. In modern war, fighting is on the level of financial war, ideological war, and strategic war, in addition to the military war." In Japan the identity between army and nation was expressed through a variety of modes: conscription, the army's transformation into a school for inculcating in the population nationalist and militarist values, the intro-

duction of reserve service, a supportive home front, and a mobilized culture, in which retired officers were catapulted into schools to serve as
teachers.[20]

Since the army played a key role in bringing about the nation-in-arms
and in forging the national sentiment, making it the property of the
whole population and exploiting it for purposes of war, it was the army
that occupied the center of the collective consciousness. The army, in effect, came to stand for all that was good and noble within the nation. This
was the situation in France, where the army-nation (*armée nation*) was the
backbone of la France Réelle (the real France), embodying all that was
good in it.[21] Naturally the army's various demands—for expansion, for
technical improvements, for munitions, and for better conditions for
its soldiers and officers—were almost always fulfilled. Who would dare
deny the embodiment of the nation its desires?

ISRAEL AS A NATION-IN-ARMS

The concept of nation-in-arms was first broached in March 1948. The
country's security chiefs met to consider what measures should be taken
to prepare for and win the coming war. Yigael Yadin said that the Yishuv
was unprepared for a war. Mobilization was slack, a guided economy was
not in place, and party considerations affected senior military appointments. Yadin proposed introducing arrangements of a nation-in-arms.
However, Yohanan Rattner, the former Haganah chief of staff, replied:
"We cannot rely on a 'nation-in-arms,' we need trained people." The
other speakers agreed.[22]

It was only toward the end of the war that Ben-Gurion acknowledged
the importance of the "nation-in-arms" concept. On one occasion, when
his advisers suggested using the army for economic purposes in industry
and agriculture, Yadin, the acting chief of staff, objected, arguing that
this would impair the army's effectiveness. In the face of the two approaches—one calling for the army to be harnessed to civilian missions,
the other advocating that military professionalism be confined to the battlefield alone—Ben-Gurion argued for a third option. His idea, he said,
did not accept conventional antitheses which had become empty phrases,
such as peace vs. war or army vs. work, but a combination of all.[23] In his
meetings with sector and brigade commanders in November 1948, Ben-
Gurion expressed doubts about the possibility that the war was ending
and shared with the officers his ideas on blurring differences between the
army and the civilian population.[24] Even though the idea of the nation-
in-arms was thus born in the war's latter phase, it was premised on the
assumption that the war would continue; even if it ended, it would soon
erupt again. Hence it was imperative to be ready for war at all times and
to keep the population mobilized, directly or indirectly.

Internal as well as national politics motivated the establishment of a nation-in-arms. Statism attested to Ben-Gurion's intention, once the instrument of the state was available to him, to organize the army as a profession which would stand above party politics. Mapam, in the opposition, tried to block this. In August 1949, when the government submitted to the Knesset the defense service bill for enactment in law, Mapam said it feared that the resulting army would become a militarist, technocratic elite, estranged from the nation's needs. As an alternative it proposed a militia—bearing a strong resemblance to the forces of the pre-state period—which would draw its strength from the people and not from the state bureaucratic apparatus which operated by law and fiat.[25] Mapam, in fact, had raised the idea of a people's army, a type of army which is based on the notion that the use of arms is determined by the people themselves, not by the state.[26]

Mapam's logic was obvious. If accepted, its proposals would bring the party a huge political advantage and dislodge Mapai's foothold in the army. Statism, in contrast, could confer on Mapai, the party standing at the head of the state, not only power but unrivaled legitimation. But not everyone grasped this fact. Mapai's functionaries were aghast at the idea of a supraparty state army. When party members discussed the defense service bill a few days before the Knesset was to vote on it, they asked Ben-Gurion: "Is it conceivable that the party will not be active in the army?" And Ben-Gurion replied: "It is for the good of the state and not to the detriment of the party." He was right. Mapai's image as a statist party, ostensibly concerned only with the general good and standing above party intrigues and the narrow view, was the source of its advantage over its rivals.[27]

There is a similarity here between the Israeli case and the political role played by the army during the period of the Meiji restoration in Japan. The restorationists sought to establish a professional, national army which would operate independently of feudal or sectorial traditions. Until then the officer corps had taken a narrow view of politics, and Japan's new rulers had prohibited it from becoming politically involved. At the same time, they wanted to ensure the army's loyalty. To achieve this, they effectively fashioned two types of political affiliation: internal politics, characterized by narrow interests and local loyalties, from which the army was ordered to keep its distance at all costs; and a general, national suprapolitics, in which the army was heavily involved. The army thus became committed to the Meiji rulers on terms that were perceived as national rather than sectorial. As Nakamura and Tobe explain, "The officers . . . did not regard their cooperation with the oligarchs as contradictory to the principle of the 'apolitical' warrior." According to their interpretation, such involvement was above politics: politics meant first of all, participating in activities of political parties opposed to the Meiji oligarchy.[28]

Ben-Gurion did not even consider the idea of establishing a people's army now that the statist apparatuses were, at long last, in his hands. A strong professional army, isolated from the society, with pronounced bureaucratic elements, also would have exposed Ben-Gurion to criticism by Mapam that he was out to create a careerist, praetorian force, oblivious to the community's needs. Israel's constitution as a nation-in-arms avoided both pitfalls. The IDF was a full-fledged army which was not a militia but displayed militialike elements. It was neither egalitarian nor based on volunteering but in it those features occupied a central place. And it was controlled by the state rather than by the people, with a broad social base enabling it to be called "the people's army."

The result was an army which was deeply involved in the statist arrangements that were meant to blur any possible separation between army, politics, and society, and which was completely immune from praetorianism. In general, armies of nations-in-arms are not inclined to foment military coups; they give an institutional seal to the inverse relationship between militarism and praetorianism. The IDF was no exception.[29] When the opposition claimed that the army had conquered and triumphed in 1948 but the government had squandered its achievements, Ben-Gurion retorted that separation between the army and the government was a hallmark of parties with a totalitarian bias: they would like to see the army become an independent body, operating at its own discretion.[30]

Party politics was only one reason for the constitution of the nation-in-arms; the other was ethnic politics. The singular circumstances were a crucial factor, just as the Prussian, Japanese, and French models of the nation-in-arms had not arisen in routine times. The more than 600,000 Palestinian Arabs who had left the country during the war were waiting for permission to return, and those who had remained were placed under the military government. This situation could be as much of a threat to Israel as the fact that its borders—which hardly resembled the U.N. partition resolution, having been redrawn according to war gains—were not recognized by most states of the international community. The leadership concluded that to prevent a reversion to the status quo ante and to be ready for the possibility of a "second round," the country must have a powerful army and a mobilized population.

There was another reason as well. Almost concurrently with the Arabs' mass exodus, Jews streamed into Israel at a rate of 15,000 to 30,000 per month, and within a few years the country's population more than doubled. The Jewish immigrants came from every corner of the world. They brought a Babel of languages, a bewildering array of customs and outlooks. Some were Ashkenazis (like the majority in the pre-state period), but most were Sephardis (from North Africa and the Middle East). Few knew anything about the Zionist movement or its relevance to Israel. Ben-Gurion explained: "Since everything depends on the people as a whole and on all the people, we must ask ourselves a question that no other people asks: Are we a nation? . . . My answer is that we are not yet a nation. . . . Jews arrive from every country on earth and they have no common language. . . . You have no idea of the remoteness and estrangement between those from the different countries."[31] Ben-Gurion's conclusion was that the new Israel lacked the unity of a nation, and that might hamper any preparation for war. Describing his impressions after visiting a battalion commanders' course in the IDF, he said that he had seen there only "one race, our Ashkenazis. . . . I see no greater danger than if the commanders are from a 'noble' race and the rank-and-file from a low race."[32]

On another occasion Ben-Gurion clearly suggested that the "pathological" social cleavage that exists in Israel might undermine the efforts to prepare the country for war. "An attempt has been made," he said, "to introduce this cleavage into the army as well. . . . And I must warn. . . . If our army has to fulfill a security role . . . it can do so only if it is united . . . subordinate to one authority exclusively."[33]

Ben-Gurion and his colleagues in the leadership viewed the army as the central mediating agent that would transform the heterogeneous Jewish population into a nation possessing the will and the ability to fight a war. The army's presence in and responsibility for the transit camps (ma'abarot) in which most of the new immigrants were initially housed was exploited to gain their support for the "security project." The army was in charge of the camps, looking after accommodations, transportation, food supplies, teaching, children's care, maintenance, medical aid, and so forth. However, its presence also bore an additional meaning. As the IDF weekly Bamahane explained, "The army's help . . . will teach the new immigrant that the army and the uniform he sees are in fact his."[34] The army was not depicted in terms of its primary function, as the instrument of organized violence in the society, but was overlaid with a civil image, as an intimate, friendly force.

On Novermber 17, 1950, when the chief of staff declared the start of Operation Ma'abarot, he stated explicitly: "It is up to us to prove to the new immigrants, who have become accustomed to viewing the army in their country of origin as an enemy and oppressor, that the army of Israel is a comfort and shelter for them."[35] Afterward, contemporary newspapers ran numerous features titled "Soldiers Take Good Care of the Kids," "Female Soldiers Teach Hebrew," and the like.[36] The implication of this deliberate blurring of the distinction between the military and the civil was clear: war is everyone's project. For now, the army was involved in civilian tasks, and the immigrants would soon become part of the military.

Ben-Gurion left no doubt about the purpose of the institutional affiliations that were forged between the new immigrants and the army. They would learn, he said, "not army Hebrew but Hebrew soldiering."[37] On another occasion, Ben-Gurion did not hesistate to insist in the Knesset that the Ma'abarot had security value: "The ma'abarot play an important role in defending the country's borders. If we do not turn every ma'abarot into a frontier post and the residents of the ma'abarot into people who are ready and able to defend themselves—our security will not be established."[38] Of course, the army's prestige was also enhanced by the fact that it took charge of the new immigrants in the ma'abarot, the more so because it followed various civilian bodies which had had little success in the same endeavor. Here was Ben-Gurion's opportunity to raise the army's prestige consciously and to enhance its standing in the society.[39] However, his major purpose was to familiarize the immigrants with the army project and to rebuild the immigrant as a new being, as an Israeli of a distinct species. The Jacobin state had constructed a new Frenchman. The ideal was described by Barere, the strong man of the Jacobin state, in his memoirs: "In France the soldier is a citizen, and the citizen a soldier." Ben-Gurion once said: "I saw these boys [the new immigrants] after their army service. . . . They are different people, they are different Jews."[40]

The new Jew was sanctified to be part of the new strong army, which is ready to battle Israel's enemies. The Defense Service Law of August 1949 and the later amendments gave legal validity to the special arrangements which were intended to establish a strong, professional, mass army in Israel. Particularly notable was the decision to create a four-tier military system: career army, regular army, reserves, and border settlements. Conscription was universal; even youths fourteen to eighteen years old were placed within a security framework (Gadna, or Youth Battalions), the better to prepare them for military service through a few hours of activity each week. Compulsory service for males was two years, which was then considered lengthy. The wording of the law was telling: "To prepare the entire nation to become, when necessity calls, a fighting nation." Ben-Gurion noted that in Israel two different concepts were mistakenly mixed: army and security. Although they were connected, the army was not the exclusive reservoir of security. The purpose of the law, he explained, was to eliminate the vile misconception that the army alone maintains the state's security.[41]

The army had one purpose only: to win in a war. Hence Ben-Gurion's reply to Mapam's proposal, deriving from the best socialist tradition, for a voluntary militia: "We must forget the romanticism of the army. . . . We will make war not with a local militia but with an army of rapid movement and heavy firepower, activating large formations, various corps . . . in combined operations . . . with uniform planning and command."[42] That was exactly the idea: a large, offensive army, trained to execute a blitzkrieg war.

The extensive army of reserves was not intended to introduce civilian patterns into the army but to bring the army to the Jewish population. So it had been in Prussia and in Japan, the latter having adopted the Prussian model of reserve service in order to expand the state's combat strength. Cumulatively, Israeli men would spend five years of their lives doing military service, trained to be soldiers in every respect and to demonstrate excellence, among other ways, by being able to shift, quickly and efficiently, whenever called upon, from civilian to soldier status.

It was in this spirit that Ben-Gurion, in 1952, explained the government's decision to extend military service by half a year. Israel's security, he stated, was based on training the entire nation—all ages capable of bearing arms—to fight when threatened. If we are not a fighting nation, Ben-Gurion declared, we will not be a living nation and certainly not an independent one. Moreover, he added, "quantity is also decisive." It was a comment in the style of Napoleon's "God walks with the big battalions." The overwhelming majority of the Israeli parliament, including the right-wing opposition Herut led by Menachem Begin, supported the motion to extend army service by six months. The lopsided vote in favor, 70-11, demonstrated the unequivocal support of the people's elected representatives for the idea of Israel as a nation-in-arms. As Yohanan Bader, a senior right-wing Knesset member, explained, "There is one element that expresses, in the most striking and concrete way, the change that occurred in the nation's life in 1948: the army. Our heartfelt love goes to the army. It is our pride and our hope."[43]

The government lost no time in implementing the 1949 Service Law. In March 1950 the press reported that citizens would be called up for reserve duty. This was explained as another important step in the deployment of all branches of the Israeli security forces to meet any situation. And to prevent self-satisfaction on the part of those not yet called up, the papers explained that until now they had enjoyed "a kind of hiatus" but henceforth they would share in responsibility for the state's security.[44]

The civil break ended quickly. In July 1950 phase two of the mass callup began. All those who had already done military service were assigned to reserve units. Now came the turn of all males up to age fifty who had not yet served (mainly new immigrants). It was no easy task to mobilize these newcomers, who were still trying to get their feet in the strange new country. Bamahane, though, saw things in a different light. The journal expressed the hope that henceforth, as the line between soldier and civilian dissolved, the imaginary barrier of a division of roles would disappear and everyone would shoulder responsibility for security.[45] So important was the motif of participation for the nation-in-arms that the army magazine devoted much space to the call-up of women,[46] vehicles—even mules, describing how the animals were incorporated in military units.[47] The implicit message was clear: if even beasts of burden were drafted, could the new immigrant men shirk their duty?

It was General Yadin who first described Israelis as full-time soldiers on ten months' leave (referring to two months of reserve duty each year). This went beyond the idea of serving in the army under legal obligation;

it implied an informal criterion of citizenship and belonging. However, not all Israeli citiznes enjoyed that privilege or obligation.

THE OTHER

The Palestinians, who in 1917 constituted about 90 percent of Palestine's population and before 1948 slightly less than 70 percent, emerged from the war as a minority, accounting for little more than 20 percent. Still, it would be incorrect to say that they were kept out of the project of building a nation-in-arms. In fact, albeit against their will, they played an important role in the process. They were "the other," "the alien," "the enemy," the foil against which the nation constructs itself and demarcates its normative boundaries. It was an image calculated to provide collective self-justification for the occupation, expulsion, and dispossession of those who had lived in the land for centuries.[48]

When the Arabs were expelled from Majdal (today's city of Ashkelon) some two years after the state's establishment, Bamahane explained: "Many of them will enjoy allocations from the U.N.'s aid institutions in Gaza. . . . [They] will enjoy the support of Egypt and will not be lacking for work; nor will the wealthy [among them] be without business there. The Arabs of Majdal have suffered quite a bit from being cut off from their families, which are in the Egyptian region. Therefore most of the Arabs of Majdal are leaving of their own volition."[49] The Palestinians thus became strangers in their own land. The Jewish attitude toward them matched their new status. It was one of suspicion and abuse. They were a potential fifth column who contributed nothing to the state, so there was no reason that they should benefit from the services and rights conferred by the state.[50]

Few took note of the fact that it was the country's leadership, with its ethno-national outlook, that prevented the Arabs from serving in the army. In 1954 all members of the minorities (as the Palestinians who had remained in Israel were called) were ordered to register for security service. The order was published at the decision of Defense Minister Pinhas Lavon. In the Arab villages it was virtually the only topic of conversation. Despite widespread objections, registration proceeded apace throughout the Arab sector. A follow-up report noted that most of the registrants spoke Hebrew, were pleased at the opportunity to serve in the army, and requested information about getting into the units of their choice. This report probably did not reflect the actual situation. Still, the registrants displayed no massive, clearcut opposition to conscription. But the registration procedure seemed to take place in a vacuum: Arab youngsters were never called up for military service.[51]

By not conscripting Israel's Arabs to the IDF, the authorities created a potent mechanism for introducing ethnic segregation in the new state—between those who belong to the nation and those who do not. Perhaps in the 1950s Israel was not a Herrenvolk democracy, the democracy of a "master race," in which the rights of other ethnic groups were utterly expunged; perhaps the situation of the Israeli Arabs gradually improved, vindicating the thesis of the Israeli sociologist Sammy Smooha, who depicted Israel as an "ethnic democracy," successfully combining viable democratic institutions and civil rights with ethnic dominance.[52] Clearly, though, the situation of Israel's Arab citizens was determined according to a potent image of the Other, in the same way that the Orient supplied Europeans with an image of the Other, a sine qua non for the articulation of their own identity.[53]

One of the main mechanisms which separated Jewish citizen from Arab citizen in the new state was the military government. It operated as an instrument of despotic rule, as an occupation force in every respect, with the goal of preserving separation and ethnic superiority. Knesset protocols reveal its operations blatantly: expulsion of Palestinians across the border, internal exile from one village to another, collective punishments, a ban on freedom of movement, censorship, restrictions on political organizing, bureaucratic arbitrariness, constraints on free economic competition. Other measures included land expropriations, trials of Arab civilians in military courts which usually handed down stiff sentences, and use of organized violence, often resulting in fatalities.[54] The Arab villages were not helped by their proximity to the border, across which refugees infiltrated in an effort to return to their villages and lands. The situation was further aggravated by the tension between Israel and the Arab states. At bottom, the attitude toward the country's Arab citizens was that "the Arabs understand only force."

The Palestinian refugees who were forced to leave their homes and were not permitted to return were also the Other—sinister, menacing, weavers of insidious plots. The press of the period continued to demonize the Palestinians and banalize the Israeli-Palestinian conflict. This too was integral to the politics of the nation-in-arms. The army journal, for example, ran a series of articles by Dr. Sasson Ashriki in which Palestinians were described as defectors and as "the wild card in the hands of the Arab states." There was no refugee problem, the writer pointed out: the refugees were not interested in returning; they were being incited by their leaders. Dr. Ashriki also had a scoop: "Forty percent of the defectors who receive aid from the U. N. do not even exist."[55] The magazine's readers, particularly the new immigrants who had not taken part in the 1948 War, could form the impression that the refugee problem was a malicious invention of the Arabs.

In fact, as Adriana Kemp points out, during the 1950s the ethnic boundary line between the Arabs "inside," who were Israeli citizens, and the Arabs "outside," those residing in the Arab states, was obscured. This period also witnessed the advent of segregation of the two population groups in Israel, Jews and Arabs. Among other methods, segregation functioned through the agency of the military government's administrative apparatus and through the demarcation of the areas along the borders as security zones, in which Israel's Arabs (but not its Jews) were subject to restrictions on their movement and other prohibitions.[56]

This attitude, this ethno-national atmosphere, led finally to the massacre in the large Arab village of Kafr Kassim. There, in October 1956, an Israeli army unit killed forty-seven people, including fifteen women and eleven children aged eight to fifteen for supposedly violating a curfew.[57] The incident was long hushed up. Finally, though, simmering rumors forced the authorities to launch an official investigation. Issakhar Shadmi, the brigade commander under whom the perpetrators of the massacre served, later claimed that the battalion commander involved, Major Malinky, had told the unit in the pre-operation briefing: "Now our time has come. We will lead the military brigade, with our two armored vehicles, to Nablus, and the Arabs will run before us." The IDF had a contingency plan for war, based on three scenarios. In one scenario the Israeli Arabs leave their villages to link up with their brethren across the border. In that event, the plan stated, "under no circumstances should action be taken which could be construed as discouraging this." According to Shadmi, Malinky knew about the contingency plan. He thought that a few deaths in Kafr Kassem would certainly not be taken as discouraging the eastward flight of the Arab population. This is a striking example of how a militaristic perception of reality brought forth ideas of ethnic cleansing in the state era. Those who took the ideas seriously proceeded to kill innocent civilians. The military tribunal sentenced the perpetrators to prison terms ranging from seven to seventeen years. In prison they received preferential treatment, and all were soon released. Afterward the leadership arranged jobs for them in various state bodies, since members of the nation must be looked after.[58]

Kafr Kassim was not the first incident of its kind. In August 1952, for example, at the end of the Muslims' holy month of Ramadan, the army killed two Israeli Arabs and wounded several women and children from the village of Ara, when they neared the border intending to meet with relatives on the other side. They were shot in broad daylight inside Israel while still a considerable distance from the border. In the Knesset Ben-Gurion was willing to admit that the soldiers had exercised poor judgment. He also promised compensation to the victims. Those responsible for the incident, however, were never questioned and never brought to trial. Nor was any meaningful compensation paid.[59] From time to time, Ben-Gurion declared that the Israeli Arabs enjoy the principle of equality before the law. Practically, the fact that he never once fought against these violations of law and that during those years, with the exception of the Kafr Kassem affair, not one soldier was tried for attacking Arabs, was an indication of how ethnic politics was central in the new state.[60] The Arabs were subjects, discrete entities, and each was judged as an individual when faced with the mechanisms of the state. The Jews, in contrast, were part of an ethno-national collective, the state was theirs and they were the state, active partners in carrying out its missions, and nowhere more so than in the major task: doing military service and preparing for war.

CHAPTER TWELVE

A Nation Ready for War

Israel's constitution as a fighting nation was underlined by a distinctive view of reality where concepts such as peace, war, emergency, and security were concerned. During the 1948 War, Ben-Gurion had endeavored to extend the security net as broadly as possible. "I have to admit," he had said in February 1948, "that I am not capable of seeing anything now other than through the prism of security. . . . Security is involved in all branches of life."[1] At that time, his description was only partially true. Now, though, in the era of statism, the defense minister sought to realize his goal fully. Security, he explained in January 1949, meant more than the army. It entailed stepping up the birthrate and populating empty areas.[2]

Accordingly, Ben-Gurion refused to view Israel as a country in a state of peace. Immediately after the end of the 1948 War, in reply to a question from the army journal, Ben-Gurion described the situation as a "temporary truce." The Arab leaders were refusing to make peace with Israel, he explained, and therefore the IDF's role had not yet ended. The truce was meant only to raise the army's efficiency level.[3] In the Knesset debate on the Defense Service Law, Ben-Gurion referred to an "armed peace." No one should harbor illusions about the future, the prime minister asserted, warning about the dangers of a "false peace."[4]

Ben-Gurion usually put the blame for the situation on the Arab countries in the Middle East. As he described it in the Knesset, they were caught up in a maelstrom of disturbances, coups, political chaos, and assassinations—a volatile situation with unknowable consequences which could spread anywhere. The demonization of the Arab states was heard in silence by the Knesset, and only one member, from the Communist Party, called out: "This is a prelude to the order; it is preparation for war."[5]

With the passing of time, Ben-Gurion's definition of security would be broadened still further, and the civil sphere would shrink correspondingly. By 1955 Ben-Gurion would be able to declare: "Security is not possible without immigration . . . security means settlements . . . the conquest of the sea and air. Security is economic independence, it means

fostering research and scientific ability . . . volunteerism of the population for difficult and dangerous missions."[6]

An example of an instrument that entailed a broad concept of security and erasing the dividing line between army and society was Nahal
(acronym for Fighting Pioneer Youth). Nahal combined military training
with agricultural work and land settlement. The country, it suggested in
an echo of earlier times, could be conquered not only by a professional
army but also by settlement. In a discussion by Mapai activists in early
1949, the idea was raised to turn from "military conquest" to "settlement conquest" as a goal that would serve the same purpose of displaying lordship over the land. This fit in with one of the reasons for Nahal's
establishment, as Ben-Zion Yisraeli explained at the same meeting: "To
grab quickly the hundreds of abandoned [Arab settlements] along the
borders."[7]

Nahal enabled active cooperation between the army and the kibbutz
movements. The cooperation was grounded in principles that were laid
down by the army. To prevent a possible friction, the he'ahzut, the "security settlement," came into being. Its rationale was entirely military; in
fact, the he'ahzut was the most complete expression of the militarization
of settlement.[8] If something of a civilian image was attached to Nahal—
in the soldiers' dress, their lax discipline, the informal, communal relations within their units—and if the army made no effort to reverse such
tendencies, the goal was clear: a penetration of the military into society.
For beneath Nahal's civilian markings was a military unit prepared for
war. Again and again, Ben-Gurion explained that Nahal would not be a
static, local defense force. On the contrary, it would play a central role
in carrying the war to the enemy's territory.[9] Ben-Gurion left no doubts
about his conception of territorial and conquest-oriented settlement when
he told the Knesset that every locality must be steeled and trained and
ready to stand in the gate, and this obligated men and women alike. The
men would make their way toward the border, he explained, and the
women would stay behind to protect the children, the elderly, and themselves.[10]

The program to turn Nahal and the agrarian settlements into a more
effective military element with an offensive orientation was realized as
the 1956 war drew nearer. Israel, led by Defense Minister Ben-Gurion
and Chief of Staff Dayan, found ways to sidestep the armistice agreement
with Egypt through the settlements. Nahal outposts were set up in the
demilitarized zones, where soldiers were prohibited, over the objections
of the United Nations and Egypt. The latter were not disposed to accept
the modern statist version of the Zionist pioneer and settler. The army
also demanded the establishment of twelve new settlement sites along the
border with Egypt, calling them by a name which disclosed their true
intent: "breakthrough points." Avraham Harzfeld, a legendary settler

in the pre-state period, and his colleagues from the Agricultural Center were eager to deal with the army's request. Harzfeld explained the approach that guided them: "It is an order and we do not consider whether it is good for agriculture or not."[11] This was the latest articulation of the concept that had emerged in the second half of the 1940s, when agricultural needs were subordinated to security considerations. In addition, as part of the war preparations, Dayan turned the "tomatoes unit," as Israeli slang dubbed Nahal, into an airborne corps and attached it to the paratroops, the IDF's elite unit. The unit that blurred the boundaries between military and civilian finally became the spearhead of the army.[12]

Mass maneuvers were another means that served to construct a broad concept of security. "Every exercise has its own mission," the daily *Ha'aretz* informed its readers in the autumn of 1953, going on to describe how that year's maneuvers differed from those of 1951 and 1952. Nor did the paper omit to publicize the army's slogan: "And you, the citizen, share in their mission and their success."[13] The large-scale maneuvers, like the reserves system, were the handiwork of Yadin. Through them he wanted to test the idea of a nation-in-arms. To dramatize his point, he sent military police in 1950 to arrest the secretary of the Finance Ministry, who was under the impression that his position exempted him from service. Yadin also demanded that at least one exercise be held with the participation of 100,000 troops—virtually the entire army that Israel would field in the event of a war.[14]

The maneuvers demonstrated the participation and involvement of the entire Jewish population in the project called war and preparation for war. The mass maneuvers also blurred the distinction between two types of time: peace and war. The press provided daily reports on the exercises: "A surprise attack by the 'Reds' on the 'Blacks' in the air force maneuvers," one paper wrote. A few days later it emerged that "paratroops from the country of the 'Yellows' have landed on the soil of the 'Blacks.' " And three days afterward readers learned that "efforts by the 'Greens' to breach the lines of the 'Blues' were thwarted."[15] The entire population was involved, as befits a nation-in-arms.

While the maneuvers were in progress, a number of incidents occurred on the Egyptian border; the line between training exercises and real attacks was blurred. The uncertainty was heightened when Israel denied, at first, that its soldiers had entered the demilitarized zone, ascribing everything to the Egyptians' overvivid imagination. The press wrote that travelers in Galilee, where the maneuvers were being held, were caught up in a war atmosphere. The country's president, escorted by the chief of staff, toured the area of the "battles." The day after his visit, the IDF raided the Jordanian village of Qibiyeh, this time for real, killing some fifty inhabitants and blowing up about forty houses. The United Nations and the Great Powers were outraged at the scale of the operation, its brutality, and Israel's violation of the armistice accord. The government, in contrast, continued to hold what it called "thorough discussions on security."[16]

REPRISAL ACTIONS

The maneuvers readied the troops for war. But no less effective for that purpose were the reprisal operations. During the early 1950s, border incidents occurred with Syria, Jordan, and Egypt, triggered mainly by conflicting interpretations of the armistice agreements, the status of the demilitarized zones, and the exact location of the boundaries. U.N. representatives had a clear stand on the question of who was violating the agreements along the borders—Israel or the Arab states. Even Arye Shalev, a veteran of Israel's military intelligence and at the time a member of the Israel-Syria Mixed Armistice Commission, has written that, contrary to the prevailing view in Israel, both countries, and not Syria alone, were responsible for the tension between them and for the violent clashes. Israel was not always the lamb, nor was Syria necessarily the wolf.[17]

Besides these confrontations between states, Palestinians continued to infiltrate into Israel. At first these were refugees trying to return to their homes, and then sabotage-and-murder squads. Benny Morris, in his extensive study of Israel's border wars in the first decade of the state's existence, shows that the majority of the cross-border infiltrations into Israel, certainly those in the first years after the 1948 War, were economically motivated. Fewer than 10 percent of the infiltration attempts were for political or terror purposes. But Israeli policy makers were not inclined to distinguish between the different types of infiltration. In fact, until 1956 most of the infiltrators were unarmed and were driven mainly by the aspiration to return to their homes. The Israelis were in no hurry to concede this fact, and in any event, from the Israeli point of view this was intolerable—so much so that the IDF maintained a policy of free fire-to-kill against infiltrators.[18]

The inevitable result was escalation. The possibility that a different policy might also be viable was not discussed, with one exception, after the U.S. and British press sharply condemned Israel's brutal attitude toward a group of deportees, some of whom had died after the Israeli authorities sent them on foot to cross the Jordan on a particularly hot day in May 1950. Apart from this incident there was only denial. As in the expulsions of 1948, some actions were committed tacitly, the army acting and the political leadership giving its approval after the fact. The inverse relationship between militarism and praetorianism did its work. And when the government was forced to justify reprisal raids, the explanation most frequently adduced was that they were carried out by vigilantes who were fed up with the infiltrations. Only Foreign Minister Moshe

Sharett seemed uncomfortable with the prevarications which had become part of Israeli policy. In October 1956, after Ben-Gurion presented his new government in the Knesset and announced his readiness to meet with Nasser for peace talks, Sharett wrote in his diary that the prime minister "did not, of course, see any logical contradiction between the verbal demonstration and the concrete military operation." Sharett was referring to a raid which had been carried out that same night by a brigade-size Israeli force against Egyptian positions in the Kuntilla region of the Sinai Peninsula.[19]

The reprisal operations were a sort of preparation for war. True, Dayan claimed that they bore a deterrent character, which would give the Arab states pause before they launched a war on Israel. But Dayan also strove for an Israeli-initiated war during these years and made good use of the reprisal raids to achieve that goal. It is important to bear in mind that following the 1948 War, many in Israel, including the right-wing Herut party and the left-wing Le'ahdut Ha'avodah, believed that the western region of Trans-Jordan (the West Bank) could have been conquered and that the work could be completed by means of another war. Herut spokesmen said that only within the historic borders of Greater Israel would the Jewish state know true peace instead of having to live by the sword.[20] To counter this, the left-wing opposition, for example, Hakibbutz Hameuhad, urged not "peace without territories" but "territories for security." Thus Allon, the hallowed commander of the 1948 War, said Israel was a "country of a narrow corridor," justified his opposition to the Rhodes armistice agreements four years earlier by saying that the "liberation of the land" had not yet been accomplished, and complained that because the "liberation" did not extend as far as the Jordan River, the country was split, had no natural border, and lacked necessary territorial depth.[21]

There was also the desire of IDF units to demonstrate determination and combat capability. From the day he became chief of staff Dayan imbued the army with this spirit. He also portrayed the reprisal raids in terms of a mechanism linking the army to the nation. The raids, he said, were the Jews' elixir of life: without them they would not have a fighting nation and without the regime of a fighting nation they would be lost.[22] The army absorbed from Dayan the militaristic spirit that the chief of staff considered vital for Israel's existence. And thus violence came to be seen as a phenomenon that had to be accepted as though it were a decree of fate, as Dayan described the Israeli condition in his famous eulogy for Roi Rotenberg, who was murdered by Arabs in the fields of Kibbutz Nahal Oz, near the Gaza Strip: "Yesterday, at dawn, Roi was murdered. . . . Not from the Arabs of Gaza but from ourselves shall we seek [to avenge] Roi's blood. How did we close our eyes and not face up to our fate, not see our generation's mission in all its harshness? . . . For we know that if the hope that we can be destroyed is to die, we must be armed and ready,

morning and night. We are a generation of settlers, but without steel hel-
met and muzzle of cannon we cannot plant trees or build homes. . . . Let
us not avert our eyes lest our hand waver. This is the fate of our generation. This is our life's choice—to be prepared and arrayed, strong and
unyielding, or to have the sword thrust from our grasp—and our lives
cut off."[23]

True to his creed, Dayan saw to it that those who bore the sword—the
army and its shock troops—also gained the highest prestige. Indeed, the
reprisals spawned a myth of heroic warriors; the paratroops became the
elite of the army. The nation esteemed its warrior-emissaries and made
them the symbols of the new Israel. Every young inductee wanted to
serve with the Red Berets (the paratroops); those who made it were the
pride of their family, kibbutz, or neighborhood. Reporters for the army
weekly accompanied raiding forces on their missions to provide authentic color stories, complete with photographs, of the heroes in action.[24]
Hardly anyone pointed out that these photos were taken in the sovereign
territory of neighboring countries and that the raids were state-perpe-
trated acts of revenge on the order of "an eye for an eye."

The raids had helped create a bellicose atmosphere and transformed
war from something distant and alien into a seemingly unavoidable
aspect of everyday life. War was no longer necessarily threatening, as a
member of the Mapai's Center explained: "[We must] remove all these
elements of mystical fear [from war] such as blood and the sound of gunfire, which have a psychological effect."[25] It was most important to implement such a conception among the new immigrants from North Africa and the Middle East. They had been turned into a living protective
wall along the borders, and they dreaded the infiltrators. Newly arrived,
sent to border settlements, forced to live on the periphery, caught up in a
cycle of organized violence and war preparation, they displayed normal
human instincts: a desire for peace and quiet and fear of a situation for
which nothing had prepared them. Some tried to find individual solutions that did not meet the "collective needs" as defined by Mapai functionaries. The latter, safely ensconced in the big cities, construed the immigrants' feelings as weakness. As one Mapai member put it, "All those
settlements may bring a great disaster on us. They are very sensitive to
gunfire, one shot and they are up on their feet."[26] But the passing of the
years did not reduce the fears, while the nation-in-arms took ever firmer
shape, ready for war.

"POSITIVE MILITARISM"

At the end of September 1955 a huge Czech-Egyptian arms deal was
made public and a wave of popular volunteerism swept the country. The
deal served as the backdrop for the events that followed. Mass patriotism
held the country in its grip, on a scale similar to the "Reveil National" in

France from 1910 to 1914: an expression of the nation's wish for war. In Israel the national awakening was triggered by a speech delivered in the Knesset by Sharett (prime minister for a time), who concluded his remarks with the words "Arms for Israel."

The next day the public began spontaneously to donate money and valuables to subsidize IDF weapons procurement. The contributions were given the name Defender Fund (Keren Hamagen). The new immigrants, the so-called Second Israel, shared in the collective national effort. The press reported the amounts donated and described the donors, noting "general enthusiasm and manifestations of mass volunteerism never before seen in the country." The papers also published price lists of weapons as though they were produce in the vegetable market, and the public began buying them virtually by weight. Thus the general public felt itself to be involved, and public organizing, which potentially could have been civilian in character, was directed toward the war effort.

The Teachers' Association contributed an amount sufficient to purchase one warplane and one tank. The Haifa City Council decided to contribute a torpedo boat to the navy. The Artisans' Association purchased a warplane. The City of Ramat Gan bought a transport plane and 100 parachutes. Discount Bank collected enough for a tank. The town of Ramleh's elected representatives decided to purchase a tank to be called Ramleh 1. At the same time the popular manifestations continued. As the cabinet was deliberating the Defender Fund, an elderly woman appeared and donated an antique Venetian glass vase. A second woman turned up at the prime minister's office with a heavy bracelet made of pure gold. Lydia Balulu, mother of ten, who had received a child-bearing prize of 100 pounds, donated it to the fund. Schoolchildren organized street parades, and Yadin, the former chief of staff, made an emotional appeal: "Parents, buy a suit of iron, a suit of armor for the defense of your children."[27]

A total of 300,000 pounds was collected on the first day of the spontaneous donations. One paper called it "the nation's finest hour." Certainly the project was founded on the public's active involvement. The prime minister's office was inundated with thousands of letters from donors. Bereaved parents gave in the names of their sons, Jews from abroad sent money, and Chief Rabbi Yitzhak Nissim, who donated 200 pounds, added a scriptural invocation: "And you shall chase your enemies, and they shall fall before you by the sword."[28] The leadership soon directed this outpouring of feelings into channels it found desirable. Parades and mass demonstrations were organized, donation booths and special offices were set up, information pamphlets were distributed, and two former chiefs of staff headed a public committee which declared its intention to raise twenty-five million pounds for weapons purchases.

The public committee, which was set up at the end of October, turned the fund-raising drive from a voluntary effort into an obligatory one. The committee supervised the contributions from the public sectors and demanded that each meet its quota. Nor did the committee neglect propaganda, or, as they called it, the renewal of the volunteering, pioneering element. Names of shirkers and "rejectionists" were published. The committee described its project as a transition "from spontaneous volunteering to organized volunteering." This was the latest version of the "duty to volunteer" which had marked the emergence of Israeli militarism in the decade leading up to 1948. In the 1950s it also became the foundation for the idea of the nation-in-arms.[29]

Another expression of the nation's will at that time was Operation Wall (Mivtza Homa). The army did not want to budget funds for saliently defensive purposes, such as protecting the civilian rear or fortifying settlements. The result was that nongovernment companies belonging to civil institutions such as the Histadrut Federation of Labor and the Jewish Agency rallied to the cause of improving the defenses of border settlements. Workers from the big cities volunteered to help with construction. The operation was made viable thanks to typical cooperation between the civilian companies and the army. Here was a clear indication that security was no longer a pure state-bureaucracy project but the people's enterprise. Gradually the campaign gathered momentum, becoming a mass movement that ultimately encompassed more than 100,000 volunteers and 300 settlements.

The Jacobins in France spoke of the need to turn houses into fortresses. In Israel a similar notion was put forward. Senior Defense Ministry official Shimon Peres explained the significance of Operation Wall in terms that shed light on its contribution to the nation-in-arms model. Peres noted that until the nineteenth century, wars had been fought by professional soldiers and the goals were military strongholds. With the emergence of nation-states and the development of national sentiment, wars ceased to be a matter for mercenaries and military strongholds were no longer their only target. Nowadays, soldiers and civilians were interchangeable. Today's soldier would be tomorrow's civilian and vice versa, just as today's civilian settlement would be tomorrow's military stronghold.[30] This was a classical expression of the idea that it is not the army alone which makes war; the state must organize the whole Jewish population according to military principles that previously had been the exclusive province of the army.

The Defender's Fund and Operation Wall showed that after years during which the state had constructed a nation, the politics of the state's leadership corresponded closely with the nation's "will." The problem of authority, which had so perturbed the leadership in the 1940s, had been resolved. The cooperation between Ben-Gurion and the army, which had begun in the 1948 War, continued. The opposition was not perceived as a significant factor liable to interfere with policy, certainly not with a war policy.

To understand how conditions amenable to war were created, it is necessary to take into account that in the mid-1950s the leadership imposed a conception which found advantages in the situation of "neither peace nor war." The idea was formulated by Dayan, one of the most prominent representatives of the native-born generation; it was the precursor of another famous Dayan epigram of about ten years later: "Better [to keep] Sharm e-Sheikh [in occupied Sinai] without peace than [to have] peace without Sharm e-Sheikh." In the meantime, he reiterated the "neither peace nor war" formula at every opportunity and extolled its virtues.

Around the same time, *Davar*, the newspaper of the ruling party, published an article explaining that the peculiar situation of "neither peace nor war" should be regarded not only as descriptive but also as prescriptive. The absence of peace, the writer stressed, was not entirely a negative condition: it spotlighted the nation's condition of mobilization, underscored the success of Israel and particularly the IDF as a melting pot for the new immigrants, and helped reduce class, communal, even party disparities.[31]

The mind-set that comes through in this article is known as "positive militarism." Its manifestations in that era were manifold, notably in the exacting and coercive recommendations made by the Emergency Committee, which was then established. The body's chairman, Pinhas Lavon, claimed that the ideas in question should not be seen as constraints, as the least of the necessary evils generated by the possibility of war, but rather as recommendations for the implementation of which the emergency situation provided a propitious moment.[32]

Possibly the most trenchant manifestation of "positive militarism" in this period was displayed by the Histadrut's Actions Committee. Its members believed that the emergency situation and the war preparations would radically boost the economy, increase tax collection, and lead to the elimination of corruption and speculation while elevating the young generation to new heights of volunteerism. Most impressive of all were the remarks made by former chief of staff Yadin at that meeting. Yadin, who headed the Defender Fund, left his audience in no doubt about the purpose of the operation: "The nation feels and knows that our strength derives not only from a regular army.... We are talking about a second round that will come. The second round has already come. We are already in the third and fourth round.... And in this battle woe is us if we fight within our country's borders.... We do not have room to fight in [this] country.... We must be ready to fight back, simply, across the border.... For that we need weapons that can carry the war ... across our borders."[33]

The existence of "positive militarism," in which people show readiness, even enthusiasm, to fight, suggested that the nation was ready for war. This should not be considered the sole causal explanation—wars are multicausal. Nevertheless, as the events described in this book have shown,

in an atmosphere of support for cultural militarism, war not only becomes possible; it is also considered reasonable and legitimate.

MILITARISTIC POLITICS

The unfolding of events within the power center—mainly the relations
between the military and political elites—produced a situation in which
war became inevitable. In other words, the thrust of the army and of its
chief, Dayan, to solve Israel's national problems by means of war was realized in full.

Did Israel have any other choice? This question can be approached
from several directions. From a sociological standpoint, the issue is
whether in the situation as it then developed there was a realistic alternative to the policy pursued by Ben-Gurion and Dayan. In fact, there was.
It was embodied by Sharett. A year after his ouster as foreign minister, Sharett described his dispute with Ben-Gurion and Dayan in terms
of two schools: "One approach maintains that the Arabs understand only
the language of force. . . . From time to time, Israel must prove clearly that
it is strong and that it is ready and able to use its strength. . . . As for
peace, according to that approach it is a dubious proposition in any case.
. . . The other approach [holds that] the question of peace must not for a
moment disappear from our calculations. . . . We must restrain our reac-
tions. And there is always the question: has it really been proved that reprisal raids solve the security problem they are meant to deal with?"[34]

Dayan was a distinct representative of Israel's native-born generation,
of those who advocated the use of force to deal with Israel's national
problems. Since 1949, serving as the general in charge of Southern Command, he had openly made known his view that there was only one way
to fight the infiltrators: by means of military reprisals, which would induce the Arab governments to keep the Palestinians in their countries
under close surveillance and prevent them from infiltrating into Israel.
To follow that logic was to walk a thin line, since it could just as easily
trigger a full-scale war. But to Dayan such a scenario was hardly problematic.

On the contrary, after his appointment as chief of staff in December
1953, he spared no effort to bring about a war. He was able to persuade
Ben-Gurion, an experienced statesman, that only war would solve the region's problems. A key turning point was the Kibiyeh operation in October 1953. In the wake of an attack by infiltrators on a house in an Israeli
village, Ben-Gurion and Dayan decided on a tough reaction. As in previous cases, the local units placed a far-reaching interpretation on the
general guidelines. The result was that more than sixty civilians—men,
women, and children—were killed when paratroopers blew up houses in
the Jordanian village of Kibiyeh.[35]

Following the Kibiyeh operation, Sharett demanded the establishment of a cabinet committee on security and foreign affairs which would give prior approval to reprisal raids.[36] However, Ben-Gurion and Dayan had long held a stereotyped view of the international arena: the Great Powers, the U.N., and indeed the entire world would always be against Israel— why, then, should Israel care what they thought? It was an outlook well suited to an orientation which stemmed from cultural militarism, insisting that Israel must rely solely on its own strength. Sharett, in contrast, although he did not balk at using the IDF as an instrument to achieve political goals, continued to take into account the attitude of the international community and the U.N., which could, he believed, create an atmosphere favorable to Israel and help bring about regional peace.[37]

On December 7, 1953, Ben-Gurion resigned as prime minister and defense minister, the two portfolios he had held since the state's establishment. The expectation, based on previous occurrences, was that the resignation would create a vacuum which would bring about Ben-Gurion's return under preferable conditions. To ensure that he would retain control, Ben-Gurion did not leave without appointing—on the day before he resigned—two members of the younger generation to key posts: Peres was made director-general of the Defense Ministry and Dayan was named chief of staff. Both were ardent advocates of an aggressive reprisals policy. In the meantime, as though to validate Ben-Gurion's assumptions, the new defense minister, Pinhas Lavon, who had been known as a moderate, became an incorrigible activist following his appointment. Indeed, his adventurist military initiatives, carried out under the motto of "an eye for an eye," caused eyebrows to be raised even within the army.[38]

Relations between Dayan and Sharett were marked by friction, suspicion, even sheer hostility. *He is still intoxicated with the victories of 1948,* Sharett wrote of Dayan.[39] A political chief of staff in every respect, Dayan indeed fought relentlessly against Sharett's policy of moderation, which sought to avert war by all possible means.[40] Dayan did not resort to a military putsch to turn his views into policy; nor did he openly challenge the government or the prime minister. The methods he relied on are typical of nations-in-arms: lobbying, pressuring, behind-the-scenes politicking, secrecy and denial, even threats, but never so much as a hint of praetorianism. The head of the Security Services, Isser Harel, reported that Dayan had told staff officers: "This government will not declare war, but we will get there by means of [border] incidents."[41] In this atmosphere we can understand why Sharett was forced time and again to give in and allow the army to operate contrary to his declared policy. The problem was compounded by the fact that in the Israeli reality every local incident that seemed to call for a tactical military response could very quickly, if the chief of staff wanted, become a tangled political-diplomatic issue, perhaps with international repercussions. Indeed, Dayan's methods gradually triumphed, as Sharett confided to his diary: "The status quo which the chief of staff advocated became an intolerable regime. The army did not cooperate, did not pass on reports about developments, confronted [me] with facts."[42]

Probably the critical juncture that did much to determine the fate of the region came in February 1955. Ben-Gurion had returned to the Defense Ministry and set up a "small forum" consisting of just three members: himself, Dayan, and Peres.[43] This trio gradually prepared the ground for war. Shortly after Ben-Gurion reassumed the defense portfolio, the IDF carried out the reprisal operation which would have the greatest impact on subsequent events: the Gaza raid. The paratroops' 890th Battalion attacked an Egyptian Army camp located in a train station north of Gaza City; eight Israeli soldiers were killed in the ensuing battle, but the Egyptians suffered thirty-eight dead. Here was striking evidence of the shift which had occurred in Israel's security policy. Egypt's President Nasser would afterward cite the Gaza raid as the turning point which had proved to him that Israel was not interested in peace.[44]

In the meantime the infiltrations from Egypt continued, and toward the end of March Ben-Gurion said he wanted to capture the Gaza Strip. For the first time, Ben-Gurion suggested an Israeli-initiated war. The fact that he could not muster a cabinet majority for the operation hardly presented an obstacle. Beginning in April, he and Dayan adopted an indirect route to achieve their goal. The reprisal raids took on a new character, becoming larger in scope, with more troops taking part, and the size and number of the targets increased accordingly. The aim was to drag Egypt into a response that would effectively trigger a war.

It is important to point out that the IDF's senior officer corps was also involved in the escalation vis-à-vis Egypt. In fact, the officers played a significant role in constituting the militaristic politics of Ben-Gurion, Peres, and Dayan. They provided the strategic imprimatur for the idea of an Israeli-initiated war. The army's strategists formulated the concept that Israel lacked strategic depth and therefore the IDF must transfer the fighting to enemy territory as quickly as possible. From this starting point the road to an initiated war was short.[45] At the same time, the flexible, expansive, and in many cases distinctly personal interpretation with which the commanding officers, especially Ariel Sharon, the chief of the paratroops, construed the guidelines of the political level had a powerful impact on events. Yet, despite everything, the founders' generation often could not help admiring the perceived audacity of the younger generation—the generation of fighters—which was taking shape before their eyes, and frequently took a forgiving attitude toward their views and escapades. Indeed, in his diary even Sharett once adopted that tone of paternal affection which was so typical of the generation of the founding fathers when referring to the native-born generation; the object of Sharett's fondness was Lieutenant Colonel Mattityahu Peled (later a major general), who in a lecture attended by Ben-Gurion and Sharett said that the army found the twisting border with Jordan impossible and demanded that it be replaced by a straight line. He added that the army was bent on a war in order to capture the rest of the western Land of Israel.[46]

Throughout this period, Ben-Gurion and Dayan continued to chip away at Sharett's policy. Dayan's standing became so strong that on one occasion, after Sharett retracted his approval for a reprisal raid in Egypt, Dayan obeyed, recalled the troops—which were already in the field—and rushed to Jerusalem to tender his resignation.[47] Dayan's gesture (the resignation was, of course, rejected) enabled Ben-Gurion to challenge Sharett openly, on an either-or basis; henceforth the militaristic policy of Ben-Gurion and Dayan would be implemented in practice.

On October 23, 1955, Ben-Gurion decided that Israel must go to war. Dayan welcomed the decision and began preparing the army vigorously. Leaves were canceled, officers' courses were postponed, the Southern Command, previously eliminated owing to budget constraints, was reestablished, and a brigade was formed to capture the Straits of Tiran. However, the government did not give the go-ahead for war, not so much because of opposition to the idea as for fear that Israel would be depicted as the aggressor in the international arena. It was therefore necessary to induce Nasser to launch a war, and to that end the army launched Operation Detonation.

On October 27–28, the paratroops attacked the Egyptian garrison at Kuntilla in the Sinai desert. Nasser did nothing. A few days later an Israeli force larger than brigade size went into action against the Egyptians at Al-Sabha in northern Sinai, in the largest IDF operation since the 1948 War. The Israeli troops wiped out a reinforced Egyptian battalion; seventy Egyptian soldiers were killed and fifty taken prisoner. Again Nasser did not let himself be drawn into escalation. Mordechai Bar-On, Dayan's military secretary, who kept a detailed diary of the events, writes that the assessment that Nasser planned to attack Israel in the summer of 1956 was without foundation. He also attributes the Czech arms deal more to intra-Arab needs than to any plan to attack Israel. However, the Israeli leadership disregarded such small details.[48]

Inexorably, the clock ran out. On the night of December 1 the paratroops, commanded by Lieutenant Colonel Ariel Sharon, attacked the Syrian fortifications overlooking Lake Kinneret. Arye Shalev's analysis of Israeli-Syrian relations has already been mentioned; this time the IDF seemed to have gone too far. It was a particularly violent raid in which some fifty Syrians were killed and about thirty captured. The attack was disproportionate to any Syrian provocations, and many in the leadership were stunned by its scale. Moshe Sharett wrote in his diary: "Again the impression of a lust for blood and provocation for war—no killing [of Israelis by the Syrians] preceded the operation."[49] Sharett and others became aware of the tenuous hold on the military and of the ease with which Ben-Gurion and the army decided on operations without consulting them.[50]

As Operation Detonation progressed, nearly all the IDF's reserve units were called up for training exercises during the spring and summer of 1956. Deputy Chief of Staff Haim Laskov had issued, in October 1955, stringent new orders, which became the talk of the army, to streamline the wartime mobilization of the reserves. The government set up two civilian committees to discuss whether to place the economy on an emergency footing, and the Knesset passed a law for greater mobilization of civilian vehicles and heavy machinery for military purposes. A Mapai committee recommended far-reaching changes in everyday life, including new taxes, moving up the final examinations for high school seniors, banning strikes and lockouts, prohibiting those bound by the Defense Service Law from leaving the country, and other measures. Not all the proposals were implemented, but they reflected the zeitgeist.[51]

But still there was no war. Ben-Gurion feared a situation in which Israel would have to fight alone. His apprehensions were assuaged when Dayan and Peres engineered an alliance with the French Army, which was looking for a way to topple Nasser because of his support for Algerian rebels against the French colonials. An alliance between armies was thus forged. Ben-Gurion felt a sense of relief, not only because of the large arms supplies that poured into Israel but also because of the Great Power auspices, afterward bolstered by Britain.

In June Sharett, the leading moderate, left the government. "Once again I asked myself," he wrote in his diary, "whether the emergence of the assumption that we are on the brink of war and instilling [that idea] in the minds of the masses may not by itself become a factor which will finally bring about war."[52] Sharett's concern was probably justified. Ben-Gurion, however, expressed the dominant policy thesis when he said: "At the moment the security problem is a serious one. . . . In our situation the Foreign Ministry should serve the Defense Ministry and not the other way around."[53]

So, from one act of violence to the next, the possibility of war loomed ever larger and more reasonable, even desirable and necessary, the product of a "no-choice" situation. This was the case on October 10, 1956, when eighteen Israeli soldiers and more than 100 Jordanian soldiers were killed in the most intensive battle since the War of 1948. This was the IDF's raid on the police station in the West Bank town of Kalkilya. The heavy price of the operation raised questions about the efficacy of reprisal raids as such. Ultimately the awareness of the reprisal raids' ineffectiveness brought about the war.[54]

When the Israeli-Egyptian war finally broke out, it was the army's hour—the nonpraetorian army-nation which, under Dayan's guidance, had become a powerful, offensively oriented war machine, able to determine political facts thanks to its considerable proficiency. But the war was also the nation's hour. Jewish citizens were quickly mobilized, with the help of civil institutions like town halls or the Egged bus company. Soon, no men of military age were to be seen on the streets. Many absented themselves from work, and public transportation came to a halt. The well-oiled machine of the army-nation and the nation-in-arms functioned efficiently to wage a quick, offensive, and successful war.

Since the victory, too, belonged to the entire nation, the nation's past was immediately evoked. Fourteen hundred years earlier, Ben-Gurion told the Knesset, Jewish independence had existed on the island of Yotvata (Tiran), south of Eilat, which had been "liberated" two days before. The IDF was extolled by the prime minister as a savior, its successes attributed to a kind of miracle: "Military historians will study closely the secret of the wonderful operation that was executed by the IDF within a few days," Ben-Gurion emoted.[55] In the press, articles began to appear about Israel's historic right to the Sinai Peninsula. *Davar*, the paper of the ruling party, described the city of Gaza and Sinai as "the cradle of our transformation into a nation and harbingers of hopes for the future."[56] The nation's historical attachment to Mount Sinai was also reiterated (notwithstanding that the exact location of the biblical Mount Sinai is unknown). But no one outdid Ben-Gurion. In a message delivered at a military ceremony summing up the fighting at Sharm e-Sheikh, he stated that the soldiers had "stretched out a hand to King Solomon" and that the occupied areas would become part of Israel, part of "the third Jewish kingdom." The message was replete with biblical expressions and images, including a quotation from the Song of the Sea which warns other nations that Israel is strong and triumphant because the Lord is with them.[57] Hadari-Ramage is probably right in claiming that the labor movement—which has usually been considered a secular, rational, and sober socialist political movement—displayed unexpected messianic characteristics. Analysis of the public thought of the Sinai Campaign reveals from the labor movement an ecstatic, orgiastic, and even "manic" outburst of feelings.[58]

In the Sinai campaign wars, religion, and territory were already closely connected. What stands out here, as well, is the absence of an alternative approach to the one that gradually took shape during the decade that preceded the state's establishment. Amid the general euphoria that reigned after the Sinai campaign, the voices of the few who were critical of the war were naturally muted. Muted too was the prophecy of Sharett, who wrote in his diary: "His [Ben-Gurion's] appetite grows with the eating. At first it was said that we had entered the fray and conquered what we conquered in order to root out nests of murderers and destroy the bases of their senders. Now, though, we have already invaded not only Sinai but the recesses of primeval history and we have forged a new Torah to prove that this territory is fundamentally ours. If these islands belong to the Jewish people from ancient times, why should the lot of

Mount Sinai itself be any less? But Mount Sinai is ours, so what about the great river, the Euphrates?"[59] Israel finally was forced to withdraw from Sinai under pressure of the U.N. and the Great Powers. Perhaps Ben-Gurion learned a lesson; his views became more moderate afterward. But the "way of the gunsight," which after the state's establishment took the form of the cultural militarism of the nation-in-arms and the militaristic politics of the leadership, continued to serve for years afterward.

Epilogue

Israeli militarism was forged in the crucible of the relationship between two groups: young fighters in status groups who aspired to achieve recognition, prestige, and political influence and the veteran leadership, which, after disentangling itself from a coil of internal political disputes, sought to impose its authority on society at large. Relations between the young fighters and the leadership, as they took shape through the decade, finally brought about a kind of trade-off, involving a connection between the existence of militarism and the nonexistence of praetorianism. The essence of the transaction was that the army obtained considerable autonomy and became an influential factor in politics but never posed a praetorian threat to the leadership. Still, to extol Israel for not having turned into a barracks state despite everything is problematic if it ignores the other side of the equation. True, praetorianism was muted, but militarism in both the cultural and the political sense was rife.

Israel's founding fathers probably believed that they could keep the militaristic thrust of the native-born generation under control. In practice, though, they themselves cultivated that frame of mind and helped institutionalize it. Militaristic ideology acquired its own dynamic and was taken for granted in the newly established state. No longer dependent on its progenitors, it served the state as an instrument in constructing the nation. The result was Israel's transformation into a nation-in-arms, perpetually on a war footing. The twenty-year period beginning in 1936 saw a shift in the Israeli mind-set: the Clausewitzian conception that war is ingrained in the political process gave way to a belief in the inevitability of war as such. Conceptually it may have been a minor distinction, but its concrete ramifications were portentous.

Militarism, as the term has been used in this book, should not be confused with a love of war. Dilating nostrils at the smell of gunpowder, machismo indifference at the sight of bloodied bodies, illusory fears and self-invented enemies, exaggerated needs of an army which demand its due—such images are off the mark. Our subject, rather, is the dynamics of social processes, practices, and interactions that render a military solution legitimate, self-evident, necessary, and desirable so that it becomes integral to the formulation of national policy.

The distinctive character of Israeli militarism as it emerges from this analysis can be broken down into several parts. First, it seeks persistently to apply military solutions to national problems, unaccompanied by coup attempts. Second, this militarism lacks class, party, or sectoral roots; it crosses borders among Israel's Jews: between Right and Left, religious and secular, Oriental and Ashkenazi, new immigrants and veteran residents. Third, it is practical and concrete—"don't talk, just do"—rather than ceremonial and declarative. Fourth, its voluntaristic nature imbues it with strength and resilience without affecting its underlying foundation of duty and coercion. Fifth, it is a militarism of the state (and previously of the state-in-the-making), bearing ethical, primordial, communal, and militialike elements; in other words, it is effectively a militarism of both rulers and ruled. Sixth, it thrives on a blurring of the distinction between the sectors of the military and the civilian. Seventh, it is a product of interaction between army and politics, often appearing as civilian militarism. And eighth, since the 1950s it has manifested itself as the nation-in-arms.

The outcome of the Sinai War did not undermine the nation-in-arms model. As early as 1959 Israel found itself involved in a series of violent clashes with Syria over control of the Jordan River waters which in retrospect could be seen as the overture to later events on a much wider scale. Indeed, these incidents represented a trial run, as it were, in advance of a comprehensive war, and gave the army an opportunity to prove itself after some years of quiet.[1] By 1967 Israel was already involved in another war.

The evolution of the nation-in-arms attained its zenith in the aftermath of the Six-Day War of 1967, though its element of cultural militarism was manifested in the weeks leading up to the war. At the time, Egypt had a defense pact with Syria obligating it to aid the latter should it be attacked. In May 1967 Egyptian forces moved into the Sinai Peninsula and ordered the United Nations force there to leave. The IDF mobilized the entire reserve army, bringing the economy to a virtual halt, but the government, under Prime Minister Levy Eshkol, equivocated and finally decided to exhaust the diplomatic process first. The government quickly discovered, however, that it was not the only player on the field.

As the waiting period dragged on, the IDF High Command put relentless pressure on the political leadership to choose the military solution. "The General Staff wavered over how much time 'to give' the government to exhaust the prospect of finding a political solution to the crisis," wrote Ezer Weizman, then deputy chief of staff, who became president of Israel in 1993. "Not, heaven forbid, that anyone imagined taking action contrary to the view of the government, should its hesitations persist . . . but only as a recommendation." Weizman backed up his recommendation by throwing his rank insignia on Eshkol's desk as he stalked out of the prime minister's office after threatening to resign.[2] Yet the army displayed not a hint of praetorianism. Generals in nations-in-arms have more effective ways to exert influence and get their way than resorting to military coups as a political weapon.[3]

The senior officers were also riding the tide of a surging public opinion, which placed little trust in the hesitant civilian, Eshkol. Under pressure of the public—which had long since become part of the nation-in-arms—the government decided to appoint Moshe Dayan as defense minister and to form a government of national unity. The native-born Dayan was the embodiment of the self-confident Israel. A political hawk and former IDF chief of staff, he had no qualms about implementing military solutions in response to political problems. The national-unity government, which included the right-wing faction led by Menachem Begin, gave expression not only to universally shared fears but also to the view that the country must unite and resolve the political dilemma which had arisen by the use of force. Throughout the 1950s the right-wing parties had urged military action to deal with political quandaries, and their co-option to the government was tantamount to approval of their demands.

The war itself seemed to vindicate this course of action. Within less than a week Israel had defeated the Arab armies and conquered huge stretches of territory. In the wake of the victory, the nation-in-arms adopted a view of reality that fused rationalization—the need for "strategic depth" or "territories as a keepsake for peace"—with a national-religious outlook. Its proponents spoke of the "liberation" of the Jewish people's ancestral land, attesting to the advent of the messianic era. Redemption was at hand. Few questioned Israel's ability to control such extensive territories and to rule another people, or called for the IDF's withdrawal in return for peace.[4]

In the "six years of empire," as one journalist dubbed the period from 1967 to 1973, the war-hero generals became objects of sweeping admiration and emulation. They were also conspicuous for their ostentatious life-style—a new phenomenon in a country which had just emerged from an extended economic crisis—marked by frequent visits to luxury restaurants, rubbing elbows with top models, hobnobbing with politicians, and being mentioned regularly in gossip columns.[5] The public atmosphere showed unmistakably that Israelis revered military solutions. The Israeli Air Force, which had excelled in the war, earned the greatest prestige; its slogan, "The Best to the Air Force," was accepted as self-evident by the Israeli public. Before the war the Israeli philosopher Natan Rotenstreich had expressed outrage at the idea of linking a universal value with a military corps, suggesting instead: "The best to the good, the pilots to the Air Force." But in the war's aftermath a local journalist, Shabtai Teveth, said that the intellectuals should get down on their knees and beg forgiveness from the air force's commander.[6]

Perhaps the most striking manifestation of the near awe in which the army was held in this period was the emergence of a fascinating pattern in which just-retired senior IDF officers made an instant transition to politics, a process which came to be known as "parachuting." Indeed, many of Israel's prime ministers and cabinet ministers had impressive military careers before entering politics. Interviews with them invariably exposed their conception that in Israel politics is the continuation of the military and that the military skills and values they bring to politics— efficiency, integrity, determination, courage, and unequivocal solutions to problems—are qualities not found in the average Israeli politician.[7]

The parachuting phenomenon exposed a flaw in Israeli democracy but generated no public backlash—the public, long habituated to the porous character of the boundaries between the military, social, and political spheres, did not view such occurrences as representing a drastic transition between two completely separate worlds. From a sociological perspective, additional mechanisms also helped dissolve the boundary between the military and the social (noncivil) in Israel. An example is the IDF's project of absorbing new immigrants and teaching them Hebrew, using specially trained female soldiers. For the "underprivileged" there were special programs to rehabilitate slum youngsters, many with criminal records, through military service. The IDF also became active in the general culture through performances by military troupes for civilian audiences in the cities and through IDF Radio, the country's most popular station, its staff a mix of civilians and soldiers. In addition, various funds were created, the most famous known as Libi (an acronym meaning "my heart"), to raise money from civilians for the army and for security needs. More informal mechanisms, such as parents' committees, enabled soldiers' parents to become more involved in the military service of their offspring. By such means the dispensing of organized violence by the society became a project shared by all, if only vicariously. Some of the mechanisms of the nation-in-arms operate to this day in Israel. But recent years have witnessed changes that are fraught with significance.

Incipient changes in the status of the nation-in-arms were discernible in the wake of the 1973 Yom Kippur War. Even the State Commission of Inquiry that investigated the army's performance in the war spoke of a "failure," which was found to stem in large part from complacency and a "misguided conception." The commission formulated its findings in military-strategic terms, but its rationale was the same cultural militarism that had viewed the Israeli as a superman who could so easily overcome his enemies that they would recoil from any attempt to attack.[8] Nevertheless, the Yom Kippur War did not cause second thoughts about the nation-in-arms model. On the contrary, the conclusion was that if Israel had been caught unprepared, the vigilance of the citizenry must be redoubled. It took the Lebanon War of 1982 and the Intifada, the Palestinian uprising in the territories in the late 1980s and early 1990s, to bring about a tangible devaluation in the model of the mobilized society. These events altered the perception of the IDF's character, status, and prestige among Israelis. The sharp decline in the nation-in-arms model was manifested in the politics that separated army from society.

Oddly, the army itself bore much of the responsibility for this situation. The trend was most pronounced during Ehud Barak's tenure as chief of staff in the early 1990s. Barak discharged thousands of career officers and civilians employed by the army and slashed rehabilitation projects and other civilian programs of a cultural or educational character in which the army was involved. In the process, some of the sacrosanct elements of the nation-in-arms were violated, most strikingly general conscription. By the mid-1990s, about 30 percent of all eighteen-year-old Israeli Jewish males were not doing army service, compared to less than 10 percent in the past. One consequence of this approach has been the army's professionalization, including its adoption of "utilitarian" criteria and techniques as indices to determine the scope and character of its involvement in the civilian sector.[9] The army's needs, however, were not the only sign of the changes that Israel underwent. At that time, it was clear that young Israelis were less motivated to do army service. In March 1995 the chief of staff, Amnon Shahak, warned that Israel could pay a high price for the continuing evasion of military service.[10] The defense minister in the Netanyahu government, Yitzhak Mordechai, a recently retired general, expressed a similar concern after he visited a new recruits' base where inductees told him frankly that they were reluctant to serve in combat units. "I don't have the energy" was a characteristic remark.[11]

These trends, while not necessarily signaling a decline in militarism, certainly show its modification. At the same time there is a thrust toward demilitarization and decolonization, which is undoubtedly related to the transformation that is occurring in the Middle East and more broadly to shifting global perceptions of war and armed forces.[12] Major triggers of these processes were the collapse of the Soviet Union as a world power and key supporter of the Arab states and the peace agreements signed by Israel with the Palestine Liberation Organization and Jordan.

The Israeli army is steadily becoming less of an army-nation, and army-society relations are being recast. One example has been mounting public criticism of the IDF. The public's willingness to speak out, coupled with the IDF's deglamorization, began to gather momentum during the Lebanon War, directed first at the army's judgment in prosecuting a classic "war of choice" and heightened by its indirect responsibility for the Lebanese Christian forces' massacre of Muslim civilians in two Beirut refugee camps, Sabra and Shatila.[13] In the late 1980s trials of soldiers for excesses committed during the Intifada were widely publicized; charges included the use of brutality, unnecessary killing, violating Palestinians' civil rights, and disobedience.[14]

The IDF's senior level has also been severely censured for training accidents in recent years. Even though statistics show a downtrend in accidents, irate parents of soldiers killed or maimed in training exercises and in some cases during combat activity have organized and gone to court against the IDF. One of their major demands is for an external, neutral body to investigate such incidents—and not the army. The passions aroused by this ultrasensitive, once taboo subject demonstrate the growing rift between army and society in Israel.[15]

Latent in those examples is the possibility that with the gradual decline in the nation-in-arms model and the IDF's concomitant transformation from an army-nation into a professional force, the army might become detached and partially alienated from society, particularly under the impact of relentless criticism. In other countries, such developments would almost certainly hasten the rise of praetorianism; in Israel that still remains a conditional scenario.

The fact is that many aspects of the nation-in-arms continue to exist in Israel, most notably conscription (even if at diminished intensity), reserve service, and the informal mechanism which parachutes former generals to the top ranks of politics. Nor, strikingly, have significant antimilitarist social forces arisen in Israel, and combat units are still glorified. As long as organized violence persists—for example, in southern Lebanon—it will be premature to speak about the disappearance of militarism in a troubled country like Israel. At the same time, even the relative decline of militarism is giving rise to an unexpected danger in the form of mounting sectarianism and factionalism in the IDF, albeit gradually and almost imperceptibly.

As mentioned, the younger generation of religious Zionists did not consider the areas which the IDF conquered in 1967—particularly the West Bank of the Jordan River—as "occupied territories" to be held as a keepsake for peace. They spoke instead about the "liberation of Judea and Samaria," the "ancestral patrimony" which was the Jewish people's by right and would never again be forsaken. Jewish settlements were established in the territories very soon after the war. Many settlers consider political changes, including wars, as portents of the Jewish people's impending messianic "redemption." They are passionately opposed to any territorial compromise in the territories, since this would be to compromise Eretz Yisrael, the Land of Israel (as distinct from the State of Israel).[16]

In recent years the settlers and their supporters have been penetrating the IDF in ever greater numbers. Many of them are involved in or graduates of the *hesder yeshiva* program, which combines religious studies with military training and active service in separate units. Some are making the army their career. There is now in the IDF a stratum of ultranationalist, religious colonels who live as settlers in the territories.[17] Will this group obey government orders to evacuate and withdraw from territories and settlements, or will they heed the injunctions of their spiritual leaders against transferring any part of the Land of Israel to non-Jews? This is no hypothetical question. Apart from the fact that military coups elsewhere have typically been fomented by full colonels, in recent years propaganda films, posters, and leaflets have repeatedly called on Israeli soldiers to disobey any order to evacuate settlers. On several occasions prominent rabbis of the settlers, who exert enormous influence, have published rabbinical edicts in a similar vein.[18]

The murder of Yitzhak Rabin provoked serious soul-searching in Israel, among both the religious and secular public. But it did not eliminate sectoralism or reduce its latent dangers. Similarly, Benjamin Netanyahu's election as prime minister perhaps slowed the Oslo process but did not immediately terminate it. Under the new system of direct election of the prime minister, opponents of the Oslo accords cast their ballots for Netanyahu, only to be angered and disappointed at his actions. The possibility of a civil war, an uprising by the settlers, even a military coup fomented by the peace rejectionists has, for the first time in Israel's history, become a concrete danger. In the terms of my analysis, the root of the problem lies in the decline of nation-in-arms-type militarism, which acted a buffer against praetorianism.

Has Israel entered a post-militaristic era? Is the time of the nation-in-arms about to expire? Does the eye that observes reality now look beyond the gunsight? Will the decline in militarism exact a price in the form of praetorianism? Such questions are more easily asked than answered. But there is no doubt that Israel's destiny will hinge on the answers. Israel has the ability to face up to its past courageously and to be a partner in the construction of a new reality.

Notes

Full citations for primary and secondary sources on which this book is based are given in the notes. The primary sources were collected from various archives. In addition, the author conducted a number of interviews. The archive material is fully referenced in the notes, except for political parties and institutions, where the reference includes the archive's name, the institution, and the date.

ABBREVIATIONS

BGA	Ben-Gurion archive in Sde-Boker
CHH	Chever Hakvutzot-Gordonia, in Kibbutz Chulda
CZA	Central Zionist archive, Jerusalem
GA	Galili archive in Ramat-Efral
HA	Hagana archive in Tel Aviv
IOD	Institute of Oral Documentation, Hebrew University, Jerusalem
JI	Jabotinski Institute in Tel Aviv
KA	Kinereth archive in Kinereth
KAA	Hakibbutz Haartzi archive in Giv'at Habiba
KMA	Hakibbutz Hameuhad archive in Ramat-Efal
LA	Labor archive in Tel Aviv
MA	Mapai archive in Beit-Berl
MHA	Hamachanot Haolim archive in Ramat-Efal
SA	State archive in Jerusalem

INTRODUCTION

1. Ben-Gurion address in the International Council for the Unification of Jerusalem, April 26, 1939, *BGA*, speeches.

2. As the philosopher Paul Mendes-Flohr wrote, "Whoever accuses the Zionists of ignoring the Arab question is misinformed. In fact ... the majority of the Zionists were painfully aware of the presence of the Arabs in Palestine, and their awareness often reflected genuine moral agonizing.... Many of them were far from holding a marginal position in the Zionist movement." Introduction to Martin Buber, *A Land of Two People* (in Hebrew) (Jerusalem: Schocken, 1988), p. 15.

3. Some observers ascribe to the Zionist movement a tactical use of the term *National Home* to conceal the ambition for a state. See Christopher Sykes, *Crossroads to Israel: From Balfour to Bevin* (London: Collins, 1965), pp. 23–24; Ian Lustick, *Arabs in the Jewish State: Israel's Control of a National Minority* (Austin: University of Texas Press, 1980), pp. 29–31. The truth, however, is more complex. Israel's founding fathers were socialists who believed in the importance of laying the infrastructure, whereas the state was perceived as being part of the superstructure. Thus the Zionist Congress at the beginning of the century rejected Theodor Herzl's statist ideas and supported "cultural Zionism."

4. Gershon Shafir, *Land, Labor, and the Origins of the Israeli-Palestinian Conflict, 1882–1914* (Cambridge: Cambridge University Press, 1989); Baruch Kimmerling, *Zionism and Territory: The Socio-territorial Dimensions of Zionist Politics* (Berkeley: Institute for International Studies, 1983), pp. 1–105; Michael Shalev, "Jewish Organized Labor and the Palestinians: A Study of State/Society Relations in Israel,"

in Baruch Kimmerling, ed., *The Israeli State and Society: Boundaries and Frontiers* (New York: SUNY Press, 1989), pp. 93–132; Elia Zureik, *The Palestinians in Israel: A Study in Internal Colonialism* (London: Routledge and Kegan Paul, 1979).

5. Baruch Kimmerling and Joel S. Migdal, *Palestinians: The Making of a People* (New York: Free Press, 1993), pp. 3–95; Muhammad Y. Muslih, *The Origins of Palestinian Nationalism* (New York: Columbia University Press, 1988); Yehoshua Porath, *The Emergence of the Palestinian-Arab National Movement, 1918–1929* (London: Cass, 1974); Issa Al-Shuaibi, "The Development of a Palestinian Entity-Consciousness," *Journal of Palestinian Studies*, vol. 9, no. 1, 1979, pp. 67–84.

6. David Ben-Gurion, *Meetings with Arab Leaders* (in Hebrew) (Tel Aviv: Am-Oved, 1967); Shabtai Teveth, *Ben-Gurion and the Palestinian Arabs: From Peace to War* (Oxford: Oxford University Press, 1985); Yosef Gorni, *The Arab Question and the Arab Problem* (in Hebrew) (Tel Aviv: Am-Oved, 1985).

7. Berl Katznelson, *Writings* (in Hebrew) (Tel Aviv: Mapai, 1947), vol. 5, pp. 16–26; Mapai Center, January 9, 1940, *MA*.

8. Yehuda Slutzki, ed., *The Haganah History Book* (in Hebrew) (Tel Aviv: Am-Oved, 1954), vol. 1, p. 175.

9. "The First Volunteers Committee in Eretz Israel," in *On the Brink: A Collection about Life and Literature* (in Hebrew) (Jerusalem: Poalei Zion Party, 1918), pp. 6, 90.

10. Quoted in Yehuda Slutzki, *Introduction to the History of the Israeli Labor Movement* (in Hebrew) (Tel Aviv: Am-Oved, 1973), p. 263. On the failure of the battalions, see Igal Eilam, *The Hebrew Battalions in the First World War* (in Hebrew) (Tel Aviv: Maarachot, 1984), pp. 324–31.

11. Meir Pail, *The Emergence of the Zionist Defence Forces, 1907–1948* (in Hebrew) (Tel Aviv: Broadcasting University, 1987), pp. 9–16, 25–47; Dan Horowitz and Moshe Lissak, *Origins of the Israeli Polity: Palestine under the Mandate* (Chicago: University of Chicago Press, 1978), pp. 50–51.

12. Ze'ev Zabotinski, *Writings* (in Hebrew) (Jerusalem: Ari Zabotinski, 1953), p. 39.

13. Yonathan Shapiro, *The Road to Power: Herut Party in Israel* (Albany: SUNY Press, 1991); Yaacov Shavit, *Jabotinski and the Revisionist Movement, 1925–1948* (London: Cass, 1988).

14. See, for example, the Zionist leader Nachum Sokolov's impressions of his visit to Poland in 1934, in Yaacov Shavit, *The Mythologies of the Zionist Right Wing* (in Hebrew) (Beit Berl: Beit Berl, 1986), p. 35. On the concept of the Iron Wall (*iron* refers to weapons), which Jabotinsky developed after the First World War, see Teveth, *Ben-Gurion and the Palestinian Arabs*, pp. 55–56, 96; Gorni, *The Arab Question and the Arab Problem* pp. 229–32.

15. Gideon Biger, *A Crown Colony or a National Homeland* (in Hebrew) (Jerusalem: Yad Ben-Zvi, 1983), pp. 12–21.

16. On the idea of a transfer, see Shabtai Teveth, *Ha'aretz*, September 23, 25, 1988.

17. Elia Zureik, ed., *The Sociology of the Palestinians* (London: Croom Helm, 1980), pp. 47–63; Ibrahim Abu-Lughod, ed., *The Transformation of Palestine: Essays on the Origin and Development of the Arab-Israeli Conflict* (Evanston: Northwestern University Press, 1971), pp. 113–17.

18. Mapai Council, July 9–11, 1937, *MA*; Shmuel Dontan, *The Partition Debate during the Mandate Period* (in Hebrew) (Jerusalem: Yad Ben-Zvi, 1980), pp. 35–39.

19. Quoted in Lustick, *Arabs in the Jewish State*, pp. 34–35.

20. On the difference between ethnic and national conflict, see Anthony Smith, "Ethnic and Nation in the Modern World," *Millennium*, vol. 14, no. 2, 1985, pp. 128–32; Peter Alter, *Nationalism* (London: Arnold, 1989), p. 17.

21. Yaacov Shavit, ed., *Self Restraint or Reaction?* (in Hebrew) (Ramat Gan: Bar Ilan University Press, 1983). For more on the restraint policy, see chap. 1.

22. Ben-Gurion's speech, May 24, 1939, *BGA*, TKK.

23. Simha Flapan, *The Birth of Israel: Myths and Reality* (New York: Pantheon, 1987); Benny Morris, *The Birth of the Palestinian Refugee Problem, 1947–1949* (Cambridge: Cambridge University Press, 1987), and *1948 and After: Israel and the Palestinians* (Oxford: Clarendon, 1990); Ilan Pappe, *The Making of the Arab-Israeli Conflict, 1947–1951* (London: Tauris, 1992); Avi Shlaim, *Collusion across the Jordan: King Abdullah, the Zionist Movement and the Partition of Palestine* (New York: Columbia University Press, 1988).

24. On some of the interpretations and debates about the New Historians, see Zachary Lockman, "Original Sin," in Lockman and Joel Beinin, eds., *Intifada: The Palestinian Uprising against Israeli Occupation* (London: Tauris, 1989), pp. 185–203; Shabtai Teveth, "Charging Israel with Original Sin," *Commentary*, vol. 88, no. 3, 1989, pp. 24–33; Benny Morris, "The Eel and History: A Reply to Shabtai Teveth," *Tikkun*, vol. 5, no. 1, 1990, pp. 19–23. N. Finkelstein, "Myth, Old and New," *Journal of Palestinian Studies*, vol. 21, 1991, pp. 66–89; N. Masalha, "A Critique of Benny Morris," *Journal of Palestinian Studies*, vol. 21, 1991, pp. 90–97; Benny Morris, "Response to Rinkelstein and Masalha," *Journal of Palestinian Studies*, vol. 21, 1991, pp. 98–114; Itamar Rabinovich, *The Road not Taken: Early Arab-Israeli Negotiations* (in Hebrew) (Jerusalem: Keter, 1991); Ilan Pappe, "The New History of the 1948 War," *Theoria Uvikoret*, no. 3, 1993, pp. 99–114.

25. Morris's classic work deals with only three years. Pappe's work deals with five years. Citations for both books are given in n. 24.

26. On comparison of the work of the historian to the sociologist, see Charles Tilly, *As Sociology Meets History* (New York: Academic, 1981); Dennis Smith, *The Rise of Historical Sociology* (Cambridge: Polity, 1991).

27. Volker R. Berghahn, *Militarism: The History of an International Debate, 1861–1979* (Warwickshire: Berg, 1981), pp. 2–3; Asbjorn Eide and Marek Thee, eds., *Problems of Contemporary Militarism* (London: Croom Helm, 1980); Michael Mann, *States, War, and Capitalism: Studies in Political Sociology* (Oxford: Blackwell, 1988), chaps. 4, 6; Emilio Willems, *A Way of Life and Death: Three Centuries of Prussian-German Militarism* (Nashville: Vanderbilt University Press, 1986), pp. 1–5; Julius Gould and William L. Kolb, eds., *A Dictionary of the Social Sciences* (New York: Free Press, 1964), pp. 429–30; Baruch Kimmerling, "Patterns of Militarism in Israel," *Archives Européennes de Sociologie*, vol. 34, 1993, pp. 196–223.

28. Willems, *A Way of Life and Death*, pp. 1–5; D. Smith and R. Smith, *The Economics of Militarism* (London: Pluto, 1983), pp. 10–11.

29. K. Skjelsbaek, "Militarism, Its Dimensions and Corollaries: An Attempt to Conceptual Clarification," in Eide and Thee, eds., *Problems of Contemporary Militarism*, pp. 77–105; David Holloway, "War, Militarism and the Soviet State," in E. P. Thompson and D. Smith, eds., *Protest and Survive* (New York: Penguin, 1980), pp. 132–33; Berghahn, *Militarism*; Willems, *A Way of Life and Death*; Geoff Eley, "Army, State, and Civil Society: Revisiting the Problem of German Militarism," *From Unification to Nazism: Reinterpreting the German Past* (Boston: Allen and Unwin, 1986); Michael Mann, "The Roots and Contradiction of Modern Militarism," *States, War, and Capitalism*, pp. 166–87.

30. Karl Von Clausewitz, "War as a Political Means," in Roger A. Leonard, ed., *On War: A Short Guide to Clausewitz*.

31. See Alfred Vagts, *A History of Militarism: Civilian and Military* (New York: Meridian, 1937), p. 15.

32. The sociological concept of institutionalization refers to a process in which certain arrangements, which are determined particularistically, arbitrarily, and

coercively, are universally assented to and accepted. It is through those arrangements that common understanding is reached on the question of what is good, what is necessary, what is essential. Consequently, these arrangements exercise considerable influence on reality, particularly as they also work against alternative interpretations and arrangements. See George M. Thomas et al., eds., *Institutional Structure: Constituting State, Society, and the Individual* (Beverly Hills: Sage, 1987), p. 36. As for the possible ways in which symbolic military practices are institutionalized into cultural militarism, see Willems, *A Way of Life and Death*; George L. Mosse, *Fallen Soldiers: Reshaping the Memory of World Wars* (Oxford: Oxford University Press, 1990).

33. On the neorealistic explanation, see Michael Howard, *The Causes of War and Other Essays* (Cambridge, Mass.: Harvard University Press, 1983), p. 22; Joseph S. Nye, "Old Wars and Future Wars: Causation and Prevention," in Robert I. Rotberg and Theodore K. Rabb, eds., *The Origin and Prevention of Major Wars* (Cambridge: Cambridge University Press, 1989), pp. 3–12; Robert O. Keohane, ed., *Neorealism and Its Critics* (New York: Columbia University Press, 1986).

34. Raymond Williams, "Base and Superstructure in Marxist Cultural Theory," *Problems in Materialism and Culture* (London: Verso, 1980), pp. 31–49; Chantal Mouffe, *Gramsci and Marxist Theory* (London: Routledge and Kegan Paul, 1979); Louis Althusser, *Lenin and Philosophy and Other Essays* (London: NLB, 1977); Terry Eagleton, *Ideology: An Introduction* (London: Verso, 1991), pp. 146–50.

35. Pierre Bourdieu, *Outline of a Theory of Practice* (Cambridge: Cambridge University Press, 1977); Richard Jenkins, *Pierre Bourdieu* (London: Routledge, 1992); Roger Brubaker, "Rethinking Classical Theory: The Sociological Vision of Pierre Bourdieu," *Theory and Society*, vol. 14, 1985, pp. 745–75.

36. On symbolic practices, see Jorge Larrain, *The Concept of Ideology* (London: Hutchinson, 1979), pp. 41–49. The use of the term *practices* derives from Marxian theory. According to Michel Foucault, the concept of practices (as distinct from the concept of social practice) suggests not only the meaning an action has but also its specific order and its place in relation to other practices. See "Questions of Methods: An Interview with Michel Foucault," in Kenneth Baynes et al., eds., *After Philosophy: End or Transformation?* (Cambridge, Mass.: MIT Press, 1987), pp. 73–94.

37. On the concept of sociological generation, see Karl Mannheim, "The Problem of Generations," *Essays on the Sociology of Knowledge* (London: Routledge and Kegan Paul, 1972), pp. 297–98. As for Israel, see Yonathan Shapiro, *An Elite without Sucessors* (in Hebrew) (Tel Aviv: Am-Oved, 1984), pp. 54–65.

38. Raymond Grew, ed., *Crisis of Political Development in Europe and the United States* (Princeton: Princeton University Press, 1978), pp. 10–12.

39. The concept of generational units is taken from Mannheim's writings; see n. 37. The concept of status groups is presented by Max Weber, *Economy and Society: An Outline of Interpretive Sociology* (Berkeley: University of California Press, 1978), pp. 302–7, 926–39.

40. John B. Thompson, *Ideology and Modern Culture: Critical Social Theory in the Era of Mass Communication* (Cambridge: Polity, 1990), pp. 56–57.

41. Eric Nordlinger, *Soldiers in Politics: Military Coups and Goverments* (Englewood Cliffs: Prentice-Hall, 1977).

42. Vagts, *A History of Militarism*, pp. 13–17. For more about the distinction between the military way and militarism, see Ernie Regehr, "What Is Militarism?" in Eide and Thee, eds., *Problems of Contemporary Militarism*, pp. 127–39.

43. Samuel P. Huntington, *The Soldier and the State: The Theory and Politics of Civil-Military Relations* (Cambridge, Mass.: Harvard University Press, 1985).

44. Morris Janowitz, *The Professional Soldier: A Social and Political Portrait* (New York: Free Press, 1960).

45. Samuel E. Finer, *The Man on Horseback: The Role of the Military in Politics* (New York: Praeger, 1962).

46. For the common elements within the civil-military paradigm, see A. R. Luckham, "A Comparative Typology of Civil-Military Relations," *Government and Opposition*, vol. 6, no. 1, 1971, pp. 5–35; Samuel Edward Finer, "The Statesmanship of Arms," *Times Literary Supplement*, February 17, 1978; James Burk, "Morris Janowitz and the Origins of Sociological Research on Armed Forces and Society," *Armed Forces and Society*, vol. 19, no. 2, 1993, p. 177.

47. For criticism of the civil-military relations paradigm, see Uri Ben-Eliezer, "Rethinking the Civil-Military Relations Paradigm: The Inverse Relation between Militarism and Praetorianism through the Israeli Case," *Comparative Political Studies*, vol. 30, no. 3, 1997, pp. 356–374. A. Valenzuela, "A Note on the Military and Social Science Theory," *Third World Quarterly*, vol. 7, no. 1, 1985, pp. 132–43; Martin Edmonds, *Armed Services and Society* (Boulder: Westview, 1988), pp. 70–112.

48. On the former Soviet Union and Eastern Europe, see William Odom, "The Party-Military Connection," in Dale Herspring and Ivan Volgyes, eds., *Civil-Military Relations in Communist Systems* (Boulder: Westview, 1978), pp. 27–52; David Albright, "A Comparative Conceptualization of Civil Military Relations," *World Politics*, 22, 1980, pp. 553–76. On the Third World see Valenzuela, "A Note on the Military and Social Science Theory," pp. 132–43; Claude E. Welch, "Civil-Military Relations: Perspectives from the Third World," *Armed Forces and Society*, vol. 11, no. 2, 1985, pp. 183–98.

49. Uri Ben-Eliezer, "The Meaning of Political Participation in a Non-Liberal Democracy: The Israeli Experience," *Comparative Politics*, vol. 25, no. 4, 1993, pp. 397–412; Rebecca L. Schiff, "Civil-Military Relations Reconsidered: Israel as an 'Uncivil State,' " *Security Studies*, vol. 1, no. 4, 1992, pp. 636–58.

50. Ben Halpern, "The Role of the Military in Israel," in John Johnson, ed., *The Role of the Military in Underdeveloped Countries* (Princeton: Princeton University Press, 1962), pp. 317–57; Amos Perlmutter, *Military and Politics in Israel: Nation Building and Role Expansion* (New York: Praeger, 1969); Victor Azarya and Baruch Kimmerling, "New Immigrants in the Israeli Armed Forces," *Armed Forces and Society*, vol. 6, no. 3, 1980, pp. 22–41; Moshe Lissak, "The Israeli Defense Forces as an Agent of Socialization and Education," in M. R. Van Gils, ed., *The Perceived Role of the Military* (Rotterdam: Rotterdam University Press, 1971), pp. 325–39; Dan Horowitz and Baruch Kimmerling, "Some Social Implications of Military Service and the Reserve System in Israel," *Archives Européennes de Sociologie*, 15, 1974, pp. 262–76.

51. Baruch Kimmerling, *The Interrupted System: Israeli Civilians in War and Routine Times* (New Brunswick: Transaction, 1985). Kimmerling apparently has changed his opinion about the role of security in Israel since writing this book.

52. Dan Horowitz, "The Israeli Defence Forces: A Civilianized Military in a Partially Militarized Society," in Roman Kolkowicz and Andrey Korbonski, eds., *Soldiers, Peasants, and Bureaucrats: Civil-Military Relations in Communist and Modernizing Societies* (London: Allen and Unwin, 1982) pp. 77–106; Moshe Lissak, "Paradoxes of the Israeli Civil-Military Relations," *Journal of Strategic Studies*, vol. 6, no. 3, 1983, pp. 6–11; Dan Horowitz and Moshe Lissak, "Democracy and National Security in a Protracted Conflict," in *Trouble in Utopia: The Overburdened Polity of Israel* (Albany: SUNY Press, 1989), pp. 195–230.

53. Yoram Peri, "Political-Military Partnership in Israel," *International Political Science Review*, vol. 2, no. 3, 1981, pp. 303–15.

54. Ben-Eliezer, "Rethinking the Civil-Military Relations Paradigm."

55. Valenzuela, "A Note on the Military and Social Science Theory."

56. On Prussia-Germany, see Willems, *A Way of Life and Death*; Eley, *From Unifi-*

cation to Nazism, pp. 85–109. On Japan, see Ivan I. Morris, *Japan 1931–1945—Militarism, Fascism, Japanism?* (Boston: Heath, 1967). On France, see C. Welch and A. Smith, "France: The Frustrations of Colonial War," in Welch and Smith, *Military Role and Rule* (North Scituate, Mass.: Duxbury Press, 1974), pp. 205–33; Raoul Girardet, "Civil and Military Power in the Fourth Republic," in Samuel P. Huntington, ed., *Changing Patterns of Military Politics* (New York: Free Press, 1962), pp. 121–49; Orville Menard, "La Grande Muette," *The Army and the Fifth Republic* (Lincoln: University of Nebraska Press, 1967), pp. 10–57.

57. On the army's contempt for politics in Germany, see Willems, *A Way of Life and Death*, pp. 72–74. On Japan, see Yoshihisa Nakamura and Ryoichi Tobe, "The Imperial Japanese Army and Politics," *Armed Forces and Society*, vol. 14, no. 4, 1988, pp. 511–25. On France, see Jean-Denis Bredin, *The Affair: The Case of Alfred Dreyfus* (New York: Braziller, 1986). It is important to point out that this book does not argue for a resemblance between Japanese and German or even French militarism and the Israeli version. The classical examples of militarism and Israeli militarism have utterly different starting points. In the classical examples the enemy is often invented, whereas Israeli militarism developed in part as a reaction to a situation in which two national movements fought for the same scarce territory. As will become clear, this different point of departure brought into being an Israeli cultural militarism which bore a different character from German or Japanese militarism.

58. One should, however, take into consideration that praetorianism does not necessarily lead to militarism and that under certain conditions it is even possible to talk about nonmilitaristic praetorianism, a situation in which military regimes are too weak to solve their political problems by military means. In these situations, some scholars claim, the generals' rule is often surprisingly "civil." See Finer, *The Man on Horseback*, pp. 149–86; Stanislav Andreski, "On the Peaceful Disposition of Military Dictatorships," *Journal of Strategic Studies*, vol. 3, no. 3, 1980, pp. 3–10; Paul Zagorski, "Civil-Military Relations and Argentine Democracy," *Armed Forces and Society*, vol. 14, no. 3, 1988, pp. 407–32; Talukder Maniruzzaman, *Military Withdrawal from Politics* (Cambridge, Mass.: Ballinger, 1987), pp. 1–12; David Rappoport, "The Praetorian Army: Insecurity, Venality, and Impotence," in Kolkowicz and Korbonski, *Soldiers, Peasants, and Bureaucrats*.

59. Berghahn, *Militarism*, pp. 7–66; Willems, *A Way of Life and Death*, pp. 76–105; Vagts, *A History of Militarism*, pp. 451–52.

60. A comprehensive perspective on the term *politics* is presented, for example, by Mildred A. Schwartz, *A Sociological Perspective on Politics* (New Jersey: Prentice-Hall, 1990), p. 11.

61. On the problem of authority in Weber's legacy, see Dennis H. Wrong, *Power: Its Forms, Bases, and Uses* (Chicago: University of Chicago Press, 1988), pp. 49–52.

62. Amos Perlmutter, *The Military and Politics and Modern Times: On Professionals, Praetorians, and Revolutionary Soldiers* (New Haven: Yale University Press, 1977), p. 13; Theda Skocpol, *States and Social Revolutions: A Comparative Analysis of France, Russia, and China* (Cambridge: Cambridge University Press, 1979), p. 24; William B. Quandt, *Revolution and Political Leadership: Algeria* (Cambridge, Mass.: MIT Press, 1969).

63. Some scholars adduce other types of militarism, e.g., Kimmerling, "Patterns of Militarism in Israel," but for the purpose of this book it will be sufficient to distinguish between the two principal phenomena, praetorianism and militarism.

64. In fact, the theoretical framework which is presented in this study does not attempt to explain, but to consider the conditions of the possibility that one particular reality rather than another will be constituted. This is, in effect, to trace

the conditions that produced a situation in which what happened in a particular historical period was the inevitable, ostensibly logical, result of singular conditions, of specific modes of operation, and of the balance of forces that existed in a certain society. The linkage of all these factors was what influenced and constituted the events. See Raymond Aron, *Main Currents in Sociological Thought*, vol. 2 (London: Penguin, 1967), pp. 202–10.

65. "Forced step by step into an ever-greater defensive effort to cope with a widening circle of enmity, beginning with the Palestinians and now including the entire Arab world forcefully supported by the Soviet Union, the Israelis have been transformed into a nation of soldiers," write Edward Luttwak and Dan Horowitz, *The Israeli Army* (London: Lane, 1975), p. xiii. See also Ephraim Inbar, "The 'No Choice War' Debate in Israel," *Journal of Strategic Studies*, vol. 12, no. 1, 1989, pp. 22–37.

66. On the problematic attitude of Israeli sociology to the Israeli-Arab conflict, see Baruch Kimmerling, " Sociology, Ideology, and Nation-Building: The Palestinians and Their Meaning in Israeli Sociology," *American Sociological Review*, vol. 57, 1992, pp. 446–60. For works that present the relationship between the Israeli-Arab conflict on one hand and Israel's internal politics on the other, see Avishai Ehrlich, "Israel: Conflict, War and Social Change," in Colin Creighton and Martin Shaw, eds., *The Sociology of War and Peace* (London: Macmillan, 1987); Yoav Peled and Yagil Levi, "The Crisis That Never Occurred: Israeli Sociology in the Light of the Six-Day War," *Teoriya Uvikoret*, no. 3, 1993, pp. 115–28; Henry Rosenfeld and Shulamit Carmi, "The Political Economy of the Militaristic Nationalism in Israel," in Uri Ram, ed., *Israeli Society: Critical Perspective* (in Hebrew) (Tel Aviv: Breirot, 1993), pp. 275–327.

1. QUESTS

1. On the Palestinian Arabs during the Arab revolt, see Yehoshua Porath, *The Palestinian Arab National Movement: From Riots to Rebellion, 1929–1939* (London: Cass, 1977); Baruch Kimmerling and Joel S. Migdal, *Palestinians: The Making of a People* (New York: Free Press, 1993), pp. 96–126.

2. Yaacov Shavit, *Self Restraint or Reaction?* (in Hebrew) (Ramat Gan: Bar Ilan University Press, 1983); Shabtai Teveth, *The Life of David Ben-Gurion* (in Hebrew) (Jerusalem: Schocken, 1987), vol. 3, pp. 162–63.

3. Avidan, "By the Sword," 1939; taken from Joseph Heller, *Lehi* (in Hebrew) (Jerusalem: Keter, 1989), p. 68.

4. The handbill can be found in *LA*, handbill files (not classified).

5. Heller, *Lehi*, pp. 53–59; Yonathan Shapiro, *The Road to Power: Herut Party in Israel* (Albany: SUNY Press, 1991), pp. 43–62; Yaacov Shavit, *The Mythologies of the Zionist Right Wing*, p. 135.

6. Sykes, *Crossroads to Israel: From Balfour to Bevin*, p. 221.

7. Binyamin Eliav, *The Jewish National Home: From the Balfour Declaration to Independence* (in Hebrew) (Jerusalem: Keter, 1976), pp. 362–63.

8. See Zvi Shrudak, *Obituary Booklet* (in Hebrew) (Givat Brener: Kibbutz Givat Brener, 1976).

9. Ben-Yehuda ("Abdu") testimony, *HA*, no. 1829.

10. M. Rabinovitz ("Batz") testimony, *HA*, no. 999, 1042.

11. Sadeh talking to the Gadna commanders, July 22, 1941, *HA*, lecture file.

12. Eliahu Ben-Hur, *Memoirs 1923–1939* (in Hebrew) (Tel Aviv: Ministry of Defense, 1985), pp. 83–84.

13. Lolik Gershonovich testimony, *HA*, no. 2423.

14. Yigal Allon, *My Father's House* (New York: Norton, 1976), pp. 165–69.

15. "Venturing outside the perimeter" was the subject of Chaim Laskov's tes-

timony on the Kol Israel radio broadcast on channel 1, September 17, 1985. See also Ben-Hur, *Memoirs*, pp. 81–82; Pail, *The Emergence of the Zionist Defence Forces*, p. 45.

16. Yisraeli's address before the annual gathering on security matters in Beit Zera, Feb. 12, 1939, *HA*, Giora Shinian Archive, file no. 1; *KA* file no. 41a (no date). On the military unit, see "A Proposal to Friends" by Ben-Zion, *BGA*, December 4, 1939.

17. *LA*, Executive Committee Protocol, July 28, 1939.

18. Ben-Zion Yisraeli testimony, *KA*, file no. 14a; Yochanan Ratner, *My Life and Myself* (in Hebrew) (Tel Aviv: Schocken, 1978), pp. 300–302.

19. On the concept of sociological generations, see Karl Mannheim, *Essays on the Sociology of Knowledge* (London: Routledge and Kegan Paul, 1972), pp. 297–98.

20. Allon, *My Father's House*; Shabtai Teveth, *Moshe Dayan* (London: Weidenfeld and Nicolson, 1972); Zerubavel Gilad, ed., *The Palmach Book* (in Hebrew) (Tel Aviv: Hakkibutz Hameuchad, 1953), p. 345.

21. Yosef Tabenkin testimony, *HA*, no. 4650. See also Yonathan Shapiro, *An Elite without Sucessors* (in Hebrew) (Tel Aviv: Am-Oved, 1984), p. 117.

22. Zvi Shrudak testimony, *HA*, no. 1459; Baruch Izhar testimony, *HA*, no. 1456.

23. Adriana Kemp, "Frontier Nationalism: The Labor Movement's Discourse on Territories and Boundaries," (in Hebrew), M.A. thesis, Tel Aviv University, 1991; Zeev Zoor, "The Wall and the Watchtower Settlement Changed the Map and Reinforced the Infrastructure for State Formation," *The 1936–1939 Disturbances* (in Hebrew) (Ramat Efal: Hakkibutz Hameuchad, 1988), pp. 22–27.

24. *The Haganah History Book*, vol. 2, p. 878. For more about the meaning of the Hanita settlement, see Israel Carmi, *The Way of the Warrior* (in Hebrew) (Tel Aviv: Maarachot, 1961), p. 34.

25. *Bamaa'le*, no. 6, April 2, 1939.

26. Nathan Alterman, "The Company Song," in *The Haganah History Book*, vol. 2, p. 459.

27. Michael E. Howard, *War in European History* (London: Oxford University Press, 1976), chap. 6.

28. Ben-Hur, *Memoirs*, p. 29.

29. The letters were written by "Hacker." The first letter is from Zerubavel Gilad, ed., *A Shield in Hiding* (in Hebrew) (Jerusalem: Jewish Agency 1950), p. 301. The second letter is taken from Ben-Hur, *Memoirs*, pp. 145–46.

30. Pail, *The Emergence of the Zionist Defence Forces*, p. 51.

31. "Report on the Fosh Situation," March 15, 1938, *HA*, 16IV, file no. 21; *The Haganah History Book*, vol. 2, p. 948; Pail, *From the Haganah to IDF* (in Hebrew) (Tel Aviv: Zmora, Bitan, Modan, 1979), p. 146.

32. Quoted in *The Haganah History Book*, vol. 2, pp. 749–54.

33. "Abdu" testimony, *HA*, no. 1829.

34. *The Haganah History Book*, vol. 2, p. 964.

35. Gilad, *A Shield in Hiding*, p. 95.

36. Christopher Sykes, *Orde Wingate* (Cleveland: World, 1961), p. 158.

37. Uri Brener, *Hakkibutz Hameuchad in the Haganah 1923–1939* (in Hebrew) (Tel Aviv: Hakkibutz Hameuchad, 1980), pp. 222–25. For more on Wingate methods, see the testimony of his deputy, Carmi, in *The Way of the Warrior*, p. 70.

38. Anita Shapira, *Land and Power: The Zionist Resort to Force, 1881–1948* (Oxford: Oxford University Press, 1992), pp. 251–53. Shapira seems to adopt Allon's argumentation on the morale of Haganah's warriors, as presented by him, for example, in the Hakkibutz Hameuchad seminar for activists, May 29, 1945, *KMA*, Security Committee, 6/105.

39. "Protocol of the Fosh Gathering," January 1939, *HA*, Galili files, no. 5.

40. Ben-Gurion's letters to Goldman and Greenbaum, *BGA*, Ben-Gurion diary, March 23, 1939. See also his words in Mapai Center, May 28, 1939, *MA*.

41. According to *BGA*, TKK, May 16, 1939.

42. Ben-Gurion diary, April 29, May 1, 1939, *ABG*. See also Galili testimonies, *HA*; Carmi, *The Way of the Warrior*, 78–79; Yitzhak Avnery, "Rebellion by Immigration: Ben-Gurion's Scheme for Illegal Immigration," *Cathedra*, no. 44, 1987, pp. 126–57.

43. As Ben-Gurion noted in his diary, *BGA*, May 27, 1939.

44. Ibid.

45. Eliakim Rubinstein, "From Yishuv to State: Institutions and Parties," in Eliav, *The Jewish National Home*, pp. 136–95. Also see S. Seger, "The Origins of the Parliamentary System in the State of Israel," *Molad*, vol. 4, no. 22, pp. 327–39.

46. Moshe Smilanski, *Haaretz*, June 6, 1939.

47. *CZA*, Jewish Agency Executive, May 28, 1939.

48. On populism in general, see Gino Germani, *Authoritarianism, Fascism, and National Populism* (New Brunswick: Transaction, 1978); George Mosse, *The Nationalization of the Masses: Political Symbolism and Mass Movements in Germany from the Napoleonic Wars through the Third Reich* (New York: Fertig, 1978).

49. *CZA*, Jewish Agency Executive, June 4, 1939.

50. *MA*, Mapai Center, October 25, 1939, May 26, 1940; Yael Ishai, *Faction B in Mapai* (in Hebrew) (Tel Aviv: Am-Oved, 1978).

51. Pail, *From the Haganah to IDF*, pp. 152–60.

52. Ratner, *My Life and Myself*, p. 272.

53. See Galili's letter to Ben-Gurion, *BGA*, correspondence, May 4, 1939; Ben-Gurion diary, June 6, 1939, *BGA*; Ratner testimony, *HA*, no. 1543. Also see *HA*, Sneh files.

54. Golomb's resignation, *HA*, no. 1052/72/36.

55. Ben-Gurion diary, April 6, 1939, *BGA*; Golomb archive, file no. 37, *HA*; Ben-Gurion diary, April 30, 1939, *BGA*.

56. See letter from November (Golomb) to Avi-Amos (Ben-Gurion), Golomb archive, file no. 29, *HA*; *Haaretz*, November 15, 19, 1940; Sneh testimony no. 4681, 2049, *HA*; Galili testimony no. 4283, *HA*.

57. On the de-authorization process in sociological generations, see Lewis S. Feuer, *The Conflict of Generations: The Character and Significance of Student Movements* (New York: Basic, 1969), p. 154.

58. For example, *Bamaale*, April 17, May 19, 1939; *Sadot*, May 26, 1939.

59. Hashomer Hatzair council, June 23–25, 1939, *KAA*, (1c).10.1.3.

60. Hamachanot Haolim council, May 10, 1940, *MHA*.

61. See the testimony of the shooter, Nechamchik Avigdor, *HA*, no. 3315. See also Golomb's attitude to the incident, Yan testimony, *HA*, no. 2044.

62. Rabinovitz (Batz) testimony, *HA*, no 967. See also Munya M. Meridor, *A Secret Mission* (in Hebrew) (Tel Aviv: Ma'arakhot, 1957), p. 34; Nechemia Brosh testimony, *HA*, no. 4300.

63. Noah Dagoni, *Notes from the Acre Prison* (in Hebrew) (Tel Aviv: Ministry of Defense, 1976), pp. 146–50; Moshe Karmel, *From within the Walls* (in Hebrew) (Ein Harod: Hakibbutz Hameuchad, 1942).

64. Letter of August 12, 1940, *KMA*, security committee 1/8. See also letter of June 25, 1940, *KMA*, security committee, 7/3.

65. *Bulletin of Hanoar Haoved Center*, March 31, 1940 (LA); Hashomer Hatzair Council in Hadera, March 29–31, 1940, *KAA*, (1b)10.1.3; a meeting of Habacharut Hasocialistit activists, March 23, 1940, *LA* 439N/3.

66. *Ha'aretz*, June 7, 1939. See also a report by Berl Reptor on the demonstrations in Haifa, *LA* 58IV/7; *Yediot* no. 5,6, on March 5,6, 1940 (LA, 58IV/5). On the

slogan, see Meir Avizohar, *The Fighting Zionist* (in Hebrew) (Beer-Sheva: Ben-Gurion University, 1985), p. 50.

67. Protocol of the meeting between Ben-Gurion and the Macabi representatives, May 31, 1939, *BGA*, meetings; protocol of the meeting between Ben-Gurion and Bnei Akiva representatives, May 31, 1939, *BGA*, meetings.

68. Protocol of the Youth Organizations Conference, *BGA* , meetings, June 11, 1939. See also Yerachmiel notebook, June 11, 1939, *LA* 87/439N.

69. See a circular by the Jewish Agency to all youth organizations, June 19, 1939, *LA*, 87/439N. Also see a report made by Ben-Gurion following the meeting of June 11, *BGA*, meetings, June 19, 1939, and other meetings, *BGA*, June 25, 1939.

70. Letter from a union of religious students, "Yavne," in Raphael Gat, "The Political Involvement of the Socialist Youth Movements in Palestine 1933-1945" (in Hebrew), Ph.D. dissertation, Tel Aviv University, 1974, pp. 356-57. See also a letter from a small right-wing organization, Hatkuma, *BGA*, TKK, June 19, 23, 1939, and Ben-Gurion's reaction in his diary, June 26, 1939.

71. On his plans, Galili testimony, *HA*; Carmi, *The Way of the Warrior*, pp. 78-79; Avineri, "The Aliya Revolt." Some historians put much emphasis on Ben-Gurion's plans while ignoring the plain fact that the Zionist leader never tried to implement them. See, for example, Teveth, *The Life of David Ben-Gurion*, vol. 3, pp. 320-21.

72. Mannheim, *Essays on the Sociology of Knowledge*, p. 309.

2. THE FORMATION OF MILITARY STRUCTURES

1. *The Haganah History Book*, vol. 3, p. 72; *Davar*, June 22, 1939.

2. Ben-Jacob testimony, *HA*, no. 2887; Hillel El-Dag testimony, *HA*, no. 3882; Zadok Eshel, *The Haganah Campaigns in Haifa* (in Hebrew) (Tel Aviv: Ministry of Defense, 1978), pp. 187-90.

3. *HA*, Golomb archive, file no. 11, July 8, 1939.

4. Baruch Izhar testimony, *HA*, no. 1456.

5. Ben-Gurion diary, June 6, 13, 1939, *BGA*; Pail, *From the Haganah to IDF*, p. 177.

6. Rattner testimony, *HA*, no. 2988.

7. Mordechai Naor, *Laskov: A Warrior, a Man, a Friend* (in Hebrew) (Tel Aviv: Ministry of Defense, 1988), p. 55.

8. Galili testimony, *HA*, Galili Archive, file no. 18.

9. Avraham Negev testimony, *HA*, no. 1467; Rattner testimony, *HA*, no. 2988; Galili testimony, *HA*, Galili Archive, file no. 18.

10. Daliya Ofer, "The Nonlegal Jewish Immigration to Palestine during the Second World War" (in Hebrew), Ph.D. dissertation, Hebrew University, 1981, pp. 55-67.

11. Mapai Center, December 15, 1940; January 9, 1941, *MA*.

12. Sykes, *Crossroads to Israel*, pp. 268-69.

13. Mapai Center, December 15, 1940, *MA*; Galili Archive, actions (no date), *KMA*.

14. Hamachanot Haolim Council, December 6, 1940, *MHA*.

15. Mapai Secretariat, January 9, 1941, *MA*.

16. Jewish Agency Executive, *CZA*, March 9, 1941.

17. Mapai Center, *MA*, October 15, 1940; Jewish Agency Executive, *CZA*, November 28, December 8, 1940, March 9, 1941.

18. Jewish Agency Executive, *CZA*, January 12, 17, 1941.

19. *BGA*, TKK, September 3, 1939.

20. Jewish Agency Executive, *CZA*, September 3, 1939.

21. Mapai Center, *MA*, September 12, 1939; Ben-Gurion diary, September 25, 1939; Histadrut Executive, September 27, *LA*.

22. Ben-Ahron in Mapai's Political Committee, November 2, 1939, *MA*. Hashomer Hatza'ir's opinion was expressed in its council, March 29–31, 1940, *KAA*, (1b) 10.1.3.

23. Ben-Gurion in Mapai Center, *MA*, September 12, 1939.

24. Jewish Agency Executive, *CZA*, September 24, 1939; summary of a nonformal meeting in September 1939, *HA*, no. 1052/79/36; *BGA*, meetings, September 15, 1939.

25. Jewish Agency Executive, *CZA*, December 3, 10, 1939.

26. Dov Berger, Socialist Youth Center, July 8, 1940, *LA*; a farewell party for Hakibbutz Hameuhad recruits, July 2, 1940, *HA*, Galili files.

27. Mapai Center, July 14, 1940, *MA*.

28. Yoav Gelber, *The History of the Volunteering*, vol. 1 (in Hebrew) (Jerusalem: Yad Ben-Zvi, 1979), pp. 334–35; 260–66.

29. For example, a letter in kibbutz Alonim diary, *Alonim Diary*, September 20, 1940.

30. "Gathering of Security Activists in Beit-Hashita," July 5–7, 1940, *KMA*, security committee; Hakibbutz Hameuhad Secretariat, July 16, 1940, *KMA*.

31. *Kibbutz Afikim*, September 20, 1940.

32. Gelber, *The History of the Volunteering*, vol. 1, p. 270; Ben-Gurion in Mapai Center, September 12, 1939, *MA*.

33. Letter from Ben-Zion Yisraeli to his children, May 27, 1941, in Muki Zoor and Aronik Yisraeli, *On a Troubled Lake* (in Hebrew) (Tel Aviv: Am-Oved, 1985), p. 238.

34. Socialist Youth Convention, May 1941, *LA*, 439N/32.

35. Letter from Ben-Zion Yisraeli to Mapai Secretariat, June 30, 1941, *MA*, file 1101.

36. Volunteer movement meeting, October 14, 1941, *HA*, volunteers files 33/6; see also volunteers files 33/8; Mapai Center, July 27, 1941, *MA*.

37. Volunteer movement Secretariat, December 1941[?], *HA*, lectures files; see also Histadrut Executive, July 31, 1941, *LA*; letter from Ben-Zion, June 30, 1941, *CZA*, S25/60562; Ben-Zion's diary, November 9, 1942, *KA*, file no. 31.

38. Mannheim, *Essays on the Sociology of Knowledge*, p. 308.

39. Ben-Zion Yisraeli in the Histadrut Council, October 19, 1941, *LA*; and in the volunteers' convention, July 10, 1941, *MA*, file no. 1101.

40. Huntington, *The Soldier and the State*, pp. 30–58, 126.

41. On professions and privileges, see Randall Collins, *The Credential Society: An Historical Sociology of Education and Stratification* (New York: Academic, 1979), pp. 1–21.

42. Yehuda Ben-Avraham, *The Struggle for a Jewish Army* (in Hebrew) (Tel Aviv: National Committee for the Jewish Soldier, 1945); *The Hebrew Soldier*, October 12, 1942.

43. Huntington, *The Soldier and the State*, pp. 9–10; Eric Nordlinger, *Soldiers in Politics: Military Coups and Governments* (Englewood Cliffs: Prentice-Hall, 1977), pp. 48–49.

44. Mannheim, *Essays in the Sociology of Knowledge*, pp. 276–322; Shapiro, *An Elite without Successors*, pp. 54–65.

45. Letter from Joseph K. (end of 1942), *LA*, 439N/69.

46. Stanislav Andreski, *The Military Organization and Society* (Berkeley: University of California Press, 1971); Bengt Abrahamsson, *Military Professionalization and Political Power* (Beverly Hills: Sage, 1972); Edmonds, *Armed Services and Society*, pp. 81–86.

47. Finer, *The Man on Horseback*, pp. 22–23; Abrahamsson, *Military Professionalization and Political Power*.

48. Finer, *The Man on Horseback*, pp. 20–21.
49. Willems, *A Way of Life and Death: Three Centuries of Prussian-German Militarism.*
50. Ben-Eliezer, "Rethinking the Civil-Military Relations Paradigm."
51. Finer, *The Man on Horseback*, pp. 54–63.
52. *CZA*, National Committee, March 17, 1941; Yehuda Ben-Avraham, *The Struggle for a Jewish Army* (in Hebrew) (Tel Aviv: National Committee for the Jewish Soldier, 1945), p. 58.
53. Two letters to Galili from Ben-Aharon, January 18, 1941, March 9, 1941, *HA*, Galili archive, file no. 7.
54. "Friends meeting in Sirrera Wadi," December 27, 1942, *HA*, lectures files; Company B Bulletin, December 27, 1942; article by A. Refaeli, *The Hebrew Soldier*, December 3, 1942.
55. "From Eliezer Harrari to Friends," May 1, 1942, *LA*, 439N/70b.
56. "Friends' speeches in the Volunteers Convention," September 24–25, 1941.
57. Letter from Socialist Youth recruits, *CZA*, April 6, 1941; see also Bankover's words to the National Committee, *CZA*, National Committee, August 25, 1941.
58. "Testimonies of friends arrested in Ashrafia," December 19, 1940, *KMA*, Security Committee, 1/4.
59. Brener, *Toward an Independent Jewish Army 1939–1945*, p. 50; *To Farm or to Arm? The Youth Movements and the Palmach* (in Hebrew) (Efal: Yad Tebenkin, 1990), p. 13.
60. *To Friends* (in Hebrew) (Kibbutz Maoz Chaim Bulletin), October 21, 1941.
61. Sizling report, *LA*, Histadrut Executive, April 29, 1941.
62. Galili testimony, *HA*, no. 4283; Sneh testimony, *HA*, no. 4691.
63. "Discussion Five," *GA*, September 14, 1942.
64. Nathan Peled testimony, *HA*, no. 2675; Sneh testimony *HA*, no. 2046; Nechemia Brosh testimony, *HA*.
65. Communes meeting of Hamachanot Haolim, *MHA*, 7/2/6.
66. Galili testimony, *HA*, no. 4283; Zerubavel Gilad testimony, *HA*, no. 2971; Uri Brener testimony, *HA*, no. 4289; Meir Rabinovitz testimony, *HA*, no. 999.
67. *HA*, no. 4333; Giora Shinan testimony, *HA*, no. 4191; Zerubavel Gilad, ed., *The Book of the Palmach* (in Hebrew) (Tel Aviv: Hakibbutz Hameuhad, 1953), p. 153.
68. Shmuel Yanai testimony, *HA*, no. 4191; Dan Ram testimony, *HA*, no. 4846; Meir Rabinovitz testimony, *HA*, no. 999.
69. David Horowitz, *My Yesterday* (Jerusalem: Schocken, 1970), pp. 173–74; Yosef Tabenkin testimony, *The Voice of Israel* (radio broadcast), September 17, 1985; Uri Brener testimony, *HA*, no. 4834.
70. *HA*, Galili files, no. 18.
71. Allon, *My Father's House*, pp. 173–77; Zerubavel Gilad, *A Talk without End* (in Hebrew) (Beeri: Hakibbutz Hameuhad, 1974), pp. 74–75.
72. Shafir, *Land, Labor, and the Origins of the Israeli-Arab Conflict, 1882–1914*, pp. 165–86; Brener, *Toward an Independent Jewish Army 1939–1945*, p. 201.
73. David Livnee, *The Order: Palmach Man Memories* (in Hebrew) (Jerusalem: Mass, 1977), p. 5.
74. *HA*, Giora Shinan archive.
75. Yitzhak Sadeh, *What Did the Palmach Renew?* (in Hebrew) (Tel Aviv: Hapoalim, 1951); Yehuda Bauer, *From Diplomacy to Resistance: A History of Jewish Palestine, 1939–1945* (Philadelphia: Jewish Publication Society of America, 1970), pp. 149–52.
76. Pail, *From the Haganah to IDF*, p. 191; Bauer, *From Diplomacy to Resistance*, pp. 185–91; *HA*, Shinian files; Galili in a letter to his wife, March 23, 1942, *HA*, Galili files no. 8; Gelber, *The History of the Volunteering*, vol. 1, pp. 615.

77. *Friends Tell about Jimmi* (in Hebrew) (Tel Aviv: Hakibbutz Hameuhad, 1966).
78. Sadeh in the Hakibbutz Hameuhad Convention, October 3–8, 1941, *KMA*; and in the Hakibbutz Haartzi Convention, April 10–17, 1942, *KAA*.
79. Nordlinger, *Soldiers in Politics*, pp. 49–51.
80. "Discussion of Commanders from Company A," July 19, 1942, *HA*, no. 4876.
81. Brener, *Toward an Independent Jewish Army*, p. 135.
82. Mati Meged in *The Palmach Book*, pp. 173–77.
83. Shmuel Yanai testimony, *HA*, no. 4191; Rabinovitz testimony, *HA*, no. 4147. See also a letter from Shmuel Zemach to Shertok, July 14, 1942, *CZA*, S25/6056a.
84. *Our War*, no. 1, October 1942.
85. Levi Shkolnik in the Histadrut Convention, April 19, 1942, *LA*.
86. *Palmach Bulletin*, no. 1, October 1942.

3. HAKIBBUTZ HAMEUHAD AND THE PALMACH

1. Yonathan Shapiro, *The Formative Years of the Israeli Labor Party: The Organization of Power, 1919–1930* (Beverly Hills: Sage, 1976), pp. 196–212.
2. Anita Shapira, *Berl* (in Hebrew) (Tel Aviv: Am-Oved, 1980), pp. 124–225.
3. Mapai Center, July 24, 1939, *MA*. For more on the struggle within Mapai in the thirties, see Ishai, *Faction B in Mapai*, chaps. 1 and 2.
4. In a meeting in Ein Harod, January 7, 1940, *KMA*, 1b/6/25.
5. Hakibbutz Hameuhad Secretariat, July 14–16, 1940, *KMA*, 5/5/5.
6. Yitzhak Tabenkin's proposals, see Hakibbutz Hameuhad Secretariat, June 3–4, 1941, *KMA*; three suggestions by Ziesling, Histadrut Executive, June 19, 1941, *LA*.
7. Dayan in the Histadrut Executive, June 19, 1941, *LA*.
8. Ziesling in the Histadrut Executive, June 19, 1941, *LA*; Tabenkin in the Histadrut Executive, July 31, 1941, *LA*.
9. Yudke Hellman in Hakibbutz Hameuhad Council, August 9, 1941, *KMA*.
10. Hakibbutz Hameuhad Secretariat, June 3–4, 1941, *KMA*.
11. "Participation of the Female Comrade in the Haganah," *KMA*, Security Committee, 7/7 (1941).
12. Hakibbutz Hameuhad Council, December 26–28, 1941, *KMA*; Hakibbutz Hameuhad Secretariat, January 11–12, 1942, *KMA*; Hakibbutz Hameuhad Council, February 6–7, 1942, *KMA*.
13. Hakibbutz Hameuhad Council, February 6–7, 1942, *KMA*.
14. As explained by one of the enlistees in the kibbutz bulletin, *Ashdot*, April 24, 1942.
15. Yudka Hellman in Hakibbutz Hameuhad Convention, October 3–8, 1941, *KMA*.
16. Mapai Secretariat, April 13, 1942, *MA*.
17. Hakibbutz Hameuhad Council, April 15–16, 1942, *KMA*.
18. Gershon Ostrovski in the Histadrut Convention, April 19–23, 1942, *LA*.
19. Eshed in Ein-Harod Diary, 1942.
20. Hakibbutz Hameuhad Council, April 15–16, 1942, *KMA*.
21. Tabenkin's lecture, May 7, 1942, *HA*, Galili files no. 2.
22. Hakibbutz Hameuhad Council, August 21–23, 1942, *KMA*.
23. Ibid. See also Hakibbutz Hameuhad Secretariat, October 11, 1942, *KMA*.
24. Tabenkin, "The School and the War," *Devarim*, vol. 3, p. 105.
25. Ishai, *Faction B in Mapai*, p. 99.
26. Histadrut Secretariat, September 6, 1942, *HA*; Histadrut Council, September 7, 1942, *HA*.
27. Hakibbutz Hameuhad Secretariat, September 14, 1942, *KMA*.

28. See Zerubavel Gilad, private archive, *KMA*; *HA*, Galili's files no. 4, a letter from December 14, 1942.

29. Hamachanot Haolim Secretariat, January 17, 1942, November 19, 1942, *MHA*, 5b/1/12; Hakibbutz Hameuhad Secretariat, December 14, 1942, *KMA*; Shlomo Shva, *Run Beni* (in Hebrew) (Tel Aviv: Hakibbutz Hameuhad, 1981), p. 109. See also a letter of April 7, 1943, which deals with Marshak's methods, *CZA* J1/3575.

30. "Before the Kfar Vitkin Convention," October 1942, *KMA*, 1/3.

31. "The Danger of a Split in Mapai (1942)," *KMA*, 13E/2; report made by Tabenkin on the meeting with Ben-Gurion, *KMA*, 13E/1/4; Tabenkin's lecture in Hakibbutz Hameuhad seminar, August 3, 1966, *KMA*, 25A/7/A.

32. Tabenkin in the Hakibbutz Ha'artzi Council, April 10–17, 1942, *KAA*, 3.20.5 (2E).

33. See chap. 9.

34. Faction B protocol, March 2, 1943, *KMA*, 13E/2; Hakibbutz Ha'artzi political community, [1942–1943?], *KAA*, 5.3.(4).

35. Bauer, *From Diplomacy to Resistance: A History of Jewish Palestine, 1939–1945*, p. 308; Uri Brener Testimony, *HA*, no. 4834, Baruch Shoshani testimony, *HA*, no. 4592.

36. *The Haganah History Book*, vol. 3, pp. 376, 401–405, 464; Bauer, *From Diplomacy to Resistance*, pp. 165–66; Baruch Rabinov testimony, *HA*, no. 5093.

37. Hakibbutz Hameuhad Council, July 5, 1942, *KMA*.

38. "Talks of Haganah's Commanders," June 7, 1942, *KMA*, 25A, 5.

39. Hakibbutz Hameuhad Council, August 21–23, 1942, *KMA*.

40. Tabenkin in January 30, 1942, Galili's notebook, *GA*.

41. *Palmach Bulletin*, no. 21, August 44.

42. Zerubavel Gilad testimony, *HA*, no. 2971; Tabenkin in the Histadrut Council, November 30, 1942, *HA*, Galili's files no. 4.

43. *Palmach Bulletin*, no. 1, October 1942, p. 23, and no. 2, November 1942; *Dapim*, no. 43; David Idlin testimony, *HA*, no. 2678.

44. Brener, *Toward an Independent Jewish Army, 1939–1945*, p. 179.

45. B Company's Protocol, October 19, 1942, *HA*, Golomb files; *HA*, Galili's files, no. 8. *Igeret*, no. 2, October 22, 1942, *KAA*, 18.1.(16).

46. *HA*, Galili's archive, file no. 9.

47. B Company's Protocol, October 19, 1942, *HA*, Golomb files; "Friends Discussion in a Convention," November 10, 1942, *KMA*, Security Committee, 1/8.

48. *The Palmach Book*, p. 184.

49. B Company's Protocol, October 19, 1942, *HA*, Golomb files.

50. "Friends Discussion in a Convention," November 10, 1942, *KMA*, Security Committee, 1/8.

51. Finer, *The Man on Horseback*, pp. 26, 35–36.

52. Shura Osharowitz in Hakibbutz Hameuhad Convention, January 1944, *KMA*.

53. Meir Davidson testimony, *HA*, no. 4637. See also Munya M. Meridor, *A Secret Mission* (in Hebrew) (Tel Aviv: Maarachot, 1957), pp. 33–34.

54. *Palmach Bulletin*, no. 4 (9), December 1942; Brener testimony, *HA*, no. 4834.

55. Tabenkin, "The School and the War," *Devarim*, vol. 3, p. 118.

56. Linda L. Reif, "Seizing Control: Latin American Military Motives, Capabilities, and Risks," *Armed Forces and Society*, vol. 10, no. 4, 1984, pp. 563–82; M. Needler, "Military Motivations in the Seizure of Power," *Latin American Research Review*, vol. 10, 1975, pp. 63–79.

57. Finer, *The Man on Horseback*, pp. 28–29; David Rapoport, "The Praetorian Army: Insecurity, Venality and Impotence," in Kolkowicz and Korbonski, eds., *Soldiers, Peasants, and Bureaucrats*, pp. 242–80; Nordlinger, *Soldiers in Politics*; S. E.

Finer, "The Morphology of Military Regimes," in Kolkowicz and Korbonski, eds., *Soldiers, Peasants, and Bureaucrats*, pp. 281–309; Talukder Maniruzzaman, *Military Withdrawal from Politics* (Cambridge, Mass.: Ballinger, 1987).

58. "Friends Discussion in a Convention," November 10, 1942, *KMA*, Security Committee, 1/8.

59. Willems, *A Way of Life and Death*, p. 38.

60. "A Meeting of Hakibbutz Hameuhad Secretariat before Naan's Convention," August 16–17, 1942, *KMA*.

61. Vagts, *A History of Militarism*, pp. 456–57.

62. T. Dye and H. Ziegler, "Socialism and Militarism," *Political Science and Politics*, pp. 800–13; J. Payne, "Marxism and Militarism," *Polity*, 19, 1986, pp. 270–89.

63. Uri Ben-Eliezer and Ronen Shamir, "The Emergence of Militaristic Nationalism in Israel," *International Journal of Politics, Culture and Society*, vol. 4, no. 3, 1991, pp. 387–93.

64. Tabenkin, "The School and the War," p. 113.

65. Ibid., p. 118.

66. Ibid., p. 114.

4. MAPAI AND ENLISTMENT IN THE BRITISH ARMY

1. National Committee, April 6, 1941, *CZA*.

2. Jewish Agency Executive, October 15, 1940, *CZA*.

3. Ibid., June 8, 1941, *CZA*.

4. Ibid., August 17, 1941, *CZA*.

5. On the quota system, Gelber, *The History of the Volunteering*, vol. 1, pp. 233–42.

6. "Consultation regarding Army's Mobilization," September 1, 1940, *BGA*, meetings.

7. Mapai Council, April 27–28, 1941, *MA*; Mapai Center, July 10, 1941, *MA*.

8. Jewish Agency Executive, March 9, 1941, *CZA*; *BGA*, speeches, March 26, 1941. Regarding Ben-Gurion's decision to be a "Zionist preacher," see the Histadrut Committee, April 8, 1941, *LA*.

9. *BGA*, speeches, March 5, 1941.

10. Shabtai Teveth, *The Life of David Ben-Gurion*, (in Hebrew) vol. 3 (Jerusalem: Schocken, 1987), p. 377.

11. Mapai Center, April 14, 1941, *MA*. See also Teveth, *The Life of David Ben-Gurion*, vol. 3, p. 380.

12. Jewish Agency Executive, March 9, 1941, *CZA*.

13. Gelber, *The History of the Volunteering*, vol. 1, p. 339; National Committee, April 27, 1941, *CZA*.

14. Ben-Gurion diary, May 5, 1941, *BGA*.

15. The document from May 7, 1941, *CZA*, S25/1856.

16. Horowitz and Lissak, *Origins of the Israeli Polity*; Itzhak Galnoor, *The Origins of Israeli Democracy* (in Hebrew) (Tel Aviv: Am Oved, 1985).

17. Ben-Eliezer, "Rethinking Civil-Military Relations Paradigm."

18. "Friends' speeches in the Volunteers Convention," September 24–25, 1941.

19. For example, Golomb in a lecture, March 16, 1942, *HA*, private archive, file no. 34.

20. Dori's letter in *The Haganah History Book*, vol. 3, pp. 1865–71.

21. Jewish Agency Executive, October 4, 1942, *CZA*.

22. "A Nonformal Discussion about the Party's Situation," October 5, 1942, *BGA*, meetings; Ben-Gurion diary, October 23, 1942, *BGA*.

23. *BGA*, meetings, October 5, 1942.

24. Mapai Secretariat, October 6, 1942, *MA*.

25. *BGA*, speeches, October 13, 1942.

26. Jewish Agency Executive, October 8, 1942, *CZA*; National Committee, October 9, 23, 1942, *CZA*; Histadrut Council, December 2–3, 1942, *LA*; Mapai Secretariat, November 9, 1942, January 16, 1943, February 9, 1943, *MA*.

27. Hakibbutz Hameuhad Secretariat, December 20, 1942, *KMA*; Hakibbutz Hameuhad Council, January 1–2, 1943, *KMA*.

28. Soldiers' Convention in Haifa, October 24, 1942, *MA* file no. 1101.

29. Mapai Secretariat, December 9, 1942, *MA*.

30. Uri Ben-Eliezer, "The Politicization of Israeli Youth Movements during the Forties," in Mordechai Naor, ed., *Israeli Youth Movements 1920–1960* (in Hebrew) (Jerusalem: Yad Ben-Zvi, 1989), pp. 127–44.

31. Mapai Secretariat, December 9, 14, 16, 1942, *MA*; Mapai Center, January 20, 1943.

32. Mapai Secretariat, December 9, 1942, *MA*.

33. Mapai Bureau, December 15, 1942, *MA*.

34. Mapai Secretariat, December 16, 1942, *MA*.

35. Mapai Center, January 20, 1943, *MA*.

36. Hakibbutz Hameuhad Council, January 1–2, *KMA*.

37. "Meeting of Faction B Activists," November 7, 1942, *KMA*, 13E/1/4.

38. "Youth in the Face of the Diaspora Holocaust," January 15–16, 1942. See also a report on that gathering, *MA*, 43/6, 2.

39. Kibbutz training groups' meeting, January 23, 1943, *MHA*, 5B/1/12.

40. Hanoar Haoved Secretariat, March 7, 1943, *LA*, 213N/29; Hanoar Haoved Secretariat, April 23, 1943, *LA*, 213N/29.

41. Brener, *Toward an Independent Jewish Army, 1939–1945*, pp. 353–56.

42. Gelber, *The History of the Volunteering*, vol. 2, pp. 9–13.

43. *Kibbutz Dafna Bulletin*, July 3, 1942.

44. "Two Suggestions for Institutionalization of the Relations between the Irgun [Haganah] and the Soldiers' Federation," June 1942, *HA*, 33/9/1517.

45. Lectures files, 23–34C, December 14, 1942, *HA*.

46. Mapai Secretariat, November 9, 1942, *MA*.

47. Protocol of the Mobilization's activists in Tel Aviv, January 12, 1943, *CZA*, S25/5063; December 25, 1942, *CZA*, S25/6056. See also exchange of letters between Ben-Zvi and Bernard Joseph, January 14, 18, 20, *CZA*, J/2235; Gelber, *The History of Volunteering*, vol. 2, pp. 18–21.

48. Eliyahu Lankin testimony, *IOD*.

49. Kenneth H. F. Dyson, *The State Tradition in Western Europe: A Study of an Idea and an Institution* (New York: Oxford University Press, 1980), pp. 101–7; Charles Tilly, ed., *The Formation of National States in Western Europe* (Princeton: Princeton University Press, 1975); Charles Tilly, "War-Making and State Making as Organized Crime," in Peter B. Evans et al., eds., *Bringing the State Back In* (New York: Cambridge University Press, 1985), pp. 169–86.

50. Ronald Zweig, "Britain, the Haganah and the White Paper," in Yaacov Shavit, ed., *Struggle, Revolt, Disobedience* (in Hebrew) (Jerusalem: Zalman Shazar, 1987), pp. 141–67.

51. Mapai Secretariat, November 16, 1942.

52. Ibid., January 12, 1943.

53. "Decisions Taken in a Joint Meeting," January 15, 1943, *CZA*, S25/9245.

54. *HA*, Galili Archive, file no. 9.

55. Volunteer movement meeting with Sneh, *HA*, volunteers files, 33/5.

56. Finer, *The Man on Horseback*, p. 22.

57. Meeting of the volunteer movement with Sneh, *HA*, volunteers files, 33/5.

58. *HA*, Galili Archive, file no. 9, January 15, 1943; meeting of the volunteer movement with Sneh, *HA*, volunteers files, 33/5.

59. Gathering of units representatives from Battalion A, March 2, 1943, *MA*, file no. 1101.

60. Gelber, *The History of the Volunteering*, vol. 2, p. 155.

61. Brener, *Toward an Independent Jewish Army*, p. 410.

62. Gelber, *The History of the Volunteering*, vol. 1, p. 671.

63. *HA*, Mordechai Hadash files, no. 3, June 27, 1944.

64. A letter from Hadash to Elik, April 28, 1945, *CZA*, S25/4971. See also Yehuda Tubin, *Between the Sanyo and the Bunker in Mila 13* (in Hebrew) (Tel Aviv: Hapoalim, 1986), pp. 135–37, 140–42, 249–55.

65. Huntington, *The Soldier and the State*, pp. 80–83.

66. Regarding the possibility of civilian control of the military in the liberal sense of a separation between politics and army, see Nordlinger, *Soldiers in Politics*, pp. 13–14.

67. Moshe Lissak, "Paradoxes of the Israeli Civil-Military Relations," *Journal of Strategic Studies*, vol. 6, no. 3, pp. 6–11, and "Convergence and Structural Linkages between Armed Forces and Society," in Michel L. Martin and Ellen McCrate, eds., *The Military, Militarism, and the Polity* (New York: Free Press, 1984); Yoram Peri, "Political Military Partnership in Israel," *International Political Science Review*, vol. 2, no. 3, pp. 303–15; Horowitz and Lissak, *Trouble in Utopia*, pp. 195–230.

68. Peter L. Berger and Thomas Luckman, *The Social Construction of Reality* (London: Penguin, 1971); George M. Thomas, *Institutional Structure: Constituting State, Society, and the Individual* (Beverly Hills: Sage, 1987).

5. "IN UNIFORM" AND "WITHOUT UNIFORM"

1. Regarding romanticization of armies in Europe, see Vagts, *A History of Militarism*, pp. 17–19.

2. Max Weber, *Economy and Society: An Outline of Interpretive Sociology* (Berkeley: University of California Press, 1978), pp. 302–7, 926–39.

3. Pierre Bourdieu, *Outline of a Theory of Practice* (Cambridge: Cambridge University Press, 1977); Richard Jenkins, *Pierre Bourdieu* (London: Routledge, 1992), pp. 66–83; Braubaker, "Rethinking Classical Theory," pp. 745–75; Frank Parkin, *Class Inequality and Political Order: Social Stratification in Capitalist and Communist Societies* (London: Paladin, 1972).

4. Bauer, *From Diplomacy to Resistance*, pp. 154–57; Gelber, *The History of the Volunteering*, vol. 1, pp. 349–50.

5. See Galili in *The Palmach Book*, p. xiii.

6. Histadrut Secretariat, December 9, 1943, *LA*.

7. *Palmach Bulletin*, no. 2, 1942, p. 1; no. 5, January 1943.

8. Randall Collins, *The Credential Society: An Historical Sociology of Education and Stratification* (New York: Academic, 1979).

9. Histadrut Council, December 2–3, 1942, *LA* (Kafri saying).

10. *The Palmach Book*, pp. xxvii–xxix.

11. Eric Hobsbawm and Terence Ranger, *The Invention of Tradition* (Cambridge: Cambridge University Press, 1992).

12. See Yehudit and Zvia in "Meeting with Women Security-Activists (1942)," *KMA*, Security Committee, 1/7.

13. For the connection between women's struggles for equality in the army and militarism, see Cynthia Enloe, *Does Khaki Become You? The Militarization of Women's Lives* (London: Pandora, 1988), pp. xv–xvi.

14. J. Manza, "Classes, Status Groups, and Social Closure," *Current Perspectives in Social Theory*, vol. 12, 1992, pp. 275–302.

15. Yitzhak Rabin, *Service Diary* (in Hebrew) (Tel Aviv: Maariv, 1979), p. 33.

16. From "Bulgarians," an article by the Palmach Information Bureau, *LA*, 16/18.

17. Allon in the Hakibbutz Hameuchad Seminar for delegates, May 29, 1945, KMA, Security Committee, 6/105. See also The Palmach Book, p. 460.

18. Zvia in "Seminar Meeting with Women-Activists in Security (1942)," KMA, Security Committee, 1/7.

19. Palmach Bulletin, no. 40, March 1946.

20. See Azriyahu Ornan, one of Palmach's "politruks, in the Hakibbutz Hameuhad Convention, January 14–21, 1944, KMA. On the difficulties of the city dwellers in the Palmach, see B. Zoor testimony, HA, no. 1103. On the difficulties of the Moshavim members, see Nechemia Ginzburg in Hakibbutz Hameuhad Convention, January 14–21, 1944, KMA.

21. S. N. Eisenstadt, Differentiation and Social Stratification (in Hebrew) (Jerusalem: Magnes, 1979), 83–93; Collins, The Credential Society, p. 58.

22. Histadrut Council, December 2–3, 1942, LA.

23. Bamahane, no. 59, May 1, 1942, no. 60, June 5, 1942. For the nationalist meaning of hiking in the European youth movements, see George L. Mosse, Fallen Soldiers: Reshaping the Memory of the World Wars (New York: Oxford University Press, 1990), pp. 114–19.

24. A letter from Hanoar Haoved Secretariat, April 3, 1945, LA, IV213, I246.

25. Hamachanot Haolim Secretariat, January 24, 1947, KMA 9/3/1.

26. Elliot Oring, Israeli Humor: The Content and Structure of the Chizbat of the Palmach (Albany: SUNY Press, 1981).

27. The History of the Haganah, vol. 3, p. 464.

28. "Haganah and Palmach Course of Indoctrination," August 2, 1943, HA, Galili files, no. 15.

29. Braubaker, "Rethinking Classical Theory," pp. 745–75.

30. Dan Even, Service Years (in Hebrew) (Tel Aviv: Milo, 1973), pp. 81–84.

31. The Hebrew Soldier, December 23, 1943; Kibbutz Yagur Diary, January 19, 1943; The Hebrew Soldier Word, April 6, 1943.

32. Arie Phichman, "A Hebrew Soldier Notebook," LA, 439N/70B.

33. See, for example, The Hebrew Soldier, December 23, 1943.

34. See chap. 12. Also see Uri Ben-Eliezer, "A Nation-in-Arms: State, Nation, and Militarism in Israel's First Years," Comparative Studies in Society and History, vol. 37, no. 2, 1995, pp. 264–85.

35. Yae'l 468 Diary, no. 50, July 9, 1943.

36. From Dany G. to officer Shlomo, December 4, 1942, HA, volunteers files, 33/10.

37. See a report from August 5, 1943, HA, Galili archive, file no. 3.

38. HA, volunteers files, 33/8 (November 5, 1943).

39. Chaim Nadav diary, October 14, 1943, HA, Nadav archive.

40. On the terms use-value and symbolic-value, see Pierre Bourdieu, "Cultural Reproduction and Social Reproduction," in Richard Brown, ed., Knowledge, Education, and Cultural Change (London: Tavistock, 1973), pp. 71–113.

41. "The Hebrew Battalions in Struggle," 1943, HA. See also a letter from G. M-b, August 1, 1943, HA, Golomb files no. 31; HA, Galili files, no. 3 a report to R. from Gershon (Dan), October 4, 1943.

42. Perlmutter, The Military and Politics in Modern Times, p. 24.

43. For the term status politics, see Seymour M. Lipset, "The Sources of the Radical Right," in Daniel Bell, ed., The Radical Right (New York: Doubleday, 1955), pp. 166–234; Richard Hofstadter, "The Pseudo-Conservative Revolt," in ibid., pp. 33–35; Joseph Gusfield, Symbolic Crusade: Status Politics and the American Temperance Movement (Urbana: University of Illinois Press, 1963).

44. Galili in the Histadrut Convention, April 19–23, 1942, LA.

45. Kibbutz Ashdot Bulletin, May 23, 1942; see also Eva Tabenkin in Kibbutz Ein-Harod Bulletin, June 1942.

46. Hakibbutz Hameuhad Convention, January 14–21, 1944, *KMA*.

47. Idelson in the Movement Center in Yagur, October 17, 1942, *HHA*, 5B/1/12.

48. Shertok in the First Seminar for Lecturers, September 28, 1942, *HA*, Shertok private archive.

49. Gelber, *The History of Volunteering*, vol. 1, p. 361.

50. *BGA*, speeches, October 30, 1942.

51. Mapai Secretariat, December 9, 1942, *MA*.

52. "Party Activists in Hakibbutz Hameuhad," *HA*, Golomb private archive, June 19, 1944 (Golomb referred to the 1942 dispute).

53. Kibbutz training groups in Yagur, January 20, 1943, *Yalkut*, no. 6.

54. "Party activists in Hakibbutz Hameuhad," *HA*, Golomb private archive, June 19, 1944.

55. Histadrut Council, *LA*, September 7, 1942.

56. Concerning this mixture of haughtiness and whining, see also Shapira, *Berl*, p. 682.

57. *BGA*, speeches, April 25, 1943.

58. A description of the "in uniform/without uniform" debate that ignores the dimension of status politics and cultural production can be found in Yoav Gelber, "Standing Army against Underground, the Constitution of the Yishuv's Military Force during the Second World War," *Kathedra*, no. 13, 1979, pp. 143–69. Cf. Uri Brener, "With Uniform and without Uniform: Hakibbutz Hameuhad and Mobilization to the British Army," *Kathedra*, no. 13, pp. 169–75.

59. Hanoar Haoved Center, September 19, 1942, *LA* 213N/23.

60. Duvdevani in Hakibbutz Hameuhad Council, January 1–2, 1943.

61. Hamachanot Haolim Center, October 17, 1942, *HHA*, 5b/1/12.

62. Gathering of Hakibbutz Hameuhad enlistees, April 21, 1943, *GA*, file no. 9.

63. Volunteers meeting, November 29, 1942, *HA*, volunteers files 5/33. See also chap. 6.

64. Hakibbutz Hameuhad Council, January 1–2, 1943.

65. A proclamation to the Hebrew Youth, *HA*, Galili files, no. 14.

66. Soldiers Gathering, January 17, 43, *KAA*, 22.1.18.

67. "Youth in the Face of the Diaspora Holocaust," January 15, 1943.

68. In Hamachanot Haolim Gathering, *BGA*, speeches, February 8, 1943.

69. Hamachanot Haolim Center, April 2–3, 1943, *MHA*, 5b/1/1.

70. On status and conventions, see Weber, *Economy and Society*, p. 324.

6. THE HOLOCAUST AND THE BILTMORE DECLARATION

1. *Bamahane* (Company 12 Bulletin), December 9, 1942, p. 3. See also S. Lavi, "To the Frontline," *Yae'l 468 Diary*, December 4, 1942.

2. Dina Porat, *The Leadership in a Trap* (in Hebrew) (Tel Aviv: Am Oved, 1986), pp. 124–50.

3. Volunteers meeting, November 29, 1942, *HA*, volunteers files 5/33.

4. *The Hebrew Soldier*, February 7, 1943.

5. Mapai Secretariat, November 24, 1942, *MA*; Histadrut Executive, November 25–26, 1942, *LA*; Jewish Agency Executive, November 29, 1942, *CZA*.

6. The leaflet appears in Porat's book; see n. 3 (no page is marked).

7. A letter to Captain Obrein (Abba Eben), *HA*, volunteers files 10/33, December 7, 1942; meeting of volunteer activists, November 30, 1942, *HA*, volunteers files, 5/33.

8. Regarding the registration, see a letter written by Shorer, December 7, 1942, *HA*, volunteers files, 10/333.

9. *The Hebrew Soldier*, December 23, 1942.

10. Manza, "Classes, Social Groups, and Social Closure."

11. "Youth in the Face of the Diaspora Holocaust," January 15, 1943.

12. Hamahanot Haolim seminar, September 20–October 7, 1941, *MHA*, 10F/1/21.

13. A representative of Gordonia in the Hamahanot Haolim Council, April 3–6, 1945, *MHA*, 2/1/4.

14. *Palmach Bulletin*, October 16, 1973 (KMA).

15. John Breuilly, *Nationalism and the State* (New York: St. Martin's, 1982), pp. 344–48.

16. "Youth in the Face of the Diaspora Holocaust," January 15, 1943.

17. *Bama'avak*, September 1946, p. 13.

18. "In the Eyes of Our Soldier," *Leachdut Haavoda*, no. 35, March 7, 1945.

19. *Bama'avak*, September 1946.

20. Communes seminar of Hamahanot Haolim, October 6, 1943, *MHA*, 7/1/1B.

21. Words spoken in 1944 and published in *Molad*, 1949, vol. 2, no. 10, pp. 226–29. See also Shapira, *Berl*, vol. 2, pp. 664–73; Avraham Zivyon, *The Jewish Portrait of Berl Kazanelson* (in Hebrew) (Tel Aviv: Hapoalim, 1984).

22. Shapira, *Land and Power*, pp. 343–45.

23. Michel Foucault, *Power/Knowledge: Selected Interviews and Other Writings, 1972–1977* (New York: Pantheon, 1980); Michael Waltzer, "The Politics of Michel Foucault," in David C. Hoy, ed., *Foucault: A Critical Reader* (New York: Blackwell, 1986), pp. 51–67. On this form of domination in the Yishuv and the Israeli state, see Uri Ben-Eliezer, "Israel's Myth of Pioneering and the Elusive Distinction between Society and State," *Megamot*, vol. 37, no. 2, 1996, pp. 207–228.

24. For Ben-Gurion's declaration, see chap. 1; for Berl's declaration, see his *Writings* (in Hebrew) (Tel Aviv: Mapai, 1947), vol. 5, pp. 16–26. Also see Mapai Center, January 9, 1940, *MA*.

25. The Zionist Executive meeting, October 15, 1942, S25/293, November 10, 1942, S25/294, CZA.

26. "The Pros and Cons in Biltmore," *Herut*, vol. 8, February 15, 1943.

27. Norman Rose, *Chaim Weizmann: A Biography* (New York: Viking, 1986), pp. 381–82.

28. Sykes, *Crossroads to Israel*, pp. 281–85.

29. Soldiers convention, January 17, 1943, *KAA*, 22.1.18.

30. Rose, *Chaim Weizmann*, pp. 381–82.

31. Bauer, *From Diplomacy to Resistance*, pp. 259–61.

32. Nachum Sarig in Hamahanot Haolim gathering, December 4, 1942, in Itzhak Kafkafi, ed., *Hamachanot Haolim's Years* (in Hebrew) (Tel Aviv: Hakibbutz Hameuhad, 1985), vol. 2, p. 335.

33. Ezra Zohar in *HA*, file no. 4766.

34. *Al Hameducha*, December 1942.

35. Essay written by Mati Meged in the prison, *HA*, Galili archive, no. 20.

36. Mapai Center, March 16, 1942, *MA*; a report on that meeting by the Socialist Youth representatives, *LA*, 439IV/69.

37. Gelber, *The History of the Volunteering*, vol. 2, pp. 23–45; *The Haganah History Book*, vol. 3, no. 1, pp. 182–86. See also Mapai Political Bureau, March 2, 1944, *MA*.

38. *BGA*, speeches, September 25, 1943.

39. Socialist Youth gathering, October 21, 1943, *LA*, 439N.

40. Communes Seminar, October 6, 1943, *MHA*, 7/1/21.

41. Ibid.

42. Yosef Idelberg testimony, *HA*, no. 3923. See also Boaz Evron, in *Yediot Acharonot*, March 2, 1984.

43. Palmach's Company E Bulletin, no. 2, August 1943 (HA).

44. Histadrut Secretariat, December 9, 1943, *LA*.

45. *HA*, Galili archive, file no. 17.

46. *Bama'avak*, September 1946.

47. *Herut*, February 15, 1943, no. 8.

48. *Al Hameducha*, December 1944, pp. 11–12.

49. Pierre Bourdieu, "The Social Space and the Genesis of Groups," *Theory and Society*, no. 14, 1985, pp. 723–44.

50. Hakibbutz Hameuhad Convention, January 1944, *KMA*.

51. Finer, *The Man on Horseback*, pp. 20–21.

52. Regarding the meeting, see Shavit, *The Mythologies of the Right*; Shapiro, *The Road to Power*, p. 67.

53. Yehoshua Porath, *The Biography of Yonathan Ratosh* (in Hebrew) (Tel Aviv: Machbarot Lesifrut, 1989). See also Yaakov Shavit, *From Hebrew to Canaanite* (in Hebrew) (Jerusalem: Domino, 1984).

54. "A Letter to the Hebrew Youth" was published in Yonathan Ratosh, *From Victory to Defeat* (in Hebrew) (Tel Aviv: Hadar, 1976), p. 349.

55. Uzi Ornan testimony, *IOD*; Porath, *The Biography of Yonathan Ratosh*, pp. 188–89.

56. *JI*, 1/3/4–5. For more on the influence of Ratosh's ideas on Lehi, see Shavit, *From Hebrew to Canaanite*, p. 83.

57. Yonathan Ratosh, *Jewish Literature in the Hebrew Language* (in Hebrew) (Tel Aviv: Hadar, 1982); Ratosh, *From Victory to Defeat*, pp. 12–13; Uri Avineri, "The Truth about the Canaanite," *Proza*, August-September, 1977.

58. Baruch Kurtzveil, "The Essence and Origins of the 'Young Hebrews' Movement," *Our New Literature: Continuation or Revolution* (in Hebrew) (Jerusalem: Schocken, 1959), pp. 270–300.

59. Reuven Kritz, *The Literature of the Generation That Fought for Independence* (in Hebrew) (Kiryat Motzkin: Pora, 1978), pp. 10–12; Nurit Gertz, *Chirbat Chizaa and the Next Morning* (in Hebrew) (Tel Aviv: Hakibbutz Hameuchad, 1983), pp. 17–18; Azriel Uchmani, "A Test of Our Literature," *Orlogin*, no. 1, December 1950, pp. 22–33.

60. Porath, *The Biography of Yonathan Ratosh*, p. 189.

61. For the content of the radio station announcement, see *LA*, 12/58. See also a report about it by the Haganah's intelligence service, January 19, 1943, *HA*, no. 1052/79/44.

62. Am Lohem (*HA*).

63. About F Company, see Mati Meged testimony, *HA*, no. 2596; Ezra Zohar testimony, *HA*, no. 7426; Israel Libratovski testimony, *HA*, no. 4631; Mati Peled testimony, *HA*, no. 4585.

64. Yosef Idelberg, *HA*, no. 3923.

65. Lisya Galili in "The Haganah and Palmach Course of Indoctrination," July 21, 1943, *HA*, Sneh files.

66. Zvi Yehuda in the Histadrut Secretariat Executive, November 11, 1944, *LA*.

67. Protocol of party members' convention in Haifa, October 24, 1942, *MA*, file 1101; Zvi Shiloah, *A Big Country for a Great Nation* (in Hebrew) (Tel Aviv: Otpaz, 1970), pp. 30–37.

68. Protocol of Revisionist Soldiers' meeting, October 17–18, 1942, *JI*, I/17. See also Gelber, *The History of the Volunteering*, vol. 2, pp. 157–58.

69. Shapiro, *The Road to Power*, pp. 63–83; Shavit, *The Mythologies of the Right*, chap. 1.

70. A report of the Haganah Intelligence Service, May 19, 1943, *HA*, 1052/79/44; David Niv, *The History of the IZL*, vol. 3 (in Hebrew) (Tel Aviv: Klauzner, 1976), pp. 256–57.

71. Letter of resignation, December 1, 1943, *HA*, Golomb files, no. 13.

72. Eliahu Lenkin testimony, *IOD*; Eliyahu Lenkin, *The Story of the Altalena Commander* (in Hebrew) (Tel Aviv: Hadar, 1967), p. 54; Eliahu Mazdi testimony, *JI*; a report by the Haganah Intelligence Service, May 19, 1943, *HA*, no. 1052/79/44.

73. Luvotzki testimony, *IOD*; Luvotzki testimony, *HA*, no. 3660.

74. *Hamashkif*, June 4, 1943 (JI).

75. Luvotzki, *IOD*.

76. Eliyahu Ravid testimony, *JI*. See also Shlomo Reznik, "An Underground Movement in a Sectorial Society: A Social Portrait of Lehi" (in Hebrew), M.A. thesis, Bar-Ilan University, pp. 169–74; Geula Cohen testimony, *IOD*; Geula Cohen, *The Story of a Warrior* (in Hebrew) (Tel Aviv: Karni, 1961), p. 74; Israel Eldad, *The First Tenth* (in Hebrew) (Tel Aviv: Hadar, 1953), pp. 93–94.

77. Report no. 10, by the Haganah Intelligence Service, November 19, 1943, *HA*, 59/79/44.

78. Am Lohem (HA).

79. Report no. 10, by the Haganah Intelligence Service, November 19, 1943, *HA*, 59/79/44; Am Lohem (HA); Ahron Ben-Ami testimony, *JI*.

80. *Herut*, November 11, 1943. The extracts in *HA*, Golumb files no. 13.

81. Lenkin, *The Story of the Altalena Commander*, pp. 61–64; Idelberg testimony, *HA*, no. 3923; Yaacov Meridor testimony, *IOD*, Luvozki, *IOD*; Benyamin Eliav (Luvozki), *Memories* (in Hebrew) (Tel Aviv: Am-Oved, 1990), pp. 163–65.

82. Ezra Zohar testimony, *HA*, no. 4726; Chaya Shtekelberg testimony, *HA*, no. 4727.

83. *HA*, Am Lohem file. The Sneh order is from December 7, 1943.

84. Igal Horowitz testimony, *JI*; Ben-Ami testimony, *JI*; *HA*, Am Lohem file; Ezra Zohar testimony, *HA*, no. 4766; Dov Chisis testimony, *HA*, no. 5008.

85. Yosef Idelberg, *HA*, no. 3923.

86. Letter from Natan [Peled] to Ezra, February 15, 1944, *KAA*, 8.1.18 (8).

7. SAISON

1. J. Murillo de Cabarello, "Political Elites and State-building: The Case of Nineteenth Century Brazil," *Comparative Studies in Society and History*, vol. 24, 1982, pp. 378–99. See also Cyril Edwin Black, *The Dynamics of Modernization: A Study in Comparative History* (New York: Harper Row, 1966), pp. 13–18. For the role of the Yishuv's political elite, see Shapiro, *An Elite without Successors*, pp. 28–65.

2. Ben-Gurion diary, November 11, 1942, *BGA*.

3. Regarding the increasing strength of the majority, see Ishai, *Faction B in Mapai*, pp. 122–23; about the declining role of Hakibbutz Hameuhad, see Hakibbutz Hameuhad Secretariat, April 4–5, 1943, September 19, 1943, *KMA*.

4. Max Weber, *Economy and Society*, p. 56; Anthony Giddens, *The Nation-State and Violence* (Berkeley: University of California Press, 1987), pp. 7–34.

5. *BGA*, speeches, April 23, 1943.

6. Ben-Gurion diary, March 8, 1943, *BGA*; Mapai Secretariat, May 5, 1943, *MA*.

7. Mapai Secretariat, December 1, 1943, *MA*.

8. See discussion about the leaflet in Jewish Agency Executive, February 6, 1944, *CZA*.

9. Niv, *The History of the IZL*, vol. 3, pp. 267–81.

10. Ibid., pp. 20–32.

11. Jacob Banai, *Anonymous Soldiers* (in Hebrew) (Tel Aviv: Friends, 1978), pp. 181–203; Reznik, "An Underground Movement in a Sectorial Society," pp. 218–34.

12. Jewish Agency Executive, April 2, 1944, *CZA*.

13. Mapai Secretariat, February 17, 1944, *MA*; Jewish Agency Executive, February 20, 1944, *CZA*.

14. *HA,* lectures files, Golomb in Mapai Council, June 19, 1944; *LA,* Golomb archive, 104N/22, June 19, 1944.
15. Dov Yoseph's report on the "Four Committee" meeting, February 22, 1944, *LA,* 104N/17.
16. Golomb report, ibid.
17. Jewish Agency Executive, April 2, 1944, *CZA.*
18. National Committee, February 18, 1944, *CZA,* J1/7256; *Davar,* February 15, 25, 1944, November 8, 1944; *Al Hameducha,* no. 2, 1944, p. 26; Histadrut Secretariat Executive, November 11, 1944, *LA.*
19. Stanley Cohen and Jack Young, eds., *The Manufacture of News: Deviance, Social Problems, and the Mass Media* (London: Constable, 1981); James Curran, Michael Gurevitch, and Janet Woolacott, "The Study of the Media: Theoretical Approaches," in Michael Gurevitch et al., eds., *Culture, Society, and the Media* (London: Methuen, 1982), pp. 11–29.
20. For more on this idea, see Howard Becker, ed., *The Other Side: Perspectives on Deviance* (New York: Free, 1964); Cohen and Young, *The Manufacture of News.*
21. Dov Yosef report in the "Four Committee" meeting, February 22, 1944, *LA,* 104N/17. See also a meeting of the IZL commanders, October 19, 1944, *Zionism,* vol. 4, p. 427.
22. Political Committee, March 27, 1944, *MA.*
23. The report in *GA,* "breakaways," April 23, 1944.
24. *JI,* 1/10/19, 4; Matityahu Shmuelevitz, *During the Red Days* (Tel Aviv: Ministry of Defense, 1978), pp. 150–68; *Bamahane,* no. 883, July 7, 1944; *Yediot Leachdut Ha'avoda,* September 26, 1944.
25. Leachdut Haavoda Council, October 27–28, 1944, *KMA,* 13F/1/4.
26. Discussion about this propaganda was held in Mapai Political Committee, November 8, 1944, *MA.*
27. Lenkin to Golomb and Sneh, protocol of the meeting, October 31, 1944, *JI,* 2/19, 4.
28. Seminar for security activists, January 6, 1945, *KMA,* Levite archive, 14/2.
29. Rephael Gat, "The Yishuv's Socialist Youth Movements" (in Hebrew), Ph.D. dissertation, Tel Aviv University, 1974, pp. 239–52.
30. Information Bulletin of Mapai Young Guard, no. 4, December 3, 1944, *LA,* 453 IV. On the statement, see *Davar,* November 21, 1944.
31. Youth Movement Council meeting, November 21, 1944, *LA,* 213IV-1-270.
32. *The Palmach Book,* pp. 244–45.
33. Golomb's letter to Yellin Mor, September 6, 1944, *HA,* 8/21.
34. *The Palmach Book,* part 1, p. 809; Yecheskel Avni testimony, *HA,* no. 2968.
35. Bauer, *From Diplomacy to Resistance,* pp. 324–25; Shimon Avidan testimony, *IOD;* Eliyahu Lenkin, *IOD.*
36. Allon in a lecture to Kibbutz functionaries, May 29, 1945, *KMA,* Security Council, 16/105. See also Nathan Shaham's testimony, *HA,* no. 2940, 4765; Yehuda Lapidot, *The Saison* (in Hebrew) (Tel Aviv: Zabotinski, 1994).
37. Randall Collins, "Three Sources of Radical Right," *Sociology since Midcentury: Essays in Theory Cumulation* (New York: Academic, 1981).
38. David R. Segal, *Society and Politics: Uniformity and Diversity in Modern Democracy* (Chicago: Scott Foresman, 1974), pp. 41–44; S. M. Lipset, "The Sources of Radical Right"; Erdwin H. Pfuhl, *The Deviance Process* (New York: Van Nostrand, 1980), pp. 147–59.
39. *Palmach Bulletin,* no. 23, October 1944.
40. Mapai Secretariat, February 17, 1944, *MA;* Jewish Agency Executive, May 27, 1944, *CZA.*
41. Sneh's report in *HA,* October 9, 1944, Jewish Agency files; protocol of a

meeting between Jewish Agency and Irgun representatives, October 31, 1944, *JI*, 2/19-4.

42. *Davar*, October 19, 1944; Jewish Agency Executive, November 7, 1944, *CZA*.

43. Histadrut Convention, November 20-21, 1944, *LA*; Yaacov Shavit, *Open Saison* (in Hebrew) (Tel Aviv: Hadar, 1976), pp. 95-96; Menachem Begin, *The Revolt* (in Hebrew) (Tel Aviv: Achiasaf, 1984), pp. 202-204; *JI*, 2/8/19-4.

44. Allon testimony, *HA*, no. 4853.

45. Shimon Avida testimony, *IOD*.

46. Allon testimony, *HA*, no. 4853; 3254; Sneh testimony, *HA*, no. 4681.

47. *HA*, Galili archive, file no. 14 (1944-1945).

48. *The Haganah History Book*, p. 539; Allon testimony, *HA*, no. 3254. Also his testimony in *IOD*.

49. Allon testimony, *HA*, no. 4853.

50. The Chief of Staff announcement on the operations against the dissidents: October 29, 1944, *HA*, Sneh files.

51. Pail, *From the Haganah to IDF*, p. 208; Nachum Sarig testimony, *HA*, no. 4536; Nachum Kahana testimony, *HA*, 2677.

52. *The Palmach Book*, p. 218. See also Mati Meged testimony, *HA*, no. 2596; Ami Amir testimony, *HA*, no. 5014; Oded Meser, *HA*, no. 4660.

53. *The Haganah History Book*, vol. 3, pp. 537-42; Jacob Meridor, *The Long Way to Freedom* (in Hebrew) (Jerusalem: Achiasaf, 1950); Eliyahu Lenkin testimony, *IOD*; *JI*, 9/19, 4, 6/19-4.

54. *HA*, Golomb files no. 13.

55. *The Haganah History Book*, vol. 3, p. 539.

56. Shimon Avidan testimony in *KAA* and in *IOD*; Allon testimony, *HA*, no. 4853; Pail testimony in *HA*; Y. Avni, *HA*, no. 2968.

57. *The Palmach Book*, p. 810.

58. Palmach commanders' meeting with Ben-Gurion, September 14, 1948, *HA*.

59. *BGA*, speeches, a meeting with soldiers, July 3, 1944.

60. *BGA*, speeches, September 23, 1944; *Davar*, September 25, 1944.

61. *Davar*, June 4, 1944.

62. Histadrut Secretariat Executive, September 24, 1944, *LA*.

63. Ibid., October 25, 1944, *LA*.

64. Ibid., November 3, 1944, *LA*; exchange of letters between Aram and Shertok (no dates), *CZA*, S25/6060, S25/6033, proves that Shertok did not want to disband the Palmach.

65. Hachadut Haavoda Council, October 27-28, 1944, *KMA*, 13F/1/4.

66. See chap. 12. See also Yoram Peri, *Between Battles and Ballots: Israeli Military in Politics* (Cambridge: Cambridge University Press, 1983), pp. 19-37.

67. *Bama'avak*, September 1946.

68. *GA*, a speech in Hachadut Haavoda Council, November 10, 1945.

69. *HA*, Galili files, no. 14 (1944-45).

70. *CZA*, Jewish Agency Executive, February 11-12, 1945.

71. Chaim Weizmann, *Masa Umaas* (in Hebrew) (Jerusalem: Shoken, 1949), p. 426.

72. Michael Bar-Zohar, *Ben-Gurion* (in Hebrew) (Tel Aviv: Am Oved, 1975), p. 521.

8. UNIFICATION OF FORCES

1. Bar-Zohar, *Ben-Gurion*, pp. 516-17.

2. David Horowitz, *The Birth of a State* (Jerusalem: Schocken, 1952), p. 7.

3. *Leahadut Haavoda*, no. 51, July 12, 1945, no. 53, July 26, 1945.

4. Hamahanot Haolim circular, September 27, 1945, *KMA*, 5A/8/6.

5. Ben-Gurion diary, October 7, 1945, *BGA*.

6. Eliezer Shoshani testimony, *HA*, no. 4735.

7. Letter from Yasha Eliav, December 28, 1944, *HA*, Golomb files, no. 13; Nathan Shaham testimony, *HA*, no. 2940.

8. *HA*, Golomb files, no. 12, February 1945.

9. Ibid., May 1945.

10. For more about Golomb's close ties with Lehi, see Histadrut Secretariat Executive, *LA*, November 11, 1944.

11. Concerning the change in Lehi, see Reznik, "An Underground Movement in a Sectorial Society," chap. 5.

12. Eitan Livnee, *The "Class," Underground, and Operations* (in Hebrew) (Tel Aviv: Idanim, 1978), pp. 132–34.

13. *The Haganah History Book*, vol. 3, pp. 850–53; Jewish Agency Executive, August 12, 1945, *CZA*.

14. For Sneh's telegram, see Niv, *The History of IZL*, vol. 4, p. 179; Horowitz, *The Birth of a State*, pp. 9–10.

15. *The Haganah History Book*, vol. 3, p. 813; Shimon Golan, "The Activism of the Labor Party and the Activism of the Breakaways," (in Hebrew) M.A. thesis, Tel Aviv University, 1979, pp. 70–71.

16. The agreement, *GA*, actions, October 1945; *The Haganah History Book*, vol. 3, p. 851.

17. Ben-Gurion diary, November 22, 1945, *BGA*.

18. *Eshnav*, November 20, 1945.

19. Histadrut Executive, November 14–16, 1945, *LA*.

20. Pail, *From the Haganah to IDF*, pp. 199–201.

21. *GA*, letter to Dori from February or March, 1946.

22. Pail, *From the Haganah to IDF*, p. 67.

23. Eliezer Shoshani testimony, *HA*, no. 4735.

24. *GA*, actions, a letter from Ram (Sneh) to Matityahu (Galili), July 20, 1945.

25. Berl Reptor, *Without Any Stop: Objectives and Actions* (in Hebrew) (Tel Aviv: Hakibbutz Hameuchad, 1976), pp. 273–75; Ehud Avriel, *Open Up the Gates* (in Hebrew) (Tel Aviv: Maariv, 1976), pp. 164–67; Mapai Secretariat, October 11, 1945.

26. *The Palmach Book*, p. 636.

27. Elam, *The Haganah*, pp. 202–5, 331–35.

28. Ben-Gurion's diary, November 8, 1945, *BGA*.

29. *Leahadut Haavoda*, no. 65, November 1, 1945.

30. See Mapai Council, November 30–December 1, 1945, *MA*; *Michtav Lameguyas*, no. 9 (16), December 16, 1945 (KMA).

31. Jewish Agency Executive, October 14, 1945, *CZA*; National Committee, December 5, 1945, *CZA*, S25/7159.

32. Jewish Agency Executive, September 23, 1945, *CZA*.

33. *GA*, actions; Golan, *The Activism of the Labor Party and the Activism of the Breakaways*, p. 100.

34. Pail, *From the Haganah to the IDF*, pp. 79–81.

35. *The Palmach Book*, p. 573.

36. *JI*, 1/5–4, 5/5–4.

37. Nathan Yelin-More, *Lehi* (in Hebrew) (Tel Aviv: Shikmona, 1974), p. 305.

38. *Herut*, November 1945, February 1946.

39. Niv, *The History of the IZL*, vol. 4, p. 239.

40. "Here Is My Opinion: An IZL Member Answers a Haganah Member," 1945, *JI*, 1/19–4.

41. Dov Chisis testimony, *HA*, no. 4380.

42. Antonio Gramsci, *Selections from the Prison Notebooks* (London: Lawrence and Wishart, 1971), pp. 332–33; Raymond Williams, *Culture* (London: Fontana, 1981), pp. 26–27.

43. *The Haganah History Book*, vol. 3, p. 859.

44. Golda Meir, *My Life* (in Hebrew) (Tel Aviv: Maariv, 1975), pp. 146–47; also her words in Hakibbutz Hameuhad Convention, June 7–13, 1946, *KMA*.

45. Sneh in his letter of resignation from the Jewish Agency Executive, September 21, 1946, *HA*, Galili files no. 13; Sneh testimony, *HA*, 4681.

46. *Bamahane*, July 28, 1946.

47. *Leahadut Ha'avoda*, July 25, 1946.

48. From Weizmann to Shertok, January 20, 1947, in Joseph Heller, ed., *The Struggle for a State* (in Hebrew) (Jerusalem: Shazar Center, 1984), pp. 424–27.

49. *Bamachteret*, no. 2, pp. 158–60. See also Shabtai Teveth, *Moshe Dayan* (in Hebrew) (Jerusalem: Shoken, 1971), pp. 241–42.

50. Meir, *My Life*, pp. 143–45.

51. *The Palmach Book*, pp. 572–73.

52. *Lephetach Ohalenu* (*HA*), pp. 27–28. See also *Palmach Bulletin*, no. 45, September 1946.

53. *Bama'avak*, September 1946.

54. *Leahadut Ha'avoda*, August 22, 1946 (I. Noded).

55. *Leahadut Ha'avoda*, October 8, 1946 (I. Noded).

56. Hakibbutz Hameuhad Council, September 18–19, 1946, *KMA*.

57. Reptor, *Without Any Stop*, pp. 275–76.

58. Nicolas Bethell, *The Palestine Triangle* (London: Andre Deutsch, 1979), pp. 240–44.

59. Kol Israel radio broadcast, August 16, 19, 26, 1946, in *Bama'avak*, 1946.

60. Weizmann in the Zionist Congress, in Heller, *The Struggle for a State*, pp. 455–61. See also Bethell, *The Palestine Triangle*, pp. 286–87.

61. Avriel, *Open Up the Gates*, pp. 220–23.

62. Nachum Bugner, *The Resistance Ships, 1945–1948* (in Hebrew) (Tel Aviv: Ministry of Defense, 1994), p. 57.

63. Yehuda Breginski, *A Nation Strives at Board* (in Hebrew) (Tel Aviv: Hakibbutz Hameuhad, 1965), p. 366.

64. The Japanese case is perhaps the best-known example. Generals explained to the emperor in the early 1940s that Japan must go to war despite the fact that it would not win. See Meirion and Susie Harries, *Sheathing the Sword: The Demilitarization of Japan* (London: Hamish Hamilton, 1987).

65. *Palmach Bulletin*, no. 49, January 1947.

66. Bugner, *The Resistance Ships*, p. 124.

67. *The Palmach Book*, pp. 581–82.

68. Breginski, *A Nation Strives at Board*, pp. 419–20; Jacques Derogy, *La Loi du retour: la secrète et véritable histoire de l'Exodus* (Paris: Fayard, 1970).

69. Vinia Hadari and Zeev Zahoor, *Ships or a State* (in Hebrew) (Tel Aviv: Hakibbutz Hameuhad, 1981), p. 94.

70. Bugner, *The Resistance Ships*, pp. 135–36; Ben-Gurion diary, November 22, 1945, *BGA*.

71. Letter from "Brith Trumpeldor in Eretz-Israel," to Hamachanot Haolim, 1946, *MHA*, 5A/8/4A.

72. *Bamivchan*, September 1944.

73. Moshe Halforn, Hamachanot Haolim Secretariat, November 2, 1945, *KMA*, 3/1/7A.

74. Kemp, *Frontier Nationalism*.

75. Hamachanot Haolim Secretariat, January 24, 1947, *KMA*, 9/3/1.

76. Document from August 10, 1943, *The Haganah History Book*, vol. 3, pp. 1876–77.

77. Pail, *From the Haganah to IDF*, p. 220. See also Yeruham Cohen, *In Daylight and in the Night* (in Hebrew) (Tel Aviv: Amikam, 1969), p. 92.

78. Sykes, *From Balfour to Moin*, p. 281.

79. Hakkibutz Hameuchad Council, September 18–19, 1946, *KMA*.

80. Mapai Council, September 5–8, 1946, *MA*.

81. Elhanan Oren, *The Settlement in the Struggle* (in Hebrew) (Jerusalem: Yad Ben-Zvi, 1978), pp. 169–78.

82. Levi Eshkol, *The Story of Settlements* (in Hebrew) (Tel Aviv: Am Oved, 1959), p. 127.

83. Oren, *The Settlement in the Struggle*, pp. 122–32; Pail, *From the Haganah to IDF*, p. 212; Kemp, *Frontier Nationalism*, p. 43.

84. *GA*, actions (1946). See also *The Haganah History Book*, vol. 3, 941–47; Meir Pail, *Haaretz*, October 12, 1986.

9. POLITICAL PRAETORIANISM IN WARTIME

1. Ben-Gurion in the political committee of the Zionist Congress, December 18, 1946, in David Ben-Gurion, *Bama'aracha*, vol. 5 (in Hebrew) (Tel Aviv: Am-Oved, 1950), pp. 135–37.

2. Pappe, *The Making of the Arab-Israeli Conflict*, p. 51; Flapan, *The Birth of Israel*, pp. 55–79.

3. "The Haganah Faces the Future," June 18, 1947; David Ben-Gurion, *When Israel Fights* (in Hebrew) (Tel Aviv: Mapai, 1950), pp. 13–18.

4. Ibid., p. 13.

5. Ben-Gurion diary, May 27, 1947, *BGA*.

6. Jewish Agency Executive, May 13, 1947, in David Ben-Gurion, *Chimes of Independence: Memoirs* (in Hebrew) (Tel Aviv: Am Oved, 1993), pp. 116–17.

7. In the Elected Assembly, May 22, 1947, in Ben-Gurion, ibid., p. 127; Jewish Agency Executive, May 26, 1947, in Ben-Gurion, ibid., p. 130.

8. Mapai Secretariat, June 11, 1947, *MA*.

9. Histadrut Executive, December 3, 1947, *LA*.

10. Mapai Center, December 13, 1947, *MA*. See also Ben-Gurion diary, December 3, 1947, *BGA*.

11. Pappe, *The Making of the Arab-Israeli Conflict*, pp. 56–60; see also Ezra Danin's report, which appears in Ben-Gurion diary, December 26, 1947, in Gershon Rivlin and Elhana Oren, eds., *War Diary* (in Hebrew) (Tel Aviv: Ministry of Defense, 1982), p. 73.

12. Morris, *The Birth of the Palestinian Refugee Problem*, p. 170.

13. Yosef Weitz, *My Diary*, vol. 3 (in Hebrew) (Ramat-Gan: Massada, 1948), p. 232, 235 (February 3, 10, 1948).

14. Mapai Secretariat, October 11, 1947, *MA*.

15. *The Haganah History Book*, vol. 3, p. 1414.

16. Ibid., pp. 1383, 1543.

17. Avraham Ayalon, *The Givati Brigade in the 1948 War* (in Hebrew) (Tel Aviv: Maarachot, 1979), p. 233.

18. *The Haganah History Book*, vol. 3, pp. 1543–44.

19. *War Diary*, December 19, 1947.

20. Ben-Gurion to Ezra Danin, *War Diary*, January 1, 1948; also, *War Diary*, January 9, 1948; also his words in January 15, 1948, in *When Israel Fights*, pp. 34–37.

21. Ben-Gurion diary, January 1, 1948, *BGA*; Ezra Danin, *Zionist without Any*

Condition (in Hebrew) (Jerusalem: Keter, 1987), p. 221; Uri Milstein, *The History of the 1948 War*, vol. 2, part 6 (in Hebrew) (Tel Aviv: Zmora Bitan, 1989); Gelber, *A Nucleus for a Regular Army* (in Hebrew) (Jerusalem: Yad Ben-Zvi, 1986), p. 402.

22. Ben-Gurion diary, February 19, 1948, *BGA*.
23. Milstein, *The History of the 1948 War*, vol. 4, p. 146.
24. Regarding the Israeli Arabists, see Gil Eyal, "Between East and West: The Discourse about the Arab Village in Israel," *Teoriya Uvikoret*, no. 3, pp. 39–56.
25. *War Diary*, p. 97.
26. *War Diary*, December 10, 1947.
27. *War Diary*, October 23, 1947. See also his words in the security committee, October 23, 1947, in Ben-Gurion, *Chimes of Independence: Memoirs*, pp. 417–21. Also his words in the Mapai Political Committee, October 30, 1947, *MA*.
28. Frank Parkin, *Marxism and Class Theory: A Bourgeois Critique* (London: Tavistock, 1979).
29. *War Diary*, January 18, 1948.
30. Gelber, *A Nucleus for a Regular Army*, pp. 15–20; Naor, *Laskov*, pp. 175–76; Anita Shapira, *The Army Controversy, 1948* (in Hebrew) (Tel Aviv: Hakibbutz Hameuchad, 1985), p. 145. For a narrative description of the "with uniform/without uniform" debate, see Gelber against Brener in *Kathedra*.
31. Memorandum from April 4, 1948, in Zeava Ostfeld, *An Army Is Born* (in Hebrew) (Tel Aviv: Ministry of Defense, 1994), p. 181.
32. "The Committee of Five Protocol," in Shapira, *The Army Controversy, 1948*, p. 116.
33. Yoav Gelber, *Why the Palmach Was Disbanded* (in Hebrew) (Tel Aviv: Schocken, 1986), p. 83.
34. Document (letter or lecture) by Galili (no date), in Zeisling archive, *KMA*.
35. About the differences between the two schools, see Yadin testimony in the Committee of Five, Shapira, *The Army Controversy, 1948*, p. 116.
36. Ben-Gurion diary, January 31, 1948, *BGA*.
37. Mapai Council, February 6–7, 1948. See also *War Diary*, p. 228.
38. Mapai Council, February 6–7, 1948. A revised version is in Ben-Gurion, *When Israel Fights*, pp. 62–74.
39. *War Diary*, April, 5, 20, 23, 1948.
40. Willems, *A Way of Life and Death*, pp. 54–60.
41. David B. Ralston, *The Army of the Republic: The Place of the Military in the Political Evolution of France, 1871–1914* (Cambridge: MIT Press, 1967), pp. 138–202.
42. Ben-Gurion diary, April 10, 1948, *BGA*.
43. The document, dated September 29, 1948, was presented by Ben-Gurion in the Histadrut Executive, in October 15, 1948, *LA*.
44. *War Diary*, February 6, 1948.
45. Ibid., February 14, 1948.
46. Ibid., March 5, 1948.
47. Ibid., March 10, 1948.
48. Uri Brener testimony, *HA*, no. 4348; Ostfeld, *An Army Is Born*, pp. 98–99; Shapira, *The Army Controversy, 1948*, pp. 88–89.
49. Yitzhak Levi, *Jerusalem in the 1948 War* (in Hebrew) (Tel Aviv: Ministry of Defense, 1986), pp. 292–93; Gelber, *Why the Palmach Was Disbanded*, pp. 113–14; see also Mapam Secretariat, June 22, 1948, Security Committee, *KMA*.
50. *War Diary*, June, 12, 13, 14, 1948.
51. Ostfeld, *An Army Is Born*, p. 235; Shapira, *The Army Controversy, 1948*, p. 105, 114.
52. Shapira, *The Army Controversy, 1948*, pp. 85–86.
53. Ben-Gurion diary, April 26, 1948, *BGA*.
54. *War Diary*, April 27, 1948, May 2, 1948.

55. Ibid., March 25, 31, 1948, April 26, 1948, May 2, 1948. See also letter from Galili (no date), in Zeisling, private archive, *KMA*, 6/4.
56. National Administration, May 3, 1948, *SA*.
57. Mapam's Political Committee, May 4, 1948, no. 3, *KMA*.
58. Histadrut Executive, May 10, 1948, *LA*.
59. Ibid.
60. Ostfeld, *An Army Is Born*, p. 235; Shapira, *The Army Controversy, 1948*, pp. 105–10.
61. Gelber, *Why the Palmach Was Disbanded*, pp. 99–117; Ostfeld, *An Army Is Born*, pp. 76–101.
62. Ostfeld, *An Army Is Born*, p. 761.
63. Gelber, *Why the Palmach Was Disbanded*, p. 139.
64. *War Diary*, p. 390, 392.
65. Ibid., May 6, 28, 1948.
66. Gelber, *Why the Palmach Was Disbanded*, p. 127; Levi, *Jerusalem in the 1948 War*, p. 335.
67. *War Diary*, May 24, 1948.
68. Lapidot, *The "Saison"*, pp. 171–246.
69. Mapai Secretariat, May 29, 1947, *MA*.
70. Avizohar, *The Beats of the State*, p. 451.
71. *War Diary*, December 2, 1947.
72. Ibid., December 12, 15, 29, 1947, January 1, 1948.
73. Letter from Lenkin to Begin, December 27, 1947, in Gil Nisim, "Altalena" (in Hebrew), M.A. thesis, Tel Aviv University, 1977, p. 39.
74. Menachem Begin, *The Revolt* (in Hebrew) (Tel Aviv: Achiasaf, 1984), p. 422.
75. Ostfeld, *An Army Is Born*, p. 628.
76. Levi, *Jerusalem in the 1948 War*, pp. 340–46.
77. Ostfeld, *An Army Is Born*, pp. 632–33.
78. Ibid., p. 630.
79. *War Diary*, June 16, 1948.
80. Ostfeld, *An Army Is Born*, p. 651; Arye Yitzhaki, *The Burma Road* (in Hebrew) (Tel Aviv: Tamuz, 1988), pp. 174–75.
81. Shlomo Nakdimon, *Altalena* (in Hebrew) (Jerusalem: Idanim, 1978); Eliyahu Lenkin, *The Story of Altalena Commander* (in Hebrew) (Tel Aviv: Hadar, 1986); Uri Brener, *Altalena* (in Hebrew) (Efal: Tabenkin Institute, 1978).
82. *War Diary*, May 16, 1948.
83. From Galili to Ben-Gurion, June 20, 1948, in Meir Pail and Azriel Ronen, *A Tear in 1948* (in Hebrew) (Efal: Galili Center, 1991), pp. 119–20.
84. *War Diary*, June 19, 1948. See also David Ben-Gurion, *The Restored State of Israel* (in Hebrew) (Tel Aviv: Am-Oved, 1951), pp. 179–81.
85. State Council, June 23, 1948, in Ben-Gurion, *When Israel Fights*, pp. 165–68. See also Shapiro, *The Road to Power*, p. 75.
86. Niv, *The History of the IZL*, vol. 6, pp. 275–76; Ostfeld, *An Army Is Born*, p. 650.
87. Niv, *The History of the IZL*, vol. 6, p. 275.
88. *War Diary*, June 11, 1948.
89. Ibid., June 16, 19, 1948.
90. Allon in Commanders Convention, June 29, 1948, *KMA*.
91. Mapai Council, June 19, 1948, *MA*.
92. Allon in Commanders Convention, June 29, 1948, *KMA*; see also his speech in Hakibbutz Hameuhad Council, November 5–7, 1948, *KMA*.
93. Palmach Commanders meeting with Ben-Gurion, September 14, 1948, *HA*. Also Allon in the Histadrut Executive, October 14–15, 1948, *LA*. Also *Without Palmach* (in Hebrew) (Tel Aviv: Mapam, December 1948).

94. Gelber, *Why the Palmach Was Disbanded*, p. 123.
95. Mapam's Political Committee, May 4, 1948, *KMA*.
96. Histardut Executive, October 14–15, 1948.
97. Ben-Gurion in Palmach Commanders meeting, September 14, 1948, *HA*. Also Ben-Gurion diary, September 7, 1948.
98. *War Diary*, June 29, 1948.
99. Ibid., July 1, 1948; Bar-Zohar, *Ben-Gurion*, vol. 2, p. 805; Ostfeld, *An Army Is Born*, pp. 605–6. Also Mapam's Political Committee, July 3, 1948, *KMA*.
100. *War Diary*, June 4, 1948.
101. Shapira, *The Army Controversy, 1948*, p. 223.
102. Ibid., p. 44.
103. Ibid., p. 242.

10. MILITARISTIC POLITICS IN WARTIME

1. The desire to gain time was presented, for example, by Galili; *War Diary*, March 18, 1948.
2. *The Palmach Book*, vol. 2, p. 189.
3. Ostfeld, *An Army Is Born*, p. 213.
4. Milstein, *The History of the 1948 War*, vol. 4, p. 146.
5. Morris, *The Birth of the Palestinian Refugee*, pp. 61–131.
6. Walid Khalidi, "Plan Dalet: The Zionist Master Plan for Conquest of Palestine," *Middle East Forum*, 1961, pp. 22–28; Gelber, *A Nucleus for a Regular Army*, p. 128; Pail, *From the Haganah to IDF*, pp. 309–19.
7. Ostfeld, *An Army Is Born*, p. 286.
8. Ibid., p. 315.
9. National Administration, May 12, 1948, *SA*.
10. Ostfeld, *An Army Is Born*, p. 307.
11. Yitzhak Laor, "The Torn Tongue," *Ha'aretz*, September 19, 1994.
12. *War Diary*, May 1, 1948.
13. Ibid., May 18, 19, 1948.
14. Ibid., December 11, 1947, January 2, 1948. See also Moshe Carmel, *The Occupation of the Arab Towns in 1948* (in Hebrew) (Efal: Yad Tabenkin, 1987), p. 43.
15. Levi, *Jerusalem in the 1948 War*, pp. 340–44. For more about the effect of Deir Yassin, see Kimmerling and Migdal, *The Palestinians: The Making of a People*, pp. 151–52. The Haganah also perpetrated many massacres. The historian Arye Yitzhaki counts ten major massacres (fifty or more killed in each incident) and about a hundred smaller massacres which, he argues, had a profound effect on the flight of the Arabs. See G. Erlich, "Not Only in Deir Yassin," *Hair*, May 6, 1992. The Arabs, too, carried out numerous massacres. One of them, the attack on a convoy of physicians and nurses who were on their way to Hadassah Hospital on Mount Scopus in Jerusalem, was a reaction to the Deir Yassin incident.
16. On the periodization that sees the second wave in April, see Morris, *The Birth of the Palestinian Refugee Problem*, pp. 61–131.
17. Ibid., pp. 101–10.
18. Ibid., p. 211.
19. Ibid., p. 235.
20. Moshe Carmel, *The North Battles* (in Hebrew) (Tel Aviv: Ministry of Defense, 1949), pp. 274–77. For more about Carmel, see Pappe, *The Making of the Arab-Israeli Conflict*, p. 82.
21. Morris, *The Birth of the Palestinian Refugee Problem*, pp. 124–27.
22. Lorech Netanel, *The History of the Independent War* (in Hebrew) (Ramat-Gan: Massada, 1989), p. 220; Zeev Sharf, *Three Days* (in Hebrew) (Tel Aviv: Am-Oved, 1959).

23. Ostfeld, *An Army Is Born*, p. 292.

24. On the importance of power on the microlevel, see Michel Foucault, "The Subject and Power," *Power/Knowledge: Selected Interviews and Other Writings, 1972–1977*, pp. 417–33; Michael Walzer, "The Politics of Michel Foucault," in David C. Hoy, ed., *Foucault: A Critical Reader* (London: Blackwell, 1986), pp. 51–67.

25. On the army's initiatives in Acre, for example, see Zadok Eshel, *Carmeli Brigade in the 1948 War* (Tel Aviv: Ministry of Defense, 1973), p. 179. On the numerical superiority, see Simha Flapan, *The Birth of Israel: Myths and Reality* (New York: Pantheon, 1981), p. 631; Pappe, *The Making of the Arab-Israeli Conflict, 1947–1951*, pp. 64–65.

26. *The Battles of the Golani Brigade* (in Hebrew) (Tel Aviv: Ministry of Defense, 1983).

27. Eshel, *Carmeli Brigade in the 1948 War*, pp. 91, 173. The Yehiam convoy was one of three major Jewish convoys destroyed during the last week of March, with the loss of more than one hundred Haganah members. See Morris, *The Birth of the Palestinian Refugee Problem*, p. 61.

28. N. A. Nazzal, "The Zionist Occupation of Western Galilee in 1948," *Journal of Palestinian Studies*, vol. 3, 1974, pp. 58–76; Erlich, "Not Only in Deir Yassin." For more on local initiatives of commanders, see Morris, *The Birth of the Palestinian Refugee Problem*, pp. 156–59; Igal Eilam, *The Executors* (in Hebrew) (Jerusalem: Keter, 1990), pp. 31–52.

29. For the case of Qusariya, see Morris, *The Birth of the Palestinian Refugee Problem*, p. 54.

30. Amos Mokedi testimony in *The Occupation of the Arab Towns in 1948*, pp. 46–47.

31. Mapai Council, February 7, 1948, MA. See also Ben-Gurion, *When Israel Fights*, p. 62. Also see his words in the Zionist Executive, *War Diary*, April 6, 1948.

32. Milstein, *The History of the 1948 War*, vol. 1, p. 141.

33. Yosef Weitz, *My Diary* (in Hebrew) (Ramat-Gan: Massada, 1948), p. 261 (April 2, 1948).

34. Histadrut Executive, June 16, 1948, LA.

35. The Temporary Government Protocol, July 4, 1948, SA.

36. *War Diary*, July 7, 1948.

37. Histadrut Executive, July 14, 1948, LA.

38. *War Diary*, July 18, 1948.

39. Ezra Danin, *Zionist without Any Condition* (in Hebrew) (Jerusalem: Keter, 1987), p. 218.

40. Weitz, *My Diary*, September 26, 1948.

41. Rabin's book was censored, but the *New York Times* told the full version. See Bar-Zohar, *Ben-Gurion*, vol. 2, p. 775.

42. See nn. 16, 23, 24 in the Introduction. Also Shabtai Teveth, "The New Historians," *Haaretz*, April 7, 14, 21, 1989; Benny Morris, "The New History and the Old Propagandists," *Haaretz*, May 9, 1989.

43. That is the claim of Shabtai Teveth and Anita Shapira. Teveth's opinions are referenced in n. 16 in the Introduction. As for Shapira, see *At the Horizons* (in Hebrew) (Tel Aviv: Am-Oved, 1988), pp. 23–81, and *Land and Power: The Zionist Resort to Force, 1881–1948* (Oxford: Oxford University Press, 1992). Interestingly, this is also Morris's claim. See Benny Morris, "Response to Finkelstein and Masalha," *Journal of Palestinian Studies*, vol. 21, 1991, pp. 98–114. This claim stands against Shaak's claim; see Israel Shaak, "A History of the Concept of Transfer in Zionism," *Journal of Palestine Studies*, vol. 18, no. 3, 1989, pp. 22–37.

44. Morris, *The Birth of the Palestinian Refugee Problem, 1947–1949*, p. 435.

45. Ibid., p. 451.

46. Histadrut Executive, June 16, 1948, LA.

47. Histadrut Executive, May 10, June 16, July 14, 1948, *LA;* Mapam Secretariat, July 13, 1948, *KAA.*

48. Weitz, *My Diary,* p. 303 (June 17, 1948).

49. For more about Mapam's attitude toward the Arabs and the 1948 War, see Yosi Amitay, *The United Workers' Party (Mapam) 1948–1954: Attitudes on Palestinian-Arab Issues* (in Hebrew) (Tel Aviv: Tcherikover, 1988); Morris, *1948 and After,* pp. 35–68.

50. Morris, *The Birth of the Palestinian Refugee Problem,* pp. 139–40.

51. Morris, *1948 and After,* p. 182.

52. Morris, *The Birth of the Palestinian Refugee Problem,* pp. 139–40.

53. Weitz, *My Diary,* p. 293. See also Ben-Gurion's *War Diary,* June 5, 1948.

54. *War Diary,* June 16, 1948.

55. Ibid., August 18, 1948.

56. Ibid.

57. Ibid., July 21, 1948.

58. Morris, *The Birth of the Palestinian Refugee Problem,* p. 149.

59. *War Diary,* July 19, 1948.

60. Ibid., October 26, 1948.

61. Ibid., April 27, May 5, 1948.

62. Histadrut Executive, November 3, 1948, *LA.*

63. *War Diary,* November 6, 10, December 23, 25, 1948.

64. Ibid., December 31, 1948, January 4, 1949.

65. Mapai Center, November 30, 1948, *MA.*

66. *The Negev Brigade in Battle* (in Hebrew) (Tel Aviv: Ministry of Defense, 1949), pp. 181–82.

67. Histadrut Executive, June 16, 1948, *LA.*

68. Cabinet Session, June 16, 1948, in David Ben-Gurion, *The Restored State of Israel* (in Hebrew) (Tel Aviv: Am-Oved, 1951), p. 165.

69. Vagts, *A History of Militarism,* pp. 452–53.

70. *War Diary,* p. 454, 722; Ostfeld, *An Army Is Born,* p. 702.

71. *The Arabs Fighting in the 1948 War* (Efal: Tabenkin Center, no date).

72. Rabin, *Service Diary,* p. 57.

73. Pail and Ronen, *A Tear in 1948,* pp. 188–89.

74. Ben-Gurion in the State Council, July 22, 1948, *War Diary,* p. 618.

75. Ben-Gurion, *When Israel Fights,* p. 275, and *The Restored State of Israel,* p. 267.

76. Gelber, *Why the Palmach Was Disbanded,* p. 206.

77. Ostfeld, *An Army Is Born,* pp. 632–45.

78. As Ostfeld claims, ibid., pp. 755–97; or as Gelber claims in *Why the Palmach Was Disbanded,* pp. 262–71.

79. Shapira, *The Army Controversy, 1948,* pp. 156–57.

80. Ben-Eliezer, "Israel's Myth of Pioneering."

81. Ostfeld, *An Army Is Born,* pp. 766–68.

82. *War Diary,* September 26, 1948.

83. Ostfeld, *An Army Is Born,* p. 768.

84. Ibid., p. 770.

85. Temporary Government Protocol, November 7, 1948, *SA.*

86. *An Army Is Born,* p. 700.

87. *War Diary,* November 12, 1948.

88. Temporary Government Protocol, November 17, 1948, *SA.*

89. *War Diary,* December 25, 1948.

90. Temporary Government Protocol, December 5, 1948, *SA.*

91. Ibid., January 9, 1949, *SA.*

92. *War Diary,* October 16, 1948.

93. Weitz, *My Diary,* September 26, 1948.

94. *War Diary*, October 7, 1948.
95. Ibid., October 7, November 27, 1948.
96. About a deterministic perception of the Arab-Israeli conflict, see Kimmerling, "Patterns of Militarism in Israel."
97. Exchange of correspondence between Brener and Dori of October 10 and afterward, *KMA*, Security Committee, 2a/19.
98. Mapam Political Committeee, October 21, 1948, *KMA*, no. 8.
99. Ben-Gurion, *When Israel Fights*, pp. 273–82.
100. Bar-Zohar, *Ben-Gurion*, p. 942.
101. *War Diary*, October 16, 1948.
102. Ibid., October 22, 1948.
103. Ibid., October 28, 1948.
104. Ibid., October 30, 31, 1948.
105. *Bamahane*, November 11, 1948.
106. Ben-Gurion, *When Israel Fights*, pp. 264–71 (November 27, 1948).
107. Shimoni to Sassun, November 2, 1948, *Documents*, vol. 2, no. 92, pp. 126–27 (SA).
108. "Ben-Gurion's Consultation with Army Commanders and Foreign Ministry Officials," December 30, 1948, *Documents*, vol. 2, no. 282, pp. 320–21.
109. *War Diary*, pp. 816–17; Ostfeld, *An Army Is Born*, pp. 774–77.
110. Rabin, *Service Diary*, p. 77.
111. *War Diary*, November 14, 1948.
112. Robert Slater, *Rabin of Israel* (New York: St. Martin's, 1993), pp. 79–84; Rabin, *Service Diary*, p. 73; Cohen, *In Daylight and in the Night*, pp. 250–51.
113. Rabin, *Service Diary*, p. 78.
114. *War Diary*, March 18, 1948.
115. Ibid., April 4, 1949.
116. *Without Palmach*. See also Shlomo Gazit and Gabriel Cohen, "The Palmach Tested by War," *Ma'arachot*, no. 62–63, 1950, pp. 75–98.
117. Rabin, *Service Diary*, p. 79; Bar-Zohar, *Ben-Gurion*, p. 816.

11. A STATE ARMY CONSTRUCTS A NATION

1. On the importance of the state as an actor, see Charles Tilly, ed., *The Formation of National States in Western Europe* (Princeton: Princeton University Press, 1975); Theda Skocpol, "Bringing the State Back In," in Peter B. Evans et al., eds., *Bringing the State Back In* (Cambridge: Cambridge University Press, 1985). Regarding the concept of a strong state and Israel as such, see Joel S. Migdal, "The Crystallization of the State and the Struggles over Rulemaking: Israel in Comparative Perspective," in Baruch Kimmerling, ed., *The Israeli State and Society*, pp. 1–27.
2. Ben-Gurion, "A Letter to a Palmach Member," *When Israel Fights*, p. 279. On statist pioneering in general, see Ben-Eliezer, "Israel's Myth of Pioneering."
3. *War Diary*, August 26, 1949.
4. See Ben-Gurion's testimony in "Committee Five," in Shapira, *The Army Controversy, 1948*, p. 421.
5. Gelber, *Why the Palmach Was Disbanded*, p. 250, and *A Nucleus for a Regular Army*, pp. 482, 554–55; Uri Brener, *The Resignation* (in Hebrew) (Tel Aviv: Yad Tabenkin, 1987).
6. Rabin, *Service Diary*, pp. 84–87; Naor, *Laskov*, p. 224.
7. Ben-Eliezer, "Rethinking Civil-Military Relations Paradigm."
8. *Bamahane*, February 1953. About the meaning of pioneering at that time and in general, see Ben-Eliezer, "Israel's Myth of Pioneering."
9. Benedict Anderson, *Imagined Communities: Reflections on the Origin and Spread of Nationalism* (London: Verso, 1983); Eric J. Hobsbawm, *Nations and Nation-*

alism since 1780: Programme, Myth, Reality (Cambridge: Cambridge University Press, 1990).

10. Mapai Faction in the Knesset, April 11, 1951, *MA*.

11. Anthony D. Smith, "State-Making and Nation-Building," in John A. Hall, ed., *States in History* (Oxford: Blackwell, 1986), pp. 228–263.

12. *Knesset Protocol*, August 8, 1952.

13. Lissak, "The Israel Defense Force As an Agent of Socialization and Education," pp. 325–39; Horowitz and Kimmerling, "Some Social Implications of Military Service and the Reserve System in Israel," pp. 262–76; Perlmutter, *The Military and Politics in Modern Times*, pp. 251–80, and *Military and Politics in Israel: Nation Building and Role Expansion*; Azarya and Kimmerling, "New Immigrants in the Israeli Armed Forces," pp. 22–41.

14. Horowitz and Lissak, *Trouble in Utopia*, pp. 195–230.

15. Mapai Political Committee, July 24, 1952, *MA*.

16. On France as a nation-in-arms, see Richard D. Challener, *The French Theory of the Nation in Arms, 1866–1939* (New York: Russell and Russell, 1965); Carlton J. H. Hayes, "Jacobin Nationalism," *The Historical Evolution of Modern Nationalism* (New York: Russell and Russell, 1931), pp. 43–83.

17. Vagts, *A History of Militarism*, pp. 130–36.

18. Willems, *A Way of Life and Death.*

19. Colmar Von Der Goltz, *The Nation in Arms* (London: Hugh Rees, 1913). For more about German militarism, see Eley, "Army, State and Civil Society: Revisiting the Problem of German Militarism," pp. 85–109.

20. On Japan as a nation-in-arms, see Theodore F. Cook, "The Japanese Reserve Experience: From Nation-in-Arms to Baseline Defense," in Louis A. Zurcher and Gwyn Harries-Jenkins, *Supplementary Military Forces: Reserves, Militias, Auxiliaries* (London: Sage, 1978); Harold Hakwon Sunoo, *Japanese Militarism, Past and Present* (Chicago: Nelson-Hall, 1975).

21. Phillip Bankwitz, "Maxime Weygand and the Army-Nation Concept in the Modern French Army," *French Historical Studies*, vol. 2, pp. 157–88.

22. *War Diary*, March 17, 1948.

23. Ibid., p. 853, and also on November 13, 1948.

24. Ibid., November 26, 27, 1948.

25. *Knesset Protocol*, August 15, 1949.

26. For example, Bar Yehuda, in *Knesset Protocol*, August 26, 1952.

27. Mapai Secretariat, August 7, 1949, *MA*.

28. Nakamura and Tobe, "The Imperial Japanese Army and Politics," pp. 511–25.

29. For more on nations-in-arms in general and Israel in particular, see Ben-Eliezer, "A Nation-in-Arms: State, Nation, and Militarism in Israel's First Years."

30. *Knesset Protocol*, August 2, 1949.

31. Ibid., August 15, 1949.

32. Mapai Secretariat, June 1, 1950, *MA*.

33. Mapai Center, January 12, 1949, *MA*.

34. *Bamahane*, November 23, 1950.

35. Dvora Cohen, *The New Immigration and Its Absorption in Israel, 1948–1953* (in Hebrew) (Jerusalem: Yad Ben-Zvi 1994), p. 281.

36. *Bamahane*, September 20, 1951.

37. *Knesset Protocol*, June 18, 1952.

38. Cohen, *The New Immigration and Its Absorption in Israel*, p. 281.

39. Ibid., p. 158.

40. *Knesset Protocol*, August 19, 1952.

41. Ibid., August 15, 1949.

42. Ibid., November 9, 1949.

43. Ibid., August 18, 26, 1952.
44. *Ha'aretz*, March 12, 1950.
45. *Bamahane*, July 20, 1950.
46. Joyce Robbins, "The Israeli Woman Soldier and the Politics of the 'Non-Military' Roles in the 1950s," M.A. Thesis, Tel Aviv University, 1994.
47. *Bamahane*, July 31, 1952.
48. Yitzak Laor, *Narratives with No Natives: Essays on Israeli Literature* (in Hebrew) (Tel Aviv: Hakibbutz Hameuchad, 1995), pp. 115–70.
49. *Bamahane*, October 19, 1950.
50. Ian Lustick, *Arabs in the Jewish State* (Austin: University of Texas Press, 1980).
51. Uzi Benziman and Atallah Mansour, *Subtenants* (Jerusalem: Keter, 1992), pp. 117–18.
52. Sammy Smooha, "Minority Status in an Ethnic Democracy: The Status of the Arab Minority in Israel," *Ethnic and Racial Studies*, vol. 13, no. 3, 1990.
53. Martin Evans, "The French Army and the Algerian War: Crisis of Identity," in Michael Scriven and Peter Wagstaff, *War and Society in Twentieth-Century France* (New York: Berg, 1991), pp. 147–61; Edward W. Said, *Orientalism* (New York: Pantheon, 1978).
54. For example, *Knesset Protocol*, July 12, 1950, January 10, 1951, January 16, 1952, December 24, 1952; March 4, 1953, June 8, 1954. Also see Lustick, *Arabs in the Jewish State*.
55. *Bamahane*, October 5, 1955, October 12, 1955.
56. A. Kemp, "Talking Boundaries: The Making of Political Territory in Israel 1949–1957" (in Hebrew), Ph.D. dissertation, Tel Aviv University, 1997.
57. Igal Eilam, *The Executors* (in Hebrew) (Jerusalem: Keter, 1990), pp. 53–70.
58. E.g., *Ha'aretz*, April 4, 1957; July 19, 1957; November 21, 1957; "Forty Years since the Kafr Kassim Masacre," *Ma'ariv* (daily), October 27, 1996.
59. *Knesset Protocol*, August 28, 1952, November 24, 1952.
60. Benny Morris, *Israel's Border Wars, 1949–1956: Arab Infiltration, Israeli Retaliation, and the Countdown to the Suez War* (Oxford: Clarendon, 1993), p. 416.

12. A NATION READY FOR WAR

1. Ben-Gurion in Mapai Council, February 2, 1948, in his *When Israel Fights*, p. 62.
2. Mapai Center, January 12, 1949, *MA*.
3. *Bamahane*, September 17, 1949.
4. *Ha'aretz*, August 16, 1949.
5. *Knesset Protocol*, August 19, 1952.
6. Ibid., November 2, 1955.
7. Mapai Center, January 12, 1949, *MA*.
8. Asnat Shiran, "The Politics of Settlement during the 1948 War and the Constitution of a State" (in Hebrew), M.A. thesis, Tel Aviv University, 1992.
9. *Knesset Protocol*, August 19, 1952.
10. Ibid., March 5, 1951.
11. Mapai Political Council, January 17, 1956, *MA*.
12. Mordechai Bar-On, *The Gates of Gaza* (in Hebrew) (Tel Aviv: Am-Oved, 1992), 94–96.
13. *Ha'aretz*, September 28, 1953.
14. Shabtai Teveth, *Moshe Dayan: The Soldier, the Man, the Legend* (London: Weidenfield and Nicolson, 1972), p. 355.
15. *Ha'aretz*, October 7, 12, 15, 1953.
16. *Ha'aretz*, October 21, 1953.

17. Arye Shalev, *Cooperation in the Shadow of Conflict* (in Hebrew) (Tel Aviv: Ministry of Defense, 1989), p. 298.

18. Morris, *Israel's Border Wars, 1949–1956*, pp. 124–31.

19. Moshe Sharett, *Personal Diary* (in Hebrew) (Tel Aviv: Maariv, 1978), vol. 6, November 3, 1956; vol. 7, December 2, 1956.

20. *Knesset Protocol*, August 18, 1952.

21. Hakibbutz Hameuchad Councils, July 2, 1953, April 9, 1954, *KMA*; Mordechai Bar-On, "The Policy of Retaliation as a System of Deterrence," in Moti Golani, ed., *Hetz Shachor: Gaza Raid and the Israeli Policy of Retaliation during the Fifties* (in Hebrew) (Tel Aviv: Ministry of Defense, 1994), p. 116.

22. Morris, *Israel's Border Wars, 1949–1956*, p. 182.

23. See ibid., pp. 379–80; Kimmerling, "Patterns of Militarism in Israel," pp. 196–223.

24. *Bamahane*, September 18, 1956, October 3, 1956, October 12, 1956.

25. Mapai Center, August 8, 1956, *MA*.

26. Mapai Political Council, January 17, 1956, *MA*.

27. *Davar*, October 21, 1955, November 6, 1955.

28. Letter from Rabbi Nisim to Moshe Sharett, October 21, 1955, *SA*, Chetz-2934.

29. Defender Fund, the National, Public Committee, May 9, 1955, *SA*, Chetz-2394.

30. Histadrut Executives, July 19, 1955, *LA*.

31. *Davar*, October 26, 1955.

32. Mapai Political Council, January 17, 1956, *MA*.

33. Histadrut Executive, July 17, 1955, *LA*.

34. Moshe Sharett, *Israel versus Arab: Two Approaches* (in Hebrew) (Tel Aviv: Center for Peace, 1990), lecture presented in October 1957.

35. Morris, *Israel's Border Wars, 1949–1956*, pp. 246–48.

36. Moshe Sharett, *Personal Diary*, vol. 1, (in Hebrew) (Tel Aviv: Maariv, 1978), October 15, 1953.

37. See Bialer Uri, "Ben-Gurion and Sharett: The Crystallization of Two Orientations," *Medina, Mimshal Veyachasim Beinleumiim*, 2, 1971, pp. 71–84.

38. Moti Golani, "The Sinai Campaign: Military and Political Aspects" (in Hebrew), Ph.D. dissertation, Haifa University, 1992, p. 11; Moshe Dayan, *Story of My Life* (in Hebrew) (Tel Aviv: Dvir, 1976), p. 140.

39. Sharett, *Personal Diary*, vol. 4, April 14, 1955.

40. Ibid., vol. 2, p. 591.

41. Ibid., vol. 5, December 27, 1955.

42. Ibid., vol. 4, May 23, 1955.

43. Golani, *The Sinai Campaign*, p. 23.

44. Ibid., p. 14; Golani, *Hetz Shachor*; Morris, *Israel's Border Wars, 1949–1956*, pp. 324–55.

45. Golani, *The Sinai Campaign*, pp. 38–42.

46. Sharett, *Personal Diary*, vol. 1, October 26, 1953.

47. Golani, *The Sinai Campaign*, pp. 34–35.

48. Bar-On, *The Gates of Gaza*, pp. 13–27.

49. Sharett, *Personal Diary*, vol. 5, p. 1307.

50. Ben-Gurion in Mapai Political Committee, December 28, 1955, *MA*.

51. Mapai Political Committee, January 17, 1956; *Davar*, January 17, 1956.

52. Moshe Sharett, *Personal Diary*, vol. 5, p. 1385.

53. Mapai Political Committee, May 15, 1954, *MA*.

54. Morris, *Israel's Border Wars, 1949–1956*, pp. 397–404.

55. *Knesset Protocol*, November 7, 1956.

56. *Davar*, November 5, 1956.

57. Ibid., November 7, 1956.

58. See also Yona Hadari-Ramage, "War and Religiosity: The Sinai Campaign in Public Thought," in S. Ilan Troen and Noah Lucas, eds., *Israel: The First Decade of Independence* (Albany: SUNY Press, 1995), pp. 355–73.

59. Sharett, *Personal Diary*, vol. 5, p. 1836.

EPILOGUE

1. See Israel Tal, *National Security: The Few against the Many* (in Hebrew) (Tel Aviv: Dvir, 1996), pp. 136–38.

2. Ezer Weizman, *You Have the Sky, You Have the Land* (in Hebrew) (Tel Aviv: Maariv, 1975), pp. 258–64.

3. Ben-Eliezer, "Rethinking the Civil-Military Relations Paradigm."

4. Gad Barzilai, *A Democracy in Wartime: Conflict and Consensus in Israel* (in Hebrew) (Tel Aviv: Hapoalim, 1992), pp. 87–123; Yossi Beilin, *The Price of Unification: Labor Party until the Yom Kippur War, 1973* (in Hebrew) (Tel Aviv: Revivim, 1985), pp. 53–57.

5. Ron Meiberg, "The Empire Celebrates," *Chadashot*, September 29, 1993.

6. In Michael Keren, *The Pen and the Sword: Israeli Intellectuals and the Building of the Nation-State* (Boulder: Westview, 1989), p. 105.

7. Among senior officers who made the transition into politics in Israel were Lieutenant Generals Itzhak Rabin, Chaim Bar-Lev, Mordechai Gur, Rafael Eitan, and Ehud Barak; Major Generals Ezer Weizman, Shlomo Lahat, Ariel Sharon, Rechavam Zeevi, and Itzhak Mordechai; and many brigadier generals.

8. Ronit Vardi, "The Blame of the 'Conception,' " *Ma'arive*, January 2, 1995. See also Charles S. Liebman, "The Myth of Defeat: The Memory of the Yom Kippur War in Israeli Society," *Middle Eastern Studies*, vol. 29, no. 3, 1993, pp. 399–418.

9. Stuart A. Cohen, "The Israel Defense Forces: From a 'People Army' to a 'Professional Military'—Causes and Implications, *Armed Forces and Society*, vol. 21, no. 2, 1995, pp. 246–54; Clyde Haberman, "Israelis Deglamourize the Military," *New York Times*, May 31, 1995.

10. *Ha'aretz*, March 22, 1955.

11. *Ha'aretz*, August 6, 1996. See also Major-General Shefer, "Draftees to Combat Unit Is in a Consistent Decline," *Ha'aretz*, October 24, 1996.

12. Martin Shaw, *Post Military Society: Militarism, Demilitarization, and War at the End of the Twentieth Century* (Philadelphia: Temple University Press, 1991).

13. Zeev Sheef and Ehud Yaari, *The Intifada: Causes and Effects* (in Hebrew) (Tel Aviv: Papirus, 1990).

14. Amnon Straschnov, *Justice under Fire* (in Hebrew) (Tel Aviv: Yediot Achronot, 1994); Menachem Hofnung, *Israel: Security Needs vs. the Rule of Law* (in Hebrew) (Jerusalem: Nevo, 1991), pp. 326–35.

15. E.g., *Ha'aretz*, May 28, 1996; June 21, 1996; July 7, 1996; Decmeber 8, 1996.

16. Ehud Sprinzak, "Gush Emunim, the Tip of the Iceberg," *Jerusalem Quarterly*, 21, 1981, pp. 28–47; Ian Lustick, *For the Land and the Lord* (New York: Council on Foreign Relations, 1988); Baruch Kimmerling, "Between the Primordial and the Civil Definitions of the Collective Identity: Eretz Israel or the State of Israel?" in Eric Cohen et al., eds., *Comparative Social Dynamics* (Boulder: Westview, 1985).

17. *Ha'aretz*, April 5, 1994; June 30, 1994; November 17, 1995.

18. *Ha'aretz*, September 31, 1994; *Yediot Achronot*, November 17, 1995.

Index

Uri Ben-Eliezer is a senior lecturer in the Department of Sociology at the University of Haifa. He is co-author (with Yonathan Shapiro) of *The Elements of Sociology*.

www.ingramcontent.com/pod-product-compliance
Lightning Source LLC
Chambersburg PA
CBHW070448100426
42812CB00004B/1235